D1647313

THE CATHOLIC REFORMATION

The CATHOLIC REFORMATION

BY PIERRE JANELLE

PROFESSOR IN CLERMONT UNIVERSITY

THE BRUCE PUBLISHING COMPANY
MILWAUKEE

NIHIL OBSTAT:

JOHN A. SCHULIEN, S.T.D.
Censor librorum

IMPRIMATUR:

✠ WILLIAM E. COUSINS
Archbishop of Milwaukee

August 2, 1963

In loving memory
of my father
ERNEST JANELLE
(1861–1940)
to whom I owe
the little that I am

© 1963 THE BRUCE PUBLISHING COMPANY
First printing in Great Britain 1971.

Collier-Macmillan Publishers, London
A Division of Crowell Collier and Macmillan Publishers Ltd.

PRINTED BY COMPTON PRINTING LTD, LONDON AND AYLESBURY

Contents

I   Anarchy, the Disease Within the Church .   1

II   Early Reactions Against Disease in the Church   17

III   Reformation Again Delayed   32

IV   Preparing for Trent   47

V   The Council of Trent   64

VI   The Religious Revival Among the Regulars   92

VII   Education and Scholarship .   115

VIII   The Catholic Reformation and Literature .   137

IX   The Catholic Reformation and Art .   159

X   Piety and Mysticism   183

XI   The Catholic Reformation After Trent   206

XII   The Catholic Reformation in France   226

XIII   The Catholic Reformation in Great Britain and Ireland .   250

XIV   The Missions   275

Conclusion .   301

Index   305

THE CATHOLIC REFORMATION

CHAPTER I

Anarchy, the Disease Within the Church

IN ONE of the scenes of Marlow's *Doctor Faustus* — here a mere reproduction of its German source — we are introduced into the pope's private chamber at the Vatican. Mephistopheles asks Faustus, who is eager to go and admire the marvels of ancient Rome, to stay awhile:

> I know you'd fain see the Pope,
> And take some part of holy Peter's feast,
> Where thou shalt see a troop of bald-pate friars,
> Whose *summum bonum* is in belly-cheer.

Then the pope and the "Cardinal of Lorrain . . . enter to the banquet, with friars attending." They sit down at table, while the friars bring in "dainty dishes" sent by the bishop of Milan and the cardinal of Florence. But Faustus, who is invisible, snatches the food from them, and is therefore cursed "with bell, book, and candle." The scene is, of course, a farce, and an unduly coarse one; yet it can hardly be termed a pure libel. That the moral condition of the clergy, and especially of the Roman Curia, had by the end of the fifteenth century become deplorable, is asserted by eminent Catholic writers of the time, whose evidence cannot be gainsaid. The spirit of lucre and sensuousness was manifested in many abuses, especially various forms of simony, which were in urgent need of reformation.

There was no need, however, of reformation such as the Protestants understood it. According to their contention, the primitive simplicity of the Church had become disfigured by manifold superstitions, these being in turn the source of the lowering of her morality. Remove these superstitions, purge Christian doctrine of an excessive belief in the supernatural and marvelous, relieve Christian discipline of the strain of excessive asceticism, and order would be restored.

Now, if such a view were true, if medieval superstition had engendered corruption, the "Eve of the Reformation" ought to appear as a particularly barren period, both in regard to devotion and virtue. A careful study of the late fifteenth and early sixteenth centuries, however, shows that there was, at the time, a flowering forth of piety and mysticism. The

1

question then arises, how could the above-mentioned abuses be met with in the midst of so much faith and charity? This strange contradiction is to be accounted for, not by false beliefs, but by defective organization, and consequently defective discipline.

The Church had become cut up into a number of independently functioning bodies; authority, jurisdiction, and possessions were divided among them, and inextricably entangled. This, on the one hand, made the enforcement of ecclesiastical canons and regulations extremely difficult, and provided numberless loopholes whereby to evade them. On the other hand, the struggle of many conflicting interests gave rise to constant litigation. It heightened, at the expense of the regular hierarchy, the importance of those officials who were empowered to settle differences and who were too often tempted to take bribes or to exact undue payments. This was especially the case when favors were sought from the Roman Curia. There was an understanding between those who sued for dispensations or exemptions from the performance of their clerical duties or the observance of disciplinary rules, and those who granted graces against payment for the benefit of the papal exchequer or to fill their own pockets. Money assumed as much importance in the Church as in any temporal state, and where money reigns supreme, sloth, lechery, pride inevitably follow.

Thus the moral disorders in the Church really had their source in the overgrown development of an officialdom, the members of which had come to identify the Church with their own class. Reformation had to hack pitilessly through a network of vested interests; it could come only from the authority that had connived at the abuses, and must now, in correcting them, correct itself. The result would be a strong papacy, supported by a strong and independent hierarchy, which would be less likely to let its own dignity and prestige be debased in the eyes of Christendom.

Unfortunately centrifugal tendencies had been at work since the time of the Great Schism, and the Councils of Basle and Constance. These two councils had met as a response to the general clamor for reform; but in fact they ushered in the spirit of nationalism, which was to be the main obstacle in the way of reform. The various European sovereigns cared little for the moral welfare of the Church; they preferred to consider her as a department of the State, to take her dignitaries into their employment, and use her preferments and benefices as rewards for their loyal subjects; thus countenancing abuses which they were later to denounce, once they had found it to their advantage to chastise the

Church by seizing her property. Even when they were not actively hostile to the work of reformation from inside, they refused to give up their private quarrels and claims in order to ensure general peace; and the correction of abuses in a divided Europe remained well-nigh impossible.

In fact, whatever may be said about the corruption of the Holy See, it was not altogether the fault of the popes if they had little time to attend to such matters as monastic discipline or the education of the lower clergy. Whether they liked it or not, their safety, their independence, nay, all but the very existence of the papacy, were involved in the wars between the European princes. They were threatened by the French or Imperial invasions of Italy, or by the Turkish advance. They had to struggle painfully to defend their temporal dominions, which alone could ensure their spiritual independence and authority. Had they not contrived to hold their own against national interests, there might never have been a Catholic Reformation at all.

They might, it is true, have taken less account of political dangers and inconveniences, and attempted to carry Christian opinion along with them, by boldly asserting their will to perform the task of reformation under any circumstances. But they had become too much absorbed in worldly matters to realize the driving force of a purely spiritual appeal. The Renaissance had not merely corrupted the personal morality of the popes and their court; it had done even worse in lowering their notion of their proper function. For apostleship, it had substituted "policy," the art of playing upon human passions and motives.

Taken as a whole, the condition of the Curia was such as to make any Christian blush. Its bureaucracy was self-centered and self-seeking; it had come to halo its privileges, its greed, and its lusts with the sacred character of Christianity itself. Only a huge evangelical revival could breed enough of the spirit of sacrifice in the Church, to sweep away all selfishness; and in fact the Catholic Reformation was due first and foremost to a reawakening of the spirit of the Gospel. But it would still have failed to achieve success if it had merely been a reversion to the intellectual and sentimental outlook of the Middle Ages. It would not have been possible to fall back upon the Renaissance; it must perforce be made use of toward a Christian end.

Such was the task of the movement known as "Christian humanism," which began about 1470 and was steadily gathering strength in the early sixteenth century. It served a double purpose: it saved the Church from paganism, while retaining, in the philosophy, literature, and art of the ancients, whatever might serve toward enriching Christian life. Hence its peculiar quality, which was new and attractive, and which St. Thomas More represents better than anyone else. It was fully flourishing before Luther arose, and was likely to blossom into further flowers of wisdom and holiness, when the religious war forced it for a time into the background. Yet it was to come to the front again with the Council of Trent and the Society of Jesus, and henceforth to be one of the chief elements of the Catholic Reformation.

*   *   *

According to early Protestant controversialists, such as Tyndale, the abuses in the Church were the consequence of false doctrine. A close study of fifteenth-century conditions brings us, however, to a wholly different conclusion. The abuses may be shown to have sprung, not from mistaken notions on justification, the worship of the saints, Purgatory, etc., but from the state of administrative anarchy which had prevailed since the Great Schism. In the early centuries, the organization of the Church, aside from the divinely instituted headship of Peter and his successors, had been modeled on that of the Roman Empire: there was a regular hierarchy, gradually descending from the pope of Rome to the primates, metropolitans, bishops, and deacons. With the advent of feudalism however, this fine architectural order had been in many ways disturbed. As in civil society, many smaller, self-governing units had been founded, which did not come under the authority of the ordinary superiors. There was not much harm in this, so long as the Holy See was strong enough to assert its general overlordship. But when it had become enfeebled by the Great Schism and the conciliar movement, it was unable to put a stop to the scrimmage which took place between all sorts of ecclesiastical bodies. The authority of the hierarchy was openly flouted by clerical or lay patrons, cathedral chapters, religious orders and houses; this being made easier by the practice of exemption, which national sovereigns naturally enough turned into a weapon against Church independence, but which the popes, in a misguided attempt to extend their jurisdiction, were themselves imprudent enough to foster.

Whatever efforts the bishops might make toward a general reformation of morals were set at naught from the fact that they were unable to compel the obedience of a very large section of their clergy. In the late fifteenth century, many parishes were really in the hands of clerical patrons, generally religious houses, which held the advowsons and drew the tithes, often from a considerable distance. Such patrons were obviously unable to help in the enforcement of Church discipline, and were mainly intent on the maintenance of their rights. In the diocese of Paris, for instance, out of 469 parishes, the bishop appointed only 215 incumbents. In Paris itself, the episcopal appointments were only 6 out of 30; worst of all, in the diocese of Lyons, only 21 parishes out of 392 were in the hands of the archbishop.

Nor was the disciplinary influence of the bishops merely countervailed by the power of the patrons. The various religious communities that had come into being inside each diocese also asserted their independence. Cathedral chapters, collegiate churches, brotherhoods of secular priests, monasteries, priories, or convents, all had their elected heads, their assemblies, their statutes, and their estates; they had vassals and tenants, and commanded considerable influence. Besides, most of the chapters, many collegiate churches, all the greater monasteries, and such religious orders as the Carthusians and mendicant friars, had been granted by the Holy See exemption from episcopal jurisdiction. Within their boundaries, they exercised sovereign powers and through the incumbents of their benefices, they held whole blocks of parishes under their sway. The authority of the bishops was threatened with total disappearance.

The practice of exemption was steadily growing in the fifteenth century, and it is but natural that the bishops should have attempted to minimize its effects. Hence a permanent struggle, which led in many cases to scandalous disorders. At Vendôme, the bishop, having entered the collegiate church by stealth, was surrounded by the monks, insulted, and mishandled; the abbot tore from him his rochet, his square cap, and "part of the hair of his head"; then he was seized by the hands and feet, and flung into the street, amidst the shouting of the mob. Similar happenings occurred, between 1470 and 1515, in a great many places in France. Cathedral chapters were equally unruly. They were composed of men of learning, and had great social influence, besides their actual share in the government of cathedral towns, and their powers over a numerous retinue. The late fifteenth century is a period of constant wrangling between chapters and bishops. Both parties go to law over the most trifling points — precedence in a procession, or the whipping of a choirboy. In 1517, the canons of Langres manifest their displeasure to the archbishop by regularly standing up and having the bells rung when they reach the following verse of Lauds: *"Fiant dies ejus pauci et episcopatum ejus recipiat alter."* Even the archdeacons try to extend their authority at the expense of the bishops. What wonder, then, that the latter should have turned in disgust from their religious duties, in which they found rebellion on every hand, to the field of political life, and willingly accepted the favor which princes offered to them in exchange for their able service?

They did try, however, to countercheck the encroachments of exempt bodies; but the means they used still further increased the disorder in the Church. Just as the popes peopled the Curia and the College of Cardinals with their own kin, because other appointments would have been unsafe, the bishops endeavored to open the cathedral chapters to their relatives, thus laying themselves open to the charge of nepotism. In regard to the religious houses, since they could not be held in curb, the simplest plan was to gain a footing inside them. Therefore, in the latter half of the fifteenth century, monastic dignities were more and more frequently conferred upon members of the hierarchy. The circumstances were in favor of such a change, for both the popes and kings wished to have the greatest possible number of benefices in their gift and discountenanced the old practice of appointing abbots, priors, and other officers by election. Thus in France the episcopate easily acquired control over the largest and richest abbeys, such as Saint-Denis, Fécamp, or La Chaise-Dieu, and even over most of the houses of the Cistercian Order. Obviously the prelates, who held abbacies *in commendam,* could not fulfill the duties of their change. Hence, the monasteries were ruled by deputies, from whom the flaming enthusiasm of the founders or reformers of religious orders could certainly not be expected.

But, it will be asked, was the increase of monastic influence in the fifteenth century necessarily an evil? About the answer there can be little doubt. In the early Middle Ages, indeed, the religious orders had spread culture and true religion everywhere, and the work they had then done toward civilizing Europe can scarcely be overestimated. But conditions had changed, and the old spirit of heroic enterprise had been largely superseded by remissness and perfunctoriness. To such decay there were, of course, exceptions, which will be mentioned in due course. In Northern Europe especially, in the Low Countries, Germany, and England, the monastic spirit had not exhausted its powers of recuperation and creation. Yet, it cannot be doubted that, as a whole, conditions in most monasteries left much to be desired. Here again, a process of administrative disorganization, far more than any "superstitions," was at the root of moral evils. Discipline could be enforced only by a central authority, which in the religious orders was that of the general chapter, held at regular intervals, and strong enough to compel obedience. Now in the fifteenth century, the general tendency is toward disintegration. The various houses of each order tended to loosen the bonds which united them to the others, and to assert their independence.

This was, of course, easily achieved in the case of the so-called "autocephalous" monasteries, which had been the earliest-founded, and mostly belonged to the Benedictine Order. The drawbacks attending their isolation had become apparent in the fourteenth century, and Pope Benedict XII, through his bull *Summi Magistri,* had attempted to gather those of France into six provinces. The system, however, soon broke down, and many large monasteries, living for and by themselves, came to assume the position of great landowners rather than of religious institutions. But the same individualism was equally at work in those monastic orders which up till then had constituted real federations, with the general abbot as their head and the general chapter as their parliament. In the late fifteenth century, the general chapters of Cluny, Cîteaux, and Prémontré were vainly striving to assert their authority. Each house claimed a right to dispose of its own property and to select its own members. If visitors are sent, the prior of St. Euverte writes, "they are received at great cost and richly entertained. Neighbors and great personages are invited to come and feast with them, and gold is freely spent to shut their mouths." The same individualistic spirit led the officers in each house to make themselves independent, to rebel against the old communal spirit of monasticism, and secure for themselves private incomes out of the common property. Thus did monastic offices become real benefices, which often fell into the hands of non-resident seculars. Here again, administrative anarchy led to a general relaxation of discipline, with the worst possible consequences in morals.

We have shown that the main obstacle to reformation in the Church was the complicated entanglement of vested interests. Now, those interests were reducible to terms of money: hence the importance of the financial aspect of the ecclesiastical problems of the time. The clergy needed resources to carry on the various phases of their work, and owing to the disorganized state of the Church, those resources were not forthcoming, or were diverted into other channels. In the case of bishops, these ought to have included the ordinary dues levied on benefices, and the chancery and law fees. But all the exempt bodies, with their dependencies, refused to pay the former; while the latter brought in far less than they ought to have done because so many people withdrew themselves from episcopal jurisdiction. In 1482, the General Chapter of Cluny forbade all the houses of the Order to pay to the bishops the usual duty on their accession to their sees, or the visitation fees. About the same period, many parish priests also claimed exemption from taxes. As a consequence, the exchequer of many sees was in a sad plight. In 1461, the revenue of the archbishopric of Rouen had fallen to the paltry sum of 2000 French livres.

It was no easy task to extend or increase the taxes on benefices; but other duties imposed upon the laity might bring in more, and the bishops turned their efforts that way, from 1450 onward. A steady effort was made to extract more from marriage fees and the proving of wills. At Paris, in 1505, parish priests would refuse to bury the deceased whose wills had not been proved. Ecclesiastical censures were used freely against those who refused to pay; and in France the evidence of royal officers — even though it should be taken at a discount — throws light upon a stupendous state of affairs. In 1500, in the Clermont diocese, if we are to believe a procurator royal, there were some thirty or forty thousand excommunicated persons. Authentic records show a steady increase at Sens from 1468 to 1505. The dignity of the Church could be no gainer by such a cheapening of her censures; and while in the long run this increased pressure on the part of the clergy did little toward improving their financial position, it paved the way for the Protestant rebellion. In England popular feeling against Church taxation was running high toward 1520; and Henry VIII made use of the leverage thus offered him in his struggle against the Holy See.

The parish clergy was even worse off. Indeed, the churchwardens had considerable resources at their disposal, in the shape both of taxes, bequests, and foundations; but these funds were reserved for the building, repairing, and furnishing of the churches. The priest himself had no claim upon them, and might in most cases be described in Chaucer's words as "a povre persoun of a toun." Here again, the root of the evil lay in the faulty organization of the Church. Lay patronage had been reduced to some extent, but clerical patronage was fast gaining ground. The monasteries or chapters to which benefices were appropriated were entitled to the tithes, on condition that they should provide a decent income for the incumbent; but in general they proved to be close-fisted, and failed to fulfill their obligations adequately. Parishes, especially in rural areas, were too numerous and too small, and in many cases the priests were literally starving. We hear of some in Normandy living on an income of less than one "sou" a day, only half the pay of an artisan. What wonder, then, that the lower clergy should have made shift as best they could to grind a livelihood out of their parishes? Some took up a trade; most raised the duties for burials and churchings, begged for Masses, quarreled over their revenues with monks or friars, and charged fees for the sacraments.

We have now reached the point where financial maladministration led to religious abuses properly speaking. The doctrinal contentions of the Reformers were, to a large extent, the translation into theological language of a protest against undue payments exacted from the laity. This applied not merely to Church taxation proper, but also to voluntary contributions. Public charity had done beautiful work in building churches, cathedrals and hospitals, roads and bridges, under ecclesiastical supervision. But toward the year 1500, amidst the general confusion which we have described, there was a scramble for alms in which the most objectionable means were used. "Pardoners" often went far beyond the letter of the bulls which authorized them, or even hawked indulgences about without any permission at all. The piety and credulity of the people were exploited by swindlers, who carried about false relics or spurious indulgences. In 1506, the chapter of Soissons imprisoned a cleric who had produced forged bulls, allowing him to beg alms for the ransoming of prisoners; and there are many similar instances. Worse still, the sale of indulgences was pushed by means of unorthodox doctrine, as for instance that "whoever paid into the almsbox for the Crusade a tester for a soul in Purgatory, would free that Soul from Purgatory incontinently."

This abuse of Christian truth was bad enough, but it was not the only moral evil that followed upon the disorganized state of the Church. We have shown how tempting it was for the members of the hierarchy to neglect dioceses in which they met with resistance on every hand, and to join the courts of princes, where their abilities would meet with recognition. Thus in every country of Christian Europe the episcopate became an aristocracy of courtiers. Too much has been made of the serious moral lapses of some of them; but the least that can be said of the others is that they led a brilliant and pleasurable life, far removed from the obligations of their charge. They entrusted the care of their dioceses to deputies and accompanied the sovereign in his wanderings from castle to castle, or even in his campaigns. In the Italian wars, three cardinals, two archbishops, six bishops, and an abbot were in the following of Louis XII of France when he entered Milan in 1507. Some of these took part, with much gusto, in the actual fighting. At a court festival, about the same time, two cardinals danced before the king. The prelates soon became accustomed to an easy and luxurious life.

Cardinal d'Amboise erected a palace at Gaillon, on which he spent no less than 50,000 French livres. Wolsey's residence at Hampton Court immediately suggests itself as an English parallel. Much money was of course needed for the life which was to be led in such surroundings. Each bishop endeavored to obtain a growing number of benefices, and the crying scandal of pluralities became quite general. "The higher clergy," the German Johann Butzbach writes, "are much to blame for the neglect of souls. They send to the parishes unworthy pastors, while they themselves draw the tithes. Many seek to heap up for themselves as many benefices as possible, without fulfilling the duties incumbent upon them, and squander the ecclesiastical revenues in luxury and servants, pages, horses and dogs." That the influence of temporal sovereigns, in attaching to themselves those whose services were due to the Church, was largely responsible for this state of things, cannot be doubted.

The lower clergy had their own reasons for disliking residence in impoverished parishes, where it was impossible for a clever man to "get along" or to proceed with his studies. Toward the end of the fifteenth century, when the archdeacon of Paris was engaged upon a visitation, he found that 36 incumbents out of 83 were nonresident, while 12 had left their cures without permission. Those who supplied their places were the poorest and least qualified of the ecclesiastical body. Indeed, no systematic provision at all was made for the religious training of the parochial clergy as a whole. Some few of them only, who belonged to the gentry or to well-to-do burgher families, were lucky enough to attend a university or a chapter-school. The others had to be content with the teaching given at a village-school, or the lessons of the rector of the parish; they gathered a few scraps of Latin, learned enough theology and liturgy to say Mass, administer the sacraments, bury the dead, and keep the church accounts. They took orders without ever leaving their native place. No effort was made to develop the priestly spirit in their souls. They considered themselves as very much on the same level as their parishioners; and this lack of clerical dignity, coupled with their poverty, caused them to lead the same life, and indulge in the same pleasures, as the common rabble. There is truth indeed in Rabelais' satire of the lower clergy.

With the regulars also, financial and moral decay went hand in hand, the main cause being, here again, administrative abuse. A growing number of religious houses were held *in commendam* by Church dignitaries or members of the aristocracy who considered them merely as sources of income, never visited them, refused to pay for necessary repairs, and reduced them to sore financial straits. In 1486, the monks of Saint-Denis lodged a complaint against their commendatory abbot. The roofs of the church, cloisters, and dorters, they said, let in the rain; most barns and manors were falling to ruin; the scholars of the college which the abbey kept in Paris had been turned out; they themselves were scarcely able to obtain the necessaries of life; the sums allotted for their clothing and wine had been pared down; and their bread was so bad that they could not eat it; all this because the abbot had built extensive lodgings for his own convenience, and granted the benefices "to strangers who let everything melt away." Such a state of things seems to have been quite general and many monasteries were heavily in debt. Financial distress, the spirit of revolt, and relaxed discipline went, of course, hand in hand. To this must be added that the feudal aristocracy had gradually found their way into the religious houses as well as into the hierarchy. Monastic dignities and offices were reserved for the younger sons of noble families. The ideal of equality and common property had therefore disappeared. At Paris, in 1481, during the public festivities of the Epiphany, a number of monks joined with the students, dressed up as fools, armed themselves, and ranged about the city, abusing and attacking the passers-by. Women's cloisters were in the same pitiable condition. At le Vergier, it was found in the course of a visitation that the abbey was not closed, that the nuns had not gone to confession for six months, and that the abbess had not received Communion for fifteen months.

*   *   *

Dioceses in which most parishes were in the hands, not of the bishops, but of distant and neglectful patrons; in which exempt bodies of all kinds asserted their independence and spent their time in private quarrels; in which the higher clergy were elegant courtiers, while the lower clergy scarcely managed to live from hand to mouth; financial conditions which resulted in increased taxation for the laity, and the peddling of holy things by ecclesiastical mountebanks; monasteries which refused to submit to the heads of their orders, and in which the offices were held either by non-resident seculars or by disdainful and profligate noblemen, while the monks and nuns were left uncared for materially and spiritually; such is the state of affairs that we are faced with on the eve of the Reformation. The surprising thing, in the circumstances, is not that the level of Christian morality should have been low, but that it should still have been so high. In any case, a general administrative readjustment was needed; but no Church assembly, however holy and well-meaning, could effect it by its own means. Only a powerful central authority would be able to override all the vested interests which were unwilling to let themselves be dislodged.

Now, it was the tragedy of the late fifteenth and early sixteenth centuries that the papacy was disabled, almost until it was too late, from undertaking the necessary work of reconstruction. Of course the Holy See would have enjoyed greater authority and heightened respect had its moral decay not made it, for a time at least, unworthy of its task; and yet, the very evils and abuses which are most frequently denounced were largely brought about by external causes, over which the popes had no control. The nationalism so prominent at the Council of Constance (1414–1417) asserted itself anew, as the century wore on, in a less democratic shape. The power of national sovereigns was fast becoming absolute, and was attempting to embrace the ecclesiastical province as well. The attention of rulers was focused upon "policy," upon what was purely human and temporal in the government of their states, and they no longer even suspected the necessity of an independent spiritual body. The administration of the Church must be solely in their hands; and the pope must be content with the part of a chaplain, who might be allowed to preach, so long as he did not make himself offensive, but who might not on any account be granted actual powers of government.

Long before such theories were expounded by Bishop Stephen Gardiner as a justification of the Anglican schism, they had been acted upon by most sovereigns in Europe, even in countries which were afterwards to be considered the stanchest supporters of the papacy. In 1498, Spain was threatening to break off its allegiance to the Holy See, and Pope Alexander VI had to placate the Spanish sovereigns by granting them supreme authority over religious affairs within their dominions. Later, in 1508, the Spanish government claimed and obtained full rights of patronage over all churches in the West Indies. France very nearly started a schism of her own at the time of the Council of Pisa, convened by Louis XII (1511–1512). Venice went almost to the same lengths. Not merely did the Signory, in the first decade of the sixteenth century, arraign clerks before its tribunals — the question of clerical immunities being a debatable one — but it went so far as to appoint to benefices and even to bishoprics, not even allowing the pope to withhold confirmation of these acts.

Nor was this struggle to maintain the spiritual independence of the Church the only difficulty that the Holy See had to contend with. Its liberty and the very life of the popes were constantly threatened, in the late fifteenth century, and within the very walls of Rome, by feuds between powerful families, such as the Orsinis and the Colonnas, who wished to have the pope in their dependence. Maintenance of order in the papal dominions, or in the Eternal City itself, was a formidable problem. The nobility of central Italy was unruly and turbulent. The papacy was no better protected against the undertakings of mightier neighbors. France, Spain, the Empire, Venice, all wanted to extend their influence in the Peninsula, nibbled at the patrimony, took cardinals or Roman noblemen in their pay, and raised rebellions against the Holy See. Italy was overrun with foreign armies. In the circumstances, since the papacy had no sufficient military force at its disposal, the only possible policy was to play off the powers against each other, a policy to which Julius II was reduced throughout the length of his pontificate (1503–1513).

Here again, the disorders of the times were reflected in a financial crisis. Huge sums were needed for the administration of the universal Church, and for its defense against the Turkish invasion. The older sources of income had well-nigh dried up. Extensive parts of the patrimony had been usurped by the local nobility; feudal dues, rents, and tributes were not forthcoming, or lost in value through being farmed out. At the end of the fifteenth century, the total produce of customs, salt taxes, and feudal dues amounted to the wholly inadequate sum of 125,000 ducats. There was but one way out of the difficulty, the same one which both parish priests and bishops had taken, and one which was not likely to make the Church popular: namely, to raise the fees which were due to the Holy See for its spiritual services. Apart from tenths, first fruits, and various duties to be paid by the holders of benefices, the fees for dispensations of different kinds were increased 100 percent from 1471 to 1515.

Unfortunately, this oppressive system of taxation, while breeding much discontent, brought in far less than it ought to have done. Sovereigns insisted on retaining their share of all subsidies granted by their clergy to the papacy; the taxpayers took advantage of the fact that as a rule no compulsion was available against them, while tax-collectors, secretaries, and notaries of all descriptions retained for their own use a large part of the sums paid in to them. Two-thirds at least of the assessed moneys never reached the Curia at all. The budget of the Apostolic Chamber, the center of papal administration, had fallen, in the space of sixty years preceding the Reformation, from 300,000 to 150,000 ducats. On the eve of the Reformation, the sum total of all papal revenues amounted only to a maximum of 450,000 ducats, while in such a small kingdom as Naples, the poll-tax alone brought in 600,000. In 1484, Pope Sixtus IV had to pawn his tiara for 100,000 ducats. From 1471 to 1520 the Holy See was constantly in debt. In fact, it had become impossible to enforce a system of papal taxation throughout Europe, at a time when the ideal of an united Christendom was being battered down by the spirit of nationalism.

The dangers which threatened the independence of the papacy on the one hand, and the financial straits to which it was reduced on the other, account for many of the "abuses" which had crept into the Curia. The position of the popes in the early sixteenth century cannot be compared to what it is nowadays. European public opinion might be devotedly loyal; but distance made it difficult for it to count in Italy, while the papacy was really dependent on the play and counterplay of intrigue and strife between Roman or Florentine factions.

It was impossible for the popes not to engage in that intricate game of local politics; and first of all, they were compelled to recruit a body of faithful adherents, who were not likely to turn traitors. Now, in a country where the ties of blood count for more than any other bond, none were better fitted than the pontiff's own kinsmen to form that body-guard. Hence arose what has been so often branded as "nepotism" — hence, too, followed even the appointment of juvenile cardinals, whom it was safe to attach to the papal fortunes as early as possible, and who did not always turn out to be scapegraces.

There is less to be said in defense of the sale of ecclesiastical offices, or even cardinals' hats, though this was but one of the makeshifts used by Alexander VI to fill his treasury. At the consistory of May 31, 1503, nine cardinals were appointed, "most of them men of slender reputation." Some of them had paid up to 20,000 ducats and more, the total sum received amounting to 130,000 ducats. Such simony, however, still failed its purpose. Sixtus IV, Alexander VI, Julius II, and even Leo X, were compelled to have recourse to bankers. In 1513, the debt of Leo X to some of these rose to 125,000 ducats. Since the bankers — such as the Medici at Florence, the Dorias at Genoa, the Fuggers at Augsburg — naturally enough wanted pledges, permission was given to their local branches to collect the papal taxes directly. They even acted as intermediate agents between suitors for papal exemptions, dispensations, or benefices, and the Holy See. Thus there arose a huckstering in properly religious favors, which could only be detrimental to the good name of the Church.

The situation was the same in regard to the head of the Church as to her limbs. The times were changing. A system of administration, which had been possible and satisfactory as long as Europe was spiritually united under the authority of the Holy See, ceased to work once the disruptive spirit of lay statecraft gained the upper hand. The worst of it was that the papacy itself, being compelled to act less as an universal spiritual power than as a second-rate Italian principality, became infected by the new spirit, that of the pagan Renaissance, and tended to model itself on temporal courts. Thus moral evils arose, which cannot be excused or justified. In fact, however, the most scandalous period was not of very long duration, since it coincided with the pontificate of Alexander VI, which lasted from 1492 to 1503. But the condition of the papal court at the time might well give rise to righteous indignation. The pope showered favors upon his children, especially on Caesar Borgia; and the worst instance of his paternal generosity is the lavish way in which he granted to his son, who needed much money for his campaigns toward the enlargement of his dominions, much of the sums brought in by the jubilee of 1500. Beside such a misuse of the pope's power and such a betrayal of the trust shown to him by the pilgrims, common immorality will fall almost flat. Yet one imagines the impression produced on pious foreigners by such events as the solemn festivities for the second wedding of Alexander VI's daughter, Lucrece Borgia, one of the shows consisting in licentious dances, at which the pope himself was a spectator.

The moral level of the Roman court was much higher during the following pontificate, that of Julius II; nepotism disappeared, and the revenues of the Holy See were no longer squandered. But administrative and financial malpractices were not discontinued. The same old means were used to fill the papal treasury: the sale of offices, of benefices, of indulgences. Ecclesiastical censures were being constantly used for temporal purposes such as the recovery of Bologna from the Venetians.

In short, the same thing had happened to the Church which happens to most human societies. Without any deliberate evil intentions on the part of anyone, abuses creep in, which are gradually sanctioned by conservative habits and become almost respectable through age. They no longer give rise to wonderment or protest, and things are allowed to glide down the slope of perdition, the more comfortably, as so many vested interests would suffer if a root-and-branch reformation were undertaken. Only a man of uncommon sanctity, enthusiasm, and clearsightedness is able to cope with such a state of things; and in fact it did take a good many such men to plan a new organization for the Church, and keep her abreast of the times. They could hardly have succeeded, however, had Christendom been really corrupt at heart; but it was not. The material was lying ready for the hand of the builders: Christian Europe was rich in faith, charity, and devotion.

CHAPTER II

Early Reactions Against Disease in the Church

HOWEVER deplorable the abuses we have described, their influence upon the faithful was far less than might be expected. They persevered in the straight path despite faulty institutions. This appears clearly from a study of the religious literature, the piety and mysticism, the parish life, and the very Church architecture and decorative art of the period. The impression arrived at is not that of spiritual impoverishment, but on the contrary, almost that of a Renaissance. Indeed we may safely draw conclusions from the books turned out by the first printers, who like those of today had an eye to sales. Out of 54 works published in England by Wynkyn de Worde between 1490 and 1500, 30 have a religious theme. While the English seem to have had a preference for the lives of saints, numerous editions of the Bible appeared in Germany, France, and Italy, where the *Fioretti* of St. Francis were also especially popular. Mystical and ascetical treatises were many, the *Imitation* being, of course, foremost among them; but there were countless other works of the same description: *Pilgrimages* and *Hills* and *Ladders of Perfection, Gardens* and *Guides* and *Consolations of the soul.*

This flowering of fifteenth-century devotion was to have a considerable influence upon the mystical writers of the Catholic Reformation, especially St. Ignatius Loyola. It is manifested not merely in printed volumes, but also in private correspondence, pious effusions, diaries, commonplace books, and the wills of contemporaries.

A quality of sweetness and peace is found in a Yorkshire will of 1507 which begins with the following words:

> "In the name of the most blessed and holy Trinity, the Father, the Son, and the Holy Ghost, one God almighty and everlasting, of whom is all, by whom is all, and in whom is all; I Walter Cawood, inwardly remembering that all men living have here no city abiding, but be as pilgrims passing toward the promised city of Heaven by this temporal and wretched life, not sure of the hour nor time when the Lord of the house shall come, late at midnight, or early; lest that death, as a thief, unawares might throw adown this house of my earthly living, that at the coming of the great Spouse, when His pleasure shall be to call me, I be not found sleeping, willing therefore to dispose me through the gracious assistance of Almighty

God in all things to His pleasure. . . . I recommend and bequeathe my sinful soul to Almighty God my maker and redeemer, to His blessed mother and virgin Saint Mary, my whole trust and succour after God, and to the holy company of Heaven. . . ."

As far as can be ascertained, all the wills of that time are couched in the same style, and begin with the same pious exhortations, followed by bequests for the churches and the worship conducted within them, for prayers and Masses, and for good works of all kinds. Nor were the well-to-do alone generous. One is touched, even now, by the will of the poor woman of Northallerton, who left "a towel to the high altar and a brass-pot to the church."

There is indeed something especially simple and graceful about the period, which is reflected in its religious architecture. The effusiveness of personal piety gracefully combined with the growing prosperity of the times to produce a new type of art, naïve and skillful at the same time, rich and yet restrained, tender and fanciful. Everywhere churches were being built or repaired; hundreds of these are still extant in central and southern Germany, while even in half-civilized northern Germany, some forty were built on the "eve of the Reformation." The marvelous church and chapels of Brittany mostly date back to the same period, to which also belongs such a finished masterpiece as Notre-Dame de l'Epine in Champagne. England, as usual more solemn and stately, evolved the perpendicular style, which is exemplified in the wonderful chapel of King's College at Cambridge, and Henry VII's chapel in Westminster Abbey. Nowhere is the spirit of the early sixteenth century better revealed than in its painted glass as found for instance in the cathedral at Moulins or in Notre-Dame church at Châlons-sur-Marne. The happy, elegant blending of late Gothic and Classical motifs in the frames and setting; the range, richness, depth, and delicacy of the coloring; the airy lighting of the backgrounds; the intense devoutness of the feeling, especially in the kneeling portraits of the donors — all these combine to produce a mixed impression of beauty, serenity, and peace; of artistic refinement and spiritual perfection, greater even than those suggested by the half-Eastern gorgeousness of the thirteenth century.

The artistic beauty of the churches had its counterpart in the spiritual beauty of the home, which remained a shelter for religious truth and piety. Many treaties and books of devotion provided rules for the every-day life of families and for the education of children. In the Austrian *Road to Heaven* the head of the family is exhorted to attend the sermon and recall it after dinner with his home-folk.

"Then he sits at home with his good wife and with his children and his servantfolk, and asks them what they remember of the sermon, and tells them what he himself remembers. He questions them also, whether they know and understand the ten commandments, the seven deadly sins, the Our Father and the Creed, and teaches them. Finally he has a little drink brought in for them, and makes them sing a charming little hymn referring to God, to Our Lady or to the dear Saints, and rejoices in God with all his home-folk."

This charming picture of an Austrian household is not the only one of its kind. Italian families were being advised, about the same time, though in a somewhat soberer key, by St. Antonine, in words like the following: "When you go visiting abroad, even to see relatives, speak as little as possible, and only if you are compelled to do so. . . . Do not fail to watch over your children, so that they may live in the fear of God, and keep aloof from evil society. Guard yourself from evil not merely in your actions, but in your thoughts as well."

The same spiritual ideal inspired the corporate life of tradesmen and craftsmen to an extent which might surprise many Christians nowadays. The guilds in which they assembled were more than trade unions coupled with mutual insurance companies: they had a higher purpose, attending to the religious as well as to the temporal interests of their members. For members who died, they had Masses sung in their own chantries. They had prayer meetings before the statues of the Virgin or saints, such as that gathering in the streets of Amiens which surprised Bucer so much as late as 1549. They went on pilgrimages. Moreover, the statutes of Italian guilds often demanded that their members go to confession two or three times a year, refrain from swearing, hear Mass on Sundays and feast days, keep a devout attitude in the house of God, and remain in it until the very end of the divine service.

Though the administrative confusion in the Church made it harder for the clergy to perform their duties, one should not believe that the churches were silent and the pulpits empty. Once again we may turn to the early productions of the printing press. In England, among the first books published by Caxton, we find a number of collections of sermons; the old *Quattuor Sermones* of 1281 ran through no fewer than seven English editions between 1493 and 1499. In Germany, the sermons of the Dominican, Johann Herolt, had been printed forty-one times before 1500, which implies a sale of forty thousand copies. Then, besides direct preaching, many other means were used to teach the lay folk. The list of early printed books includes catechisms, such as that of the German friar, Dederich Cölde, which dates back to 1470.

At no period of Church history had the *biblia idiotarum,* the "books of the unlettered" — painted windows, frescoes, tapestries, and particularly stone carvings — assumed such importance in church decoration. The vanity of this world and the supreme importance of the hereafter is especially insisted on, as in the frequent theme of the "dance of death," of which the wonderful wall-painting in the abbey of La Chaise-Dieu in Auvergne provides such a haunting instance. At the same time religious drama was reaching a high degree of perfection. The mystery plays flourished in the late fifteenth and early sixteenth centuries. The huge composition known as the *Old Testament* was published in France about 1500, while the still vaster *Acts of the Apostles* of Arnould and Simon Gréban were printed in 1538. The parliament of Paris stopped the performance of mystery plays only in 1548, while in Italy, as late as 1517, a guild of religious players was founded by the Dominicans at Pistoja, and performed the life of the Virgin Mary, to the great edification of the townspeople.

In a Europe so deeply imbued with the spirit of the Gospel, it would be surprising indeed had no reforming efforts been made prior to the advent of Lutheranism. In fact, such efforts were constantly being made between 1450 and 1520, and often with a measure of success. They were a prefiguration of the Trentine plan, but they were frustrated by political circumstances, and most of all by the temporal and spiritual weakness of the Holy See. Among the huge body of the regular clergy, the monastic ideal was far from having spent all its strength. The Carthusians were famous for the holiness of their lives both in England and in Germany, where the Charterhouse at Cologne was considered as "offering to all religious orders a pattern of perfect ascetical discipline." The attraction of their spiritual life was felt at the English court; and it will be remembered that St. Thomas More spent "four years among them, dwelling near the Charterhouse, frequenting daily their spiritual exercises . . ." and that "for the religious state he had an ardent desire, and thought for a time of becoming a Franciscan."

In Italy, the movement which was to bring about the birth of new orders amidst the very turmoil of the battle against Luther, had begun twenty years at least before the Reformation. At Vicenza in 1494, at Genoa in 1497, brotherhoods had been founded, which were a link between the Franciscan and the Jesuit schemes of religious life. It is significant that the "Oratory of Divine Love" of Gaetano da Thiene, which was to develop into the Theatine Order and exert such an influence upon the Catholic Reformation, was founded just one year before

Luther posted his theses on the gates of Wittenberg university church. The partiality shown by the popes themselves to various religious orders may well be an instance of mistaken zeal, since it led to the weakening of the authority of the hierarchy. Yet the Holy See was no doubt right in thinking that the vitality of monastic life, if maintained, would strengthen the militant spirit in the Church. It would be tedious to rehearse the many favors granted to the regulars, even in the darkest days of pagan sensuousness at Rome, by Sixtus IV, Alexander VI, and Julius II. It seems obvious that the popes, especially while protecting the friars, wished to further the work of the most active section of the Church; and one is struck by the fact that in many cases, the orders which they encouraged followed an austere rule inspired by burning piety. Such was the case of the Minims, the Tertiaries attached to them, the Brothers of the Common Life, and the Apostolic Brothers. Besides, reform and re-union were frequently attempted by the popes in the case of the larger orders: the Franciscans (under Sixtus IV), the Dominicans (under Alexander VI), the Benedictines (under Julius II).

However, no real reformation of the regular clergy was possible so long as the practice of exemptions made each order — and within each order each house — practically independent. In fact, in granting favors to individual monasteries, the popes, far from strengthening their authority, really played into the hands of what remained of the conciliar party. Viewing things as a whole, the conciliar movement had tended to the breaking up of the Church, not merely into nations, but also into numberless separate units. Those who stood against the supreme authority of the pope and hierarchy were generally defending privileges which in most cases were no better than abuses. At all events, they were providing safe hiding holes for all kinds of moral evils. The point is an important one, and is perfectly illustrated in the happenings of the mid-fifteenth century, when Pope Nicholas V attempted with great earnestness the general reformation of the Church. But both the evils to be amended and the resistance to correction on the part of privileged bodies are best revealed in the mission of Cardinal Nicholas de Cusa, a Rhinelander, who in his capacity as papal legate ranged over the whole of Austria and Germany in the years 1451 and 1452.

The main object of his mission was to proclaim and distribute the indulgence granted for the Jubilee of 1450; but he had received extensive powers of visitation and reformation and, in a series of provincial synods, issued many drastic regulations. The evils he had to deal with were those which have been described above. He took steps against the exactions of secular or regular patrons and endeavored to improve the financial condition of the parish clergy, who in their turn were to refrain from simony in every shape, such as the receiving of fees for confession. The practice of keeping concubines had become widespread, especially among cathedral chapters, the members of which belonged to the nobility. Nicholas de Cusa forbade it under the severest penalties. Spurious indulgences, miracles, and pilgrimages, the unnecessary swarming of brotherhoods which withdrew their members from parish life, and generally all petty devotions inspired by superstition, were summarily dealt with. Visitors were sent to many monasteries, reforming movements were encouraged. Where compliance was not forthcoming, new abbots were substituted for those who refused to obey. A further impulse was given to preaching; all parish priests were ordered to have a copy of St. Thomas Aquinas' *Summa of the articles of the faith and of the sacraments of the church*. Rules were prescribed for the dignity of public worship and against the undue exposition of the Blessed Sacrament.

That all those decrees might actually be enforced, Nicholas de Cusa did his best to strengthen the powers of the pope and of the hierarchy. He ordered all priests to recite after every Mass the following invocation. "O Lord, guard from all adversity Thy servants our pope and our bishop, as well as the whole Catholic Church." He safeguarded the rights of bishops' courts against archdeacons. He compelled non-exempt monks to acknowledge episcopal authority, and in one case, at least, made use of the latter even for the reformation of exempt monasteries.

All in all, his work anticipated, on many points, that of the Council of Trent by a hundred years. Why, then, was its effect only temporary? The reasons for its failure are easily ascertained, and provide food for thought. In fact, the very causes which stood in the way of Catholic Reformation in the fifteenth century were to bring about the Protestant revolt in the sixteenth. It was greed, the thirst for power, and the lusts of the flesh, which induced one generation of princes to support every local resistance to Rome, and perpetuate abuses which no centralized Church would have tolerated. It was greed, the thirst for power, and the lusts of the flesh which induced another generation of princes to take the so-called Reformation into their own hands, and to tear up the body of the Church. In either case "independence" meant freedom from all spiritual restraints.*

---

* The above judgment applies to temporal rulers only. The real moral earnestness of many reformers, especially after the first phase of the religious struggle was over, will certainly not be questioned here.

Despite the efforts of Nicholas de Cusa, the nationalist spirit would not allow of any sums being sent to Rome for indulgences or otherwise; the mendicant friars were hostile; so was the conciliar party. Besides, those whose conduct had been reproved often put up a more or less open fight. Hemold, abbot of St. Godeshard at Hildesheim, after having sworn obedience, went on living in his old way. At Deddingen, when a reformer was sent to the monastery, the monks broke his carriage to pieces; at St. Ulric, Augsburg, an emissary from the reformed abbey of Melk was imprisoned for a fortnight. The alliance between the vested interests of the clergy and the secular power appeared clearly when Nicholas de Cusa as bishop of Brixen in the Tyrol, tempted to correct the abuses in his diocese. He made it compulsory for his parish clergy to meet in chapters thrice yearly; unified the liturgy; and warned the faithful against the beautiful tales of the *Golden Legend*. But when he undertook to reform the nunnery at Sonnenburg, where many daughters of the nobility had found a home, he came up against the determined will of Sigismund, the duke of Tyrol, who refused to acknowledge any authority but his own. In the quarrel which ensued, the duke more than once had recourse to violence; it was to assume huge proportions and to last many years, and we are not concerned with its history. But Nicholas de Cusa's own view of the position is significant. In his mind, the freedom of the Church was the necessary condition of its reformation; no reforming bishop ought to be a court prelate, the compliant servant of a temporal ruler. He induced Pope Nicholas V to define in the following words the duties of the bishops of Brixen: "They shall be neither the chancellors nor chaplains of secular princes, but will be bound to reside in their diocese."

*   *   *

The efforts of Nicholas V were continued by his successor Pius II (1458-1464) under whose pontificate Cusa administered the papal states in the same spirit in which he had governed his diocese and composed a plan for the reform of the Curia. Unfortunately, the evangelical ideal was gradually being smothered at Rome by the enthusiasm which ancient literature, philosophy, and art were arousing, and various feeble attempts to improve the state of the Church at large proved abortive. Alexander VI, when struck with awe and repentance by the murder of his son, the duke of Gandia, resolved to mend matters. He called a committee of cardinals to prepare a general reformation, and drafted a bull against abuses (1497). But it was never to take effect. At last a sincere and well-meaning man, Pius III, was raised to the papal throne; but his untimely death (1503) frustrated his plans. When reading the history of the period, one has almost the uneasy and painful impression that a perverse fate was set on defeating all reforming efforts, and that things would never come to a head.

Yet, in the absence of guidance from above, individual movements for the betterment of conditions had begun in several countries. These movements anticipated the Catholic Reformation proper, insofar as they tried to restore morality in the Church; but they differed from it, in that they merely looked backwards, expecting salvation from a general restoration of the old forms of discipline, especially in the monasteries. They took no account of altered conditions, which made adaptation a necessity. Savonarola's attempt to establish the kingdom of Christ at Florence (1481–1498) was in fact but the reaction of mediaevalism against the Renaissance. In France, the conservative wing of the reforming party could think of no remedies but a reinforcement of the strict rule in the religious orders, and a reversion to the old system of elections throughout the Church, culminating in general councils of a parliamentary type. And yet, though it was not realized that a new world demanded new methods, important results were obtained; and it is not a little significant that this true reformation should have taken place twenty years at least before Luther.

At the French States General of 1484, the representatives of the clergy raised a protest against those very administrative malpractices which were the cause of corruption, ignorance, and superstition in the Church. The Provincial Council of Sens (July, 1485) issued a set of canons on public worship, monastic discipline, against excessive taxation and the disorderly life of clerics. In Paris, the principal of Montaigu College, Jean Standonck, mystic and scholar, gathered around him a circle of reforming spirits. Similar groups began to appear everywhere, with abbots and bishops as their heads. Their influence soon spread to the civil authorities and to royalty itself. It culminated in the general assembly of the French clergy which met at Tours on November 12, 1493. There the sores of the Church were laid bare: the peddling of holy things, the abuse of indulgences and collections, various forms of simony, the wandering about of monks, the ignorance of preachers, the exactions of ecclesiastical judges; all these being due originally to the neglect of old canons, to the fact that no synods were held, to the granting of benefices to unworthy persons, to exemptions and dispensations, and the holding of benefices *in commendam*.

At the same time the French king, Charles VIII, applied to the pope for help toward the enforcement of the decisions of the assembly; and on July 24, 1496, Alexander VI appointed three Benedictine abbots as visitors of all the French houses of the order. But spontaneous reformation had already begun. Several bishops called synods, as at Langres, Chartres, Nantes, Troyes, and undertook to improve matters in various monasteries. The movement was gathering momentum among the religious communities themselves. At Cluny, from 1481 to 1486, the general chapters undertook the work of concentration. In 1486, statutes were issued for the restoration of the rule, the re-enforcement of fasting, silence, and the common life. Steps were taken to help materially decayed houses, and to apply part of the revenues to the repair of monastic buildings. In 1494, the chapter organized visitations and prescribed a minute inquiry into every detail of life in the monasteries. The visitors were empowered to suspend and excommunicate abbots or priors if they rebelled. Still harsher measures were taken in 1499. The reforming action was continued right up to the appearance of Protestantism. A similar process took place at Citeaux, Tiron, and elsewhere.

The pressure brought to bear on Rome by the reforming movement made itself felt increasingly after 1500. On the request of King Louis XII, Pope Alexander VI granted to Cardinal d'Amboise full powers as legate in France in 1501. The Cardinal undertook the reformation of the mendicant orders. He had to struggle against huge difficulties, and had recourse more than once to main force. In order to effect the reformation of the Benedictine abbey of St. Germain in Paris, he sent to it two religious from Cluny accompanied by a party of men-at-arms, who forcibly and without any parley expelled three recalcitrant monks. In the case of the Paris Franciscans, he had to send to them a company of one hundred archers and several sergeants, who put them under arrest and threatened them with expulsion. The method used by him in France was the same as was being used beyond the Channel: it consisted in furthering the action of reformed branches, such as that of the Observant Franciscans. In England King Edward IV had established them at Greenwich in 1480. Henry VII founded another house at Richmond, and another again at Newark, in 1499; then turned out unreformed Conventuals to make room for them at Newcastle, Southampton, and Canterbury. In 1502, the Greenwich Observants prevailed upon the Conventuals to "change their religious habits" for coarser ones. In France, Cardinal d'Amboise introduced small groups of them into each Franciscan house. He did the same thing in the case of the independent Benedictine abbeys, restored moral and financial discipline among the nuns of Fontevrault and other houses, and finally gathered detached monasteries into unions or bound them to existing orders. His religious dictatorship, which lasted nine years, produced lasting results.

As the Protestant outbreak drew near, the Church in France, as in England, seems to have been, not on a downward, but on an upward slope. New ecclesiastical buildings of all descriptions were being built or repaired. The number of ordained clerics, secular and regular, was steadily increasing. The progress was no less notable in regard to quality, the proportion of university graduates and members of the bourgeoisie and nobility also rising higher and higher.

Yet the regular clergy had put up a hard fight against Cardinal d'Amboise; and once the reforming movement had spread to Rome, and had brought about the gathering of the Lateran Council, that same resistance of vested interests was to immobilize its impulse. The council first met on May 2, 1512, and after lasting through twelve sessions broke up on March 12, 1517. It was clear from the first that the Fathers were alive to the needs of changed times. Two points were made clear by the speakers: first, that the temporal overlordship of the Holy See had to be set aside, to be replaced by agreements made with each sovereign and safeguarding the interests of religion; secondly, that the spiritual supremacy of the papacy was a necessary preliminary to any general reformation. In his sermon at the opening of the first session, Giles of Viterbo advised the Church to give up the use of material weapons, and to confine herself to that of spiritual weapons, piety and prayer, the cuirass of faith and the sword of light; while on May 10, the Venetian, Bernardino Zano, preached on the unity of the Church, which could only be ensured, he said, through the submission of the members to their head, the Vicar of Christ. On May 17, Thomas Cajetan further stressed the necessity of papal authority, and made an onslaught upon conciliar theories, and especially upon the council of Pisa, which had been called by the French king, Louis XII. No voice among the assembled Fathers was raised to assail his views.

In fact, the Lateran Council did succeed in giving effect to these two principles when sanctioning the Concordat of 1516 with France, which gave the death-blow to conciliarism there, and ensured spiritual supremacy to the Holy See. But in regard to Church reformation, it did not probe the sore to the bottom, and was content with timid, though well-meaning, recommendations. It did pass a decree with the following provisions: that bishoprics and abbacies should be conferred only upon worthy persons and according to canonical rules; that resignations, transfers, dispensations, and reservations should be limited; that cardinals and members of the Curia should adopt a stricter rule of life. But when thorough reformation of the administrative and fiscal systems of the Church was suggested, the assembly split into two parties, and it was clear that nothing drastic would be done. A quarrel arose between seculars and regulars, especially over the bull *Mare magnum;* eventually the powers of the bishops were somewhat strengthened. But the general atmosphere seems to have been lukewarm. It was a pity that France, England, and Germany should have been practically absent from the council; their moral earnestness and their critical temperament might have altered matters. But the Italian wars allowed of no general gathering.

While the Lateran Fathers struggled feebly with the difficulties of the hour, things were developing on new lines elsewhere. Leo X was giving proof of his clearsightedness and political sense in the matter of the French Concordat. It seems surprising, at first sight, that he should have relinquished into the hands of a temporal ruler so much of his properly spiritual authority. The king of France was henceforth to appoint to all ecclesiastical livings and preferments, while the pope would be allowed to veto such appointments only if the canonical rules had been infringed. The moral influence and wealth of the Gallican Church were thus placed at the disposal of the sovereign. At the same time Leo X, while striking a bargain of doubtful advantage to the future interests of the Church at large, was trying to turn it to the best possible account, by inserting clauses which were to ensure the reformation of the French clergy, even more so than the Lateran decrees. The very nature of the agreement did away with all papal reservations and expectative graces. University graduates were to have one third of the benefices. Excommunication and interdict were henceforth to be used only in specified cases. The most important provision by far was that which forbade seculars to hold regular benefices and the reverse. Steps were taken against concubinary priests. In each cathedral or metropolitan church, a canonry was reserved for a graduate in theology, who was bound to lecture to the faithful at least once a week on Holy Scripture.

Leo X dealt similarly with other countries. Though temporal princes were later to make use of his very concessions to bar the way to the reforming action of the Council of Trent, for the time being at least, his policy had beneficial effects. In the case of France, by granting the king wide powers over his Church, it took away from him the main reason he might have had of joining hands with the German princes or with Henry VIII and declaring a schism; it also bound him to the interests of the Holy See, and made him the foremost instrument of re-formation in his dominions. Besides, by ensuring the removal of the most blatant abuses, it deprived Protestantism of its chief grievances, and made it difficult for it to gain a firm foothold in France. In the case of Spain, Leo X respected the ecclesiastical independence of the realm, thus attaching it to the papacy. He granted many privileges to Portugal, and concluded an agreement with Poland, much on the same lines as the French Concordat. Had the latter been extended to England and Germany, the greed of princes would have been everywhere sated, and the theological revolt of Luther would have been deprived of all state support. Within its limits, the policy of Leo X appears as wise, and it did much to lessen the effects of the Protestant outbreak.

*   *   *

"Policy" alone, however, could not repair the ruins heaped up by more than one century of maladministration and moral decay. Devotion, sacrifice, enthusiasm were needed, as also a feeling of deep remorse for what had been wrong in the past. These fine qualities indeed had not disappeared, since the spirit of reform was at work everywhere; but they would not have been sufficient, if men had looked only backwards, had only attempted the re-enforcement of the old rules and canons, a re-version to early monasticism and to the disciplinary practice of the Middle Ages. Changes had taken place which could not be ignored, and reformation must now develop along new lines. It had to take into account, not merely the division of Europe into national units, but also the cultural, literary, and artistic development brought about by the Renaissance, which could not be ignored.

In other words, while no amendment of Church conditions was possible without an evangelical revival, that revival must consist mostly in chastening the spirit of the times, must be a combination of a cultured Christianity and a christianized Renaissance. This combination, which was to be the essence of the Catholic Reformation, had its root as early as the late fifteenth century in the movement known as Christian human-ism. It was the natural reaction of the genuine piety of the body of the Church against corruption in its head. Its progress was to be simul-taneous with the progress of the reforming party; its representatives were slowly to force their way into the College of Cardinals, the curial offices, and eventually to conquer the papacy itself; and it was then that their efforts were to mature and bear fruit in the Council of Trent, while they also inspired the work of the Society of Jesus.

The task which the Christian humanists set out to perform was a new and original one. The harm done by the Renaissance, they thought, must be undone by the Renaissance. Nor was the duty thus to be fulfilled such an ungracious one; for there was much which was of lasting value in the speculative philosophy and practical everyday wisdom of antiquity, in its perfection of literary form and artistic beauty. There was much also which might be used to help in the strengthening and spreading of Christianity. For one thing, the labors of profound study might be reconciled with Christian seriousness of mind. Then again, antiquity might be viewed as having had at least glimpses of the absolute truth; and to that extent, its teachings might still be profitable. The poets of ancient Greece and Rome were in various respects worthy of imitation, for despite the pagan fables in their works, they had felt, at least obscurely, the beauty of divine things. Ancient philosophers yearned for communion with the absolute perfection of the Godhead. St. Paul himself was a Greek writer of note; and the first Christian interpretation of the ancient world was supplied by the Fathers of the Church. The Christian humanists of the late fifteenth and early sixteenth centuries were but following suit: they gathered, from antiquity before the Revelation, enough knowledge to serve as a guide for the study of antiquity after the Revelation — of the sacred texts and patristic literature.

This attempt to seek Christianity even in pagan Greece and Rome, to rescue the Church through the very means which had produced her downfall, may seem somewhat paradoxical; and indeed it did, upon occasion, run to lengths which are to be deplored, were it but in the name of good taste. Besides, it was to be feared that the flaming ideal of apostleship might be damped by the classical philosophy of the golden mean. But the danger was not as yet a real one. The Christian humanists ardently wished for a religious revival. They aimed at a true reformation — not merely a correction of abuses, but a cleansing and a lifting up of hearts, grounded on a more sincere acquiescence in the Gospel, a deeper love of Christ. They did not want every man to set up as a theologian; but they wanted him to read the Bible humbly and piously, and to gather from it spiritual truths. They insisted on the importance of preaching — the right sort of preaching: not by means of divisions and distinctions of the scholastic type, but sweetly, kindly, in words that all might grasp, that might win through love rather than strike with fear. In this respect they were decidedly different from the early Protestants, both in Germany and England; though they have often been said to have unwittingly been their forerunners.

Calling "Pre-Reformers" all those who attempted to improve the state of religion before Luther is a common enough mistake. But whatever we know of the deeper feelings of the Christian humanists runs clear against such a view. It cannot be shown that they ever took up the theological position of the Protestants, or that they shared their political or social views. Erasmus clearly asserted that works must be joined with faith in the task of salvation, and both he and Lefèvre d'Etaples looked to the pope as the supreme head of Christendom. It is true that they themselves as well as their school devoted much time to the critical study of the Scriptures. But what likeness is there between the patient efforts of scholars to elucidate, through linguistic and historical research, the true meaning of the sacred texts, and the free interpretation of those same texts, through the "Spirit," which the Protestants claimed as a right for everyone of the faithful, however unlearned he might be? It is true also that the Christian humanists denounced intellectual evils, and attempted to substitute for the debased remnants of mediaeval theology a new type of religious culture, both more enlightened in its thought and more evangelical in its spirit. In so doing however, they laid the groundwork, not for the Protestant but for the Catholic Reformation.

Thus were the gentle wisdom, the temperate persuasiveness of the best among the ancients — outward tokens, now, of a love of Christ which was anything but merely moderate — made to spread the teachings of Christ. The aim which the Christian humanists had before their eyes, when reviving classical studies, was strikingly expressed by the German scholar, Trithenmius: "The ancient authors we are engaged in reading," he says, "should be for us but the means of reaching a higher goal. We may with a clear conscience recommend the study of such books to all those who wish to take it up, not in a worldly spirit and with a view to witty trifles, but for the earnest development of their intellectual faculties, seeking in it, according to the example of the Holy Fathers, ripe fruits for the improvement of Christian knowledge. Nay, such studies, in our judgment, are necessary for this purpose." Indeed there are — thus spoke Johannes Butzbach — "in the ancient authors many descriptions which hurt moral delicacy, but we may not on that account dispense with the study of the classics. Only we should as far as possible, and according to the advice of St. Basil, go to work as the bees do, that do not suck in the whole of the plants or the poison that is in them, but absorb only the honey."

Three quarters of a century later, one of the refugees at Douay College was to use words almost similar to these, when referring to the educational scheme of the Jesuits. Grounding the teaching of the young upon the study of the classics, and especially of classical form rather than substance, might — and did eventually — lead to superficiality and dryness. But the point is that the Jesuit plan, in its essentials, was already outlined in the educational practice of the Christian humanists.

Many treatises were printed to teach adult or juvenile scholars the principles of grammar and eloquence, as expounded by the ancients. Thus the French humanist, Gaguin, the author of a poem on the Immaculate Conception, also wrote a handbook for poets called *Ars versificatoria;* and another French humanist of a somewhat later generation, Clichtoue, who was to wage a controversial war against the Lutherans, published with his own commentaries the *De eloquentia* of Stefano Fieschi and the *Opusculum in elegantiarum praecepta* of Agostino Dathi. Schoolboys and students soon had at their disposal a number of fine editions of the classics, of dictionaries and grammars. That this was not merely a lay movement, and that pagan antiquity was made to help in the study of Christian literature, appears from the syllabus of a German parish school, of the year 1500 or so; it included the *Iliad*, Aesop's *Fables*, Terence, the *Aeneid*, Cicero's *De Amicitia* — but also the historical part of the Old Testament, the Gospel and the Acts, works of Boece, St. Jerome, and St. Basil.

Though "imitation" might become superficial after a time, the mingling of what was best in classical culture with all that was best in Christian piety, on the "eve of the Reformation," produced a particularly attractive type of religion. Clear minds, freed from all the lumber of decadent scholasticism, temperate, reasonable, and elegant in expression; kind hearts, imbued with all the sweetness of the Gospel, eagerly spiritual, trusting and humble; both minds and hearts filled with the supreme thought of peace, and therefore disinclined from all social or political troubles, averse to individual selfassertion, to rebellion against the established order, whether in society or in the Church; conservative in their actions, and yet free in their thoughts; trusting enough in the permanent unity of the Christian commonwealth to allow themselves surprising flights of imagination — as in the *Utopia* — or outbursts of satire — as in the *Encomium Moriae* — which they never thought of turning into explosive charges toward the disruption of the Church; such were the contemporaries of More and Clichtoue about the year 1500. That their "moderation" was not exclusive of absolute devotion to their Christian ideal, the martyrdom of More, like that of John Fisher, was to show.

CHAPTER III

Reformation Again Delayed

THE administrative results of the Lateran Council were not such as might have been desired; but it was the outcome of a reforming movement which could not be withstood, and which had borne fruit long before Luther's protest was heard in Germany; it created a new spirit, which made itself felt very soon in the government of the Church as well as in the intellectual and artistic life of the Roman court. Granted that the pontificate of Leo X was not a pattern of Christian austerity, yet the time of the worst abuses was now past. The state of Christianity was improving; and it would have improved much faster, and wholly forestalled the Protestant upheaval, had the papacy been free to concentrate upon home problems. Unfortunately, the correction of abuses, even indeed, some years later, the suppression of the German revolt, ranked only second among the difficulties which Rome had to contend with. Just about the year 1517 the whole of Christendom was threatened with a Turkish invasion, which might have done away with Western civilization altogether; while the ambition of various Christian princes constantly endangered the independence of the Holy See. Thus the popes were compelled to turn most of their attention to international politics, and to play the part of temporal rulers rather than that of religious leaders.

On the other hand, it is true that they also lacked the necessary insight to anticipate the Lutheran uprising. Not, indeed, that lukewarmness prevented them from understanding its religious motives, but that the spirit of the North was foreign to men who were surrounded by the exuberance of Italian art and culture, with all the wealth of external expression these possessed. The Renaissance was no longer responsible for monstrous crimes; but its intellectual and moral ideal still inspired the life of the Roman court. Man's highest pursuits were still held to be, in the natural order, the acquirement of knowledge, the erection of monuments, the production of works of art, and the government of states. Such an ideal, indeed, might be reconciled with the Christian spirit, and was no bar to personal devotion; but its outward splendor made it difficult for the Curia to understand the puritanical mysticism of the North, to realize its explosive force, and to obviate its consequences. Something has been said in the preceding pages of the pontificate of Leo X (1513–1521). Contemporaries described it as being the reign of Minerva succeeding upon that of Venus. The rising soberness and seriousness thus denoted were not confined to the intellectual sphere. Abuses current but one generation before had now become unthinkable. Bribery had been made impossible at papal elections by a bull of Julius II. At the conclave which chose Leo X, the personal virtue of the candidates was taken into account. The new pope himself, however cultured and refined in his tastes, was sincerely devout. Every day, even in the midst of pressing business, he would hear Mass and read his breviary. His moral character, both before and after his election, remained unspotted. In his appointment of cardinals, he was not always, it is true, guided by the highest motives. The first batch, in 1513, included worthless relatives or associates, one of them being the scandalous Bibbiena. But the second batch, a few months before Luther defended his theses at Wittenberg, showed marked improvement. Some of the new cardinals owed their appointment to their high connections or to their kinship with the Medici family, to which Leo X belonged; but the others were men of great learning and personal dignity. Such were Tommaso de Vio, better known as Cajetan, the general of the Dominicans; and Egidio Canisio, often called Giles of Viterbo, the general of the Augustinian Hermits, and reformer of his order, a man of undisputed moral and intellectual eminence. The college of cardinals was now open to rejuvenating influences.

That the age of Leo X should be considered as a preface to the Catholic Reformation will, it is true, give rise to some wonder. The material prosperity and the artistic magnificence of Rome at this time seemed to some contemporaries, and still seem to many nowadays, hard to reconcile with the soberness and lowliness of the true Christian spirit. On the other hand, the period was profusely praised by humanists and artists as a kind of golden age, and its memories were later treasured and cherished by them, after the sack of Rome in 1527 had put an end to it forever. And yet all this refinement and splendor were not, as Luther thought, tantamount to moral depravity. It was possible for refined Romans to lead sincerely pious lives. That very beauty of outward form of which they were so fond might be made to glorify Christian truth. The example of Leo X himself is typical. He ate but one dinner a day; and fasted three times a week; yet he delighted in listening to music after his meals. A composer himself, he spared no expense to attract performers from various parts of Italy and from abroad. His private chapel included singers from Italy, Spain, France, and the Netherlands. But his purpose, in thus encouraging the musical art, was the beautifying of public worship. The Renaissance was still there, but it was being Christianized.

It is true that pagan forms of speech and pagan motives in painting, sculpture, and decoration were still freely used. When Leo X took possession of the Lateran after his election, triumphal arches were raised in the streets through which the procession was to pass. One of these, built at the expense of the banker, Agostino Chigi, was adorned with the figures of Apollo, Mercury, Pallas, of Nymphs and Centaurs. Another had a statue of Moses between those of Perseus and Apollo, Mercury and Diana. The paintings in the *loggie* at the Vatican, completed under Leo X, exhibited the same abundancy of profane motives: the legends and even the lighter side of classical mythology revived there, with Venus and Jupiter, Bacchus and Ariadne, Apollo and Marsyas, Medea, the Sphinx, Centaurs, Satyrs, Nymphs, Harpies, frolicsome Eros, Tritons fighting with marine monsters. Yet the very fancifulness of such a decoration shows that it should not be taken too seriously. It testifies mostly to a taste for playful amusement, and to antiquarian curiosity, the latter being evidenced by pictures representing sacrifices, an augur, a ruined temple, the Appian way, etc.

In fact, the pious inspiration due to the reforming movement was already present in the major compositions of Raphael (1483–1520), who was entrusted by Leo X with the supervision of all building and decorative work at the Vatican. Pagan motifs had not wholly disappeared from the tapestries of the Sistine Chapel, the cartoons of which are now preserved in South Kensington Museum: the Parcae, the labors of Hercules, were strangely mixed with Faith, Hope, and Charity; but the central spaces were occupied with subjects taken from the Old and New Testaments, and especially from the lives of SS. Peter and Paul. Though the intimate, naïve, and somewhat awkward devotion of an earlier age had now given place to perfection and magnificence, yet such pictures as the *Sistine Madonna* or the *Transfiguration* testify to the depth of Raphael's devout feelings, and to the influence of the Lateran Council.

The revival of devotional art was paralleled with a similar revival in the world of letters. Among Raphael's friends was the Christian humanist, Sadolet, one of the most prominent and attractive figures of the time: a man of sober, earnest piety, whose presence at the Roman court, and whose favor with Leo X, show that life in early sixteenth-century Rome was far from being an orgy of pagan revelry.

Sadolet, who stood high among contemporary Latin writers, and wrote Ciceronian epistles, had achieved fame through his poem on the discovery of the Laocoon group of statuary. He spent his time in serious studies; from time to time he would gather his literary friends for tranquil debate. After a plain meal in some place reminiscent of the classical age, poems were recited and orations were read. Years later, Sadolet would cast a glance of melancholy regret upon those happy hours. Indeed, the period just preceding the Protestant Reformation seems to have been, in Italy as well as in England, bathed in a golden light: the general atmosphere was not one of riotous sensuousness, but rather one of self-denying industry, of patient research, in which men freely, quietly enjoyed the pleasures of intellectual enquiry. The charm of literary pastimes was no bar to personal holiness. Sadolet was concerned with the amendment of Church conditions; he took no advantage of his influential position, rejected the gifts that came to him from every hand, and sought no benefices. In him enthusiastic appreciation of classical letters was perfectly blended with ardent piety; and if he happened, in his Latin writings, to use such expressions as "by Hercules" or "ye immortal gods," it was, he said, to give greater force to his style, so as to make it fitter to serve justice and truth, and to urge men to righteousness.

Many believed, like Sadolet, that classical elegance and purity of style were necessary for the fostering of Christian piety. This was not altogether an illusion in an age which set such store by purely literary accomplishments, and the notion was to inspire Catholic methods of education for centuries after the Council of Trent. It might lead to exaggerations, as when Zaccaria Ferreri, at the bidding of Leo X, recast the hymns of the Breviary, substituting for their robust roughness and fervor smoothness which betokened the polished craftsman more than the ardent worshipper.

Thus, in Italy as well as in France and in England, Christian humanism was the keynote of the age. Leo X was consistently friendly toward Erasmus, whose scholarly work on Scripture and the Fathers he encouraged. The learned Dutchman was allowed to dedicate to the pope his edition of St. Jerome and his Greek New Testament; and the pontiff was unwilling to believe the charge made against Erasmus, of having secretly connived at the Lutheran heresy: thus showing that, in his mind there was no necessary connection between Scriptural scholarship and new-fangledness in doctrine. Leo X also granted privileges to Aldo Manucci, the Venetian printer of Greek books, and founded in Rome a Greek college, with Jan Lascaris as rector. Christian poetry was no less encouraged than Christian scholarship. In 1521, the pope hastened the publication of Sannazaro's Latin poem *De partu Virginis,* and he befriended Marco Girolamo Vida, a young priest who, before the end of Leo's pontificate, set to work upon his fine Latin epic on the Gospel story, the *Christias.* Nor were Roman circles incurious in regard to the higher mysteries. Giovanni-Francesco Pico della Mirandula was the main representative of that Christian Platonism which was to last on through the century, and dedicated to Leo X, himself a former pupil of Marsilio Ficino, his treatise on divine love.

*   *   *

Thus the spirit which was to inspire the Catholic Reformation was already present in all its essentials. Deeply devout men were at work everywhere in Western Europe extracting from the Renaissance what was of lasting value, and molding anew the intellectual, the artistic, and even the devotional life of the Church. But individual efforts were of little avail against the unwieldy system of ecclesiastical government. Administrative abuses continued which, it must be repeated, were the real cause of moral corruption, and which only drastic action from above could remove. These abuses were the more bitterly resented, as they were of a financial nature. Huge sums of money had to be levied to satisfy the universal wish to beautify public worship. This was felt not merely at Rome, but also in Germany, France, and England, in the early sixteenth century. But the Roman Curia, like all bureaucracies, was slow of mind and lacked imagination; and the collection of money by means of indulgences was allowed to go to extremes which met with opposition even in the Latin countries. In Spain, a protest was raised by Cardinal Ximenes against the indulgence published toward the completing of St. Peter's Church; and Venice, independent-minded as usual, forbade it altogether. We need hardly recount here the causes of the Lutheran revolt. The essential point is that a religious practice, first created as an incitement to repentance and moral improvement, was now being used as the equivalent of any other money-raising device.

Thus were financial abuses continued in the Curia, in the shape of indulgences, taxation, duties, the sale of offices, etc., at the very moment when Christian humanism was refining and purifying an *élite* of worthy souls. Their aspirations found too little satisfaction in the reality around them. Many voices — not of rebels, but of devoted adherents of the papacy — began to complain of the existing state of things. In his *Storia di Milano*, Giovanni Andrea Prato denounced those monks who, "having nothing, yet own everything." The Sienese canon, Sigismondo Tizio, inveighed bitterly against financial malpractices. The illustrious Pico della Mirandula, a layman, in his address to the Lateran Council, shortly before its close in 1517, uttered severe warnings and demanded, not merely the proclamation, but also the enforcement, of reforming regulations.

But such complaints and denunciations failed, throughout the reign of Leo X, to bring about the long-desired Reformation. When all has been said about the pope's love of "honor and glory," the luxury of the Roman court, the loose living of some of its members, the corruption and bribery, the main cause of the delay still has to be mentioned. It is hard to realize today that the Turks were pressing hard on Hungary and Poland, that European civilization stopped at the Adriatic, and that Italy and Rome were threatened with an Ottoman conquest. Yet this was the situation the popes had to face from 1500 to 1530. The policy of Leo X aimed first and foremost at bringing about the union of Christian princes against the invader; but the sovereigns appealed to seemed to care little for the common welfare of Christendom, and were governed by only the most selfish motives. They sought the favor of the papacy to use it as a weapon in the game of political and armed warfare, and tried to win it at the small cost of protestations of friendship and promises; accepting the pope as an ally, but steadily refusing to grant him any real freedom of judgment or action, or even the territorial independence which alone would have enabled him to play the part of an umpire and leader: thus making either a crusade or a real reformation of the Church equally impossible.

From the beginning of Leo X's pontificate, the Turkish peril weighed heavily upon his mind. The new sultan, Selim, was of a warlike temper. The Polish ambassadors soon reported on the danger which their country was in, and the pope was moved to tears and sobs. And now, throughout the remainder of his pontificate, the thought of a crusade remained uppermost in his mind, and whenever the international situation seemed to clear up, he reverted to it. As early as 1513, money and encouragements were sent to Poland, Hungary, and Rhodes. In 1516, the French king, Francis I, was appealed to. In the autumn of 1517, a congregation of the Crusade was formed, with representatives of most European powers; every aspect of the campaign was fully discussed, from its finances to its tactics. In March, 1518, the Crusade was preached in Rome amidst great religious festivities.

Unfortunately, despite the sending of legates, the various princes of Christendom displayed no eagerness to follow the pope's lead. Venice might have put at his disposal the most powerful fleet in Europe, but she had a treaty with the sultan which safeguarded her trade, and kept him informed of all papal preparations. Henry VIII, then the ally of Spain, thought that Leo X would be better employed in siding with him against France. The French king was equally lukewarm. As for the Emperor, he was unwilling to grant the pope a free use of the sums collected for the Crusade in Germany, part of which he hoped to turn to his own purposes. Thus at the very moment when the Lutheran outbreak made it more necessary than ever to reform the Church, Leo X was compelled, in order to save her from complete destruction, to struggle against the nationalism of every country in Europe.

This nationalism, or more accurately, this exaltation of the State as personified by its sovereign, was just then finding expression in Machia velli's treatise on the *Prince*. In this work the interest of the State was considered as sufficient justification for even the most immoral acts, whereas on the contrary, when the pope proclaimed the ideal of united Christendom, he appealed to a common moral ideal. It may therefore rightly be said that the Machiavellian spirit — which was in existence long before the Italian writer gave it a name — was in its essence contrary to that of the Catholic Reformation. Besides, it was directly responsible for its postponement.

Each sovereign was seeking his own aggrandizement, and that even at the expense of the Church. The Emperor Maximilian still viewed himself as the overlord of Europe and the supreme temporal governor of the Church. He considered himself entitled to take the reformation of the Curia into his own hands, and in no friendly spirit either. He said that "before warring against the Infidels he would have to prune God's vineyard." He was constantly bringing pressure to bear upon the pope in favor of Spain, whose king claimed sovereignty both upon northern and southern Italy. The French kings, Louis XII and Francis I, also wished to lay their hands upon Milan and Naples as well. Now if both the North and the South of the Peninsula were in the same hands, there was an end of territorial independence for the Holy See, and consequently of spiritual independence also. Therefore Leo's efforts were constantly directed toward avoiding such a reunion, and the story of his pontificate is mostly a tangled tale of intrigue and petty warfare, in which he was constantly attempting to play off France against the Empire, siding now with one, now with the other, according to circumstances.

It was indeed to be regretted that the papacy should have to mix in the game of international politics. Its spiritual prestige could only lose from the fact that religious and temporal issues were constantly being mixed up: examples of this are the French secession and the Italian wars in the early days of Leo X's pontificate. Later on the emperor was constantly urging him to use ecclesiastical censures against Francis I, and in fact the French general, Thomas de Foix, who had invaded the States of the Church, was threatened with excommunication and interdict. And yet, though Leo X might take a part in the political fray, there is no doubt that from the first and ever after, his aim was to be a mediator between all European princes, to establish peace and to rescue Christendom from the Turkish invasion. That he was not unduly engrossed by the thought of external dangers, the events which followed hard upon his death were to show. Internal reformation could hardly be attempted while the very well-being of the Church was at stake.

*   *   *

The task that the refined and lovable Medici had been unable to perform, was taken in hand firmly by his successor. Adrian VI (January 9, 1522 — September 14, 1523) was the first pope who attempted a root-and-branch reformation; and though he did not succeed, he has a particular claim upon our attention. In most respects, Leo X and Adrian VI stand at opposite poles. While the former was in every respect a southerner, the latter was no less typically a northerner. He was a native of the Netherlands, and had been educated in a school of the Brothers of the Common Life. He imbibed their sober, grave, mystical piety, their evangelical spirit, their love of biblical and patristic studies. Yet he was not, properly speaking, a Christian humanist. He had spent ten years in the old-fashioned University of Louvain, where he read in theology, philosophy, and canon law. He himself was medieval in his tastes, and had no love for the Renaissance. His distrust of classical culture seems to have extended even to Sadolet, whose help might have been useful for the work of reform, but remained unemployed.

No wonder, in the circumstances, that Adrian VI should have met with all but general opposition among the Italians. As soon as his election was known, the satires which were pinned on to Pasquino's statue called him a "Barbarian." Nor was he disliked merely because of his aversion for the Renaissance. The prosperity of Rome was largely linked with those very abuses which he had set out to correct. The lavish distribution of papal favors to worthy and unworthy suitors alike attracted crowds both from Italy and foreign countries. Trade flourished, money flowed in freely. The city had become a nursing-bed for all the fine arts. All this seemed threatened. All through his pontificate, and even after his death, the mob of Roman poetasters kept baying at him; they called him an ass, a wolf, a harpy, compared him to Caracalla and Nero. In fact, the story of his pontificate is a sad tale of reform undertaken in the face of popular hostility, of high ideals struggling with overpowering difficulties.

Nothing else, indeed, was to be expected; for how could a purely moral reformation arise from the selfishness of vested interests? But among men of real culture and virtue, Adrian VI met with ready support. As soon as it was known that the new pope took a serious view of Church matters, all the reforming aspirations that had been lately gathering strength came to light, and advice began to pour in from every hand.

When the college of cardinals was first introduced to the pope, one of them, Carvajal, addressed him in a set speech, in which he outlined his future policy. It would be necessary, he said, to do away with simony, ignorance, tyranny, and the other vices which disfigured the Church; to appeal to righteous advisers; to keep the officials in curb; to honor and promote right-minded cardinals and prelates and to take care of the poor; to bring about a truce among Christian princes, and gather funds toward a crusade.

From various parts of Europe, many memorials were sent in to Adrian VI. One, composed by the Spanish humanist, Luis Vives, who had settled down in the Netherlands, called for peace among Christians, and a reform of the clergy. This, he said, might be effected only by a general council. In another writing, Cardinal Schinner, a Swiss, recommended a reform of the Curia. The pope was to reduce his household and thereby set an example for the cardinals. The selling of curial offices was to be discontinued, and those who held them were to receive no other fixed salaries. Chancery duties were to be reduced to a minimum, and no other payment was to be exacted.

The fullest scheme of reform came from Cardinal Campeggio, a devoted adherent of the Holy See, and began with an assertion of the supreme power of the papacy. But such power, he said, implied duties as well. He advised a remodeling of the system of benefices. The holding of plural benefices was to be proscribed, and that of benefices *in commendam* regulated. The appointment of foreigners should be avoided in each country, and only honest and virtuous candidates should be selected. All rights of patronage should be reserved for the Holy See, and all concessions made to princes in that behalf should be deplored. The memorial further showed the unwisdom of allowing the Franciscans to dispense indulgences freely, and the necessity of a sounder plan for the jubilee year, 1525. Lastly it considered the financial problems with which the papacy was faced, and the means of obtaining money hitherto resorted to. The creation and sale of new offices, Campeggio thought, should be given up, and a voluntary contribution should be obtained from Christendom at large. Like the other advisers of Adrian VI, he referred to the Turkish peril, which weighed heavily upon men's minds. Most memorials, it should be noted, expressed the wish that work on St. Peter's Church should be continued, thus showing that the nascent Catholic Reformation was not puritanical, and was willing, in regard to art, to walk in the footsteps of Julius II and Leo X.

Adrian VI himself was more indifferent to artistic beauty; but he realized from the first that only a strong pope would be able to correct abuses, and he struck the right path at once. Even before he had left Spain he ordered that all vacant offices should remain at his disposal, and that the cardinals should not sell, give away, or promise them to anyone. As soon as he arrived at Rome, he issued an edict which forbade the carrying of arms, expelled all loose livers from the city, and made it compulsory for clerics to be clean shaven, lest they look like soldiers. In his first consistory, on September 1, 1522, he made it clear to the cardinals that he wished to carry out a thoroughgoing policy. Rome, he said, quoting St. Bernard, was so inured to sinning that its people did not even notice the evil odor of their lives; its corruption had become a byword throughout the whole world. He entreated the cardinals to turn out all lewd persons from their households, to give up excessive luxury, and to be content with an income of 6000 ducats each. Nor was Adrian VI slow in enforcing his own advice. All cardinals, except Schinner who was an outstanding reformer, had to leave the Vatican, and their retinues were forced to comply strictly with the order against carrying arms. Cardinal Cibo, a scandalous liver, was denied access to the pope.

At the beginning of 1523, Adrian VI undertook, much to the dismay of his Roman environment, to abolish all new offices created by Leo X, a congregation of six cardinals being appointed to that effect. In regard to appointments to benefices, he was equally firm: all candidates had to

satisfy him as to their age, morality, and learning, and he dealt vigor-
ously with pluralities and simony. From the first he had selected his
advisers from the reforming party, with a preference for northerners; he
later realized that he ought to conciliate Italian public opinion, and
called up to the Vatican Gian Pietro Caraffa and Tommaso Gazzella to
help him in his work of correction. But as his brief pontificate was
drawing toward its close, he seems to have lost heart in his struggle
against the huge administrative machine which he had set out to remodel.

A religious bureaucracy, Pastor says, is the worst of all bureaucracies.
The pope's difficulties and his concessions began when he applied himself
to the reform of the datary. Since the treasury was empty, it was
hardly possible for the Holy See to give up the fees for bulls and
dispensations; and Adrian VI had to be content with lowering the latter
as much as possible. In March, 1523, in order to finance the Crusade,
he reverted to the practice of his predecessors, when hard pressed for
money, and resumed the sale of offices and dignities.

Meanwhile Adrian's attention had been drawn to the conditions in
Germany, where the Lutheran movement was spreading rapidly. As
early as November 25, 1522, the nuncio, Chieregati, appeared before
the Diet at Nuremberg, in order to explain to the assembly the reforming
intentions of the pope. "You will promise," the latter said in his instructions, "that we shall apply ourselves with all our strength to the
amendment, first of the Roman Curia, from which maybe all the evil
has sprung; and so too the healing, like the disease, will come thence."
Unfortunately, Adrian VI found no response among the German bishops,
who lacked the necessary energy. Rather than firmly oppose the
Lutheran movement which threatened their very lives, they pursued the
suicidal policy of letting things shape their own course and forgetting
the imminent danger amidst feasts and dances. The pope's eyes were
fully opened when Johann Eck, the famous Catholic reformer, arrived
in Rome early in 1523, and made clear that the decrees of the Lateran
Council had not been observed by the German clergy, and that a new
gathering of the whole Church was necessary. He further made suggestions for the correction of abuses: papal visitors with full powers
should be sent to every country; the holding of provincial and diocesan
synods should be resumed; the number of pensions and expectancies
should be reduced; no benefices should thenceforth be granted *in
commendam*.

Here again, Adrian VI was prevented by his untimely death from
carrying out his plans. But in any case, one wonders whether he would

have been successful. We are apt to be given the curious impression that he was both ahead of his times and lagging behind them. Roman society was not ready for the Catholic Reformation. It had not been chastened by suffering. Besides, the people of Rome greeted with ill-humor a pontificate which they considered as a descent of the barbarian North upon Italy. Nor was the opposition wholly unjustified. The Italians, however pious, were conscious of the intellectual and artistic enrichment which had accrued to them through the Renaissance. The pope, on the other hand, fell into the same mistake as Savonarola, viewing the fine arts and classical literature as needless and even harmful luxury. Before the Catholic Reformation could mature, it was indeed necessary that the easy attitude of the age of Leo X should give place to a more militant and bracing atmosphere; but it was no less necessary that the value of classical antiquity, even for the Church, should be recognized.

"Woe! how even a most righteous man's power to act depends on the times in which he happens to live!" This epitaph on the grave of Adrian VI is even truer if applied to his successor, Clement VII. He was a well-meaning and virtuous pope. But his good intentions were frustrated from the first by a succession of calamities which make his pontificate the darkest period in the history of Christendom. Within the space of a few months, the national Lutheran Church was founded in Germany; the Hungarians were beaten at Mohacs by the Turks, who entered Buda-Pesth on September 10, 1526; and Rome was sacked by the imperial armies (May 6, 1527).

But the saddest feature about those sad events was that they were to be put down to one and the same cause: the utter selfishness of Christian princes, and the predominance of State over spiritual interests. We are here faced with a general European movement of national self-assertion. The custom had grown among sovereigns to view the religious power of the papacy merely as a means toward the attainment of purely temporal ends. The pope might be made to confirm territorial conquests, to prevail upon the clergy to part with their income for the benefit of royal exchequers, or to confer ecclesiastical promotion upon royal favorites. If he complied with the wishes of one prince, he became tied to him and incurred the enmity of all others; if he refused to obey, he was first emphatically reminded of the benefits that had been showered upon him, and which were so many titles to his favor; then he was threatened with a national schism, and lastly with an appeal to that general council which all Europe was eagerly awaiting. Thus the assembly of the Church, from which everyone was expecting the correction of abuses, was turned into a club for the use of kings; it might, they suggested, remember the tradition of Basle and Constance, and depose a recalcitrant pope. The religious ideals of the age and the very hope of a Catholic reformation were made to subserve the political schemes of princes, and thus lost much of their spiritual efficiency.

The process of alternate cajoling and intimidation outlined above was that which Henry VIII of England used in the years 1527 to 1534, to induce Clement VII to annul his marriage with Katharine of Aragon. But it would be a mistake to think that he had invented it. Most European sovereigns, about the same time, were alternately flattering and bullying the pope to enlist his support toward their own personal ends. The French wished to retain Milan, which the emperor also demanded; and when Adrian VI, in 1523, became reconciled with Charles V and proclaimed a truce in Italy, Francis I wrote the pope a long letter of recrimination. He reminded him of the services rendered by all the French kings to the Apostolic See. Those who ought to have been grateful for such services were now preventing France from availing herself of her rights upon Milan. The Pope ought to have justice and equity before his eyes, to think of the salvation of souls, of his own honor, of his approaching end. Should Adrian VI seek to enforce a truce through ecclesiastical censures, he might fear the fate of Boniface VIII, who had tried the same thing with Philip the Fair and had had to suffer for it. The pope would do no more than his duty if he granted to Francis I, as he did to his enemies, subsidies out of the revenues of the clergy. These threats succeeded in terrifying the pope, who was afraid lest the French king should favor Luther's heresy and establish an independent Gallican Church. In fact, the sending of moneys to Rome was forbidden in France shortly after.

The reverse happened in 1525, when Clement VII sided with the French in order to prevent the Emperor from seizing the kingdom of Naples. Charles V then exclaimed "that Martin Luther might, now or later, be a valuable man." One year later, when the pope had, for the same motive joined the League of Cognac, headed by France, the Emperor addressed him in a severely worded letter. He insisted on the fact that the pope, being the supreme pastor, had no right to unsheathe the sword; that when a cardinal he had been shown much favor by the Emperor; that when conspiring against the latter he forfeited his right to be called a pastor and a father. Clement VII ought to remember that he drew most of his income from the empire. If he persisted in having recourse to arms, the Emperor would appeal to a general council that would settle all pending differences.

In fact, the imperialist theories of the Middle Ages had not wholly died out. The Fraticelli and Marsilius of Padua, two hundred years before, had granted to the Emperor wide spiritual powers, with a right to convoke general councils. Charles V still considered himself to a large extent responsible for the spiritual welfare of the Church, and entitled to take the work of reform into his own hands. Before the expedition against Rome, the extent of his duty toward the pope was freely discussed; and it was considered moot question whether he ought to submit to ecclesiastical censures. The other European princes, just as they aspired to the imperial dignity, also shared the pretensions of the Emperor in regard to ecclesiastical matters. Wolsey was trying to make England the hub of the Christian world. When Clement VII was imprisoned by the Emperor after the sack of Rome, the cardinal assumed quasi-papal powers, took the whole of Church administration for France and England into his own hands, and called up a gathering of the Sacred College at Avignon. These attempts to rob the papacy of the government of the Church were similar in all European countries; they ended in schism in Scandinavia, Germany, and England, and might well have done so elsewhere. They made it practically impossible for the Holy See to proceed with the work of reform.

And yet Clement VII did his best, even during the distressful years 1523 to 1528, to make the Catholic Reformation possible. He was himself a Christian humanist, and immediately took Christian humanists, such as Giberti and Sadolet, into his service. He had a sincere wish to maintain peace between the Powers. Whenever it seemed possible he reverted to the policy of papal neutrality, and even succeeded in effecting a short-lived reconciliation between Charles V and Francis I in 1533. Unfortunately, as Bishop Stephen Gardiner said, he was of a weak and wavering temper, giving the impression that he was irresolute rather than peace-loving. He was indeed a true Christian, but he did not take the ample view of the situation which was then necessary; he behaved like a man who, in a huge conflagration, would only be anxious to save some trifling item of his possessions. He was rightly desirous to preserve the independence of the States of the Church; but his wish to recapture Ravenna and Cervia, which Venice had taken, assumed in his eyes an inordinate importance and governed his external policy for many years. In 1530, Clement VII induced the emperor to lay siege to Florence in order to restore the power of the Medici in the city. The fall of the city, he wrote on June 3, would enable the Emperor to turn his attention to the Lutheran heresy and to the Turkish peril!

No dwelling on the rights and privileges, however legitimate, of the the Holy See, could save the Church from impending disruption and ruin. It would have been necessary to proclaim in a ringing voice a spiritual ideal that would have carried away the whole of Christendom. Unfortunately Clement VII did not seek salvation outside and above the ordinary game of international politics. His attempts to play off the powers against each other eventually involved him in the most terrible calamities. When he had joined the League of Cognac, Charles V, for revenge, entrusted Ugo de Moncada with the task of raising a rebellion in Italy. The pope had made an alliance with the powerful Roman family of the Orsini. Moncada joined hands with their enemies, the chief of whom was Cardinal Colonna. The latter gathered an army of five thousand men, and took Rome by ruse on September 20, 1526, while Clement VII was fleeing to Castel St. Angelo. The soldiers plundered the Vatican, stole the relics, the crosses, the sacred vessels and vestments, even the precious ornaments on St. Peter's altar; "the artillery drivers," a German diarist says, "rode along in the purple robes of the Holy Pontiff, and others, having put on his hat on their heads as a sign of contempt, gave benediction. . . ."

The worst, however, had yet to come. On May 6, 1527, Rome was taken by storm by the imperial armies, which had been largely recruited among the German Lutherans, but included Catholic Spaniards as well. The sack of the city lasted for one whole month. Twenty thousand mercenaries, together with the riff-raff of army followers, went roaming about the city looking for gold and silver. They set fire to the houses, tortured the inhabitants, raped and slaughtered women before the eyes of their husbands, girls before the eyes of their fathers. Some of the townspeople were shut up and starved to death. After clothing a donkey as a bishop, some soldiers tried to compel a priest to incense the animal and give him Communion. As he refused to do so he was cut to pieces. Innumerable works of art were destroyed; tombs were opened and searched; nuns were sold on public squares for a couple of ducats.

Never had Christianity fallen so low. Never, it seemed, would the Church flourish again. And yet, forces had been slowly gathering which now, braced by suffering, were to make it young again. In the very hour of its direst distress, the tide was turning, and the Catholic Reformation was at hand.

CHAPTER IV

Preparing for Trent

THE Sack of Rome sharply divided one period from another: it put a sudden end to the golden sunset of the Italian Renaissance, and introduced a period of stress and strain which was to be that of the Catholic Reformation. The latter had been prepared for by the Christian humanists, and was gaining ground even before 1527; but its necessity had not yet been brought home to the papal court and to the Italian people at large. Such a dreadful calamity as the Sack was needed to shake them out of their ease. A new religious earnestness spread to all classes. Many men and women of the nobility retired to monasteries in order to bewail their past transgressions. At the meeting of the Council of the Rota, on May 15, 1528, Bishop Stafileo described the sufferings of the capital of the world as a visitation for her sins. She had been struck, he said, "because all flesh had given itself up to corruption, because we no longer are the inhabitants of the holy city of Rome, but of the perverted city of Babylon." He and others, however, could see a new hope dawning ahead. "If we satisfy God's wrath and justice," Sadolet wrote to Clement VII, "if those terrible punishments open the way for purer manners and juster laws, perchance our misfortune will not have been so great."

Some years were still to elapse, however, before the Catholic Reformation was in full swing. Many reasons account for this delay. The chief agent in the correction of abuses could be no other than a general council. It had been in men's minds for many years, and especially since the outbreak of Lutheranism. It was appealed to on every possible occasion, by sincere reformers, by heretics, by self-seeking sovereigns. Though most people disagreed as to its desired composition, location, and syllabus, its authority was as a rule undisputed. Its very name was one of those which, although (or perhaps even because) their meaning is but dimly grasped, rouse the enthusiasm and hopes of a whole generation.

Now before a general council could be held, many difficulties, mostly of the political order, had to be cleared away. The mutual jealousy of the chief European princes stood in the way of any great international undertaking. Each one of them objected to the holding of the council in the dominions, and consequently under the influence, of his enemies. Each one of them made the holding of the council dependent upon satisfaction, to be obtained by the pope, regarding his own political claims. The dispute between the Emperor and France over the possession of Milan was the cause of years of delay. The prelates could hardly be gathered during a war; hence the establishment of peace was necessary. To that end, the pope himself must keep out of the wrangle, but take up the superior position of a disinterested umpire. Lastly, the Lutheran revolt in Germany had given rise to further problems. The Emperor needed the help of his Protestant subjects to fight the Turks and was unwilling to irritate them. At first he hoped that a general council would placate them and bring them back to the Fold, but later, finding that they would have nothing to do with the Holy See, he resorted to direct negotiations with them in political assemblies, in which religious matters were the object of mutual give-and-take. His high estimate of his own power and function induced him to try to settle the religious difficulties by his own means and apart from the pope. Therefore after first agreeing to the council, the mightiest sovereign in Europe kept putting it off for many years.

To overcome all these obstacles, as well as the resistance of the Roman bureaucracy, a strong hand was needed. Unfortunately Clement VII was ill-suited for such a task. A serious and well-meaning pope, neither lax nor wanting in dignity, he was still a man of the past. He still belonged to the political age, and looked for salvation to the old policy of balance, to close diplomatic fencing now with one, now with the other party in the European struggle. He did not realize that the papacy now had to play another part, that it ought boldly to assert its spiritual authority. His attitude toward Henry VIII is typical in this respect. About his opinion on the divorce matter there can be no doubt; nor did he give in to the threats and blandishments of the English king. Yet he failed to understand that by making, at the very outset, an open declaration of right and wrong, he would have carried the English people with him and won the day for the English Church. He preferred an attitude of diplomatic shilly-shallying, which deprived him of all his advantages and allowed him to be fooled by his adversary. The same was true of the council: instead of attacking the obstacles in a spirited way, he stood weighing difficulties, and was at best but lukewarm.

It should be owned that there was, for the pope and the Roman court, no lack of justifiable reasons why the council should be put off. The memory of the assemblies at Basle and Constance was still alive in men's minds. The attempt to establish democracy in the Church might still be renewed at the expense of that very papal power which was needed more than ever for the correction of abuses. The mere announcement of the council had brought about a fall in the price of venal offices in the Curia. Who knew but that the financial position of the Holy See might be seriously threatened?

Besides, the attitude of temporal sovereigns might well give rise to concern. In the past, they had so repeatedly clamored for a general council whenever they thought themselves wronged by the pope, that one might be forgiven for viewing it as a means of dispossessing the papacy of its authority for the benefit of princes. This was true even of Charles V. It was now clear that they had been insincere, and that they wanted no general assembly of the Church in which their privileges might be curtailed. This latter attitude, however, was no less dangerous than the former; for Henry VIII and Francis I threatened schism if any attempt were made to compel their attendance. Lastly, the Protestants insisted that their ministers should be admitted on equal terms; but if the Holy See had granted such a request, it would have granted thereby that the Lutheran revolt was legitimate. All these obstacles were so formidable that more than common faith in the likely benefits of the council was needed; but Clement VII had more of worldly prudence than foresight or enterprise.

Nor were circumstances otherwise as favorable as they might have been for a Catholic reformation to be effected either by the pope himself or by a council. For one thing, it is easy to issue reforming decrees, but they are not worth the paper they are written on if the will to enforce them be lacking. In other words, it was not enough to forbid the continuation of abuses, since the administrative personnel of the Church which profited from them could easily nullify any prohibition. It was necessary that the said personnel should be gradually renewed, so that it might give up of its own accord advantages which the older generation were unwilling to relinquish. Hence the slow progress of the reforming movement, and the futility of the Lateran regulations. The seed that was sown by the Christian humanists of 1510 was to take thirty years to ripen into fruit; long enough, that is, for people inspired with the new spirit to reach positions of authority in the Church. Between 1517 and the first session of the Council of Trent, the Catholic Reformation, like a rising tide, slowly submerged the college of cardinals and higher offices in the Curia, until it could be withstood no longer.

This tide was already fairly high in the days of Clement VII, though the cardinals he created were "no saints," as the Venetian ambassador described them, "but lords, true and worthy gentlemen." The pope did in fact give some satisfaction to the general wish for a council. He was sincerely desirous to effect a reconciliation between Francis I and Charles V. He urged both sovereigns to agree to the council. In the consistories of December 16 and 20, 1532, the various means of restoring unity and discipline in the Church were discussed. The majority of the cardinals advised a council; and it was finally agreed that it should not be a national assembly to be held in Germany — for then Henry VIII and Francis I would have declared that it was under imperial influence and would have rushed into schism — but a general gathering of the whole of Christendom, to be called in a suitable place, after all the Christian princes had given their assent. The decision was an important one, though its effect was to be suspended for twelve years. It would now have been impossible to go back upon it. Pursuant to the vote of the cardinals, the Emperor's agreement was first sought and obtained, and then briefs were sent to the kings of France and England, and to the other Christian princes, including the imperial electors.

No sooner had this step been taken, however, than further difficulties began to arise. The Emperor, in order to quiet the Lutherans, wished for immediate action, contrary to his later policy. The pope preferred to wait for the universal agreement of the sovereigns. That this might be obtained, nuncios were sent, in February, 1533, to Germany, France, and England. But the Lutherans refused to bind themselves to compliance with the decrees of the council, while Francis I and Henry VIII returned dilatory answers.

Meanwhile, the king of France held out hopes to the pope of easing the difficulties between England and the Holy See, if the latter sided with the French against the emperor. The pope, who feared Charles V's power in Italy, agreed to an interview with Francis I at Marseilles in October and November, 1533. In his conversations with Francis I, he did try to bring about a reconciliation between him and the emperor, and pressed the matter of the council; but as the French king obstinately advised delay, the weak-willed pope let the matter drop. In March, 1534, he wrote to Charles V's brother, Ferdinand, king of the Romans, that he meant to put off the council to better and less troublous times. In such circumstances, the great historian of the papacy, Ludwig von Pastor, considers it fortunate for the Church that Clement VII's pontificate did not last much longer. The pontiff died September 25, 1534, leaving Christendom in a more critical position than it had perhaps ever been.

And yet, while the pope's adherence to the political traditions of the past, and his waverings compromised what hopes might be left of preserving the unity of the Church, the reforming movement was gaining strength, both inside the Curia and out of it. "Reformation," like "the council," had become one of those words which, in a given generation, will not bear discussion. Such was the very spirit of the age. Even before the Sack, Clement VII himself had attempted to correct abuses. He advanced the question of the reform of the Curia in the consistory of January 18, 1524, and a commission of cardinals was appointed to that end. On September 9, in view of the coming jubilee of 1525, the pope suggested that a visitation of the Roman clergy should take place; that all Roman secular clerics should undergo an examination, and that those who failed it should be forbidden to say Mass; that good confessors should be sought for the holy year. The visitation was carried out, and though many worldly prelates grumbled, they had to submit to it. It is significant that Sadolet, together with Giberti, the reforming bishop of Verona, gave full support to the efforts of Clement VII.

The pope also issued directions against simony and in some cases declared against pluralities. A number of papal decrees of 1524 provided for reformation, not merely in the Italian dioceses of Florence, Parma, Naples, Venice, and Milan, but also in those of Burgos and Mayence, and in the Carmelite Order at large, the same being done in 1525 for the Humiliati. Unfortunately the conflict between the Emperor and the Holy See in 1526 and 1527 interrupted all activities of the kind for the space of several years. They were resumed in 1529 and 1530, and many ordinances were issued. Some were aimed at the reformation of the secular clergy in various towns (Padua, Trevisa, Parma) but most of them referred to religious orders in Italy and out of Italy, even as far away as Poland. The same policy was continued until the end of Clement VII's pontificate, particular decrees dealing with individual cases. For the year 1532, no fewer than twenty-three such decrees, mostly bearing on the reform of regulars, especially of the mendicant orders, are extant in the papal registers. This was a heartening symptom: unfortunately it was not enough to cope with the situation. The pope was but nibbling at the abuses: these had spread so far that little could be done without general legislation of a more drastic character.

While Rome still shirked the main issue, and was slow in taking the lead, individual reforming movements were springing up everywhere, thus heaping up fuel which the spark of the Council of Trent was to kindle into a mighty blaze. Much of that work was done in the field of the regular life, either through the reformation of orders already extant, or through the foundation of new ones. Older forms of monastic discipline were re-enforced, or new institutions and a new spirit were resorted to in order to cope with the difficulties of the hour. This side of the early Catholic Reformation will be dealt with in one of the following chapters; but something must be said here of the work done in the secular field, and especially of that accomplished by Gian Matteo Giberti, bishop of Verona (1495–1543).

Giberti — the fact is worthy of note — had spend his youth at the court of Leo X and had been prominent among the Roman humanists. Clement VII made him his datary, that is, in fact, his chief secretary, and in 1524 appointed him to the bishopric of Verona. The Sack had the same effect upon him as upon many others, and in 1528 he sought permission to reside in his diocese, the condition of which might well give reason for concern. Many priests were living out of their parishes and were replaced by unworthy deputies. Some of them were so ignorant that Giberti had to get the Latin rubrics of the Missal translated into Italian for them. In many places, preaching had been given up, confessions were slack, and the churches looked like cattle sheds.

Giberti began reformation at home, and the amiable and temperate humanist he had been turned to a pattern of austerity and asceticism. He resigned most of his benefices and resolved to undertake in his own person the correction of abuses. In January, 1529, he began the visitation of his whole diocese, no easy task apparently, since once he was nearly drowned in a swollen torrent. He went from parish to parish, found out about the life of the clergy and the state of the churches, got into talk with the lowliest, and composed differences among them. He compelled the priests to reside in their parishes and to lead spotless lives; while in addition he prevailed upon Rome to withdraw the benefices with cure of souls which had been granted to nonresidents. He used compulsion whenever necessary, and as early as November, 1528, "the dungeons were full of concubinary priests." It is particularly striking that he should have striven to restore the vitality of parish life, the dignity and beauty of worship, to have discouraged attendance at Mass in chapels and private oratories, and freed the parish clergy from the encroachments of regulars. He gave great attention to the moral worth of confessors, and is said to have established confessionals in their present form.

Preaching was of paramount importance as a weapon against Lutheranism, which Giberti had severely condemned in 1530. He insisted that the people should be addressed "with charity and simplicity of heart," without unnecessary quotations from the poets or theological subtleties. Licence to preach was to be granted by the bishop. Catechism classes were founded for the children. Giberti obtained powers from Clement VII for the reformation of religious orders within his diocese, and went about it with a strong hand. He firmly repressed the abuse of indulgences and collections. As might be expected, he ran up against violent opposition from wealthy families, whose influence was supreme in some monasteries of women, and from his cathedral chapter, who pleaded exemption and held their own for several years. He founded orphanages and Sunday schools, houses of refuge for poor innocent girls or for those who had lapsed, popular banks to rescue the people from usurers, and an association (the *Societas pauperum*) for the relief of the poor — a prefiguration of the later Society of St. Vincent de Paul. Lastly, it should not be forgotten that in his palace at Verona, Giberti welcomed many of those humanists whom the Sack had scattered through Italy and induced them to apply their gifts to the work of reformation. In a word, all that was later to be essential in the work of the Council of Trent was already extant in his diocese, before the death of Clement VII; and, in fact, many of his enactments were embodied word for word in the Trentine decrees. Many bishops followed his example, and St. Charles Borromeo did his best to imitate it. The seed was sown, and was soon to fructify.

* * *

Whatever Clement VII's failings, he did the Church exceptional service by recommending a man of strong character and serious intent, Cardinal Alessandro Farnese, as his successor. The Sacred College followed his advice; they were by now firmly convinced that only an out-and-out reformer could deal with the situation; and Paul III (1468–1549) was elected within the space of a few hours. In his own person he provided an instance, both of the culture and moral laxity of the Renaissance period, and of the remorse for the Renaissance brought about by Christian humanism. He had been educated at Rome, where he was in touch with the neo-pagan philosopher, Pomponius Laetus; at Florence, in the house of Lorenzo di Medici; and at the University of Pisa. Under Alexander VI he was promoted to many benefices and dignities and was made a cardinal deacon in 1493. For some years his life was most irregular; he had four children (though it should be mentioned that he was not yet in priest's orders) the eldest being the famous Pier Luigi Farnese.

He was soon, however, to turn to more serious ways; and it is significant that this should have taken place at the height of Christian humanism, shortly before the Lateran Council, in which he took a prominent part. In order to enforce the decrees there issued, he made a visitation of his diocese of Parma in the year 1516, and gathered a diocesan synod in 1519. Nonetheless he took part in the brilliant life of the court of Leo X, and gave ample proof of his administrative abilities.

His election as pope was greeted by universal applause. Sadolet saluted him with a long letter of praise, in which he thanked God for entrusting the helm of Christendom to such a wise and excellent pilot. All those who wished for the council hailed the advent of a pontiff who was known to favor it.

All the ability and energy of Paul III were indeed needed to cope with the dangers which threatened the Church. We know from the words of a contemporary Catholic reformer what feelings the situation of Christendom gave rise to in 1534: "I could see in my mind," Giovan Battista Caccia writes, "the supreme emperor of Asia (the sultan) the enemy of Christ, lifted above the heads of the Christian people; I beheld the German secession; I recalled to memory that my holy mother the Church, before the black and Tartarean fog of Mahomet had blinded Asia and Africa, had embraced within her most holy bosom the whole of humankind, and that now she was forced back within that narrow space of Europe, torn about by various opinions, and so disfigured by the cutting off and breaking of her joints, that she seems to be rushing to her utter ruin."

In fact, while the pontificate of Paul III offers, in certain respects, a peaceful, reassuring appearance, the dangers which beset Christendom on every hand were greater than they had ever been. Despite the capture of Tunis by the Emperor in 1535, the Turks were making headway in the Archipelago and on the shores of the Adriatic, and threatening Italy and Rome herself. In July, 1536, they landed in the Peninsula, near Otranto, and began raiding the country and carrying away the inhabitants as slaves. A European league against them was formed, including Venice; but the Emperor and the king of France were so jealous of each other that the operations were delayed. When at last, in September, 1538, Andrea Doria with a fleet attempted the relief of Corfu, he was shamefully routed at Prevesa. On August 26, 1541, the sultan took Ofen (Buda), the capital of Hungary, and extended his dominions right up to the Danube. When finally an imperial mixed force of Catholics and Protestants came to the rescue in September, 1524, it was so lacking in unity and discipline that it retreated without having done its work.

It is not certain that the town of Perugia, which revolted against the pope rather than pay heavy taxes, sought Lutheran support; yet, what happened there in the year 1540 provides a striking instance of the confused influences which tended to bring about the breaking up of the Church. The rebellion soon assumed the same character as that of Florence under Savonarola. The chancellor publicly asked for the help of the Savior, to whom he offered the keys of the city; coins were minted with the inscription: "Perugia, the city of Christ." The treasures of churches were seized; and order was only restored after a regular siege.

One sees how evangelical phraseology was then naturally resorted to. Protestantism was a rallying-point for revolutionary agitators. In Venice, its swift progress was due to another reason: the city had long been jealous of its ecclesiastical independence. An event which took place in 1542 was even more painful for the Catholic-minded than the sporadic spread of Lutheranism in Italy. Bernardino Ochino, the most famous preacher of his time, renowned for his spiritual gifts, had been elected vicar-general of the Capuchins in 1536, and was very nearly made a cardinal in 1538. But at the same time he was imbibing Protestant doctrine, and soon sought refuge with Calvin at Geneva, together with the Augustinian, Pietro Martyr Vermigli. For some years he had been hovering between orthodoxy and heresy. The need for a clear statement of the Catholic position was becoming more pressing than ever.

Both for the purposes of definition and reformation, therefore, the council was urgently needed. But its gathering could not be immediate. The action of the papacy was needed, both to call it up, and to solve the numerous problems that were involved in its preparation. The pope alone could provide the necessary driving force, and first of all in the field of international politics, in which, from 1536 to 1545, he had to struggle against the divergent efforts of the various sovereigns. The selfish, short-sighted view which they took of their national interests was in every case responsible for the delay of the council, and no one among them can be exculpated from guilt in this respect.

Henry VIII, needless to say, would hear nothing of a Church assembly in which his matrimonial conduct and his assumption of ecclesiastical supremacy might be condemned. But as he was a valuable ally for either of the two chief continental powers, he could make his help conditional upon their rejection of the council. As a matter of fact, up to about 1540, Francis I was in league with him as well as with the Turks and the German Protestants, to whom the very name of a papal council was hateful. A Gallican schism might be feared, and Charles V denounced the disloyalty of the "most Christian king" toward the Holy See. But the situation was soon to be reversed. Despite his professed championship of the papacy, Charles V did not scruple to enter into close confederacy with Henry VIII. As a matter of fact, he largely shared the latter's notions of the part to be played by a king in religious matters. He did not, indeed, make himself "supreme head of the German Church," but he did attempt to establish a common rule of faith for all his dominions, and kept nudging the pope out of assemblies gathered to that effect. Things went so far that, in 1544, shortly before the Council of Trent assembled, he recalled his ambassadors from Rome, and the pope had to issue a severe warning to him. Ecclesiastical and political questions were inextricably mixed up. The tangle of conflicting interests confused the religious issues. In 1539, the Catholic princes of Germany, both lay and ecclesiastical, in fact sought an agreement with their Protestant neighbors, rather than side with their natural ally, the Emperor, whose power they feared might become overwhelming.

As long as the powers were at variance, the holding of the council appeared well-nigh impossible. How were the "fathers" to be gathered, if each sovereign was to refuse permission to his bishops to attend, unless the pope backed his temporal claims? Peace, it seemed, or at least a truce, must first of all be established; and to that purpose Paul III's efforts vainly tended for several years. Gradually, however, he found that his attempts were doomed to be futile, and that if the princes were allowed to have their own way, the issue would be perpetually shirked. Then he began to assert his own will more and more firmly, until at last he decided to call the council on his own authority, without waiting for anyone else's consent. This change of attitude, however, was only completed in little under ten years. As early as May 29, 1536, a bill of convocation had been approved in consistory, and the council convened to Mantua, for May 23, 1537. However, local and international difficulties soon made it necessary to prorogue the assembly twice in succession, and the place of meeting had to be shifted to Vicenza in the territory of Venice. On May 12, 1538, the legates appointed for the council made their solemn entry into the town, but the "fathers," bishops, and others, who were to make up the gathering, failed to appear; and two further prorogations ensued, the latter, on May 21, 1539, being *sine die*.

In fact, the policy of *colloquia* between Protestants and Catholics had then been inaugurated by the emperor; and Paul III for some time indulged in the hope that papal representatives might do useful work in such purely German conferences. He soon learned however, that attempts at conciliation only sharpened the aggressive spirit of the Lutherans and enabled them to extend their influence. We need not enlarge here on the Diet at Spires and the religious debate at Ratisbon — the nearest approach to an understanding between Christian sovereigns for the extension of the English plan of Church organization to the whole of Europe.

Paul III had by now made up his mind to act independently. On July 6, 1541, the question of the council was again raised in consistory; and on June 6, 1542, the assembly was called at Trent for All Saints' Day in the same year. In the bull of convocation, the pope recalled the efforts which he had made till then, and declared that he had resolved to wait no longer for the consent of any prince, but to consider only the will of God and the weal of Christendom. This manly decision was, however, frustrated for some time still. On October 28, the legates specially appointed left for Trent; but once more no "fathers" were forthcoming, owing to the opposition of the princes; and Paul III was compelled to suspend the council again. War was raging anew between Francis I and the Empire, and the problem of Milan was still unsolved. Peace, indeed, was made at Crèpy-en-Valois on September 17, 1544, but Charles V was more unwilling than ever to relinquish his religious policy. So Paul III once again took things into his own hands and convoked the council for March 15, 1545. He was determined that it should now be held under any circumstances; and in fact his energy had won the day.

*   *   *

But a general council could not be extemporized; and in fact it could not have been held at all if the long years of waiting had not been years of preparation as well. Many problems had to be solved. There were no set rules to determine what members were to compose the assembly, who was to preside over it, what matters it was to discuss, or how its decisions should be arrived at. The Councils of Basle and Constance, of which the memory was not yet lost, had attempted to alter the government of the Church according to democratic and nationalist principles. Among their "fathers" were members of the lower clergy, of the universities, and even laymen, whose votes were of equal value with those of the bishops and abbots, and actually outnumbered them; while the debates were carried on and concluded within each national group, final decision being taken by a majority, not of individuals, but of "nations." No real reform could be effected under such circumstances; and the assembly, lacking an arbiter and head, could only register the clash of conflicting interests. Paul III realized that, if the new council was to perform its task, it must be presided over and directed by himself. In the "congregations" that were preparing its work, it was decided that bishops only should be *definitores,* that is entitled to settle the points at issue, other ecclesiastics, theologians, and canonists being reduced to the part of *consultores* or advisers. The council was indeed to be free in its decisions, but its debates were to be prepared by the pope and committees of cardinals and curial officials. Learned specialists would sit together and draft articles to be approved by the pope, and sent to the assembly for discussion. In fact, while it lasted, Rome was enabled, if not to direct its proceedings, at any rate to guide them, and make her voice heard whenever necessary, both through the papal legates and through almost daily correspondence. Hence there was, between the "teaching Church" and the Holy See a close co-operation which the princes did not interfere with, for they were out of humor with the whole undertaking and kept sulking. The authority of the pope was left undisputed, and was able to sanction decrees which otherwise might have lacked force, since the gathering of the bishops at Trent was to be far from universal.

Not merely rules of procedure, but also the very substance of the debates had to be prepared beforehand. This could be performed in two different ways: either by beginning reformation at Rome, and thus setting an example which could not but be followed, or by ascertaining through committee work how such reformation could be extended to the whole of Christendom. Such tasks, however, could only be entrusted to right-minded men. Therefore Paul III's first move was to introduce members of the reforming party into the Sacred College and the curial offices. In his first batch of cardinals, in May, 1535, was included the Venetian statesman Gasparo Contarini. He was a virtuous layman, a Christian humanist, and had studied philosophy as well as theology at the university of Padua. He had formed around himself a circle of men of the same school. As soon as he was created a cardinal, he took orders, and engaged upon the work of reform in the Roman Church. A commission for that purpose had been appointed in the previous year, and strengthened by the bull *Sublimis Deus* on August 27, 1535.

Contarini now proceeded to lend them his support, and thanks to his influence, a series of decrees was published on February 11, 1536. The obligation to wear clerical dress was recalled; the use of the breviary was enforced anew; all holders of benefices were compelled to sue for confirmation within the space of four months, so that unqualified persons might be got rid of. Canons and prebendaries were now to take a personal part in solemn public worship; priests, to attend to the cure of souls, to say Mass at least once a month, and go to Communion on all feasts of obligation; clerics in minor orders were to receive Communion at least four times a year; all ecclesiastics were forbidden to enter public houses, gambling dens, and theaters. Preachers now had to seek guidance from certain superiors before refuting heretical doctrine. Mendicant friars were prevented from straggling about and collecting excessive alms. The very fact that these decrees were so moderate shows how much a restoration of discipline was needed.

The reformation of Rome and that of Christendom in general could scarcely be separated. Paul III soon tried to form a kind of "precouncil," which might set up an inquiry into Church conditions at large, and make suggestions for their improvement. In the latter half of July, 1536, the most notable among the members of the reforming party were, for that purpose, called to Rome: Caraffa, Giberti, the English refugee, Reginald Pole, and other Christian humanists, such as Sadolet and Federigo Fregoso. They were formed into a committee of nine, under the chairmanship of Contarini. Three of its members, Caraffa, Sadolet, and Pole, together with a batch of similarly minded men, were soon after raised to the cardinalate, and the resistance of the die-hards was consequently weakened. About mid-February, 1537, the committee handed in their report. It was entitled *Consilium delectorum cardinalium et aliorum praelatorum de emendanda ecclesia* (Advice of the cardinals and other prelates chosen [by the pope] toward the reformation of the Church). This document, which is extremely severe in tone, begins with a few lines of thanksgiving for the good will of Paul III, who wishes to "restore the Church of Christ, which was crumbling down, nay had almost fallen in headlong ruin."

The evils, which the *Consilium* denounces, all spring from one common source: the transformation of a spiritual society into a venal administration. The popes have, like all rulers, given a ready ear to flatterers. They have found councilors prepared to declare that "they might do what they pleased," especially in the matter of benefices, which, according to those doctors, they might freely dispose of in every case. Now, ownership implies a right to sell; hence the pope could take money for benefices without incurring the blame of simony. This, the report says, is the root of all abuses, the main cause of the Protestant revolt. It is needless to question the primacy of the pope; but he must not make use of it for gain. "Christ's order is: freely ye have received, freely give." The spiritual needs of the faithful must alone be considered, not the pecuniary interests of the Curia or of private persons. Now, it is at present common practice to select unqualified candidates, and to put them in wrong places; to allow them for their personal convenience or profit to draw pensions out of benefices — where none should be granted except for charitable purposes; to exchange benefices; to bequeath them, notably to their children; to take advantage of expectation, reservations, and pluralities.

What is worse, the *Consilium* continues, the cardinals themselves thirst for gold. They forfeit their independence through making suit of princes for bishoprics. They ought to give these up and receive regular and uniform emoluments. Nonresidence is general. Many cardinals live away from the papal court, and fail to perform their proper duties as advisers. They ought to dwell near the pope, while their sees should be occupied by resident bishops. The most important passage deals with exemptions. It should be quoted in full:

"There is another abuse, which ought not to be in the least tolerated, and by which the whole Christian people is scandalized: it consists in the obstacles which hinder bishops in the government of their flocks, especially in the chastising and correcting of criminals. For, to begin with, wicked men, especially clerics, find many ways to exempt themselves from the jurisdiction of their ordinaries. And again, if they are not exempt, they forthwith fly to the Penitentiary, or to the Datary, where they immediately find a way to impunity, and what is worse, in return for cash. . . . Let these blots, we beseech your Holiness, by Christ's blood, . . . be removed; the which, if they were at all allowed in any Christian commonwealth, it would . . . by no means be able to stand any longer; and yet we think it lawful to introduce such monstrosities into the Christian republic."

The *Consilium* is drastic on the question of the regulars. The monastic orders, it runs, are a cause of scandal, and ought to be allowed to die out, while the novices should be sent home. As to the friars, they should not be permitted to preach or hear confessions unless fully qualified, and with the consent of the bishop. Papal legates and nuncios should take no gratuities; their disinterestedness would edify the people wonderfully. In the monasteries of women in charge of conventual (or unreformed) friars, scandals are rife; these monasteries should be handed over to the ordinaries or to other directors. The spirit of the pagan Renaissance is at work in the schools, in which impiety is taught, while irreverence prevails in public debates held on religious subjects. Such disputations ought to be private, while profanity should be banished from the schools. The printing of books should be watched over.

Monks should not be granted permission to cast off their regular dress on payment of a certain sum of money. Those who go about hawking indulgences in the name of the Holy Ghost, of St. Anthony, "thus deceiving the simple people of the country," should be prevented from doing so. No dispensation should be granted for the marriage of persons "in sacred orders," nor for the marriage of lay people related in the second degree, who should only be fined if the marriage has been solemnized in defiance of the rules. Steps should be taken against another crying abuse: "the absolution of simoniacs. To what extent this pestilent vice prevails in the Church of Christ! So much so, that some are not afraid to commit simony, and then forthwith to apply for absolution from the penalty incurred. Nay, they buy such absolution, and thus retain the benefice which they have bought." The pope ought on no account to remit the punishment for simony, for no crime "is more pernicious, or more scandalous."

Confessionals and portable altars are granted too freely, sacred things being thus cheapened. Only one indulgence a year ought to be proclaimed in each important town. No commutation of vows ought to be allowed, "except for an equivalent good." The wills of testators should be adhered to, whereas at present pious bequests are often transferred to private heirs who plead poverty. Turning to Rome itself, the *Consilium* points to the fact that even in St. Peter's Church are seen disreputable priests, "filthily clad and ignorant," who would disgrace the poorest churches; and that courtesans parade about on mules in the streets, "followed in full daylight by noblemen, members of the household of cardinals, and clerics. In no other town, the report adds, have we seen such corruption." Reference is also made to the necessity of composing private feuds, and of creating charitable institutions to be put in the charge of cardinals. To finish with, Paul III is besought to behave like another St. Paul.

The picture of the Church offered by the *Consilium* is a sad one indeed: no wonder that Protestant propaganda should have turned it to good account. That it should have been written at all, however "without respect of the pope's, or anyone else's advantage," and that the work it outlined should have been performed within the space of a few years, is proof that the spiritual resources of what was now to be known as Catholicism were far from exhausted. They were only smothered by the weight of administrative corruption.

The most urgent task was to improve the government of the Church; and while some of the suggestions of the report — for instance those bearing on the residence of cardinals or on religious orders — were disregarded, the others were to move the Holy See to immediate action, and to the resumption of reform in Rome itself. In the consistory of April 20, 1537, a congregation of four cardinals, Contarini, Caraffa, Simonetta, and Ghinucci, was entrusted with the correction of abuses in the curial offices, and to begin with, in the Datary. The latter was so-called from the fact that it dated and authenticated all the documents referring to spiritual graces granted by the pope, charging fees for the service. Unfortunately payment was exacted before the favors could take effect, and the sums charged were much in excess of the actual expense entailed. To the chancery duties, which were paid into the papal treasury, the curials added, as a salary for their own pains, "compositions" or "taxations." These ought to have been settled according to a fixed scale, but the rise in the cost of living consequent upon the Sack of Rome was a pretext for increasing them out of all rule or measure, and demanding additional sums to be paid as extras or personal gratuities. As a remedy for this abuse, the reforming congregation suggested that "compositions" should be abolished, and that the pope should grant regular salaries to his officials, or, at any rate, that the fees charged should correspond to the actual outlay.

But the curials were to put up a hard fight. They had telling arguments to use: if the compositions were suppressed or reduced, they said, the Holy See would lose most of its revenues, and would also forfeit its prestige. They were greatly helped by the dangers which threatened the papacy on every hand, and made it necessary to postpone the work of reform. It was making headway slowly, however. In 1539, Paul III, leaving the Datary aside for a time, appointed commissaries to deal with the Penitentiary, the Roman tribunals, the Chancery, the Rota. On December 19, a new group of reformers were raised to the cardinalate, including Federigo Fregoso, a survivor of the court of Leo X and of the Oratory of Divine Love, a humanist too. For five or six years past, he had been at work transforming his diocese of Gubbio, and was known there as "the father of the poor." Even the older cardinals were touched by the new enthusiasm. On April 21, 1540, the pope declared that he was going to remodel all the curial offices at once. On August 8, Cardinal Pucci, the head of the Penitentiary, finally gave way and allowed a free hand to the papal commissaries. A bull of May 12, 1542, was to simplify procedure in the Roman court and fix duties at a reasonable level; but as early as 1541 the congregation of reform had extended their action much further, and obtained considerable results.

"They have done away with expectations," a contemporary wrote, "with the ordaining of unqualified persons against payment, with dispensations from the *clausura* or the wearing of the religious habit, and the plurality of benefices with cure of souls, even in the case of cardinals; dispensations in general have been notably reduced, for marriage especially, also the confirmation of titles acquired through simony, and resignations entailing pensions or reservations; such dispensations as have been retained now merely contribute to the support of pious undertakings."

Thanks to the will and perseverance of Paul III, Rome was no longer a disgrace, but, in the words of Contarini, a model for Christendom; the ground was now cleared for the Council of Trent.

CHAPTER V

The Council of Trent

THE Council of Trent, seen from afar and judged by its results, looks like one of the noble, stately edifices of the Catholic Reformation period; it impresses one by its mass, its duration, its weightiness, by the harmony between the various parts of its work. It is hard to realize that it was not always engaged in grave and sedate discussion; that it was a struggle, a long and dramatic one, between the papacy, which made for the permanency of the united Church, and short-sighted local interests; that its members were mere men, with all their weaknesses, pettinesses, rivalries, their lack of foresight, their insistence on private claims; that only the compelling force of necessity, and the contagious enthusiasm of a superior ideal, carried them on almost despite themselves; while their assembly, which might have ended in a hopeless muddle, was directed to the completion of its task by the guidance and leadership of wise, far-sighted popes.

The essential point in the history of the Council of Trent is the part which was played in it by the Holy See. This was made necessary by the very circumstances in which it had met. Unlike previous councils, it could lay no claim to universality. Efforts were made, indeed, to gather representatives from all parts of Christendom. A deputy was sent in 1551 by the patriarch of Constantinople, and later, in 1561, Pope Pius IV applied to the Greek and Russian Churches, to the Balkan princes, and even to the emperor of Ethiopia; but in vain. It had been hoped that at least the Protestants, who had been so long clamoring for a council, would take part in the debates. Safe-conducts were offered to them; and Sleidan, the Strasbourg theologian, and ambassadors from Wurtemberg did put in a belated appearance under Julius III. But they peremptorily rejected the authority of the Holy See, and of the council in its previous sittings, and refused to accept any basis for discussion apart from "pure Scripture." Even when most numerous, the assembly represented only a fraction of Christendom. To lend force to its decrees, confirmation was needed from some higher spiritual authority. This was felt by the Fathers, who kept referring all doubtful points to Rome and finally submitted the whole of their work to Pius IV for his approval.

But the authority of the papacy was even more needed to induce the Fathers to forget their own national claims in favor of the Church as a whole. The weal of the latter required a stringent condemnation of Protestantism; for reformation implied a declaration of abuses, especially of those which arose when Christian dogma was misinterpreted, as in the case of indulgences. It was necessary to affirm that dogma anew, to make a statement of orthodoxy. Now the assertion of clearly defined truths was opposed, or seemed to be opposed, to local interests. For it touched and angered the Lutherans and Huguenots, who were not merely heretics in the eyes of the Catholic Church, but also subjects of the Emperor and of the king of France, and rebellious subjects at that. If dealt with harshly, they might prove troublesome. The sovereigns, there-fore, set about protecting the antipapal sections of their peoples, while, strangely enough, insisting on national privileges which they held from the authority of the Holy See. Their bishops followed in their steps, kept exerting pressure upon the council to retard its work and put off all drastic reforming action which might either irritate the heretics or encroach upon the rights of the princes. Even those of Spain, where Protestantism was scarcely to be feared, made up an independent group which steadily opposed the influence and authority of the papacy; and the latter needed all its perseverance and energy, all its diplomatic skill also, to bring the council to its epoch-making conclusion.

Nor were the material difficulties less trying than the ill-will of the princes. It was no easy task to gather an assembly of bishops, many of them elderly men, in an age when travelling was slow and devoid of comfort. Many of them were unwilling to leave their dioceses, where they were loath to interrupt the struggle against Protestantism, even to go and conduct it on a larger scale at the council. Besides, people as a whole had become rather skeptical about the latter, which had given rise to so much talk and yet been put off so repeatedly. It took fifteen years — from 1546 to 1561 — to force general belief and acceptance upon the reluctant prelates.

Local conditions, too, were not as favorable as might have been. Trent had been selected for its proximity to Germany, where the religious diffi-culties had sprung up, where reformation was mostly needed, where the Lutherans were to be found, whom the council might reconcile to the Church. Also, the town lay within the dominions of the Emperor, whose support was sought above all others. But it was also deep in the Alps, and its severe winter was especially painful for the Italian majority of the assembly; while its sultry summer made work almost impossible, the more so as no sufficient accommodation was available, either for official purposes, or for the private requirements of the Fathers, their theologians, secretaries, domestics, or the ambassadors and their train — which must have numbered thousands of people, many of them of high rank and accustomed to luxury. The curial bishops had much rather stay in Rome than risk discomfort and disease in cramped and insanitary quarters.

It was an arduous task for three successive popes, first to get the Fathers on the move, and then when they had at last reached Trent, to keep them there. Circumstances were far more adverse — what with the wars of religion and the dangers lurking on every road — than they had been at the time of the Lateran Council, or even of Basle and Constance; and they would have ruined the whole undertaking, had it not been for the persistent and powerful action of the papacy.

This action and the gradual progress due to it are revealed by the facts and dates in the history of the council, which falls into three periods, separated by long intervals. The assembly first sat continuously for two years in the pontificate of Paul III. A few of its members met at Trent in March, 1545, their numbers slowly increasing to seventy-two in the winter of 1547. Then an epidemic broke out in the town and many Fathers took to flight and the legates pronounced the transfer of the council to Bologna. But the imperial bishops, mostly Spaniards, declared against this move; their sovereign's interests, they thought, would not be sufficiently safeguarded outside his dominions; and they remained in Trent, while forty-five Fathers only moved to Bologna, where the assembly dragged on its languid life until October, 1549, shortly before the death of Paul III. It was suspended for eighteen months and called again in Trent by Pope Julius III, who, as Cardinal del Monte, had presided over it during the first period. It met on May 1, 1551, and lasted for one full year; but the times were troubled, with war in northern Italy and a Lutheran advance in southern Germany, which eventually compelled the Fathers to scatter in May, 1552. This accounts for their small number, barely fifty-nine of them, including six deputies of German bishops, being present at the most favored sitting.

Then followed a long interval of eleven years. The troubled state of Italy lasted until the death of Julius III in 1554, and precluded the resumption of the council. Nor was the imperious Paul IV, who succeeded to the papal throne after the brief pontificate of Marcellus II, inclined to gather it anew. He viewed it as a ready instrument for the machinations of princes, and preferred to continue its work by his own means. For a general assembly sitting far from Rome, and comparatively independent, he substituted committees sitting in Rome, and appointed by himself. The correction of abuses was undertaken unflinchingly, as well as the suppression of doctrinal novelties; with such severity, indeed — as when the Inquisition was made to try Pole and Morone for heresy — that Paul IV defeated his own purpose, and that his enterprise roused discontent and ended in failure. After his death, it was felt that the council, which allowed of the airing of grievances, was a necessity. Besides, circumstances were growing more favorable for its recall.

Formidable obstacles to the pope's reforming work were removed in 1559, when both Charles V and the French king, Henry II, disappeared from the stage carrying their imperialist pretensions with them. Accordingly Pope Pius IV, who was endowed with all the qualities of a statesman, opened negotiations, soon after his election (Christmas, 1559), with the various European sovereigns, in view of a new gathering of the council; and despite many difficulties, the assembly was called for Easter Sunday, April 16, 1561, on which date the legates arrived in Trent.

The third period of the council lasted for two years and eight months, the closing session taking place on December 11, 1563. Its course, if not uneventful, was at any rate peaceful. The attendance now became far more numerous than it had been. On July 15, 1563, it rose to two hundred and thirty-five, including six cardinals, seven generals of orders, and six procurators of bishops. We have a full list of the Fathers on that day, the diocese, abbey, or order of each being mentioned; yet it is not easy to determine the national groups into which the assembly had fallen, and to weigh the influence of the pope and of the various European sovereigns. Many of the bishops resided at the Curia, and can hardly be considered as belonging to the countries in which their episcopal sees were situated. The difficulty of long journeys accounts for the fact that the assembly was mostly made up of those Fathers who were near at hand: Italian names are in a majority. This, however, is not, as one might think, equivalent to papal preponderance; for, as far as reckoning is possible, out of one hundred and thirty-five Italians, forty-six only depended upon the pope directly, as having their sees in the States of the Church. Among the rest, sixty-five were the subjects of three sovereigns — the king of Spain, the Emperor, the Venetian republic — who had not been noted lately for oversubmissiveness toward the Holy See. In fact, the Emperor and Spain together could more or less command ninety-five votes (the Spanish group alone numbering seventy-nine Fathers, if Naples is counted in), while the king of France had sent twenty bishops, many of them strong Gallicans. The Germans — whether they were lukewarm toward the council, or kept at home by the religious troubles — were practically absent; but there were a good few representatives from the Venetian colonies of Crete, Cyprus, Dalmatia, and the Greek Archipelago; together with a sprinkling from Portugal, Hungary, Croatia, Poland, Scotland, Ireland, Switzerland. Altogether, it would be a mistake to think that the pope had the assembly at his beck and call. It was frequently restive, and submitted to the authority of the Holy See only because the latter had taken the lead in regard to reformation, and gained considerable moral prestige.

*　　*　　*

Indeed, despite occasional outbursts of ill-humor, the opposition was divided, and could not but submit most of the time to the steady, persevering guidance of the papacy, which alone was in a position to "run" the council. The actual "running" was done by the cardinal-legates and presidents, and mostly by the one among them who was entrusted with superior authority — Cervini in the first period, Crescenzi in the second one, and Morone at the end. They enjoyed constant advice and support from Rome, where a special congregation of the council was sitting. In the third period Pius IV's nephew, Cardinal Charles Borromeo, who had been made secretary of state, was the daily correspondent of the legates. The latter settled the agenda, as well as the method, of the debates.

Despite the interruptions of the council, continuity in its management was ensured: the archives were kept during the intervals, and duly handed to the presidents at the next gathering. He who knew them best, the chief secretary, Massarelli, retained his functions throughout. It meant much for the influence of the Holy See that its officials should be the only permanent elements at Trent. The real work was done most of the time in committees. At one time the assembly was divided into three sections, at other times, a selection was made of the most eminent or representative members of each group. The Fathers only — archbishops, bishops, abbots, heads of orders, and a few procurators — were entitled to vote in the full sessions, in which final decisions were reached, and were therefore known as *diffinitores* (definers of dogma); but in the committees, advisers or *consultores* were admitted as well. Each cardinal or bishop had brought his theologians along with him, and the total number of such helpers was considerable. Some of them attained to great eminence, such as the Jesuits, Salmeron and Laynez, the latter the general of his order, who appeared on behalf of the pope.

Had the Fathers and theologians been left to themselves, the debates would probably have proceeded much faster, despite the strength of national feeling; but according to ancient custom, the various ambassadors were allowed, if not to vote, at any rate to sit in the council, and to state before it the grievances and objections of their sovereigns. They used to stand on ceremony a good deal, and the assembly was pestered with endless conflicts of precedence between Portugal and Hungary, between France and Spain, between Bavaria, Switzerland, Venice, and Florence. The activity of the ambassadors was even more troublesome behind the scenes. They were constantly, though not always successfully, egging on their national bishops to put forward the claims of their princes. In fact, they found their minds ready prepared; for the old conciliar spirit was still alive in the assembly, and stood in strong opposition to the centralizing influence of Rome. Many of the Fathers insisted on local independence in the Church, while the Holy See emphasized the necessity of subordination. Nor is it really possible to blame either side, for both were actuated by creditable motives. It is but too true that the past corruption of the Curia justified distrust on the part of the hierarchy, and many sincerely believed that no reformation was possible unless the bonds were somewhat loosened between the local churches and the papacy. At the same time, it so happened that their attitude favored the unanimous efforts of princes to make themselves, to all intents and purposes, the heads of their national churches, and to use such overlordship for other than religious purposes. Therefore, it cannot be doubted that their policy ran counter to that very reformation of the Church which they were no less anxious to bring about than their adversaries; and that Rome alone, once purified, could undertake the cleansing work which was highly unpalatable to most sovereigns in Europe.

From the very first the conciliar party began to raise difficulties, and there followed bickerings which kept recurring from time to time, right to the very end. The articles which rule the proceedings used the words *proponentibus legatis*, thus denoting that the legates alone could submit proposals to the vote of the assembly. This was considered as curtailing the initiative of individual members, and was attacked again and again. On the other hand, several fathers insisted upon the insertion of the phrase *universalem ecclesiam repraesentans*, as qualifying the council, in the heading of its decisions, thus in their minds, implying that the council was superior to the pope. On neither point, however, could the opposition prevail. On several occasions they tried to induce the assembly to revert to the practice of Basle, and vote by nations; but here again they failed. The most serious differences, however, arose in connection with the national policy of the various sovereigns.

During the first period, the Emperor Charles V had no wish to let a council headed by the pope deal with the religious dissensions in Germany. He objected to any debates bearing upon dogma, because he thought that the Lutherans might be antagonized thereby. From the very first he demanded "that the Fathers should begin with Reformation and disciplinary questions . . . and abstain from definitions which would interfere with, or altogether preclude, any agreement with Luther." When the sittings of the council had already begun, he made a further and desperate attempt to conciliate the Protestant League of Smalkalden, and called a "colloquy" at Ratisbon in the winter of 1546. Its failure did not change his mind. He kept exerting pressure at Trent in order to avert solemn condemnation of Lutheranism. Unable to put off the debate on justification any further, he followed the same method as Henry VIII on a different occasion, and insisted that the universities of Cologne, Louvain, and Paris should first be consulted. When at last he realized that conciliation was impossible, he took up arms against the Lutherans, and completely vanquished them.

He did not, therefore, relinquish into the hands of the assembled Fathers what he considered to be his own spiritual prerogative. He deemed it his right to call the council in whatever town he chose, and solemnly protested against the moving of the assembly to Bologna. He got his protestations printed and scattered about profusely, which was tantamount to a declaration of war upon the papacy. He set to work at the Diet of Augsburg (January, 1548) with the help of his own theologians, to prepare a confession of faith which would serve for all his German subjects, Catholic and Protestant alike, pending the decisions of the council. This confession, known as the "Interim," was too vague to satisfy the Catholics, and was finally considered as binding the Protestants only. In drafting it, nevertheless, the Emperor had assumed quasi-papal powers and had gone almost as far as Henry VIII himself.

Nor were pretensions to spiritual supremacy within a certain territory confined to Charles V alone. No sooner had he disappeared from the stage than Henry II of France began to make trouble. He was imbued with the Gallican spirit. In his eyes the council enjoyed no real freedom, and was dependent on the emperor. Besides, at the very moment when Julius III was gathering the Fathers anew, he sent troops into Italy (February, 1551) to support the claim of Ottavio Farnese to Parma and

Piacenza, the fate of which the pope wished to settle in negotiation with the emperor. Hence the usual blustering threats on the part of the French king, who declared he would convoke a national council, stopped the sending of moneys to Rome, hinted at Gallican independence and the creation of a patriarch of Gaul. After 1560, French policy became an almost exact counterpart of imperial policy as it had been under Charles V. The strength of the Huguenots had increased so much that they were in a position to demand a national assembly in France for the settlement of religion. This was granted to them in the summer of 1561, when a "colloquy" met at Poissy, to no great purpose it is true. The king of France was the ally of the German Protestants; the Imperialist party in Germany was paralleled by the Gallican party in France, who were inclined toward toleration and a kind of "Interim." They refused to recognize the validity of the sessions of the council held under Paul III and Julius III, which they considered as not "general" enough. Later on, when at last a delegation of French bishops had appeared at Trent, they supported the representatives of the Empire and Spain in their opposition to papal overlordship. While praising the work done at Poissy, and advocating conciliation, they defended the privileges of the French crown and the "liberties of the Gallican Church" — in other words the maintenance of the authority of their sovereign over his clergy, and his right to appoint to benefices, episcopal sees, and other ecclesiastical offices; which meant, though they might deny it, the continuation of manifold abuses.

The question which exercised the council most, and repeatedly endangered its harmony, concerned the rights and powers of the episcopate. The curial party believed that the bishops held delegated powers from the pope. Their opponents — whom we may for the sake of convenience call the episcopalians — on the contrary claimed that the bishops held their powers directly from God, and were accountable to Him only. The practical importance of this difference appeared in the long-protracted debates on residence, and on the privileges of exempt bodies. If the bishops were instituted by God directly, they were bound to reside in their sees, and to refuse employment at the Curia, rather than to govern their dioceses through deputies. If, on the other hand, they were instituted by the pope, the latter might dispense them from residence according to the requirements of the Church at large. Again, in the former case, episcopal jurisdiction could not be curtailed by intervention of the Holy See, such as exemptions implied; in the latter case exempt bodies, cathedral colleges, religious orders and houses might appeal to Rome for the maintenance of their privileges. Both parties invoked the superior interest of the Church. The episcopalians recalled the numberless abuses to which the practice of exceptions had given rise, and asserted that only an independent and powerful hierarchy could restore discipline; while the curials pointed out that the independence of the hierarchy really meant its subjection to the will of princes, who derived much profit from the abuses and had no real desire of reformation; also that the Church neded a central administration, and required for headquarters the services of her most valuable helpers, even if they belonged to the episcopal body.

The contending opinions were not always, however, so clear-cut as might appear from the above summary. It is true that part of the assembly — mostly the Spaniards, afterward supported by the French Fathers — kept up almost throughout the council an agitation in favor of the divine right of episcopacy: that they refused to allow of any absence of a bishop from his see, even for legitimate reasons, and would not even permit the practice of pastoral letters as a substitute for personal preaching; that they proposed heavy penalties against nonresident prelates and even cardinals; and that while asserting that the bishops were in one sense the equals of the pope, they implied that the council was superior to the Holy See. But much of that heckling of the papal legates might really be described as "letting off steam." When the council came to practical problems, the various parties felt that there was more to unite than there was to divide them. Even the Spanish and French bishops needed the help of the Holy See against kings who made free with the rights and property of the Church, and against the inferior clergy who asserted their own privileges. Even the papacy knew that the enforcement of residence was necessary to the program of reformation: "No one," as the legate Cervini replied in 1547 to the bishop of Huesca, "questions the obvious necessity of residence; the whole point is to know how it should be observed."

Though years of work were needed to make an end of contention, agreement did come at last, on most of the points submitted to the council. Not, indeed, that it fulfilled its whole purpose. It was able to take steps toward the reformation of the Church at large, but not to enforce its decisions outside the papal states. Many of the Fathers — more than one hundred patriarchs, archbishops, and bishops — declared on September 11, 1563, that they refused to take any further part in the proceedings, if the Reformation was not extended to the princes as well. The latter, they said, ought no longer to take advantage of flagrant abuses, and should therefore be deprived of their rights of patronage and forbidden to appropriate Church property to their own uses. The Church was to be independent of the civil power. This, however, was more than the council could effect, and it had to be content to leave its task unfinished, and to trust the Holy See to enforce its decrees as far as could be done. The work completed was nevertheless considerable; and so, though in the midst of bickering and strife, a great body of legislation had gradually shaped itself, which was to be the charter of the Catholic Reformation and direct its later progress.

* * *

On the termination of the council, one of the bishops present, the Venetian, Hieronimo Ragazzoni, gave expression to the general joy in a long oration which, though most classically polished and elegant, was nevertheless exultant in tone.

"Earlier councils," he said, "have done their best to correct our faith and correct our manners; but I doubt whether they performed their task as diligently, or as brilliantly, as we have done. Everyone's sores have been laid open, everyone's life brought to light: nothing has been dissembled. The arguments and reasonings of our adversaries have been handled as if in the interests of their cause, not of ours. Some points have been discussed thrice, or even four times; and often the highest pitch of contention has been reached; but in such wise that, as gold is tried by fire, the strength and sinews of truth were, so to say, tried by wrestling. For indeed what real discord could there exist between men who were inspired by the same convictions, and who had the same end in view?"

Indeed, it is, humanly speaking, hardly believable that an assembly, torn by conflicting tendencies, should have shown itself so unanimous and so clear about its own mind, in its *Canones et Decreta*. This work, despite the lapse of eighteen years between its inception and termination, is a forcible, coherent body of doctrine. It is fairly equally divided into two parts, the dogmatic and the disciplinary decrees, between which there is, of course, no absolutely clear-cut distinction. The former refute the new heresies, and strongly, uncompromisingly assert the orthodox faith. They are a mere naked, austere exposition of the Catholic Church's teaching; but there is something bracing about their very severity, a driving force which was bound to carry wavering opinion along with it. Amidst the confusion of thought which prevailed in the mid-sixteenth century, a definite statement of the Church's position was a rallying point for many bewildered souls. As for the disciplinary decrees, they deal with moral abuses as being the outcome of faulty administrative practice; they bring the necessary correctives to the anarchical state of the Church; they make her government, hierarchy, and system of jurisdiction into a harmonious whole.

Such strength of thought and steadiness of purpose would be wholly unaccountable had the council been merely a scrimmage between contending parties. But in truth all its members shared the same high ideal and had a noble conception of their own duty and of the function of the Church. Of course they did not express their feelings and enthusiasm through oratorical speeches or gushing sentimentalism. But their warm piety breathes forth from many a passage of sober and restrained beauty.

In the *Canones et Decreta,* there is a mingling of quiet and stately dignity, of burning charity, of fervent piety. The council, after advising bishops not to be overbearing with their flocks, warns them against fawning upon princes, their ministers, and their barons; and asks them "to bethink themselves of their order and degree, both in their churches and abroad, and remember that they are fathers and pastors." This warm, sincere piety is evident in the passage which recommends frequent Communion: "The council warns, exhorts, beseeches, entreats all and sundry . . . to believe and venerate those holy mysteries of the body and blood of Christ, with such constancy and firmness of faith, such devotion of the heart, such piety and honor, that they may often receive that suprasubstantial bread, and that it may truly be to them the life of the soul, and the perpetual health of the mind."

Such spiritual fervor was bound to be reflected in the ethical field; nor should what has been said above of administrative reform be taken to mean that the council was indifferent to moral evils as such. Its legislation against laxity of manners is quite as rigorous as that of the most severe Protestants. Like the Presbyterians, the council condemned organ music in churches in which it was undoubtedly ill-advised; like the Presbyterians again, it advised public penance for public sinners, so that "he who had through his example drawn others to evil manners, should recall them to an upright life through the witness of his correction." Some exaggerations may indeed be accounted for by the reaction against Renaissance lasciviousness; but the action of the council was of the happiest when it forbade dueling, and ordered that those who countenanced it, be they emperors or kings, should be excommunicated; when it took stringent measures against concubinary priests, "of whatever degree, dignity, or condition"; when it prescribed decent behavior in the house of God.

The moral ideal of the Council of Trent strongly recalls that of the Christian humanists of the early sixteenth century, many of whom had, as a matter of fact, lived long enough to take part in the debates. It is an ideal of earnest soberness, of decent temperateness. The following rules are laid down for all clerics:

"It altogether behooves all those who are called to act in the name of God, so to compose their lives and manner, that in their outward bearing, their deportment, their gait, and their speech, they show nothing but what is grave, moderate, and full of piety." In preaching as well as in conduct, the Christian humanists advised decent plainness; they recommended sermons in the vernacular, simple and homely, without any unnecessary refinements of eloquence and logic. The same spirit appears in the Trentine canons bearing on the subject. Lest, in the words of Jeremiah, "the little ones ask bread, and no man break it unto them," all archbishops, bishops, archpriests, and priests are requested to address their flocks in person, no exemption of any kind being allowed; but they should do so "in words brief and easy." When explaining the "force and use" of the sacraments, as they ought to do before dispensing them, let them do so "in the vernacular, if need be," and "in words suitable for the understanding of those who are to receive, . . . piously and wisely." On Sundays and feast days, they should comment, "also in the vulgar tongue," on "the holy discourses, and their intimations of salvation"; but here again, they should, "when striving to plant them into the hearts of all, and make the people learned in the law of the Lord . . . leave aside any useless disquisitions." Purgatory should be taught, but, "with the ruder sort of people, the more difficult and subtle questions, which do not tend to edification, and through which most of the time piety is not augmented, should be left out of the sermons."

Generally speaking, the council, like the Christian humanists, believes in plain, honest common sense. The carrying of the Sacrament to the sick, one of the decrees runs, is an ancient use, and should be retained: "Besides, it is consonant with the highest equity and reason." Whenever a point of dogma or canon law is demonstrated, there is the same appeal to plain, balanced thinking. Some idea of this may be gained from the following lines on confession. After recalling that Christ gave to his priests and vicars the power of the keys, they proceed: "It is obvious that priests cannot pronounce judgment without knowing the cause, and that in fact they cannot preserve equity in the imposing of penalties, if the faithful declare their sins only in general, and not in detail, and one by one. It follows that the penitents must needs review in confession all their mortal sins, of which they have become conscious after diligently examining themselves."

The very style of the *Canones et Decreta* agrees with the thought. It is terse, forcible, seldom allows itself any artifices of rhetoric, but often rises to great dignity. Its latinity is pure, elegant, and sometimes slightly affected. The literary ideal of the Fathers finds expression in their rules on forbidden books. "Such as deal with lascivious or lewd subjects . . . should be altogether prohibited. But if they are ancient works written by Gentiles, they are permitted, on account of the elegance and propriety of their speech; though they must on no account be read to children." And yet their appreciation of classical models has a higher purpose; they should lead to a better understanding of the sacred texts. In cathedral churches, when a reader in Scripture cannot be afforded, there should at least be "a master, appointed by the bishop . . . to teach 'grammar' gratis to the clergy, and also to poor scholars; so that they may with the grace of God, pass on to the study of Holy Writ." "Grammar," which should be taken in a broad sense, is also part of the syllabus of the new seminaries which are to be created in each diocese: as well, it is true, as singing and reckoning. Altogether, the council's wish to maintain classical culture cannot be doubted, possibly out of respect for the spirit of the age, but more probably to fulfill the purpose of the Christian humanists, and turn the Renaissance to a religious use.

*   *   *

There was no reason why the Fathers should have added to the *Canones et Decreta* considerations expressing the moral ideal which animated them; the latter chiefly appears in the rules which they laid down for the welfare of the Church. Nor was their work of a random or haphazard nature. They went on a very definite plan, which is never declared as such, but which unmistakably emerges from the *Canones et Decreta* taken as a whole: that of strengthening the authority of the hierarchy, both secular and regular, in conjunction with that of the papacy. The two might, on first glance, seem to be antagonistic; and no doubt many of the Fathers, still imbued with the prejudices of the conciliar party, tended to look askance at papal overlordship; while many curialists might consider episcopal independence an undue limitation of the papal prerogative. That both were, however, mistaken was soon made clear. Neither the bishops without the support of the Holy See, nor the pope unaided by the bishops, could deal satisfactorily with the abuses. Mutual correction and mutual help were needed; and such were, in fact, the lines on which the council went, establishing a firm interdependence between a purified papacy and a purified episcopacy.

The decrees as a whole bring about a general clarifying and disentangling of the various jurisdictions. There are to be two of these only, saving the superior rights of the Holy See: that of the bishop within his diocese, and that of the head of an order within the same. The bishop is to be untrammeled by the numberless individual privileges which till then had set his authority at naught. No one, secular or regular, is to preach without his license. In regard to visitation and the correction of manners, his rights are absolute; nor can his action be stopped by any exemption or appeal, even to Rome; he is expected to visit his whole diocese every two years, including his own cathedral chapter, all hospitals, colleges, and brotherhoods; also such religious houses as are not visited by the head of an order, and all benefices, secular and regular, with or without cure of souls, even those held *in commendam* or exempt; nor can the canons, archdeacons, and deans under him exercise similar powers without his permission. His jurisdiction does not merely extend only to all seculars, but also in a number of cases to religious persons as well, especially those living outside their monasteries. The provision according to which he alone can allow other than parish priests to hear confessions is obviously meant chiefly for regulars; and his authority over women's convents is shown by his right to send to them confessors extraordinary.

The Trentine legislation makes the bishop supreme in the matter of ordination or the conferring of benefices. Therefore, he has a right to select candidates to minor orders, to send aspirants to the priesthood to universities or seminaries, and to examine them before ordaining them, which ordination he must confer himself. On the other hand, should he interdict a priest, his decision is final; and if a priest has been ordained without his consent, he has a right to suspend him. He alone is entitled to confer orders within his diocese. Bishops *in partibus* are debarred from trespassing upon this privilege; and abbots and other exempt prelates, colleges, or chapters are forbidden to confer the tonsure, or allow anyone, through dimissory letters, to receive holy orders. As for candidates to benefices, whoever may have presented them, be it even a papal nuncio, they are not to be admitted, "even on account of any privilege, or custom, even immemorial," if they have not been examined and found worthy by the ordinary of the place. Besides, the same has a right to check all titles to patronage acquired within the last forty years, even through the authority of the Holy See, and, if he does not find them lawful, to revoke them.

Thus the bishops are allowed to take action, even in cases in which they may seem to infringe the privileges of the Holy See; nor would they enjoy the necessary authority, if they did not have superior powers delegated by the pope. That they are deemed to have them is clear, since they are repeatedly mentioned as acting "as the delegates of the Apostolic See." As for the papacy itself, it relinquishes the use of its right to interfere with the lower degrees of jurisdiction, and is content to be the head of the hierarchy, and the supreme court of appeal. Thus limited, its rights are maintained in the frequently used phrase, *"salva Sanctae Sedis auctoritate,"* saving the authority of the Holy See. The pope retains his powers as the chief authority in the Church. He alone is to weigh the merits of men proposed by provincial councils for the episcopate, and to appoint bishops, though the council gravely admonishes him "to put at the head of the several churches good and capable pastors; and this the more so as our Lord will call him to account for the blood of Christ's sheep, that will perish through the evil government of pastors remiss and forgetful of their duty."

That gigantic system of administration and taxation through the Curia, which the Avignon popes had perfected, which superseded the authority of the hierarchy and drew everything up to Rome, the council fells to the ground at one blow. "The Holy Council decides that provisions and expectative graces will not be granted henceforth to any one . . . even by the name of indults, or for a fixed sum, or for any other reason whatsoever." The rejection of papal exemptions is even more severe: "Since it is known that the privileges and exemptions, which are granted to many on various accounts, give rise to perturbations in the jurisdiction of the Church, and afford to exempt clerics an occasion of loose living," all those who have been granted honorary titles by the Holy See, if they are not actually resident in the Curia, are to remain subject to the authority of the ordinary.

No part of the Church, whether secular or regular, is now to claim dependence upon the papacy as a means of withdrawing itself from the normal system of jurisdiction. All those monasteries which used to be governed "under the immediate protection and direction of the Apostolic See" must now be formed into diocesan or provincial orders, with their general chapters, and their own visitors; or if they fail to do so, they are again to fall under the authority of the ordinary. Regulars are forbidden to attach themselves, without license from their superiors, to any prelate, prince, university, or community. If they leave their houses without permission, they are to be punished by the ordinary. The transfer of monks from order to order, which allows of "wandering about and apostatizing," i.e., returning to secular life, is not to be allowed. The heads of orders are enjoined to visit the monasteries and priories placed under them; nor can local superiors refuse their visitation. Secular and regular functions are not henceforth to be confused. A canon henceforth is not allowed to be at the same time an abbot or a prior.

The independence of cathedral chapters and their assumption of episcopal powers had been the cause of long-standing differences, even inside the council itself. The decrees, duly weighing the claims of both parties, make the bishop supreme: "He is to be shown honor consonant with his dignity, to occupy in the choir, chapter or processions, and other public acts, the place which he has chosen, and to have the chief authority there as to what is to be done." Yet he is to take the advice of the canons, especially in the matter of trials, in which they form a sort of judicial court. At the same time, cathedral chapters, which had been a hotbed of abuses, must now agree to be cleansed. Their members mut be fit for their task, at least twenty-five years of age, and commendable through their learning and virtue. All bartering of canonries, all promises made by candidates to pay for their prebends out of the revenues, are declared simoniacal and forbidden. Canons are not allowed to absent themselves from their churches for more than three months each year; they are requested to take part in the divine service in person, not through deputies, and to sing in the choir. Similar rules apply to the prebendaries in collegiate or parish churches.

As for cathedral chapters, so for all beneficiaries. The restoration of episcopal jurisdiction necessarily carried along with it the restoration of discipline. To begin with, pluralities share the fate of exemptions: "Many," says the council, "thereto driven by insatiable covetousness, and deceiving themselves, though not God, have through various tricks eluded wise rules, and blush not to own several benefices together." This is now to be strictly forbidden, even to cardinals, at least in cases where residence is necessary. Then, again, benefices are not to be conferred except "upon worthy and capable persons, who are able to reside, and perform their duties by themselves." They may be granted to young men who have received the tonsure or minor orders, the minimum age being fixed at fourteen; but in such cases, they are to be considered as a means to support the incumbent while he is preparing for the priesthood — after being first examined by the bishop — at a university or elsewhere; nor can he be otherwise entitled to the privileges of the clerical state. In no case is a benefice to be considered as an heirloom, to be bequeathed by the holder; even the coadjutor of a bishop or abbot is not to count upon his succession. If a parish is to be provided with a priest, the bishop alone, despite all privileges, even granted by Rome, is to find candidates and to bring them before a board of examiners of unimpeachable honesty, appointed by himself.

One of the main cares of the Council of Trent was the recruiting of a qualified clergy, and the keeping out of undesirable persons. Hence the fulness of the canons bearing upon ordination. At the time, many priests were unprovided with decent means of sustenance, and wandered about in search of employment which the council declares, "is not fitting." Therefore all candidates for the priesthood, unless they can depend upon their personal income, should be provided with a benefice; and all those who are promoted to holy orders, whether subdeacons, deacons, or priests, should be appointed to a definite function. Minor orders are to be granted only to those who appear worthy to rise higher, and who know Latin; a subdeacon must be at least twenty-two years of age, a deacon twenty-three, a priest twenty-five; this also applying to regulars, who must be examined by the bishop. One year's diaconate is necessary before priestly ordination; nor should anyone be chosen for the latter unless he knows all that is needed for preaching and the administration of sacraments, and "is thus noted for his piety and chaste conversation, that an excellent pattern of good works, and an exemplary life, may be expected from him."

Lastly, the upbringing of future priests is not to be left to chance; and here we come to the most original and probably the most important creation of the council, that of the seminaries. These are to be veritable "nurseries" for the clergy, in which likely boys will be trained from the age of twelve in the practice of virtue and piety. The regulations and the syllabus are outlined by the council; but the details of the organization are left in the hands of the bishop. The sons of poor families are to be admitted in preference to rich boys. The pupils are to be divided into classes, and to study the liberal arts — grammar, reckoning, singing, etc. — as well as Scripture, the Fathers, and liturgy; to attend Mass every day, and to go to confession and Communion at least once every month. The professors must be doctors, masters, or licenciates in Holy Writ or canon law, or at least fully qualified. There is to be one seminary or more in each diocese, and considerable attention is granted to the financing of the whole system. Revenues already devoted to the education of the clergy are to be turned over to the new institutions. In addition to this, there is to take place a general levy on all benefices without exception. Bishops who fail to comply with these provisions may be deprived of their revenues.

It was not enough, however, to provide for the education of the priests of the future. There were abuses in the life of the clergy that clamored for immediate correction. The council deals with them firmly. All persons in orders, all the holders of ecclesiastical benefices or dignities are requested to wear clerical dress, under penalty of suspension, or in case of relapse, of deprivation. Drastic action is taken against concubinary priests; the council deprives them, first of part, and then if they do not amend of the whole, of their ecclesiastical incomes, and of the right to occupy any charge or benefice; eventually they may be cast into prison. The right of punishing concubinary bishops is reserved to the pope. Especial attention is given to the vice of covetousness. "Since the ecclesiastical order must be free from any suspicion of avarice," no money is to be taken by bishops for the conferring of orders, or any of the ceremonies therewith connected; even spontaneous gifts are to be refused. The same applies to visitations, the appointment of canons, and the examination of future parish priests. The letting of Church property is severely forbidden.

Thus we are brought again to those abuses born of greed, which led to the encouragement of superstition by unscrupulous dealers in holy things, and were at least the immediate occasion of the Lutheran revolt. The council shows no leniency toward those who had well-nigh brought about the downfall of the Church. One of the very first decrees passed in its early sessions is directed against the *quaestores eleemosynarii*, commonly known as *quaestuarii*, who went about begging for alms in the name of saints whose intercession they promised to the donors, and hawking indulgences; they are absolutely forbidden to preach. A further decree does away with them altogether. The burning question of indulgences is dealt with in the same spirit. The right of the Church to proclaim them is maintained, within the limits "of moderation, and custom"; but "the wicked gains obtained from those who acquired them, from which has sprung among the Christian people the source of manifold abuses, are altogether to be suppressed." As for other corruptions, "due to superstition, ignorance, irreverence, or other causes," they are to be firmly corrected by the bishops and provincial councils. The decree on the abuse of images deserves especial attention. The people are to be taught that statues and pictures have no divine character in themselves. "All superstition in the invocation of saints, in the veneration of relics, in the use of holy images, must be done away with; all shameful gain must be removed; all lasciviousness must be avoided; so that no images of a wanton beauty be painted or represented; and that in the celebration of saints' days, or in the visit of relics, people fall not into the abuse of orgy and drunkenness." Just as the worship of saints ought not to be an occasion for greed, pious foundations should not be turned into a commercial enterprise. The will of testators, "in regard to prayers, alms and works of piety," ought to be executed with earnestness and devotion.

The foregoing is enough to give some idea of the vast scope of the task accomplished at Trent; still many points have been left in the dark. The corrective, the properly reforming side of the council's work has perforce been insisted on. Its constructive side can barely be mentioned here. Much was done for the redistribution of parishes, and the relief of poor prebends and benefices. Regulations were laid down for tithes and mortuaries, for marriage dispensations, and for the registration of weddings and christenings. Bishops and priests were reminded of the duty of preaching, and of preaching sound doctrine; this being the link between the disciplinary and the theological labors of the council. For it should not be forgotten that much time was devoted to the defining of dogma, and the refuting of heresy. This, however, consisted mostly in reasserting tenets already affirmed by previous councils. It helped considerably in the work of Catholic reformation, by providing a firm intellectual basis. But it was not its most original element, and we need not enlarge upon it.

All in all, the Trentine *Canones et Decreta* display a striking combination of spiritual ardor and earnestness, and of temperate, sober reasonableness; as, for instance, in the regulations referring to public worship. There should be in churches, we read, "nothing disorderly, nothing arranged preposterously or hurriedly, nothing profane, nothing indecent; for holiness is fitting in the House of God." And the spirit of the council's work, which is also the spirit of Christian humanism, is expressed fully in the decree concerning Mass. In its celebration, three things should be avoided at all costs: greed — or all that savors of simony; irreverence — the ministration of unworthy priests, lascivious music, profane or vain talking, walking about in church, loud noises or crying; superstition — unwarranted rites, the use of a fixed number of Masses or candles. Holiness and decency: how truly Christian, and yet how different from the rough-and-tumble of the Middle Ages, from their easy familiarity with holy things, from their lack of self-restraint, from their truculent crudity. Indeed, the temperate wisdom of classical antiquity had left its mark upon the Catholic Reformation; it had brought to it a color and a temper of its own.

*   *   *

Though the council had covered considerable ground, it could not, by its own means, complete the task it had begun. For one thing, there was no reason why the work of reformation undertaken by the Holy See as early as the days of Adrian VI should fall into abeyance while the assembly sat; and in fact the popes kept up their battle against abuses, with varying fortunes, throughout the sittings at Trent; nor did they wish to let the Fathers interfere with the reform of the Curia, which they repeatedly reserved for themselves. Then, again, the council was not an executive body: it could lay down principles, but not apply them. The enforcement and interpretation of the decrees rested with the papacy. Lastly, on many points, though the way had been pointed out at Trent, no definite steps had been taken. It was left to the popes to fill in the general framework. We shall not here describe at large their protracted fight against the many-headed hydra of Roman corruptions. The essential is that it was conducted on lines strikingly parallel with the action of the council. Among some fifty reforming briefs issued by Julius III, in the years 1550 to 1554, over half concern monastic discipline; a number deal with exempt bodies; others enforce the wearing of clerical dress, limit the use of interdict, recast the Dominican liturgy, take steps against vagrant monks and nuns, forbid the cession of benefices, and otherwise emulate the Trentine legislation.

There is something admirable, and occasionally pathetic, in the ups-and-downs of the papal struggle against abuses, especially in the long interval between the second and the third periods of the council, under the pontificate of Paul IV. This pope, a worthy successor of Adrian VI, undertook a root-and-branch reformation of the Curia and of the Church in the papal states. He was not content with issuing regulations; he actually enforced them, irrespective of all personal considerations or interests. The police were set on the vagrant monks in Rome; one hundred of them were arrested, part of these being imprisoned or condemned to the galleys. It was found that one hundred and thirteen bishops were present in the Curia; a dozen of them only, who had duties there, were allowed to remain; the others had to rejoin their dioceses under pain of deposition. The pope's own nephews, who occupied high posts in his court, had proved unworthy of his trust and perpetuated the scandalous abuses of previous times; they were deprived of their dignities, turned out of Rome, and reduced to misery.

Paul IV's main purpose was the total suppression of simony in every form. He resolutely overrode the usual objection to reform, namely that the impoverishment of the Holy See which was sure to follow would no longer allow it to make its weight felt in international politics. He compelled the Datary to deliver graces gratis, and to make up for the loss, reduced his expenses and those of the cardinals. He was prepared to fulfill his reforming designs, he said, "even at the peril of his own life." He prevented by all possible means the traffic in benefices. He was an austere and rigid moralist, and succeeded in purifying the life of Rome by his legislation against lewd women, usurers, comedians, and buffoons. He even went so far as to forbid hunting and dancing — an unwise and unfortunate reaction, though one which can be understood, against the laxity of the Renaissance. Even when enfeebled by disease and urged by relatives and friends to compromise with the times, he stood firm; and there is no doubt that his action achieved notable results, and greatly strengthened that of the council.

Paul IV's successor, Pope Pius IV, was of a less thoroughgoing temperament, and more inclined to further the fortunes of his relatives. However, the most striking instance of nepotism which he gave led to the most beneficial results, and ensured the permanency of the Catholic Reformation. Soon after his accession he appointed his nephew, Charles Borromeo (1538–1584), Secretary of State (1559). The young man, then only twenty-one, belonged to a noble family of Milan, and though devout and serious-minded, showed a partiality for pomp and sumptuousness at the outset. Sobered, however, by the death of his brother, Federigo (November 19, 1562), in whom rested the hopes of secular aggrandizement of the Borromei, he refused to step into his brother's place as head of the family, and resolved to strike a more religious course. After going through the *Spiritual Exercises* of St. Ignatius, he took priest's orders and reduced his life to ascetical simplicity, much to the disappointment of the party of abuses, who were beginning to raise their heads anew. The part he took in directing the debates of the council from Rome has been pointed out. No sooner had the decrees been issued, than he began to apply them wherever his authority extended, i.e., mostly in the papal states, thus setting an example to all Christendom. His work of reformation in the Eternal City proceeded much on the same lines as under Paul IV, and it would be tedious to rehearse the various steps taken for the uprooting of simony, the visitation of churches, the cleansing of the Curia. The change in the atmosphere of Rome was noted by visitors. Fortune-seekers no longer flocked there; the cardinals led a more austere life; societies were founded for the relief of the poor and for the education and protection of young girls; regulations were issued against excessive luxury, the pope himself, in August, 1564, dismissing over four hundred courtiers. The reform of religious orders was undertaken anew, and most important of all, seminaries were founded, largely under the guidance of the Jesuits.

Borromeo, who had been created archbishop of Milan, had long besought the pope to let him return to his see, according to the duty of residence; but Pius IV was not to be moved. His successor Pius V, however (elected on January 8, 1566), gave the permission. Charles had already undertaken, from Rome, to rejuvenate his diocese in accordance with the Trentine decrees. He now applied the regulations on provincial and diocesan synods, and held seven of the former at regular intervals, and eleven of the latter. He set up three seminaries at Milan, and three more, for younger boys, inside the diocese. He had first asked the Jesuits to provide the staff; but as they were reluctant to continue, he founded a new order of his own, on the model of the Society, but limited to his archdiocese, the Oblates of St. Ambrose. They were a company of secular priests, who took vows to devote themselves wholly to the archbishop's service and to afford him help wherever he should need it. Borromeo also established a Society of the Schools of the Christian Doctrine, which in its turn created seven hundred and forty schools. His helper in his work of reform was a simple priest, Niccolò Ormaneto, who had been trained under Giberti, and had accompanied Pole to England, being thus a link between the older generation of Christian humanists, and that of the Council of Trent.

The task of the papacy and its helpers would have been much simpler had the decrees been complete in themselves and ready for enforcement. But they were not. In order that the reforming legislation might be applicable to the whole Church, it had first to be confirmed by the Holy See, according to the express request of the council. This gave rise to more difficulties than might at first sight be expected. The Curial officials, whose incomes were threatened by a decrease in the appeals to

Rome, tried to brake down the impulse, or at any rate to obtain mitigations. Pius IV disregarded their opposition, and in a bull dated January 26, 1564, but really issued on June 30, confirmed the decrees fully. At the same time he forbade the publishing of commentaries and annotations upon them without the consent of the Holy See, and reserved their interpretation for the latter. This provision ensured uniformity in the application of the decrees, and disposed of the Gallican claim, according to which the pope was inferior to the council, and subject to its enactments. In order to deal with the numerous practical questions which were sure to arise, Pius IV created a commission of cardinals, later to be known as the Congregation of the Council, whose powers, however, did not extend to the dogmatic field.

The work of Trent was continued in many directions under the pontificates of Pius IV and his successor Pius V. The first Index of Prohibited Books, compiled under Paul IV, was unduly severe, and had given rise to many protests. In the council it was pointed out that many of the condemned writings were indispensable for literary or scholarly studies. Accordingly a specially appointed commission undertook the correction of the Index. Whereas the works of Erasmus had previously been rejected *en bloc,* a distinction was now made between them, and Boccacio was only forbidden pending emendation. After the close of the council the Trentine Index was again examined in Rome, and published by a papal brief of March 24, 1564.

The Fathers at Trent had also been anxious, as early as 1546, to draft a catechism, or rather two catechisms, one in Latin for the learned, and one in the vernacular for the unlettered and the young. They addressed themselves only to the former task. In the following years, a model was supplied by the catechism of Peter Canisius, composed at the request of the Emperor Ferdinand. When the assembly broke up, however, the new manual of doctrine had not been completed. A commission of theologians was appointed at Rome to put it into final shape, while the humanist, Giulio Poggiani, was to polish its Latin. Eventually, under Pius V, the Roman catechism was published. Soon it was translated into Italian, German, French, Polish, and Spanish.

While the council had simplified and harmonized the system of Church jurisdiction, it brought the same spirit to bear on the reform of the liturgy in the Missal and the Breviary. The latter especially had become lengthy, entangled, and overloaded with lives of saints, many of them apocryphal or fantastic and couched in wretched Latin. Little room was left for readings from Scripture, and there was no clear system for the ordering of prayers. All these things were obnoxious to the Fathers at Trent, who, true to the traditions of Christian humanism, made meditation on the Gospel the center of their devotion, and believed in applying textual and historical criticism even to sacred documents. Accordingly, after rejecting the Breviary of the Spanish cardinal, Quiñones (1535), in which correction had overshot its mark, they chose as a model that which the Theatine, Gian-Pietro Caraffa — the future Pope Paul IV — had compiled for the use of his order. This task, too, they were to leave unfinished, and it was to wait for completion until the days of Pius V. The revised Breviary was published at last by a bull of July 9, 1568, and the revised Missal two years later. The Council of Trent had prescribed a similar work of purification on the text of the Vulgate, and in 1561 the printer, Paulus Manutius, was called to Rome to prepare correct editions of the Bible and the Fathers of the Church. However, the work dragged on through the pontificates of Pius IV and Pius V, and the Vatican edition of the Vulgate was not published until November 9, 1612 by Pope Clement VIII.

* * *

Such were the lines along which the work of the council developed and fructified. Unfortunately, out of the papal states, one major obstacle stood in its way — the rights of patronage which were in the hands of temporal sovereigns and had been frequently condoned by the Holy See itself. Princes were wont to reward their servants with the benefices they had in their gift, irrespective of the requirements of Church discipline; hence they were responsible for exemptions, pluralities, and other abuses, no less than Rome herself. If they did not submit to the Trentine decrees these would lose most of their efficiency. In fact, in its last sessions, the council had attempted the reform of princes, which it felt to be necessary. There was, however, such opposition on the part of the various sovereigns, some of them threatening schism, that it had to desist and be content with exhorting them. Now that the sittings were over, the only thing to do was to persuade the civil power to ratify the legislation passed at Trent. This was no easy task, and in many cases the churches had to make shift to apply the decrees without any help from the temporal rulers.

In Italy things went smoothly enough. The various states of the Peninsula readily promulgated the Trentine decrees, foremost among them being Venice. But in other countries the obstacles which had so long prevented the meeting of the council, now retarded its enforcement.

Ferdinand's successor, the Emperor Maximilian II, persisted in Charles V's illusion that he could effect a religious pacification in his dominions through doctrinal and disciplinary concessions to the Protestants; besides he wanted their help against the Turks. The Trentine legislation was too square-cut for him, and he refused to let the decrees be confirmed at the Diet of Augsburg in 1566. Together with him a number of men in Germany and even in Rome formed what has been called the "irenical" party, and were prepared to meet the Protestants halfway. They failed to realize that in periods of moral and mental confusion, a determined and clearly defined policy acts as a rally point and as a heartening influence, whereas compromise is viewed by hostile extremists as the equivalent of weakness. The peacemakers were nevertheless inspired by the most praiseworthy motives. They thought that if the German laity were granted Communion under both kinds, Protestantism would lose most of its hold upon the people; while the marriage of priests would enable the German Church to tide over the dearth of qualified clergy. Pius V let himself be persuaded to grant the cup to laymen within the Empire. No very definite results followed, and the concession was gradually allowed to drop and was finally canceled in 1621. Meanwhile, however, the Trentine decrees had not been ratified; nor was the Empire as a whole ever to endorse them. Happily, as early as 1566, the legate, Commendone, had induced the German Catholic princes, especially the duke of Bavaria, Cardinal Truchsess, bishop of Augsburg, Cardinal Mark Sittich von Hohenems, and the three ecclesiastical electors, besides others, to publish the legislation of the council within their states, and to undertake the work of reformation, which was soon to bear fruit in plenty.

In France, objections were raised from the outset by the king and his supporters. The council was considered to have failed in its main purpose, since it had not brought about the reconciliation between Protestants and Catholics which it had been counted upon to effect. The decrees could not be accepted, for they would incense the Calvinists, whom they had severely anathematized; besides, they forbade the holding of benefices *in commendam*, and made it impossible for the sovereign to reward influential men whose help he needed. Lastly, national pride had been hurt by the precedence granted to the imperial ambassador. But the chief obstacles to the promulgation were twofold: on the one hand, while the whole of the French Church was agreed on the necessity of the dogmatic decrees, there was no such unanimity in regard to the disciplinary decrees; the cathedral chapters feared for their jurisdiction and privileges, and the poorer clergy viewed with alarm a condition of things in which they would no longer be able to make up for the poverty of small benefices by holding several of them. Therefore in the States General, in the Church assemblies, the acceptance of the decrees was at first proposed with reservations. On the other hand, the high court of judicature known in France as the Parliament was imbued with the old Gallican and conciliar ideas, and though convinced of the necessity of the reformation, wished to effect it, not in the pope's name, but in that of the king; and their opposition to the Holy See became even more settled at the time of the controversy between King James I of England and Cardinal Bellarmine on the power of princes and the temporal claims of the papacy. Despite the efforts of the papal legates during the forty years which followed the break-up of the council, it was never officially confirmed by the French sovereigns.

The Estates General of 1595, called up by the Catholic League, did proclaim them, but in the absence of a lawful king. Meanwhile, the idea of reformation had been slowly gathering momentum, and the French clergy were coming to feel that it behooved them, and not the prince, to take a decision on purely spiritual matters. Therefore, at the Church assembly of 1615, acting on their own responsibility, they subscribed a solemn declaration which "received" the Trentine decrees and promised compliance with them. This was in France the official beginning of the Catholic Reformation, which actually had been in progress for some time past, and which produced magnificent results in the spiritual, intellectual, and literary fields. Yet it was crippled by the king's refusal to join in. The abuses connected with benefices were perpetuated all through the seventeenth and eighteenth centuries. The entanglement of jurisdictions remained what it had been before Trent, and gave rise to scandalous quarrels, such as when monastic offices, considered as private property, were bitterly contended for by two opposing parties among the monks. It is hardly a paradox to repeat, in the words of the late Fr. Wernz, S.J., that the reform of the system of benefices according to the Trentine decrees was the meritorious work of the French Revolution.

Whereas the king of Portugal, writing to the pope on October 2, 1564, promised "to observe the Decrees . . . so as to ensure their undisputed and inviolate integrity," and forthwith signified as much to all his servants, things did not run so smoothly in Spain. Philip II was in a paradoxical position: he considered himself as the most Catholic sovereign in Europe, and yet, rather than relinquish what he regarded as his rights over the Church, he was willing to put off the enforcement of the Trentine legislation in his wide dominions of Spain, Naples, Milan, and

America. After some shilly-shallying, he published the decrees on July 19, 1564, but with the proviso that this was "without prejudice to his royal rights." What he meant thereby appeared clearly in his long struggle against Pius IV and Pius V for the maintenance of ecclesiastical powers scarcely less than those which Henry VIII of England had claimed a few decades before. Pius IV complained that Philip II had assumed the right of interpreting the Council of Trent, and that "he meant to be pope as well as king." The Spanish sovereign deemed himself entitled to withhold all papal bulls or briefs, even on purely spiritual matters, which he happened to disapprove of, and allowed his clergy to appeal to the crown when threatened by any decision of the Holy See. This could not but perpetuate the abuses; in fact, in the kingdom of Naples, bishops were prevented from proceeding against laymen guilty of usury or concubinage, and no clerics were allowed to take possession of their benefices without royal permission. At Milan the chapter of Santa Maria della Scala, who badly needed reformation, tried, with the help of the governor and the senate of the town, to evade visitation; they slammed their door in the face of Archbishop Charles Borromeo, excommunicated his judicial officials, proclaimed that he had made himself liable to ecclesiastical penalties, and posted up their claims. These quarrels dragged on for years, and had not ceased at the death of Pius V.

In Poland it was touch-and-go whether the country would turn Protestant altogether; however, the able Nuncio Commendone succeeded in persuading King Sigismund Augustus to accept the decrees personally on August 7, 1564, and was happy enough to witness in 1565 a renewal of piety among the people. As to the Protestant countries proper, England especially, we shall later see how the Trentine spirit managed to permeate them, despite anti-Catholic legislation. Altogether, the importance of Trent can scarcely be overestimated. It far transcends that of any other Church assembly, however notable. It was, in a way, the heir to the Renaissance, for it borrowed all that was best in it, the classical ideal of order, reasonableness, temperate wisdom, fittingness, and decency, and applied it to its task of rejuvenating the huge, cumbrous, and entangled organization of the medieval Church. Its decrees are a model of clear, forceful thinking, as well as of literary composition. They brought about a wonderful religious revival, both in Europe and elsewhere. Had they been applied everywhere, the whole system of abuses in regard to benefices would have been done away with, and the French Revolution, which was largely a reaction against clerical opulence, might never have happened. It would be a mistake, however, to narrow down the Catholic Reformation to the enforcement of a set of rules. The Trentine legislation itself was but the outcome of a spiritual movement which had begun early in the century, the most striking instance of which was the renewal of devotion and sacrifice among the older religious orders, and the foundation of new orders adapted to the needs of the times.

CHAPTER VI

The Religious Revival Among the Regulars

IT SHOULD again be emphasized here: the Council of Trent was indeed a dividing line and a starting point, but it was not a sudden revolution. The men who drafted the decrees were most of them elderly; their ecclesiastical careers had generally begun early in the century; they had been engaged in reforming work for ten, twenty, or thirty years.

At the very time when the Church is supposed to have been most corrupt, Rome itself was fermenting with devotion and charity. There is no better proof of this than the revival of spiritual life among the regulars, who through the influence they exerted both upon the secular clergy and the laity, created the atmosphere and provided the driving force for the Catholic Reformation. This was performed to some extent by the older orders, some of which did their best to get rid of the abuses which disgraced them. In their case, however, the initiative frequently rested with the papacy. Not so with the new orders — the Theatines, the Oratorians, and above all, the Jesuits; for whatever favor they may have later enjoyed from the Holy See, the merit of their creation must rest with their founders. These were far-sighted men, who had specially in view the needs of the times. They really took the lead in the reforming movement, and played a decisive part.

Yet in regard to the origin of both the older and newer orders, the beginnings were the same. Reference has already been made to those pious brotherhoods which were founded in several parts of Italy, as early as the last years of the fifteenth century. A more important foundation of the same type appeared at Rome some time before 1517, in connection with the renewal of religious fervor brought about by the Lateran Council. It was called *Compagnia ovvero Oratorio del Divino Amore* — the Oratory of Divine Love. It was not a numerous body, nor did it seek to increase its numbers much. There was an intimate quality about it. The attention of its members was turned inward. Their idea was that the best way to spread reformation abroad was to begin it in themselves, through pious exercises, through prayer and exhortation, through frequent confession and Communion, and through the performance of works of charity. Humble and modest, they merely wished to set a good example. Their retiring temper, contemplative rather than militant, was that of the Christian humanists, several of whom, like Sadolet, belonged to the Oratory. Altogether, morally, socially, and intellectually, their body, which rose to the number of fifty or sixty, was distinguished and aristocratic. It was soon joined by two men of widely differing character, who were both to exert a deep influence on the future of the Church, Gaetano di Thiene and Gian-Pietro Caraffa.

The former's upbringing and temper were quite in keeping with the spirit of the Oratory. The son of a noble family of Vicenza, he was brought up, his chief biographer says, *liberaliter et ingenue*, as befits a man of rank. He studied at Padua and became a scholar, a doctor in civil and canon law, and then turned to philosophy and theology. He had been early noted for his charitableness and for his piety, which was of a mystical kind. He "chose secret places to meditate on divine things." He had visions, notably one in which he was allowed to carry the infant Christ in his arms. The Oratory of Divine Love suited him admirably. That it should also have attracted Gian-Pietro Caraffa casts light on the devotional possibilities even of strong, active characters. Caraffa belonged to a noble family of Naples, had early proved his combative zeal by escaping from his home at the age of fourteen to join the Dominicans. Prevented from achieving his purpose, he became an official in the Curia. He lived chastely and purely throughout the scandalous pontificate of Alexander VI. He was entrusted by Julius II with several diplomatic missions, and in England made the acquaintance of Erasmus, whom he encouraged to publish the works of St. Jerome, and who in return praised his classical scholarship. Meanwhile he had been made bishop of Chieti in the Abruzzi, and set about the reformation of his diocese with a firm hand. He joined the Oratory in 1520 during a stay in Rome.

These two men and their friends were to initiate the religious revival among the regulars. Both before and after they had struck a line of their own, they fostered the new spirit among the older orders which were being leavened by small groups of the more eagerly devout among their members. As early as the reign of Leo X there was a movement among the Camaldolese to seek peace and perfection in retirement. The reform was continued and completed under Adrian VI, who for that purpose called to Rome Gian-Pietro Caraffa, a kindred spirit to his.

Various orders were similarly reformed, on the lines of the old rules and according to the primitive spirit of each, between the pontificate of Leo X and the Council of Trent. Caraffa's sister, with her brother's help, improved conditions among the Dominican nuns at Naples in 1530. The Dominican Order itself was only purged of Lutheran preachers and *gyrovagi* by two visitations, under Paul III, in 1543 and 1547. Early in the century Giles of Viterbo (Egidio Canisio), the outspoken orator of the Lateran Council and general of the Augustinian hermits, was at work among his own brethren. His efforts were bravely continued, two decades later, in accordance with the definite orders of Paul III, by his successor, the outstanding classical scholar Girolamo Seripando. In 1539 he began a visitation of all the houses of his order, throughout Italy, France, Spain and Portugal; but it took years to get rid of heretical elements. For the Franciscans, it was a case of a reform within a reform; the revival took place among the Observants, who themselves had, in the fourteenth and fifteenth centuries, seceded from the representatives of the original community, or Conventuals; and it eventually gave birth to a new order, that of the Capuchins, which however remained true to the Franciscan tradition.

Under Leo X, the general of the Observants, Francesco Lichetto, had founded houses of recollection for those among the religious who wished to lead a stricter life; and as the movement spread, the members of the new communities had gained some independence and become known as *Riformati*. The real reformer of the Franciscans, however, appeared a little later; he was Matteo da Bascio (1495–1552), a native of Umbria, where the memories of St. Francis of Assisi were liveliest. He first attracted attention by his heroic behavior during the plague at Camerino (1523 or 1524), and soon became the protégé of Caterina Cibo, duchess of Camerino, the niece of Leo X and Clement VII, and of Vittoria Colonna, two women of the Renaissance who joined fervent piety with elaborate classical scholarship and literary ability. Having returned to his convent of Montefalcone, Matteo, meditating among the solitary woods, felt a stronger and stronger impulse to model his own life wholly on that of St. Francis; this longing taking shape in his resolve to wear a pointed hood or *cappuccio* similar to that which he believed to have been worn by the saint. He was soon joined by Lodovico and Raffaele da Fossombrone. The movement spread rapidly, but its career was a checkered one. The Observants considered the secession as treachery, and succeeded in obtaining from several popes decisions in their favor, which hampered the recruiting or reduced the independence of the new order. Their complaints gained a readier hearing from the fact that Lodovico da Fossombrone, now vicar-general of the Capuchins, had taken a defiant attitude toward the Chapter of 1535, and had had to be expelled, while his successor, Bernardino Ochino, went over to Calvinism in 1542, with a number of his brethren.

At the same time, as early as 1526, Caraffa had taken the founders under his protection and secured for them some measure of freedom. Besides, the Capuchins soon gained popular favor by their eminent virtues. They walked barefoot, slept on a plank, and fasted rigorously; their churches were utterly simple and unadorned, in contrast to those of the Theatines — this being an illustration of the variety of religious tempers, and therefore of the spiritual richness of the Catholic Reformation. They were fearlessly devoted to the sick during epidemics, and attracted crowds by their sermons. Matteo da Bascio, who held up a crucifix above the heads of the people while preaching, used to cry out: "To Hell with usurers, to Hell with concubinaries, and the same for the other vices"; such was his freedom when in the pulpit, that he spared no one, and was for that reason often despised by people of little sense. The Capuchins "preached Holy Writ, chiefly the holy Gospel of our Lord Jesus Christ." One recognizes here all the main features of Franciscan oratory, which was popular both in its violence and theatrical effects and in its genuine simplicity and homeliness.

The Capuchins were the most vigorous offshoot of the older orders in the age of the Renaissance. Their merits were great, and their apostolic labors among the people were rewarded with success. And yet, while they had been well adapted to the spiritual needs of the unsophisticated Middle Ages, they were not wholly fitted to cope with those of the sixteenth century. Something more was needed in a highly refined society, which had developed new intellectual and artistic cravings; where, besides, the influence of the aristocracy was such that the heads must be gained before any enduring work could be done. A new formula was required in the field of religious life. Many pious men were groping for it between 1520 and 1540. Their successive attempts were, on the whole, directed the same way, until they culminated in the most striking and lasting creation of the times, the Society of Jesus. Before the latter came into existence, however, some of its essential principles had already been applied in the various orders of clerks regular.

*   *   *

In the case of the Theatines, the Somaschi, and the Barnabites, the idea behind the foundation is the same. The times, with their changed social and cultural conditions, called for something other than the old cloistered monasticism; they required active spreaders of the faith, who would indeed form organized and disciplined bodies, but who would mix with the world and deal with the world. Hence the double nature of the three orders of clerks regular here mentioned. Their members were true religious, who took the three vows of chastity, obedience, and poverty; their forsaking of worldly goods was even more absolute than that of the Franciscans, as a reaction against covetousness, the mother of all evils in the Church; they were even forbidden to beg and were to look for sustenance to God's Providence alone. They lived in common, and austerely too; they fasted and abstained from meat and mortified themselves. But they all wore the black cassock of secular priests; they all engaged in the same kind of outside work, and their apostolate, while first attending to the material needs of the sick, the poor, and the illiterate, found a way to their souls and raised them up toward God. Finally, they realized that the papacy alone could effect a thorough reformation, and therefore made themselves the direct helpers of the Holy See, upon which they immediately depended.

Nevertheless, each of the three orders had its own history, which accounts for its definite personality. The Theatines were the continuation of the Oratory of Divine Love, and retained its character. Gaetano di Thiene, after seeking his true path from 1519 to 1523 and after being compelled to leave Rome, had attempted to develop the action of the Oratory in provincial towns. He reconstructed and united two brotherhoods at Vicenza and Verona, and reorganized a hospital in Venice. He felt, however, that this was but nibbling at the great problem of reformation; that "the corruption of manners and of souls, which had spread far and wide among the Christian people, was a greater evil than could be cured by the means or efforts of a mere brotherhood of secular priests, which besides could not last for ever." Hence his plan for a new order that would set up a model for the imitation of the secular clergy.

The idea was imparted at first to Bonifazio da Colle, then to Gian-Pietro Caraffa. The latter understood that all attempts at reformation would be futile unless the secular clergy were provided with leaders that would carry them along; he enthusiastically declared his wish to join hands with Gaetano. His position as a bishop, however, stood in the way, and Gaetano was unwilling to accept him. And here follows a moving scene, in which both characters stand out strikingly: after many words had passed, Caraffa, "suddenly falling down upon his knees, with a somewhat angry and almost threatening countenance, affirmed that on Doomsday he would, in the presence of Christ his judge, ask Gaetano to render account of his soul, if he refused to admit him forthwith, from the turmoil of worldly cares, to the quiet of religious life. Then Gaetano . . . himself fell on his knees, and clasping him lovingly, said to him: 'My Lord, I shall never forsake you.' "

In 1524, Clement VII allowed Caraffa to give up his two bishoprics and authorized the new community of Clerks Regular. The latter were soon called Theatines, from Theate, the Latin name of Caraffa's bishopric of Chieti. Although they were to do the work of secular priests, even taking charge of parishes, they retained the exclusive and aristocratic character of the Oratory of Divine Love. Two houses were founded besides that of Rome, at Naples and Venice, but the effectives of the order never rose very high.

In 1533, there were twenty-one Theatines all told. However, Gaetano's purpose was not that they should swarm and spread, but that their communities should be fed by choice vocations, and become a nursery for leaders. In the words of Caraffa's biographer, Caracciolo, they were not "seminaries for priests," but "seminaries for bishops" — and in fact many of their members later became prelates. The success of such a reduced phalanx is an instance of the driving power of small resolute bodies. Its influence was out of all proportion to its numbers. It represented the new spirit to such an extent in the eyes of the public that any strict moralist, any man with a reforming bent, came to be known as a Theatine. The new order enjoyed the friendship and support of many eminent men who longed for the purification of the Church. In Venice, it numbered among its helpers Reginald Pole, Gasparino Contarini, and Gregorio Cortese, the reformer of the Benedictines. In Rome, Giberti used to see Caraffa daily. Tommaso Campeggio, who held the bishopric of Feltre, but had not yet been consecrated, was moved by the latter's example to take a conscientious view of his duties, and to seek consecration at his hands.

The origin and purpose of the Somaschi were somewhat different. They were founded about 1528 by a noble Venetian, Girolamo Miani (Hieronymus Aemilianus). He had been an officer — a brilliant and dissolute one too — in the army of Venice. Two wonderful escapes which he had, the one from captivity and the other from a dangerous illness, turned his mind to spiritual things. Henceforth his life was devoted to the care of the sick, the foundation of orphanages, and the rescuing of fallen girls in various towns of northern Italy, including Milan. To help him in his work, he gathered a body of pious laymen, and established his headquarters near Bergamo, in the village of Somasca, which gave its name to the new community. Yet right up to Miani's death, in 1537, the Somaschi failed to become a religious order properly so called. They became one only in 1568, when Miani's successor Angelo Marco Cambarana obtained a brief which settled their constitutions. Their particular name was "Clerks Regular of San Maiolo," which recalled the church which had been granted to them in Milan by Charles Borromeo. Their work was more particularly the relief of the poor. During the famine of 1528 they won universal admiration.

The third order of Clerks Regular — if one goes by dates — is that of the Barnabites, so called from the church of San Barnaba in Milan, which they occupied from 1545 onwards, though their real name was that of Clerks Regular of Saint Paul. It was founded in 1530 by Antonio Maria Zaccaria (1502–1539), a gentleman of Cremona, who had given up the study of medicine for theology and the priesthood; but his first two companions, Bartolomeo Ferrari and Jacopo Antonio Morizia, were, it should be noted, members of an earlier brotherhood, the Confraternity of Eternal Wisdom, which had been established in Milan by the French in 1500. The Barnabites belonged to the same circle of devotional feeling as the Somaschi; and as in the case of the latter, the leading thought of their founder was to repair the material and moral ruins left by the disasters of 1528 and 1529. Their institute was approved by Paul in 1535. They were most unlike the Theatines in their conquering spirit and their desire to expand. They devoted themselves especially to missions. Their sermons were popular and recalled those of the Franciscans. They used to hold up a crucifix to the people while addressing them; or to carry a heavy cross in church while beseeching God; or to wear a rope round their necks, and, thus attired, seek the most despised forms of employment. Their center at first was Milan; Charles Borromeo esteemed them highly, joined their retreats, and chose his confessor from among them. Afterward they spread rapidly. They founded houses, which went by the name of *colleges,* in most parts of Italy, in France, in Germany, and Bohemia, and very largely brought the province of Béarn back to the fold in the early seventeenth century. They also developed in a different way. They needed female auxiliaries for the conversion and instruction of women in the course of their missions; therefore an association of pious ladies, known as the Congregation of the Holy Angels, or Angeliche, was founded in 1535 by Luigia Torelli to help them; but it remained confined to northern Italy.

*   *   *

There is a striking contrast between the above-mentioned communities and two movements which appeared soon after, and which are by far the most original creations of the sixteenth century, those of the Oratorians and of the Jesuits. The Christian ideal of all was of course the same, and individual variations implied no mutual disapproval; yet, in their common wish for reformation they laid stress on different things. For the Theatines, Somaschi, and Barnabites, external action held a subordinate position; though they might be in charge of hospitals, colleges, or missions, their essential purpose was to sanctify themselves by chastising the flesh and curbing the spirit; they thought that personal mortification and prayer were the most powerful means to help the Church. Nor would the Oratorians and Jesuits deny the truth of such a view. Only they were more practical-minded, and, however little they might otherwise have in common, they both agreed that the most important task was the apostolate; that all else should lead up to it; that those who were to undertake it should be, like a skirmishing party, unencumbered by the heavy burden of monastic obligations; that they should be alert and alive, and have full bodily and intellectual strength at their disposal. Of the two, the Jesuits are somewhat earlier in date; yet the Oratorians, however effective their work, do not hold such a prominent place in the history of the Catholic Reformation, and we shall therefore consider them first.

The Oratory was not, in its inception, a religious order at all. It developed out of the spiritual action and sacerdotal practice of an attractive, exceptional, and even extraordinary personality, St. Philip Neri. Philip was born at Florence in July, 1515, the son of an ancient family whose fortunes had decayed. His youth was spent in his native town, in an atmosphere in which the gaiety and pastimes of a cultured aristocracy were strangely mingled with the spiritual earnestness of the people, who still remembered the fiery Savonarola. After leaving his home at the age of eighteen, he experienced a "conversion," which turned his thoughts wholly toward some sort of religious life; and he then left for Rome, where he arrived in 1534. There he was for some time tutor to the children of a Florentine customs official, and also attended lectures in philosophy and theology; but he soon became impatient of such a plodding course, and his mystical leanings, as well as his thirst for spiritual action, led him about 1537 to take up the life of a "hermit" — somewhat in the style of the Capuchins. Yet he did not retire from the world, but on the contrary began to gather around him a group of young men, mostly custom-house clerks and Florentines, to whom he provided religious guidance. He would join in their games, chatter away with them in their hours of idleness, chaff them and be chaffed, ending up with some devotional advice delivered with gay heartiness. His surprising personal influence, as well as his "method" of sanctification through cheerfulness, are already present here.

Nevertheless, something more than the sporadic efforts of hermits was needed for the reform of the Church. Philip saw that it was necessary to join an existing movement or to create one of his own. He did not feel attracted by the soldierlike discipline of the Society of Jesus, which was making headway in Rome at that time. He preferred to follow the lead given by his confessor, Persiano Rosa, a cheerful soul of his own type. Together they founded a confraternity known as the Trinità de' Pelligrini, which soon consisted of twelve laymen. Every Sunday and feast day they went to Communion, and assembled for religious exercises; for pious talks also, in which each one spoke in his turn simply and freely. These talks developed into something more definite when Philip was ordained priest and in 1552 was made one of the chaplains of a devout and charitable association, the Confraternità della Carità, which in 1524 had taken over the church and convent of San Girolamo.

He now started upon his fruitful career as a confessor, and began to direct the exercises which were soon called the "Oratory." These were afternoon meetings, at first in his own room. Their spirit as well as their devotional character are suggested by the choice of books which were selected for free discussion — saint's lives; devotional works; works of Gerson, of St. Catherine of Siena; and other mystical treaties. After the *ragionamento* had ended, the associates strolled out for a walk, still talking and singing, often going on pilgrimage to one of the Roman basilicas. On Sundays, after vespers, they would go to some ancient site or religious house on the outskirts of Rome; and there, while they sat on the grass, a new "oratory" would take place, of a more solemn, literary, and artistic kind. The musicians present would perform a motet, and one of the company, possibly a child, recite a sermon which now was not plain and homely, but in agreement with the contemporary standards of stylistic elegance. Or else, the whole party might adjourn to a hospital to comfort the sick.

Thus the Oratory, in its beginnings, was first and foremost the immediate field of action of Philip Neri. A change came when several of his companions — Baronius for instance — became priests and began to form a small community at San Girolamo, with a branch at the Florentine church of San Giovanni. At the oratory meetings, debates were no longer held between the laymen present, who were now far more numerous, but before them; their share in the exercises was reduced to listening and singing. The exercises lasted for three hours, and everyone in the audience was free to come and go as he wished. The "brothers" would first read the selected book, and discuss it *extempore* in a dialogue; then one of them would preach a set sermon, and others spoke on the history of the Church and the lives of the saints; last of all, canticles were sung, this being the origin of the musical "oratorio," which however appeared in its full-blown form only in 1619.

The community at San Girolamo was becoming more and more of a regular "congregation"; and it was in fact established as such by Pope Gregory XIII in 1575, when he granted to Philip and his companions the church of Santa Maria in Vallicella. It was now necessary for the community to choose its own form of government. On March 15, 1577, Philip was elected provost, while five fathers, known as deputies, were chosen as a permanent administrative committee. The drawing up of actual constitutions began in 1583, the model selected being the rule of the Oblates of St. Ambrose at Milan — the order founded by Charles Borromeo. However, the work had to be taken up anew in 1588 and 1595, and the final version was not approved by the pope until 1612. The delay is accounted for largely by a conflict between two opposing tendencies. Philip believed in the paramount efficiency of almost playful freedom in action. He shrank from rules and set discipline, and he had no desire to see his community of secular priests develop into a centralized organization with branches outside Rome. He agreed, it is true, to the foundation of the Naples house, but this ran against his grain. He preferred to see new oratories, modeled on his own but unrelated to it, spring up at will.

These views were opposed by one of his companions, Antonio Talpa, a man of a different type, rigid and violent, who wished the Oratory to become a real religious order and to expand like the Clerks Regular. He insisted that at least a vow of stability and a vow of poverty should be taken, the latter implying the giving up of all personal property; and that the office should be recited in choir. When entrusted with the government of the Naples house, Talpa adopted a kind of regular habit, decreed that the fathers should not go out alone, and separated the novices from them.

Talpa's views, however, did not prevail and the Oratory retained its character as a "congregation of secular priests and clerics," in other words, a free association of priests, who wished to enjoy the advantages of common life while remaining unfettered by any permanent obligation: who lived out of their own income, and who bound themselves only to the observance of a few simple rules. According to the constitutions of 1583, they were to refuse any benefices or prelacies; to have no servants of their own; and to live on a footing of perfect equality. Frequent confession and mental prayer were early practices. They might engage in various forms of work, including visits to the hospitals; but their essential task was to take their part in the oratory meetings, of which the Church of the Vallicella was the center, and which now assumed their final form. Improvisation, dialogue, sermons delivered by laymen, familiar talks with the audience had given place to set preaching, not dramatic like that of the Capuchins, but free from all rhetoric, simple and familiar. This was the most original innovation of the Oratory, and was later imitated in France by St. Francis de Sales and St. Vincent de Paul. The evening walks and Sunday outdoor meetings were retained. There were special exercises for young people, of whom Philip was exceedingly fond, and over whom his influence was great. Thus his foundation continued to bear his stamp, and his share in the Catholic Reformation remained essentially personal, even after his death at the age of eighty-two, on May 26, 1595.

His success, in fact, is almost paradoxical, and can only be accounted for by uncommon attractiveness and virtues. In an age in which everyone looked to a strengthening of authority for an improvement of Church conditions, he stood almost alone for individual liberty. As a director of conscience he was strikingly different from Ignatius Loyola; he prescribed no set rules, no fixed exercises; he left his penitents to find out for themselves what suited them best, under the guidance of the Holy Ghost. In fact, he believed strongly in inspiration; he even distrusted reason when unaccompanied by motions of the heart, and above everything else, he detested intellectual pride.

The main features of his spiritual ideal were humbleness, lovingness, cheerfulness. Some of his characteristic oddities are accounted for by his wish to strengthen the virtue of humility both in himself and in his disciples. He would dress with his clothes inside out, or introduce barbarisms and solecisms into the liturgy of the Mass. He would send Baronius to a tavern with a twelve-gallon pitcher, command him to have it washed and taken down to the cellar, then to buy a pint of wine and pay for it with a gold coin; whereupon the tavern keeper would of course be moved to abuse and blows. He was, however, of uncommon affability, and always ready, whether in good or in bad health, and even after he had gone to bed, to receive visitors, and listen to them patiently to the end, giving them all possible satisfaction. "Wherefore," his biographer adds, "it was incredible how he would bind to himself the minds of all men."

But what is most striking about his devotional life is the Christian cheerfulness, ease, and liveliness which appeared at all times in his actions. He hated to seem sanctimonious, or even to be taken too seriously. He was once chided for not having, by his attitude, sufficiently edified a Roman nobleman. "Would you have me," he replied to the disciple who made the complaint, "talk with raised eyebrows, so that people may say: 'Look at the famous Father Philip, who in harmonious speech pours out memorable words and sayings'?"

He impressed people less by his natural talents than by his almost preternatural spiritual powers: he could read the hearts of men and was famed for his gifts of prophecy and healing; and though he tried to restrain his mystical life, he had visions and ecstasies. It was magnetic personality which gained him the trust and love of his disciples, not his intellectual originality. He was not even a good public speaker, would merely listen to the sermons at the Oratory, and confine himself to familiar talk with members of the audience; but he knew how to clothe old truths in a new garb. His virtues were, in many ways, exceptional, yet his meekness, simplicity, and modesty were those very qualities which had distinguished the Christian humanists, and had been bequeathed by them to the Catholic reformers; while on the other hand his quaintness and fancifulness, his Italian mobility and familiarity, seem strangely unclassical in the age of neo-classicism. That he should have had such a share in the improvement of Roman society and of the Church at large only illustrates the extreme variety of temperament among the Catholic reformers.

*   *   *

What St. Philip Neri succeeded in achieving in a limited circle and by personal means, the Society of Jesus performed throughout the world, thanks to its discipline and organization. It was so well adapted to the needs of the time, it spread so rapidly, it grew to be so important, that all contemporary movements dwindle when compared with it. It was the main prop and the chief instrument of the Catholic Reformation. Its founder, Ignatius Loyola, was the very opposite of Philip Neri. Far from trusting to fancy and individual inspiration, he was a believer in discipline, organization, and hierarchy; and before these were established in the field of outward action, strict inward order was to be established in the soul of every member of the Society. The method, which Ignatius conceived for himself first, and which afterwards ruled the spiritual life of his disciples, accounts for everything, from the *Constitutions* of the Jesuits, to their scheme of education, to their spirit and policy, and to their heroic work in missionary countries. The *Spiritual Exercises* are at the root of all the surprising results obtained by the Society.

It is needless to enter here into a detailed study of this book. Although short and seemingly simple, it is in fact too intricate to lend itself to ready analysis. Its practical working cannot be easily understood without the help of that tradition, thanks to which the Jesuits of today still apply St. Ignatius' plan for the spiritual improvement of his disciples, be they clerics or laymen. Suffice it to say that the *Exercises* proceed on two parallel lines. On the one hand, they provide a course of regulated meditations, divided into four "weeks," and arranged on the whole in a regular progress from remorse to heavenly joy, from the sorrowful to the joyful mysteries. On the other hand, the active faculties of the soul are trained to progress from resolve to resolve, beginning with the purely negative detestation of sin, and continuing, in the second week, with the momentous decision of wholly casting one's lot with God and his servants; while in the third and fourth weeks this decision is put to the proof and confirmed.

In other words, meditation, or the exercise of the intellect and imagination, is made to take effect at once in the exercise of the will. In fact, the whole trend of St. Ignatius' teaching is directed toward a strengthening of the will. This is, of course, largely accounted for by the needs of the times; nor should we forget that the founder of the Jesuits had begun as a soldier, and consequently as a man of action. It is possible, in his view, for man wholly to master his spiritual faculties and to steer them toward the sole desired purpose. He turns meditation itself into an act of the will, and this is why he directs it so precisely and methodically. The mind should not be left to wander at random, but should be compelled to apply itself to certain persons, objects, or ideas. When some scene of the life of Christ, the Virgin Mary, or the saints has been selected for contemplation, a voluntary act of the imagination conjures it up in every detail of its physical circumstances. This is what is known as the *compositio loci;* while the *applicatio sensuum* suggests mental images referring to each of the five senses in succession. For instance, in the exercise devoted to the Nativity, one ought to "consider the cave where it takes place, and how large, how small, how low, how high it was; how it was furnished." The picture thus evoked is so real that one seems not merely to be beholding it, but to be acting in it as well.

The same method is adapted to the consideration of purely spiritual beings or truths; and, in that case, recourse is often had to images, as in the famous meditation of the two standards, in which Christ and Lucifer are represented, the One as leader of the army of the righteous; the other as dispatching the demons on their tasks. And spiritual preparation is not confined to suggestions for the imagination; the will also appears in declaring beforehand the effect it seeks, and to which it must apply its efforts; for instance, when meditating on the Ressurrection, it is essential "to ask for what one has the will to obtain, which will mean here asking for the grace to exult and rejoice intensely over the glory and joy, which are so great, of Christ our Lord."

The will is indeed triumphant in St. Ignatius' scheme. Nothing is to be left to the obscure, subconscious forces of the soul; everything must be clear, fully realized, and planned out, not in meditation only, but in the daily practice of ascetical life. One, for instance, who is for the time being in a state of "consolation," should look ahead to the time of "desolation," and lay up courage for the coming trial. The amendment of one's faults cannot be achieved haphazardly; a strict method is necessary, which goes the length of recording one's lapses by means of graphs, thus checking one's improvement from day to day. Indeed, St. Ignatius' constant wish to guide the soul in its every step may seem to lead at times to some exaggeration. It would be too much to say that each of the divisions and distinctions in the contemplations and accompanying remarks is the result of inner logic. For the author of the *Exercises* the point is not to provide an intellectual analysis of the matters considered, but to enable the soul to gain full control of itself, and to become, as he says, "its own master."

Perfect control of self means freedom from excess; and St. Ignatius repeatedly states his preference for the "golden mean." This preference, however, does not apply to the spiritual side of life, and no moderation is recommended in self-abasement or love of Christ. But in everyday actions, or even in religious practice, exaggeration is to be avoided. In the fourth week, when the joyful mysteries are contemplated, "instead of giving myself up to penitence, I shall aim at preserving temperance and keeping a middle course in all things." Similarly, in alternate temptations of overconfidence and timorousness, "the soul ought to establish itself firmly and wisely in a middle position." This tallies with St. Ignatius' belief in the value of reason. Not, indeed, that his work in the least assumes the nature of an apologetic demonstration. He takes the essential truths for granted, and sets out firmly with bold assertions. Nevertheless, practical reason plays a considerable part in the working of his spiritual scheme. In the meditation on the "election," or choice of a manner of life, we are told, one should "examine the question in its various aspects, and consider which way reason inclines most." Reason, here, really means common sense; and it is this same common sense which induces St. Ignatius to refrain from fruitless discussions on predestination or justification by faith alone.

The practical wisdom of the author of the *Exercises* is again manifested in a feature which is typically his own, which was to inspire the whole of the activities of the Society of Jesus and the new school of spirituality which it founded. This feature can best be defined by the word "adaptation." The one thing which really matters is the end in view, "to honor and serve God, and save one's soul." The means used should be subordinate to this end. Each man should be placed in the best possible conditions to fulfill his divine purpose on earth. He should not waste his strength uselessly. Bodily mortification is good, up to a point; it should, however, be exactly proportioned to one's resistance, and in no case endanger one's health or impair one's powers. Mental mortification, which in that respect is harmless, and even profitable, should be preferred. "Adaptation" is also extended to the practice of meditation: the number of the daily exercises, their themes, their petitions, are to be suited to each person's needs.

Let each one, further, find out by experience what has been hurtful to him — as in the case of excessive discouragement or scruples — and avoid it; what has been helpful, and dwell upon it. Here is the corrective to what may appear excessive in St. Ignatius' spiritual drill: the seeming rigidity of the theory is happily corrected by a keen sense of the useful and feasible.

That the reality of the material world, in and outside ourselves, has to be taken into account, is again evidenced elsewhere in St. Ignatius' directions. He who meditates, he says, should provide for himself a physical environment suited to his thoughts and feelings — "adaptation" once again. There is nothing compulsory about one's posture when praying. In the first week, which is devoted to remorse and a consideration of the hatefulness of sin, he who meditates will remain in the dark, with doors and windows closed; light and darkness will alternate in the second week, as they did in Christ's preaching life; in the fourth week, the thought of Jesus' resurrection and glory will incline one to seek "the light of the day or the pleasantness of the season, the cool in summer, and in winter the warmth of the sun or of a fire." In a word, St. Ignatius marvelously realizes that man is neither angel nor beast, and that both sides of his nature should be taken into account, and made to cooperate.

Method, directed meditation, "adapted" discipline, outward helps, all these are made to concur in the same purpose, which is, we repeat, the fortifying of the will. This, however, is not an ideal in itself, and should not be understood in the stoic sense; for the absolute end which St. Ignatius has in view is not the glorifying of one's personality, but on the contrary humbleness and self-renunciation. "I shall consider who I am," one of the exercises runs "endeavoring through various comparisons to appear smaller and smaller in my own eyes." Jesus, as St. Ignatius pictures Him, addresses all His servants. "He advises them to help all men, by attracting them first of all to an entire spiritual poverty, and to real poverty as well, if the divine Majesty is thus served, and wishes to call them to such a state: secondly, to the desire of obloquy and contempt, for of these two things is born humility." Spiritual poverty includes detachment, which is to be achieved at all costs, beginning with minor matters, such as that of food, and going on to meditation and prayer, in which "desolation" guards the soul from overweening pride.

No commonplace motive would justify such a total forgetfulness of self: only love can call it forth. And here St. Ignatius, true to the tradition of the Franciscan mystics and of the *Imitation* (which he expressly recommends) insists that love is the chief element in the relations between the soul and God. "God is love," he repeats after the Apostle John; and love can only be repaid with love. Such divine love inspires the bold ideal which the author of the *Exercises* proposes to him who will "receive" them: "He must enter into them with great bravery and great generosity toward his Creator and Lord, offering up to him his whole will and his whole freedom," for "love should consist in works far more than in words."

From this brief résumé it is clear that the whole spiritual discipline, the whole action and policy, and the very educational methods, of the Society of Jesus are clearly outlined in the *Exercises*. Total renunciation of self; total abandonment to the will of God, as personified by one's superiors; a practical bent, the belief that "God will help those who help themselves"; the striving with all one's efforts toward the attaining of actual results; a proportioning of the means to the end, a sense of the real and possible; all these were present from the first in St. Ignatius' mind, even before his order was founded. It is no less clear that many features of his spiritual ideal made it easy for him to make use of classical antiquity in his pedagogy, and thus follow in the tracks of the Christian humanists: the strengthening of the will, the *aurea mediocritas,* might readily be supported by the study of Cicero or of Seneca. Even what came to be known as Jesuit art largely rests on the principle expressed in the *Exercises,* that prayer and meditation are dependent on outward environment; also, on St. Ignatius' support of all the traditional rites and customs of the Catholic faith, in his directions on *Submission to the Church,* as against the dryness of Protestantism. Nor should we forget, finally, that, in the ascetical field, the *Exercises* were to lead the way for many generations. This simple, slight, unassuming book was to make its weight felt to the ends of the world.

* * *

St. Ignatius had conceived the plan of the *Exercises* during his retreat at Manresa in 1523, shortly after Luther had come out of his own retirement at the Wartburg, and while the unfortunate Adrian VI was vainly attempting a root-and-branch reformation of the Church. He still had no thought of founding a new religious order. The next ten years were years of preparation, with a pilgrimage to Jerusalem, spiritual work in Spain (where he had trouble with the Inquisition), and studies, philosophical and theological, at Paris University. The Society of Jesus began, potentially at least, on August 15, 1534, when Ignatius, with his first six companions, took his first vows in the chapel at Montmartre. This was more than ten years before the first sessions of the Council of Trent. When the great assembly of the Church finally gathered, the founder of the new order had just begun work on its *Constitutions* in 1544. Three years were to elapse before they were completed in 1547; six, before they were approved by a congregation of the professed fathers in 1550.

Ignatius was over fifty years of age when he undertook to provide the Jesuits with a rule; and the time he spent in drafting this comparatively short work of less than three hundred octavo pages bears witness to the unusual care, patience, and attention which he gave to it. Besides the general principles already present in the *Exercises,* the Constitutions embody the experience of his whole life, while testifying to the astounding powers of his intellect and his knowledge of the human heart. From the first, he foresaw the future development of the Society as a world-wide institution and he legislated for it as such. His organizing ability was equal to his foresight. He sees to every detail, and yet avoids excessive minuteness and rigidity. The firmness and clearness of his thought are enough to make the *Constitutions* a work of great literary value; though bare and unadorned in style, they go straight to the point; and they have a severe, soldierlike beauty of their own. Altogether, they appear as the work of a mastermind; and when ranking their author among men of genius, one can hardly be taxed with exaggeration. The *Constitutions*, indeed, are a work of striking originality, at least in regard to the means proposed. The end in view is common to all Christians — to procure "the honor of God and the universal weal of men"; but the way in which it is constantly reasserted, and the manner in which it is interpreted, make it almost into a new precept. The stress is laid on its altruistic implications, "to procure the salvation and perfection of one's neighbors" — corrupt Churchmen or misguided heretics; also on the fact that action is no less necessary than prayer, and that Providence "asks for the co-operation of God's creatures." Now, action will be fruitless if directed at random against particular abuses, which are sure to crop up again; it should spring from the source of all authority and influence in the Church, from the papacy itself. Hence the fourth vow which all Jesuit professed fathers have to take, putting themselves unreservedly at the disposal of the Holy Father, to be sent whithersoever he may choose. The spiritual principles of the Society, as expressed in the other three vows, also tend to facilitate efficient action; poverty will leave the Jesuits free from the shackles of worldly cares; obedience and humbleness will ensure perfect cooperation and the easy working of a central command; while the supreme purpose remains the training of the will, which enables each one to accept his appointed task readily, and to perform it steadfastly.

Ignatius clearly realized that no little moral corruption within the Church derived from the system of benefices, which allowed of self-seeking, ambition, and greed. Therefore the members of the new Institute were warned that, "once incorporated into the Society, they were not to hold any benefices whatsoever, but to return them to their patrons, or give them away for pious works"; also that they might pretend to no ecclesiastical dignities, and that they were to get rid of any property they might own; not, however, by making a present of it to their kin, from whom they should be wholly detached. The rules on poverty, indeed, seemed to Ignatius of such importance, and he was so much afraid lest they might be canceled, as they had been among the Franciscans, that he took special steps to ensure their permanency. Each father, on being admitted to profession, was to take a vow that he would never agree to have them relaxed. The author of the *Constitutions* also understood that the fees charged for spiritual services had led to many abuses, and had been one main cause of the Protestant outbreak; hence the Society was to accept "neither alms nor stipends . . . for masses or preaching, or reading or administration of the sacraments, or any other pious office," and its houses and churches were to have no revenues of their own. The only exception made was in favor of the colleges and houses of probation, which could hardly exist without some permanent income.

As in the *Exercises,* poverty is still more important in its spiritual than in its material shape. Humility is an essential virtue of the Jesuit. He must be prepared "patiently to bear injuries, revilings and obloquy"; and if selected for the least flattering kind of work, that of a temporal coadjutor, "to spend in it all the years of his life." Indeed, the Constitutions repeatedly forbid any member of the Society to express discontent with his present post, or any wish to be promoted. Even at the election of the general there must be no candidates, no canvassing. Each must be a ready instrument in the place to which he is appointed; an obedient instrument too — on no point is greater emphasis laid. And obedience does not mean mere compliance with orders: the inferior must train his will to become identical with that of his superior. "He must let himself be carried and ruled by his superior, as if he were a dead body"— these famous words, *perinde ac cadaver,* are borrowed from the rule of St. Francis —"that lets itself be carried anywhere and handled anyhow, or like an old man's staff, which he who holds it in his hand may use to help himself wheresoever and howsoever he may wish." Such a relinquishing of one's own personality can be accepted only if both the inferior and the superior are animated by the same over-powering ideal. Both must "tend in all things to serve and please the divine goodness for its own sake, and for the sake of its love and blessings . . . more than for fear of punishment or hope of rewards." As in the *Exercises,* the prime motive is love.

The absolute identification of the will of the subject with that of the superior is not to be left, however, to the chance working of feelings, however powerful. It is ensured by a strict, and, to outsiders, formidable, spiritual discipline — means both internal and external being used to guard the Jesuit from any faltering. He must first of all use the ordinary helps recommended in the *Exercises,* examine his conscience daily, go to confession and Communion every week, keeping as far as possible to the same confessor. In addition to this, the superior must have "full knowledge of the inclinations and motions of those in his charge, and of the faults and sins to which they are more liable and inclined; so as to be able to direct them the better accordingly." He is further to proportion the use made of them to their abilities. Whenever a probationer is about to become a scholastic, or when a scholastic is about to take his vows as a professed father, or generally when a Jesuit is going to be promoted to another post, or again on request, at stated intervals or otherwise, he must "manifest his conscience to his superior, without concealing anything which might offend the Lord of all men; and give an entire account of his past life." In the houses of probation, the master of the novices must be loved and confided in, and everyone must disclose his temptations to him. Finally, since no reliance can be put on one's unaided strength, the Jesuit, whatever his rank, must agree to be, not merely advised, but even forcibly kept in the straight path. His correspondence, his relations with others, and his very conversations are liable to supervision by his superior. His equals may observe his behavior, remonstrate with him, and even report him; a system of discipline which might give rise to indignation, but of which the force lies in the fact that it is willingly accepted, in a spirit of utter humility and love.

No second-rate personality could possibly agree to such abnegation, coupled with such burning zeal and such untiring energy. The founder of the Society realized that he ought to admit none but finely tempered souls; the morally, intellectually, physically, or even socially, unfit had no room in his Institute: able workers only could cope with the gigantic task before them. Consequently, the conditions for admission are incredibly strict. At every step in the postulancy and the novitiate, the applicant is fully informed as to what awaits him, and repeatedly, almost tiresomely asked whether he is willing to face the full consequences of his vows. He is subjected to a series of trials, as for instance to go on a pilgrimage with an empty purse, or to perform the meanest offices in the house and obey the orders of the cook, or before his last vows to go begging from door to door for three successive days. His spirit also is tried. He is warned that he will have to forget his former associates and relations, who will henceforth be mentioned only in the past tense; that he must forsake his own judgment wholly, and be prepared to spend his whole life in the humblest of occupations.

Nor is this all. The postulant must be qualified for his future task, and his task must be strictly "adapted" to his possibilities. Hence, he may be shunted on to the office of a coadjutor temporal, with only physical work to do, or to that of a scholastic, with studies to pursue;

and the scholastic himself, according to the degree of his learning and virtue, will become one of the professed fathers — the marrow and soul of the Society — or a coadjutor spiritual, entrusted with apostolic or teaching work. This adaptation of means to the end is an essential element of the Jesuit spirit. "Idleness," we read in the *Constitutions,* "which is the origin of all evils, has no place whatsoever in a Jesuit house." Not only idleness, but attention to irrelevant matters must be avoided; and so that no man may waste his time and strength, strict division of labor is to be established. The general must not be kept from the important business of central government by trifling administrative details; he must have a secretary to serve as an aid to his memory, and specialized advisers to discuss important decisions.

The Jesuits must not be kept from their proper activities even by pious exercises or subsidiary tasks. There is no choir duty for them — a strikingly new departure from the practice of all earlier orders — almost a revolution, which gave rise to no little opposition in the Curia. Nor can they be burdened with the pastorate of souls in parishes or the care of women's convents. Devotional practice must be suited to the requirements of each individual case; and St. Ignatius' breadth of view is exemplified in his use of "adaptation."

The Society must not be merely a sort of foraging party, free from all *impedimenta;* its efforts must be used to the best possible effect, thanks to a wise economy of strength. The maximum leverage must be sought in every undertaking. "One ought," Ignatius says, "to prefer such persons and places as, after gaining spiritual improvement, cause the profit to spread to others that obey their authority or follow their directions." Therefore, one should give attention first and foremost to influential people, ". . . eminent for their learning or authority." Nor is working from above the only condition of efficiency. As in the *Exercises,* Ignatius stresses the necessity of husbanding one's strength by being *sui compos,* free from all excess, and accordingly of submitting to the wise discipline of the golden mean.

Finally, efficiency in a body of men united for the same purpose, in a real army such as the Society, requires co-ordination and the hierarchy which alone can enforce it. Here Ignatius was faced with a formidable problem. He had to draft a constitution in the political sense of the word, and to guard against the evils of representative government, no less than against those of tyranny, both having been recently exemplified in the Church. He obviously did not believe in parliamentary institutions, and understood that in his Society as well as in the Christian body at large, some kind of monarchy was necessary. At the same time, he could not but realize that the central power must not be allowed the free exercise of its *bon plaisir,* and that it must be accountable to someone. Hence the remarkable system which his imagination conceived, and which bears the stamp of his genius. He retains, indeed, in the Society, a gathering of representatives sent up by the provinces, the "general congregation"; but this assembly is never allowed to indulge in the parliamentary game of cross talk, questioning, and idle oratory. It is to be called up by the general, but "seldom, except in case of necessity," or by the vicar after the death of the general, for the election of his successor. In the latter case, it is an extremely strict conclave, for the Fathers are locked in and bound to keep silence. If there is no clear majority, the decision is left to an elected committee of three or five. When general topics are discussed, the members of the assembly are free to move about, but "all that there is to be handled must be concluded as quickly as possible." To this purpose, each one of the Fathers must give his opinion *in writing* on the points at issue; and after the dumb debate is completed, if there is no unanimity or quasi-unanimity on one side, four *definitors* are elected, to settle the matter finally with the general.

The latter, therefore, is not in the position of a constitutional premier, who has to play the parliamentary game, and whose position is always insecure. His authority may even, at first sight, appear unlimited. It is stressed at every page of the *Constitutions,* to this extent that, although the necessity of a system of rules, "full, clear and brief," be forcibly asserted, there is practically no regulation from which the general may not dispense if he see fit; the same absolute powers being vested in each superior within the range of his own government. There is, however, a check upon abuses — and this is where the originality of Ignatius' political thought appears. The general, as we have said, has four assistants, whose election takes place at the same time as his. The function of these assistants is not merely to help him in his work, but also to see to it that he keeps in the straight path of wisdom and virtue. He must obey them in the matter of dress, food, and personal expenses; of his health, "so that he may fall into no excess of work or mortification"; of his spiritual welfare, "so that he may be admonished as to what tends to the greater service and glory of God." Lastly, if he has committed any crimes, the four assistants may call up the Congregation general, and have him deposed and replaced. The same principle is applied to each of the lesser superiors, who may, if necessary, be provided with a collateral, both to advise and to guide him. It is almost unthinkable, in such conditions, that authority might fall into any abuse; while the fact that in the long run, it is not a cut-and-dried printed rule which governs the Society, but a man who can take circumstances into account, makes for "adaptation" and permanency.

In fact, Ignatius' main thought was to ensure the duration of his Society, and the last part of the *Constitutions* is entitled: "How this whole body will be conserved and augmented in its well-being." Various means to this end are here rehearsed, beginning with the spiritual help of prayer and the *Exercises,* going on to poverty, to strictness in the choice of postulants ("It is good not to keep the door wide open"), to the necessity of authority, and, last but not least to the importance of union and unity. These are grounded on charity and moderation in discipline. The Society, besides, must be independent. Thus, the honors granted to the founder of a college do not imply any rights of patronage on his part. In short, there again appears, in Ignatius' conclusion, this mingling of inspired enthusiasm and practical common sense, of burning charity and staid self-restraint, of passion and reason, of abnegation and efficiency, which is the main feature of his genius and the cause of the greatness of his order. Even within his own lifetime the Society was to spread to the whole of Italy, to Spain, Portugal, France, Flanders, and Germany, and even to Africa, South America, and the Far East. The Jesuits Le Fèvre, Laynez, and Salmeron took part in the Council of Trent as theologians. Jesuit missions were founded in Morocco and in the Congo in 1548, in Brazil in 1549, while St. Francis Xavier, the apostle of the Indies, had planted Christianity in Japan during the same year. Jesuit houses began to spring up everywhere. The Roman college was founded in February, 1551, the German college in 1552, the college at Billom in 1555. This rapid expansion to which we shall revert in greater detail, bears witness to the driving force of the Jesuit movement. It was largely due to the original and progressive system of education which the Society adopted, and which was to be one of the chief instruments of the Catholic Reformation.

CHAPTER VII

Education and Scholarship

THE Catholic Reformation penetrated into every sphere of human activity. It was both a spiritual revival and a movement for the moral and material improvement of society; and in either of these aspects, was bound to be interested in the upbringing of youth. Besides, the Council of Trent had brought educational questions to the fore by prescribing the creation of seminaries for the training of priests. The facilities thus provided for the clergy were soon to be extended to the laity as well, in response to the universal demand for Christian schools. In this field as in others, however, the work of the Catholic reformers was not an absolute novelty. It had been begun, if not fully developed, before Luther arose, and had already assumed its proper shape and character. From this early period, there is evident that same blending of Christian doctrine and devotion with the almost exclusive study of classical "grammar" and literature, which was later to distinguish the Jesuit and Oratorian colleges, and constitute the chief reason of their success.

In the early sixteenth century Erasmus advocated the creation of humanistic schools (*ludi literarii*), which should be open to all, irrespective of social class. "If there be a school at all, let it be public." The studies are to begin with "language," i.e., Latin and Greek grammar, then go on to "Poetry," this including eloquence. Use should be made of commonplace books, lists of proverbs, etc. The pupils should remain under the same *praeceptor* as long as possible. The matters taught should be fully digested. "The best means of remembering consists first in understanding thoroughly; then, once things are understood, in setting them in order; and lastly, in repeating them in succession." But harshness and tediousness should be avoided. There are things "which one learns through play rather than labor." Physical exercise is neglected: "The harm done to the body seems to be amply made up for by the gain of the mind." In regard to discipline, Erasmus is as progressive as the Jesuits were later to be. The teacher, he says, should be a father to the boys. Whipping or threats should be done away with, and replaced by sweetness. Emulation will be ensured by blame and praise.

The idea that literary knowledge and moral improvement walk hand in hand is repeatedly insisted on.

Such Christian humanistic notions had inspired, at the end of the fifteenth century, the plan of studies and the discipline in the schools of the Brothers of the Common Life. The latter were a real religious order, established in the Low Countries, whose main task was education. We have fairly full particulars of their school at Liège, founded in 1496. We know more, however, about the teaching proper than about the discipline, though there is no doubt that "sweetness" prevailed. Throughout the whole succession of forms (classes), numbered from one to eight, the chief subject was Latin. The declensions and conjugations had to be learned in the first; the second, third, and fourth were devoted to grammar, the explanation of authors, and stylistic exercises; Greek was begun in the fourth. The fifth was reserved for rhetoric, while in the upper forms, the students stepped into the realm of dialectics and theology.

The general progression here, from letters to philosophy, prefigured the later organization of the Jesuit colleges; but the likeness appears more striking still when one comes to detail. The exercises were composition (the writing of essays), declamation, and disputations. For scholastic and disciplinary purposes, self-governing groups of ten were formed among the pupils, and headed each by one of their number, who went by the name of *decurion*. No one could be promoted to a higher form without an examination; and at the solemn "promotion" ceremony, those who had been rejected were allowed to put questions to those who had been passed. There were yearly prizes for the most proficient, and also prizes in term time for those who had the best marks. Plays, ancient and modern, were performed. Finally, the rector was subject to the authority of the superior of the local house of the Brothers to which the school was attached.

The schools of the Brothers of the Common Life may not have directly inspired the Catholic Reformation; but they certainly did so through an offshoot of theirs, the community of Montaigu. The latter was a religious body created by one of their number, the Fleming, John Standonck, for the upbringing of the clergy. It owed its name to a residential college of Paris University, founded in 1402 for poor scholars, later opened to students of means as well, and reformed by Standonck in 1499–1502, so as to become the head house of his new order. The college, with which Ignatius Loyola was thoroughly acquainted, combined many interesting features. It included both secondary classes devoted to letters, and university classes devoted to philosophy and theology.

Indeed the notion, later adopted by the Jesuits, that literature must be made to subserve religion, is forcefully stressed in the reformed statutes of the college. These inveigh against the "desolation" of the Church, against the pagan Renaissance, which induces men "diligently to acquire letters and sciences . . . for vanity merely." They announce their purpose "to raise a new generation, who will be taught to embrace mortification and virtue together with knowledge, whose letters will be proved by their lives."

What is more, the main purpose of the Montaigu community — which later founded houses in Flanders, Cambrai, Valenciennes, Malines, and Louvain — foreshadows that of the Society of Jesus; and even apart from the field of education proper, we must notice in passing that Ignatius certainly derives many features of Jesuit life and discipline from the practice of Montaigu. He did away, it is true, with some of the rules imposed by Standonck upon his poor scholars, such as the saying of liturgical hours in chapel at night, and excessive mortification; but he retained most of the rest. The reformer of Montaigu had insisted, as Ignatius was himself to do repeatedly, that the members of his community were not merely "to work out their own salvation, but that of others as well," through controversy and preaching. He insisted on the necessity of material and spiritual poverty, and of obedience. The students and masters at Montaigu were in duty bound "to accept smilingly and to perform faithfully" any work allotted to them by their superiors. The effective direction of the college was in the hands of a committee of three that might overrule even the decisions of a general assembly, as in the case of the election of the rector. The practice of daily meditation on spiritual things was prescribed, as well as that of examination of conscience in the evening. Idle talk was forbidden, and the scholars were strictly enjoined to report each other's failings.

As regards tuition, Montaigu forestalls St. Ignatius' colleges, insofar as there might be question of the literary and theological formation of future Jesuits. Each student, before being admitted, must reside for some time in the house, "so as to become acquainted with it, and to make himself known" to his superiors. Then he must undergo a severe examination on his physical health, his doctrine, his knowledge of grammar, and his inner dispositions. He is asked — the likeness with a Jesuit college being here striking — whether, in the event of his being found "indifferently gifted for letters," he is willing to serve the community in some humbler form of employment. After taking an oath of absolute obedience, he is switched to the branch of study for which he is best suited, and his future prospects are determined. General discipline is ensured, as in the schools of the Brothers of the Common Life, by some of the students themselves, specially selected for the purpose. In the present case, they are called not *decuriones,* but *decani* or *notati,* and they must render account to the rector or "father of the poor" of the behavior of ten or twelve of their fellow scholars.

Classes are held in the morning and afternoon, while on Fridays and Saturdays recitations and "construction" take place, in French for the lower forms, in Latin for the higher. After Vespers, disputations are held on points of "grammar" (a word which covers what we call "literature") under the chairmanship of the teachers or "regents"; they also take place in a more solemn way on Sundays, in the presence of all the *artistae,* after being prepared for on half holidays or vigils. There is even a kind of Jesuit "academy" among the theologians, who assemble at night to discuss the lessons of the day. Religious instruction is given each Sunday by way of a sermon, also on vigils before confession.

In the literature classes the syllabus included the study of Latin grammar and literature, both poetry and prose, but not of Greek. "Lascivious poets" were to be excluded, "whatever the beauty of their style." The use of Latin was compulsory among the pupils, who passed through seven classical forms, and could not be promoted from a lower to a higher one without being examined. They were listed according to merit by the regents, who, it seems, stayed with them in their upward progress. On the whole, Montaigu supplies the best possible proof that an educational movement for the purification of the Renaissance was afoot before the Lutheran outbreak; a movement which, if we judge by the devotional practice of the college, in no way anticipated the innovations of Protestant theology.

*   *   *

And yet, we are faced with a definite fact: when the Protestants, three decades later, began to develop their system of education, they did so on lines which strikingly recalled the Brothers of the Common Life, while their adversaries were slower in moving in the same direction. The school system of the Catholic Reformation has therefore often been said to lack originality, and has even been taxed with plagiarism. The charge cannot be ignored, and we must now review the facts.

Protestant education began with the Rhinelander, John Sturm (1507–1589), who was educated in the school of the Brothers of the Common Life at Liège, then moved to Louvain, where he was engaged in humanistic teaching and printing for some time. He came to Paris in 1529, and from 1530 to 1536 was a professor there in the Collège de France, where he lectured on Cicero. He accepted an invitation of the magistrates of Strasbourg to come and reorganize education in their city. The latter had then adhered, under Martin Bucer, to a modified form of Lutheranism verging on Zwinglianism. Sturm founded the Strasbourg Gymnasium in 1537, and in his book *De literarum ludis recte aperiendis* ("How Properly to Open Literary Schools," 1538), explained how closely he had followed the model of his Liège masters. His example soon bore fruit, and was imitated in many towns of Lutheran Germany, where colleges were created or reorganized, from 1541 onward. Calvin himself became acquainted with Sturm's work during his stay in the Alsatian capital, and reproduced its main features in the Academy at Geneva, which dates back to 1559. Last of all, the French Protestant towns followed in Calvin's steps, and established academies or colleges on the same pattern, from 1561 to 1630.

On the Catholic side, in regard to the education of boys at least, nothing was done before the Council of Trent. It is true that in 1542 the Jesuits began to accept lay pupils in one of their houses; but it was only in 1552 that they opened a school definitely meant for nonclerical students, at Billom in Auvergne. Their colleges soon swarmed over the whole of Europe, and achieved signal success; and their likeness to Sturm's own plan was such that the Strasbourg headmaster himself was moved to notice it: "I have seen," he wrote, "what writers they explain, and what method they follow in their teaching; they keep so close to us in their precepts and rules, that it looks as if they had derived them from our own spring."

Sturm, however, did not claim that it was a case of actual imitation. Actually, of course, there was a common source in both cases. Ignatius Loyola had been subjected to precisely the same combination of Flemish and French influences at Sturm himself, and much at the same time. He came to Paris in February, 1528, expressly to improve his knowledge of classical letters, which he deemed essential for his apostolate; and he remained there until March, 1535. He first attended the classes of the Collège de Montaigu, then of the neighboring Collège Sainte-Barbe. As he was most impecunious, he used to take trips to Flanders during the holidays to solicit grants from Spanish merchants there.

As likely as not, he may have touched at the branch houses of the Montaigu community. We know, in any case, that he came into touch with Flemish humanism. The Spanish scholar, Luis Vives, a friend of Erasmus, and, like him, a theorist of the new education, had settled at Bruges, where he entertained Ignatius and made much of him.

It is clear that the spirit of the Brothers of the Common Life and also of Paris University, which had inspired Sturm, also imbued Loyola, and that he derived from it much of his devotional ideal, his school discipline, and his plan of studies. The Catholic Reformation, as represented by the Jesuits, did not imitate the Protestants: like them, it followed the trend of contemporary educational thought. But even actual imitation of a suitable model would not be damning; it would at any rate imply wisdom. Besides, whatever may be owing to the influence of earlier movements, the educational work of the Catholic reformers has merits of its own; its very importance, its success, prove that it had some original elements. And it is a fact that it spread out of all proportion to its Protestant counterpart. In France alone the number of Protestant academies and colleges never rose above twenty-five, whereas the schools of the Jesuits and Oratorians reached a total of about one hundred and five; and the schools of the other orders ought to be added as well. This expansion cannot be explained merely by a vague, general acceptance of prevailing standards on the part of the teaching staff. There must be a constructive system of pedagogy to give the necessary impulse; and it was the merit of the Jesuits, first among the Catholic reformers, to build up such a coherent system — a system of remarkable psychological insight and keen intelligence — in their *Ratio studiorum*. Lastly we should not forget that literary education was, for the Catholic reformers as well as for the Protestants, not an end in itself, but a means of edification; and here again, the former were remarkably successful, and managed to regain a considerable amount of lost ground.

There is yet another remark which suggests itself. It is true that both Catholics and Protestants followed in the wake of the Christian humanists, and that there is, for instance, a striking likeness between the "laws" of the Protestant Academies of Nîmes (1582) or of Montpellier (1608) and the Jesuit *Ratio studiorum;* and it cannot be denied that on either side, the schools turned out scholars famous for their knowledge and elegant use of both Latin and Greek. But was the neo-classical plan of education as congenial to the holders of the new tenets as it was to the representatives of the "old religion"? Did it tally as well with the spirit of Protestantism as with that of Catholicism? There is some reason to doubt it. For one thing, Sturm cannot be considered as having been typically Lutheran or Bucerian. He belonged to a period of intellectual confusion, in which no clear-cut line had been drawn between contending parties, in which ever reviving hopes of reconciliation might allow a man of an irenical disposition, like himself, to remain in the employment of Protestants without altogether breaking with Catholicism. In fact, Sturm had been recommended to the magistrates of Strasbourg by the Catholic bishop, Erasmus of Limburg. He was found fault with by the Lutheran Marbach for "having praised the Jesuit schools and pedagogy"; he accepted Catholic pupils in his *Gymnasium*, even from France and Italy; he contemplated a redistribution of the staff, in which half the teachers would be Catholics; he advised Catholic towns to devote prebends to the creation of grammar schools. He was knighted by the Catholic-minded Emperor Charles V. His attitude was that of a classical scholar, not that of a religious controversialist: "What is there that is of more advantage in this life," he wrote, "than a pure mind and pure speech? What pleasanter, than an elegant life and elegant language?" This is the spirit of Erasmus, not that of Luther. In a word, Sturm's work was that of a Christian humanist: it can scarcely be called that of a Protestant.

Lastly, there is some reason to think that, from the very first, Sturm's scheme of education was regarded by the founders of Protestant schools as being too purely classical. Nor is this surprising, when one remembers that, while Christian humanism had undertaken the explanation of the original text of Scripture through "grammar," that is, philological science, Lutheranism had insisted on its being turned into the vernacular, and interpreted even by the unlearned. Add to this that Latin, as the language of the Catholic Church, was obnoxious to Protestants. The authors of the Jesuit *Ratio studiorum* of 1586 realized this perfectly, when they wrote that Latin was necessary in transalpine colleges, "to make relations easier between different nations, and to keep as far away as possible from some heretics, that do their best to abolish the Latin tongue, so as to prevent an intercourse with Catholics."

These reasons account for the importance given to the vernacular in some of the Protestant schools. The statutes of the Academy of Geneva already stress the importance of French, and do away with Latin verse. At the Academy of Nîmes, the pupils were to learn reading in French, not in Latin, and French was the first subject taught in the first three school years. These facts should not be overstressed; yet they help to understand how it is that the educational ideal of the Christian humanists found its fullest development with the Catholic Reformation.

From the first, the fulfillment of the prescriptions of the Council of Trent on education was mostly entrusted to the Society of Jesus. Of course, it was not alone in the field. There were schools founded by the Barnabites and the Capuchins, in Italy and France, about which printed literature is regrettably silent, and concerning which one wishes one knew more. In the seventeenth century, the colleges of the French Oratory were to gain a great and deserved renown. Nor should one forget the diocesan work done by St. Charles Borromeo in Milan, or the later institution of Sulpician seminaries in France. Yet, at the time of Trent, the Jesuits were the only organized body of sufficient size, energy, and scholarship to undertake educational work on a large scale. One of them, Fr. Le Jay, had been the first to suggest at Trent, as the representative of the bishop of Augsburg, Otto Truchsess, that special schools should be founded for the training of the clergy; and when these were in fact, created, they were largely entrusted to the Society, which alone could staff them. The council decided that the Jesuit colleges already extant should be considered as complying with its decrees on the training of priests, and dispensed from contributing to the upkeep of diocesan seminaries.

St. Ignatius' first thought had been to found houses of education for members of the Society only; in fact the first colleges were mere hostels for Jesuit students who attended classes at the local universities. But soon, a double change took place. On the one hand, non-Jesuit pupils were admitted into those purely residential institutions; on the other, "colleges" in the wider sense of the word, i.e., real schools and universities, were offered to the Society by their founders or benefactors. This induced St. Ignatius to reconsider his position; he resolved to adapt himself to circumstances, and to let the Society take charge of educational work properly so-called, first of all for the clergy at large. The first move in this direction was the foundation of the Roman college, which was meant as a model for the whole Jesuit Order. It was a non-residential university, where students attended classes only, while they boarded at various houses, also termed "colleges," but different in nature, such as the *Germanicum*, founded by the Society in 1552, or non-Jesuit houses, such as the Roman seminary or the English college.

As yet, however, nothing had been done for the laity. It was in France that the first attempt to teach laymen was made. Guillaume du Prat, the reforming bishop of Clermont-en-Auvergne, had been anxious for some years past to plant the Jesuits in Paris, where he had given them his town house or Hôtel de Clermont. But as early as 1546, at the Council of Trent, he had offered to Fr. Le Jay to take over the then decayed university at Billom. The proposal was accepted in 1553, and the "college" at Billom soon became one of the most flourishing educational centers in Europe. The Collège de Clermont in Paris, despite a good deal of opposition, also rose to prosperity and fame. Gradually the range of studies was extended downward, and made to include what we now call secondary or even elementary forms; while a certain proportion of the pupils, instead of boarding, according to medieval practice, in the houses of "pedagogues" outside the colleges, were admitted to reside there as *convictores*. Thus the typical Jesuit college was gradually evolved: a combination of a residential university for clerics who read in theology or philosophy, and a secondary boarding-and-day school for lay pupils, who studied grammar, humanities, and rhetoric.

Once settled upon, this formula met with extraordinary success. Jesuit colleges swarmed over the whole of Central and Western Europe, and even as far as India; and there were new foundations throughout the sixteenth, seventeenth, and even eighteenth centuries, right up to the suppression of the Society. This is especially striking in the countries which were threatened by the spread of Protestantism. Owing to the variations in the political divisions of Europe, it is no easy matter to make an exact statement of the national distribution of colleges. We know, however, that in Poland three had been created by 1565, at Braunsberg, Wilna, and Pultusk. In the somewhat uncertain boundaries of the Holy Roman Empire, about the beginning of the seventeenth century, we find between 1551 and 1650, about 155 foundations, the majority being in Germany proper (76), and Flanders (31); while there were 12 in Austria, 6 in Hungary, 5 in Switzerland, 4 in Holland, and 10 in various outlying districts. In France, counting neither Flanders nor Alsace, but including Lorraine, Savoy, and Franche-Comté, the foundations, from 1551 to 1643, rose to the number of 68. The word "foundations" should not, however, be taken in too literal a sense. In the majority of cases, the Jesuits — and for that matter, the Oratorians as well — were called in by city authorities, not to establish new schools, but to restore old ones, many of those colleges created in the enthusiasm born of the humanistic movement, but which had fallen into decay. Out of 68 Jesuit colleges in France, no fewer than 39 succeeded to previous educational institutions. Such was the case at Auch (founded in 1543, taken over by the Society in 1588); at Sens (1537 and 1623); at Nîmes (1539 and 1634); and in other places. The fact is one of great importance. Local bodies, when asking for the help of the Jesuits, knew that they were bringing into their schools the spirit of the Catholic Reformation: order, hierarchy, and methodical organization, as well as a severe type of moral discipline, resting on ardent piety.

The plan outlined by Erasmus and embodied in the statutes of Montaigu, was to reach its full development in the stately monument of Jesuit pedagogy. The latter was in all its essentials present in the mind of St. Ignatius when he wrote the section of the *Constitutions* devoted to colleges and universities; but it was gradually brought to perfection as a result of experience gained in the first colleges of the Society. The conclusions finally reached were expounded in great detail in the famous document known as the *Ratio studiorum,* which in a slightly modified form still governs Jesuit education today. The first draft of this work was a report prepared in 1585 by an international committee of six Fathers — one Spaniard, one Portuguese, one Frenchman, one Austrian, one High German, one Roman. It then really appeared in the nature of a discussion of the topics proposed, and was printed in 1586 as a list of suggestions, to be examined by the various provinces. The final set of rules for Jesuit schools was printed, under the same title, only in 1599. Whatever its debt to previous systems of education, it goes beyond anything that had appeared before.

The essential purpose of the *Exercises* and of the *Constitutions* had been among the Jesuits the fortifying of the will. That of the *Ratio studiorum* is the building up of a strong moral personality among their pupils. Therefore all that would tend to enforce passive and servile obedience is discarded; everything is to be done to ensure willing acceptance of the rules, and active co-operation on the part of the boys. Discipline and government are as much as possible placed in their own hands; they are made to acquire a sense of responsibility. Similarly, in the intellectual field, the pupils should not be merely receptive; they should be made to think anew by themselves, to knead and knead again, so to say, the substance of what has been taught to them. Such a conception of education implies psychological insight, wide experience, and an intelligence in advance of the times; in fact it is strikingly modern, and forestalls, in regard to the building of character, the methods of Thomas Arnold and the Rugby School, and in regard to the building of the mind, the teaching practice of the French Lycées.

Pedagogy as such, however, is only an instrument in the Jesuit scheme, the main purpose being always to build up in each student a strong religious personality. Hence originated the plan adopted for the organization of each college of the Society. Beginning with knowledge accessible to all and with students of all descriptions, it ended up with the study of theology carried on by a select few. The college was divided into two parts. The lower one was open to all pupils, whatever their prospects. It included five forms: rhetoric, humanities, higher, middle, and lower grammar; but each of the latter three comprised two halves, which the less gifted could go through at the rate of one a twelvemonth; so that this cycle of studies extended to a maximum period of eight years (the total course, exclusive of university classes, was of similar length at the Liège school of the Brothers of the Common Life). The higher part of the college was reserved for clerics, especially those who were already scholastics in the Society. In it the students went through one year of philosophy, two of theology, and were allowed to stay on for another two years for private study of the latter science. We are now accustomed to consider a secondary school and a university as things apart. St. Ignatius combined them into one, true to the tradition and practice of medieval Paris: the wholly secular "philosophy" class of the French Lycées at the present day being a legacy of the Jesuit colleges.

The staff of a school, thus constituted, includes a rector, who is supreme; a prefect of studies, who actually supervises the whole of the teaching, inspects each class at least once a fortnight, "guides and cheers" the teachers, and sees to it that they enjoy due esteem and authority; sometimes also a prefect of the inferior studies, specially in charge of the lower part of the school. Great attention is devoted to the recruiting and training of capable masters. Certain colleges prepare students for the functions of *praeceptores* in the purely literary forms. These students, toward the end of their course, are bound to gather three times a week to practice the duties of their future calling, "lecturing, dictating, composing, correcting," etc.; this under the guidance of one "most skilled in teaching." When they are put in charge of a class, the latter must be no higher than their present abilities; afterwards they rise from form to form with their pupils, gaining knowledge as they dispense it. They are advised to follow the tradition and habits of their predecessors, so as to avoid any break in the continuity of school-life. The rector himself should have had some teaching experience, so that, the *Ratio studiorum* of 1586 adds, with a touch of humor, "he may, from what he himself has suffered, learn to pity others." This is also necessary to ensure his authority over the other masters, who otherwise would grumble at being ordered about by one ignorant of their trade. The professors of theology themselves must be sent to teach grammar for some time. In fact there should be no difference in honor between the teaching of letters and that of the "higher faculties." St. Ignatius was especially insistent that both should be put on the same level. If any masters, "through fatigue or weariness," should flag in their zeal, let them be granted one year's leave; if they fail to recover the necessary energy, let them be employed in other than school duties.

One recognizes here one of the fundamental ideas of the Society, that a man's work should not overtax his powers, that there should be an exact adaptation of the former to the latter. The same principle is applied to the pupils. Vacations are brief: one week in summer in the lower and middle grammar forms, a fortnight in higher grammar, three weeks in humanities, one month in rhetoric and above; the other holidays aggregating some twenty-three days. But then there are a number of religious feasts; and, besides, each week one day must be given to rest, "or at any rate one afternoon." Nor are the pupils to overstrain themselves: "No one should apply himself to his work, reading or writing, for more than two hours running, without a break of some little time." All must be taught by the masters how "to distribute their time to the best advantage for private study," during which they should enjoy perfect peace, as the *Constitutions* themselves insist.

Nothing could be farther from the stupid and brutal cramming of children which Montaigne denounced among the pedagogues he had known in his early years; nor could the Jesuits be said "to fill up memory only, leaving the understanding and conscience empty." On the contrary, the *Ratio studiorum* insists that the pupils should first of all be made thoroughly to grasp the texts on which they work. The basis of the teaching is the *praelectio,* which still survives as *explication de texte* in modern French educational practice, of which it is the main asset. The master should first of all read the passage to be elucidated; then he should "expound its subject, and connect it up with what comes before."

The same experienced wisdom appears in the way in which the matters taught are made to sink into the mind of the boys. After class, the master stays on for a quarter of an hour, and all are free to question him. But a better plan is recommended. A proficient pupil repeats the lesson for the benefit of his comrades; some of the latter put questions, to which others reply, or the master himself. Similar "repetitions" take place in the boardinghouse, the *praeses* questioning at least three of his comrades in the space of fifteen minutes.

Another means to make the students understand and remember is the disputation, bearing on theological or literary subjects, and already in honor in Paris University in the Middle Ages. As at Montaigu, such debates took place on Saturdays and Sundays. The *Ratio studiorum* has no pity for bookworms, who are incapable of expressing themselves in public. "One disputation is of more avail than many lessons" — the Society's purpose, to defend religion through controversy, being always kept in mind. The rector or the prefect was, however, to be present and discreetly guide the discussion, keep it in its proper channel and to a proper length, dispense praise, and sum up the argument, "neither keeping silent for long, nor talking all the time."

*   *   *

If not wholly original on the subject of discipline and emulation, the Jesuit scheme elaborates the principles asserted by Erasmus in every one of their implications. The *Constitutions* forbid any chastising of the students by the masters, the latter must "exhort" delinquents "lovingly," with "mildness and charity"; "observance of the rules is to be obtained," the *Ratio studiorum* adds, "more through the hope of honor and distinction and through the fear of disgrace, than by blows." The master should "refrain from insulting the boys by word or deed; and never address them otherwise than by their name or surname." If bodily punishment is necessary, it should be meted out by a special official, the "corrector," who is not a member of the teaching staff.

Emulation is encouraged by every possible means. The pupils of each form are divided up, for the sake of competition, into two groups, in either of which the most brilliant pupils, after a class examination, are appointed *magistrates,* and take the names of Latin or Greek civil or military dignitaries. Each pupil in one half of the class has his corresponding number in the other half, whom he is supposed to keep an eye upon, and correct whenever necessary. Seats are assigned according to merit, and the "most ignoble" part of the classroom is reserved for the "form of sloth" to which "the laziest boys are sent" — only to be "frequently shamed, blamed, and scolded." There is a further division into *decuriae,* also graded according to proficiency, each pupil being allowed to challenge another one in a superior *decuria,* and change places with him if he conquers. The *decuriones* are responsible for the behavior of their comrades, and may indicate them for some slight punishment. They are also expected to supervise the work of those under them. Badges or small rewards are given to distinguished students, and a number of means are used to bring their work before the public eye. And of course there is the yearly distribution of prizes.

This fostering of emulation is consonant with the main intention of the Jesuit scheme: that of picking out the most gifted boys and developing them to the best of their capabilities, so as to bring them to influential positions either in or outside the Society. Unpromising pupils are only a hindrance, and should be gently, but firmly, eliminated; hence the continuous sifting, which begins with the admission of a pupil, and lasts to the very end of his studies. To start with, the selection of candidates should be made on as broad a basis as possible, since merit is not limited to any social class. But the would-be pupil is to be examined, and accepted only if his intellectual and moral aptitude is deemed sufficient. Afterwards he undergoes a new testing, as a rule at the beginning of each school-year, before being promoted to a higher form. Great wisdom and experience are again evidenced in these examinations. The regulations are to be read to each class two or three days beforehand. The subject for the written part should be worded briefly. The examiners should be three in number, including the prefect, but no masters; the majority carry the decision in each case. The school marks of the candidates are to be taken into account. When three of them have been subjected to oral interrogation, their fate must be settled forthwith, "while the judgments of the questioners are still fresh." In doubtful instances, the whole examination may be gone through again, the age, aptness, and diligence of the boy being considered. All preliminary discussions should be kept secret; and no external influence should be allowed to interfere.

The intelligent teaching, the humane discipline, the helps to emulation, the gradual process of elimination, everything in a college of the Society makes for practical results. The Jesuits were so bent on efficiency, so averse to useless expenditure of strength, that they made the very leisure hours of the pupils to contribute to their main purpose. This was done by means of voluntary associations inside each school, which being an élite within an élite, still further reinforced emulation, in the devotional, moral, and intellectual field. Pious students enrolled in the Congregation of the Blessed Virgin Mary, whose members alone could be admitted to the literary or philosophical debating society known as the Academy. The latter was placed under the supervision of a special prefect, and had a branch in each class, in which *magistrates* were appointed. In the course of the meetings, the pupils again went through "the repetition or applying of those matters, which had been expounded in class," their exercises being made as pleasant as possible, so as "to excite their minds to study." Here again we find public debates and recitations, prizes, and the posting up of poems. Not in vain had the *Constitutions* stated that studies "in a certain way require the whole of man."

They ought not, however, to absorb him for their own sake; they should be, according to the Society's purpose, a means of sanctification. Great attention is therefore paid to the devotional life of the students, though the *Constitutions* wisely prescribe that no compulsion shall be used. The scholastics of the Society, in the philosophy and theology classes, ought to go to Communion every week but the pupils in the "inferior classes" should only confess every month, and receive Communion "on solemn feasts," being exhorted to this on vigils, as at Montaigu. At the beginning of each lecture prayer is said on bended knees, and the teacher crosses himself before speaking. Catechism is taught on Fridays and Saturdays; but there are also daily exhortations, even in private colloquies, in which, however, no attempt should be made to induce pupils to join the Society. If they feel attracted toward it, their confessor alone is to advise them. Spiritual readings are to be recommended; while great care should be taken not to leave immoral books in the hands of the boys. Altogether, they should be constantly incited to virtue and piety, but without undue rigidity; devotional practice being here "adapted" almost as much as in the case of the Jesuits themselves.

As for the syllabus of studies, it is, in fact, for the lower classes, very similar to that of the Christian humanists, some of whom the *Ratio studiorum* mentions as examples to be followed, in their love both of the Latin and of the Greek tongue: "Sigonius, Muretus, Petrus Victorius, Manutius."

It is the same, we might say, but with some improvements, and with one exception, that of lewd authors. Johann Sturm had taken no exception to the plays of Terence; there was no danger, he said, in performing them in school, if they were properly explained; the spectacle of vice side by side with virtue was a moral lesson for the audience. The enthusiasm of the Jesuits for classical literature was subordinate to their religious purpose, however, and they showed no such leniency. Otherwise, the Jesuit syllabus is even more classical than that, for instance, of Trithemius. Teaching in the Society, in respect of language, is directed toward a single aim: to enable the pupils, in the interests of religion, to speak and write pure, elegant Latin and Greek. No decadent model should therefore be selected. In regard to Latin, Cicero, the master of perfect speech, takes up most of the space, leaving some room, however, for Virgil, Horace, Ovid, Catullus, and Tibullus, but none whatsoever for patristic literature, the latinity of which is unsafe. On the Greek side, the Fathers are not open to the same objection, since their grammar is faultless, and their style often admirable; therefore, together with Homer, Hesiod, Pindar, Thucydides, Plato, Demosthenes, and Isocrates, we find St. Gregory Nazianzen, St. Basil, and St. John Chrysostom. In both languages the exercises prescribed are of the same kind, and are meant to loosen the tongue and sharpen the pen of the students. The latter must first of all acquire a stock of words and phrases, which they gather in their commonplace books. Then they make use of it, not merely for the writing of prose essays, but also for poems, or even for fanciful trifles such as epigrams, conundrums, enigmas — all of which make for nimbleness of speech.

Fault has often been found with a system of studies in which science was reduced to a few lessons in mathematics and cosmography, in which modern history was a secondary subject, and in which the knowledge acquired was of words, not of things. The essential purpose of education, however is not to stock the mind with miscellaneous information, but to enable it to reason clearly and straight, so as later to take advantage of any branch of study, whether literary or technical. Now, the exercises prescribed by the Jesuits were meant — like the oral correction of tasks, for instance — to make the pupils use their reflective faculties. And there can be no doubt that the colleges of the Society turned out generation after generation of strongly built minds, able to write and to speak well because they thought well. The intellectual results thus obtained were all to the advantage of the Catholic Reformation movement; and the Jesuits must be praised for the way in which they brought mere theories or aspirations into the realm of fact, and understood that the only way to attain practical results was to give a firm and direct lead by means of a fixed set of rules, and by a complete and coherent system of pedagogy.

*   *   *

In fact, the methods and practice of the Jesuits spread their influence far beyond the Society proper. Advantage was taken of them in the reformation of Paris University, begun in 1595 after the wars of religion, by Henry IV. They were praised and recommended in 1600, in regard to the teaching of Latin, by the Sorbonne professor, Edmond Richer, in his treatise on education entitled *Obstetrix animarum*. Most important of all, they were closely imitated by the Oratorians.

The French Oratory, founded in 1611 by Pierre de Bérulle, had grown rapidly, and after showing some unwillingness to take charge of colleges, had finally decided to engage in teaching work. Between 1616 and 1649, it founded or restored 26 colleges, these being framed exactly on the same plan as those of the Jesuits, in other words, beginning with a secondary school to end up with a seminary or university. The Oratorians, who never refused to acknowledge their debt to the Society, adopted most of its school organization: the examination before admission, the class entrance examinations, the *decuriae* and decurions, etc. The masters, in turn, were to rise from form to form, to use Latin in their correspondence, and to refrain from inflicting bodily punishment. Except in cases of utter necessity, no fees were charged for tuition; variety and interest were introduced into school life by means of public declamations and college plays; emulation was fostered by the distribution of prizes. The very purpose of education was the same: "Public studies should be for us," Fr. de Condren wrote, "but a means of exercising charity, and the outward service rendered to the people, and occasion to serve them through the instruction of souls."

Fr. de Bérulle had been exceedingly anxious not to hamper the work of the Jesuits, whom he greatly esteemed; in fact, the apostolic zeal, the spirit of devotion and humility, were equal on both sides. At the period now under consideration, that is, up to 1650, there had not yet broken out between the two orders those lamentable quarrels connected with the Jansenistic movement, which were to last on right up to the French Revolution. At the same time there was a divergence, due possibly to the original difference between the Society and the Roman Oratory, whose lead de Bérulle had been following, but mostly to the national reaction against the international character of the Society of Jesus. It is true that the French Oratory felt no partiality for the military spirit and discipline of the Jesuits, and that, with typical Gallic individualism, it believed far more in the value of independent effort than in the power of organization. It was, like its Roman predecessor, an association of free priests, in which, to use the words of Omer Talon, "everyone obeyed though no one commanded." And yet, uniformity was enforced upon the Oratorian colleges by means of visitations, and a *Ratio studiorum* was made compulsory in 1645.

The main point of opposition lay elsewhere. Exception had been taken to the number of foreign masters in the Jesuit schools, for instance in the Collège de Clermont in Paris; the Oratorians, on the contrary, were recruited in France and their staff was consequently French, the point being expressly insisted upon at Marseilles in an agreement with the Corporation, when the local college was handed over to them. As a matter of fact, the Oratorians did not claim the same distinctive originality as the Jesuits: they merged more easily in organized public life; they were anxious to comply with the wishes of municipal bodies, to whom they granted extensive rights of inspection and supervision. In regard to the use of Latin in school there was some hesitancy; French was preferred for catechism and for the "explanation" of classical texts, even in the higher forms; and translation, as an exercise, gradually ousted prose and composition. In 1640 there appeared a Latin grammar in French by Fr. de Condren. History was taught, but it was the history of France, which also supplied themes for school tragedies. The contrast between the attitude of the Oratorians and that of the Jesuits was not due, in the case of the former, to motives of policy or national interest. The Catholic Reformation had had its inception in France, with the Christian humanists; it was bearing wonderful fruit in France in the early seventeenth century. The French contribution to the welfare of the Church was of value precisely because its spiritual quality was national and peculiar. The Oratorians were conscious of this, and their patriotism, far from being directed against the universal Church, tended to its enrichment.

Whatever opposition in temper at the outset, and whatever differences later, might separate the Oratorians from the Jesuits, there was absolute agreement between them when the future of the Church was at stake. This cordial union appeared when an order of nuns, specially founded for the education of girls, that of the Ursulines, was introduced into France. It had taken birth in Italy, thanks to the charitable efforts of St. Angela Merici. The latter was born in Lombardy in 1470, and her activities had started as early as 1516, when she had begun to establish Christian schools in Brescia. The teachers whom she had gathered about her were not cloistered, and lived with their parents or relatives. In 1572 St. Charles Borromeo, who had employed them a good deal, bound them to common life and the three vows. Late in the sixteenth century an Ursuline convent, modeled on those of Italy, was created in the papal enclave in France, near Avignon. Soon another one was established in Paris by Madam de Sainte-Beuve. This noble lady was much attached to the Jesuits, one of whom was her confessor, and who had been allowed to come back to France by King Henry IV, thanks to her personal intervention; she also belonged to the pious circle which gathered in the house of Madame Acarie, around M. de Bérulle, the founder of the

French Oratory; and advice and help were sought on either hand. The Ursuline movement spread rapidly throughout the kingdom, the number of houses, shortly before 1650, rising to 255 in eight independent "congregations."

The spirit of the Catholic Reformation is beautifully illustrated in the Ursuline schools which, *mutatis mutandis,* have much in common with the Jesuit colleges. Yet there is an essential difference, which lies in the nature of the teaching. It had been a fashion of the Renaissance to bring up female scholars who could discourse in Latin or Greek; but the Ursulines had no wish to turn their pupils into *femmes savantes,* and deemed that a sound knowledge of reading, writing and reckoning, needlework and housekeeping was all that even society women needed, "since it was more pleasing to our Lord, and more useful to them, to be virtuous than to be learned." But every care was devoted to the building up of their moral personality, according to principles which bring home to us the religious atmosphere of the period: "I advise you," St. Angela had said to her spiritual daughters in her will, "to lead your pupils with a soft and gentle hand, . . . like true mothers." This suavity, akin to that of St. Francis of Sales, by no means excluded firmness and energy: "The true and proper devotion of the Ursulines," Madame de Pommereu wrote, "is not a devotion of tenderness, ravishings and ecstasies; it is a strong and solid devotion . . . which rouses the pupils to generous and warlike virtues; thus they reach those practical ecstasies which are indeed the best of all."

The use of the word "practical" points to a conception of education related to that of the Society, which in fact many features recalled: girls of all social classes, however poor, were admitted; there was to be no excess in devotional practice — though the point at which excess began was set much higher than nowadays, and the lives of the pupils were steeped in piety; no choir duty at any rate, no properly monastic exercises; undue asceticism was carefully avoided. The rules, according to St. Angela's own advice, were not cut-and-dried, but the product of gradual experience and adaptation. Idleness was to be shunned.

The aim of the Ursuline schools was to turn out that fine social type which is still found in the French *bourgeoisie* of today, a thrifty, pleasant-mannered housewife, able to "run" a middle or even higher class home, to make a little go far, and to fulfill both her domestic and social obligations, while at the same time preserving her virtue unsullied and her piety sincere and fervent.

The practical organization used to obtain such a result was apt and efficient. The "general mistress of the boarders" was to examine candidates for admission; to keep in touch with the superior and the girls' parents; to inspect the classes, dormitories, and refectories; to read the rules to the school twice a year solemnly. Discipline was to be ensured through rewards rather than punishments; bodily chastisement, when necessary, was to be dispensed "with a serene and tranquil mind," but as a rule other means were to be used, in accordance with the character of the pupils. Great attention was granted to the health of the girls, and those who showed a tendency to curvature of the spine were to be kept from writing much. The form mistresses were to keep company with the boarders throughout the whole day — as in present-day Salesian practice — to take part in their meals, recreations, and even games. They were in charge of catechism and of the pious exercises, which culminated in the yearly First Communion, a ceremony which was first imagined by the Ursulines, and which has remained a central feature of the devotional life of the French youth. In a word, the Ursuline school produced that fine combination, a saintly woman of the world; a combination typical of that pluckily heroic age, when elegance was deemed a necessary accompaniment of bravery.

*   *   *

The Jesuit and Oratorian colleges were not merely "classical" schools. Their higher forms were more like universities, in the medieval sense of the word, or seminaries, in which the chief matters taught were philosophy and theology. We need not here consider the doctrine of the Oratory, which developed an originality only after 1650, when it embraced Cartesianism. But, from the first, the Jesuits had their own views on the teaching of divinity, and here again followed in the footsteps of the Christian humanists. They expressed their disapproval of decadent scholasticism, with its elaborate *quaestiones*, restored the authority of Thomas Aquinas, and made Scripture, as interpreted by scholars, the basis of all theology. The *Ratio studiorum* of 1586 expresses itself on the point in an uncompromising way:

"We must strive with might and main, so that the study of Holy Writ, which is languishing among ourselves, may be aroused and flourish. . . . Those who [nowadays] give themselves up wholly to theology seem to follow commentaries, leave aside the text . . . and take little account of the solidity of Scripture. Such an upbringing produces, as it were, mutilated and crippled theologians."

Scripture is to be explained clearly, intelligently, and without undue lengthiness, "according to its true and literal sense" — a reaction against the *allegories* and *anagogies* of late medieval theology — in a way that much recalls the *praelectio* on classical authors. The essential point is to drive home the moral or spiritual lesson to be learned. One need not indulge in linguistic disquisitions for the love of "grammar." As to scholastic theology, the Jesuit attitude was inspired by the wish to establish in the order one only thought and will, as well as to revert to the sources of firm, direct reasoning: "Let all our members follow the doctrine of St. Thomas and consider him as their own teacher. . . ." In regard to philosophy, the same unity is to prevail. "In logic," the *Constitutions* run, "in natural and moral philosophy, and in metaphysics, the doctrine of Aristotle is to be followed." Here again, a thorough understanding of the text itself is to be preferred to silly or abstruse *quaestiones*.

Unity, straight thinking, concentration upon essentials, both morally and intellectually, such are, in theology no less than in classical letters, the main features of Jesuit teaching. Such an intellectual discipline was bound to bear fruit, and did bear fruit of exceptional value in a whole series of theologians, some of whom appeared early at the Council of Trent; while in the following generation, the most prominent among them was undoubtedly St. Robert Bellarmine (1542–1621). The latter was a character of extraordinary richness and completeness. Famous as a controversialist, he could also write elegant Latin verse, such as the hymn of St. Mary Magdalen's day, *Pater superni luminis*. He shone in the diplomatic field, and also distinguished himself as a Jesuit provincial and as the archbishop of Capua. He should not be given the whole credit for the Thomist revival, which had begun before him in the University of Salamanca; but he confirmed it, and gave it its final impulse, when insisting that St. Thomas should hold a central position in the *Ratio studiorum*. His work ranged from the emendation of the Vulgate (from which he removed errors brought in by Pope Sixtus V) to the reform of the Breviary, from the writing of a catechism, the *Doctrina christiana*, to disputations with James I of England on the power of kings. He appears as one of the most universal men of his own time, joining wide scholarship with deep piety; and one can hardly blame Clement VIII for prevailing upon him to swerve from the rule of his order, and accept the cardinalate in March 3, 1599.

The Pope had, in this matter, taken the advice of another and scarcely less illustrious member of the sacred college, the Oratorian scholar and historian, Caesar Baronius. The latter is one of the most lovable and admirable figures of the Catholic Reformation movement. Though less fanciful than St. Philip Neri, whom he was to succeed as the superior of the Roman Oratory, he was akin to him in his genial and honest simplicity. He was born in the kingdom of Naples in 1538, and when a student in Rome, became a disciple of St. Philip and joined his congregation. His spiritual father discerned his abilities, and directed him to the study of ecclesiastical history. "He, who was then our father," Baronius himself wrote in his good-natured preface, "induced me to undertake this work, though I was unwilling to perform it, for it loaded me with a heavier burden than my weakness could bear; and so I have sweated in it for some thirty years to the best of my ability, God's grace favoring me; for I was almost beardless when I began, and now I am all hoary as I write this."

The outcome of Baronius' efforts was the monumental compilation known as *Annales ecclesiastici* — to some extent a refutation of the Protestant *Centuriae*, written at Magdeburg in 1552. The *Annales* were published from 1588 to 1607 and reached back to 1198. Though marred by errors, especially in the Greek part, they are a work of painstaking and conscientious erudition, provided with a very full system of references. Baronius was a man of transparent intellectual probity, and was acknowledged as such even by his venomous adversary, Fra. Paolo Sarpi. He loved his task: "Nothing could be sweeter," he wrote, "for the enjoyment of my own mind. . . . The contemplation of the Church . . . is like a wide door opening out on a vast plain, through which my speech may career and joyfully bound." Such alacrity was not exclusive of patience; and in fact the *Annales* provide an instance of critical treatment not unworthy of Baronius' humanistic predecessors. In fact, we may best conclude the present chapter with the very words with which Baronius invoked the blessing of the Holy Ghost upon his work, so that he might "through his words, writings, and most of all through his manners profess, attest and preach the truth." The enthusiasm of the Catholic reformers was not merely expressed by "the virtues of their souls," but as we shall now see, by "their tongue and their pen" as well.

CHAPTER VIII

The Catholic Reformation and Literature

WHEN leaving the field of precise legislation — whether bearing on the Church at large or on religious orders — to enter upon that of literature and art, one must use new methods of approach. The former subject lends itself to exact and comprehensive study; the latter's boundaries are not easily defined, and it might be pursued to an almost unlimited extent. No attempt will therefore be made in the following pages to give an exhaustive and systematic account of the influence of the Catholic Reformation upon letters, painting, architecture, and music. All that can be done is to state the principles which the Catholic reformers laid down as a starting-point, and to trace out certain general lines of development. First of all, it need hardly be pointed out that the need of reformation concerned the literary life of Christendom no less than ecclesiastical discipline.

The Renaissance of the *quattrocento* had forgotten the inner and deeper sense of religion. This is strikingly revealed by the life and works of the greatest Italian humanist and Latin poet of the period, Jovianus Pontanus (1426–1503), founder of the Naples Academy. He enjoyed extraordinary repute among his contemporaries; kings and princes bowed to him, showered favors upon him, raised him to the highest state appointments, on account of his classical scholarship. Yet he had imbibed the spirit of antiquity so thoroughly as to become almost a neo-pagan. Many of his poems are full of the luscious sensuousness of the ancients. True Jovianus Pontanus also wrote sacred poetry; but the very fact that his religious lyrics should be printed side by side with his licentious compositions, shows how far the period was from Christian earnestness.

The distance covered in the next hundred years appears when one considers the attitude of a namesake of the Naples humanist, the Jesuit poet, Jacobus Pontanus (1542–1626). He inveighed against those who wrote "things far removed from virtue, some of them filling up whole books with amatory lewdness." Poetry, he said, is "an art, which depicts the actions of men, and unfolds them in verse, in order to teach them how to live." These words give expression to the dominant thought of the literary theorists of the Catholic Reformation. They reject that ideal of "art for art's sake," which was that of the pagan Renaissance. In their eyes, poetry is not an end in itself. It is meant "to teach while it delights, but to teach more than it delights." Men, however, are weak; they must be enticed to righteousness by literary beauty, by *the* literary beauty which their present-day tastes lead them to prefer. Their partiality for Renaissance standards should therefore be gratified. Antiquity will remain the model to be imitated *par excellence,* but in its outward form only, not in its inward spirit of sensuousness. Thus a classical garb will be made to clothe religious truth, and what was poison will now become an aid to spiritual health.

There was, indeed, nothing new about the plan. In literature, as in monastic life and education, a reaction had set in, owing to the influence of the Christian humanists.

One is naturally tempted to trace back the birth of the literature of the Catholic Reformation to the Council of Trent. It is a fact that the great Church assembly was steeped in an atmosphere of classicism — one finds the legate, Cervini, quoting Horace — and that it was careful to ensure for its enactments the benefit of humanistic editing. Its respect for classical form is revealed in its treatment of lewd books: they are to be "prohibited altogether; and yet, such works, if ancient and written by pagans, are allowed on account of their elegance and propriety of style, though they are not to be read to children on any account." In other words, the Council, while rejecting pagan immorality, sanctions the literary ideal of the Renaissance.

No wonder, therefore, that the Jesuit critics of the late sixteenth century should have done the same, and attempted to connect classical forms with Christian beliefs so closely that they could not be separated, an effort that was unanimously supported by the literary theorists of the Catholic Reformation. The languages and style of the ancients assumed some of the hallowed character of religion itself. They were set up as models which could scarcely be improved upon. Hence, we have the principles which governed the literary production of the post-Trentine age, and especially its Latin verse for the space of two centuries, and of which some remote effects may occasionally be felt even now.

These principles are best expounded by Jacobus Pontanus in his *Institutiones poeticae,* published in 1594. He grants, it is true, at the outset, that poetry may consist in the direct "imitation" of nature, its purpose being "to represent the actions of men," according to the classical ideal which Pope later expressed in his famous line, "The proper study of mankind is man." But very soon the Jesuit critic alters the sense of the word "imitation," which he now refers to the reproduction of a model. "Let us propose to ourselves," he says, "some illustrious examples . . . having grasped their images with our inward sense, transfer them to our own writings. . . . We should however," he adds slily, "expend our whole labor so that those things should seem not theirs, but ours; although learned men cannot be taken in by our borrowings." What is more, the pleasure reaped from reading poetry is not due to its originality, but on the contrary to its likeness with known types.

Obviously such a theory, if strictly adhered to, would have done away with inspiration. Now there were, in the literary life of the Catholic Reformation, two conflicting tendencies. On the one hand, the Catholic reformers were so averse to the licentious freedom of the Renaissance, its unrestricted enjoyment of nature and the senses, its sporting frolic-someness and brutal lusts, its worship of glory and exaltation of human pride, that they advised restraint in every form of human activity, in-cluding literature. They distrusted passion; they preferred poetical forms in which the mind alone displayed its ingenuity, to those in which the heart unburdened itself of its burning feelings. They favored the ideal of the golden mean, the composed and balanced attitude of the classical writer. They were often partial to preciosity, to *concetti* and mannerisms, as against spontaneity and lyricism. They treated poetry, not as the free outpouring of men's emotions, but as a technical exercise, in which success was to be ensured by sedulous study and strict discipline.

But, on the other hand, they belonged to a militant movement ani-mated by soldierlike alacrity. Whatever they did, even in the field of poetry and eloquence, was done with fiery enthusiasm. They felt an ardent love of Christ, an ardent desire of His glory, an ardent craving for mar-tyrdom. Passion, which had been rejected in its purely human shape, reappeared in the expression of religious feeling. Hence a twofold aspect in the literature of the Catholic Reformation. Much of it brings into play mere skill and ingenuity: such is the case, though not uniformly so, for the lighter forms of lyrical poetry. But in epic poetry and the drama, where men and women are made to feel and to live before us, where the theme is generally provided by heroic actions performed in obedience to the call of God, no such frigidity prevails, and the highest pitch of emotion is often reached. We shall turn first of all to the former class of produc-tions, which, whatever its merits, is certainly the less remarkable of the two.

The main element in the composition of such pieces is, according to

Pontanus, the following of carefully chosen models. Now, it is easy to protest indignantly against such a literary ideal, and to denounce it as artificial and scarcely honest. But after all, is not every poet, however spontaneous his art, formed largely by imitation? How else is the technique of the literary craftsman to be acquired? And it cannot be denied that the Latin poets of the Catholic Reformation were remarkably successful in reproducing and adapting to Christian subjects the composed harmony of Virgil, the sweet plaintiveness of Ovid, or the terse wit of Martial. At the same time, however, they were also at a disadvantage. Their means of expression was not plastic enough; their very adherence to "pure" latinity tied them down to a fixed literary language which was necessarily stilted and precluded homeliness. Nor was variety or innovation allowed in metrical forms either. Hence it is that the humanistic hymns of the sixteenth century, though in better Latin than those of the Middle Ages, scarcely equal their pathetic intensity. Add that the Catholic reformers' distrust of passion led to a concept of poetry in which beauty came not from inside, but was added on from outside in the shape of "ornaments"; in which it was the product, not of genuine emotion, but of sedate, quiet, methodical reflection. "The poet," Possevinus writes, "is not only an imitator, but a man of surpassing ingenuity, and carried away by his mind; who does not use trite and colloquial words, but words . . . sought from afar; who represents great things, things admirable, abstruse things, out-of-the-way things."

The lighter poetry of the Catholic Reformation was therefore most successful where skilfulness and wit came into play, and its chief beauties were found in conceits and preciosity.

The Latin poets of the Catholic Reformation tried their hand at every one of the classical *genres,* at epics, odes, epigrams, elegies — each of these being extended to a surprising variety of themes. Thus there is an epigram, by Franciscus Raimundus, *On a certain young man, who rushed away from the paternal home, and fled to Rome, to seek admission in a religious order;* and among the odes, we find one by Franciscus Torsellinus, also a Jesuit, entitled: *Cradle-Song of the Virgin Mary to the Infant Christ,* which is touching and sweetly motherly, with its refrain, "Now sleep, my life, my light, o sleep." But however varied in inspiration and mood, most of this literary production is scriptural, and unceasingly reverts to the various parts of the Gospel story, unless it occasionally wander to the lives of the saints. A list of sacred subjects supplied by Father Jacobus Pontanus more or less coincides with the liturgical cycle. It was, of course, easier to establish unity of purpose and matter among the writers — mostly ecclesiastical — who wrote in Latin, than among those who used their mother-tongue, and who were distracted by worldly interests. Nevertheless, these also followed suit to a large extent, and we may say that the Latin compositions of the Catholic reformers really set the tone for the vernacular devotional poetry of the period.

*   *   *

Italy would, of course, be the first to come under the influence of the new spirit; and, in fact, no sooner had the Council of Trent come to a close than the leading writer of the time, Torquato Tasso (1544–1595), gave expression to the literary ideals of the Catholic Reformation, in his *Discorsi*. He quotes Horace on *prodesse* and *delectare,* and like the Jesuit critics, emphatically declares for the former purpose. "Poetry," he says, quoting Eratosthenes, "is the first philosophy, which from our tender years, instructs us as to good manners and right living. . . ." "A good poet," he adds with Strabo, "must needs be a righteous man."

What is true of verse in general is even truer in the case of that *genre* which was most in keeping with the conquering ardor of the Trentine generation, the *poema eroico*. "Epic poetry," he says, as contrasted with the drama, "requires the highest degree of all virtues; for the characters are heroic like virtue itself." Tasso feels less scruple than the Jesuits in regard to love, which he introduces into his compositions on account of its "great beauty"; but if it be not directed toward Christ himself, or toward a brother-warrior, if its object be woman, let it at any rate be "knightly love . . . , not merely passion and sensual desire, but, according to the words of St. Thomas, a most noble behavior of the will." Generally speaking, for the heroic poem "an action of the utmost nobleness" should be chosen.

While writing his *Discorsi,* Tasso was laboring to apply his own principles. His purpose was to write a Christian *Iliad,* and in fact he closely followed the model given by Homer in his *Gierusalemme liberata* (*Jerusalem Delivered*) which was completed in 1575. He chose for his subject the first Crusade, which he dealt with in a highly fanciful way, introducing classical "episodes," defiances, and single fights, Goffredo and Solimanno replacing Achilles and Hector. Nor is the stage machinery of antiquity absent. Supernatural powers intervene in the fight for Jerusalem. Pagan deities had, of course, to be eliminated from the divine hosts, and thus the crusaders are assisted by God, St. Michael, guardian angels, and holy hermits. But there was no harm in enlisting the false gods of pagan mythology among the infernal army, and thus we find Alecto side by side with Beelzebub, and the enchantress, Armida, who bears a close likeness to Circe. The Christian character of the poem is, however, very strongly asserted: before facing the prodigies of the enchanted forest, Rinaldo confesses his sins to Peter the hermit, and goes to Mount Olivet to pray at dawn. The spirit of the old medieval romance of chivalry here rejoins the heroic mood of the Catholic Reformation.

But even more than in heroic poetry, the direct influence of the Catholic Reformation is manifested in what we might call the "cycle of remorse," which had its birth in Italy and spread to the whole of Western Europe. The tearful expression of contrition was, of course, no new thing in Christian literature. The twelfth-century *Archithrenius* or archweeper of Jean de Hantville had been shown as roaming all through the world, lamenting the sins and vices of man. Nevertheless repentance was not prominent even among the religious compositions of the Renaissance poets, who were pleased with life as it was, and did not consider this earth as a vale of tears. But it reappeared in full force after the Council of Trent, when the Church had made its children rueful for their past lasciviousness. The two main themes of the "cycle," which provided poets with endless variations, were the remorse of St. Peter after he had denied Christ, and the remorse of St. Mary Magdalen after her conversion; and the works which respectively headed the two long files of poems on each of the two subjects were Luigi Tansillo's *Lagrime di San Pietro* (*St. Peter's Tears*) and Erasmo de Valvasone's *Lagrime della Maddalena* (*The Tears of St. Mary Magdalen*).

Luigi Tansillo (1510–1565) himself supplies an instance of a conversion from Renaissance paganism to Trentine Catholicism. The most famous one among his early poems, *Il Vendemmiatore* (*The Grapegatherer*), was licentious, and the author was placed on the index, and "had to drink for some time the wine of his Mother's wrath." He made amends, however, by writing *Lagrime,* the beginning of which was published in 1560. The amatory vein of his first compositions still inspired parts of his devotional poem, which was expurgated and recast by a Roman commission of Jesuit Fathers. Tansillo had compared the glance which Christ cast on Peter, thus silently rebuking him, to lovers' looks, which speak without words: the whole stanza was done away with. Owing to this and similar corrections, the *Lagrime* bear almost an official stamp; they may be considered as a model proposed by Rome to Catholic poets. Of course, Tansillo's personality is not wholly obliterated; it appears to us as quite Italian. He is garrulous, as in Peter's endless soliloquies; his descriptions — that of the sculptures in the temple of Jerusalem for instance — are pictorial and brilliant. He loves tawdry ornaments, and takes pleasure in displaying to us the riches of Isaiah's apparel when he meets Peter:

> To him he comes in garb of richer kind
> Than lord's or royal king's, of wealth untold;
> Afire with purple his gown, with purple lined,
> Studded with costly gems, and hemmed with gold.

Obviously Tansillo views poetical expression as something more external than intimate, and is partial to exuberant mimicry and lively color. So much for the negative side. But on the positive side, his talent and facility as a versifier cannot be denied, and his poem contains more than that "tinsel" which, according to Boileau, was the sole beauty of Tasso's *Gierusalemme*. Tansillo is admirable as a painter of nature, whether he describe a summer night or a spring storm in an Alpine wood. But the value of his poem should be assessed in connection with its purpose, which is essentially religious, as he himself declares, when about to recount the sufferings of Christian martyrs: "That ancient piety be renewed . . . and men aroused to follow blessed tracks."

In fact, the *Lagrime* are not only a Christian epic, they are the epitome, the condensed sum total of all possible Christian epics. This long poem of nine hundred and ten stanzas in *ottava rima*, or 7280 lines, is not a continuous whole, but a succession of episodes, in which is reviewed the whole history of the Church, from the Creation down to the author's own time. St. Peter is represented as wandering disconsolately during the three days between his denial of Christ and the Resurrection. He has a number of adventures, which provide for so many digressions. He first repairs to the Garden of Olives, then to the house of the Last Supper, then gets a glimpse of the procession of the Cross. Afterwards he visits the temple, which is adorned with stone carvings representing the chief events of the Old Testament, and, symbolically, the history of Christendom. Eventually he retires to a cave outside the town, and during the night he has visions and dreams which are a succession of pictures from the New Testament. After the shepherds who worshiped the infant Jesus have been made the occasion for a pastoral passage in the *O fortunatos* vein, in compliance with contemporary tastes, Tansillo brings Isaiah upon the stage. The latter shows Peter visions of the martyrs, and describes Christ's descent into hell and the joy of heaven on welcoming the souls rescued therefrom; and here, as a tale within a tale within a tale, Solomon sings the Creation and Fall of man. Lastly, Peter meets St. John, who tells him the story of the Passion, bringing it down to Mary Magdalen's visit at the tomb. The poem, which is unfinished, breaks off here: one wonders what further developments its author may have contemplated.

The faults of such a composition — its lack of unity, its incoherency, its artificiality — are not lacking, especially in the *Pianto primo* — the first lament or book — which was published separately at first, and is far simpler and more direct in its emotion than the rest of the work. But the chief interest of the poem lies in the fact that it is a model and a starting-point. It met with extraordinary favor. Together with Erasmo de Valvasone's *Lagrime della Maddalena*, it was printed in its final, though incomplete, form, in 1585, then again in 1587, 1592, 1598, and 1599. The fragment which had first appeared in Italy in 1560 was freely translated into Spanish by Luys Galves de Montalvo, under the title of *El llanto de Sant Pedro* (1598); in French by Robert Estinne (*Les larmes du Sainct Pierre*, editions of 1595 and 1606) and by the illustrious Malhebe (*Les larmes de S. Pierre imités du Tansille*, editions in 1587, 1596, and 1598); in English by the Jesuit father, Robert Southwell, who afterwards kept the *Lagrime* in mind when writing his own *St. Peters Complaint* (editions in 1595 [twice], 1597, 1599, 1600, 1602 [twice], 1615, 1616, 1620, 1634 [twice], 1636). There were numerous imitations, which traded on the success of Southwell's work, such as *Saint Peters Ten Teares* (1597, 1602), *St. Peters Path to the Joys of Heaven* (1598), Samuel Rowlands' *Betraying of Christ* (1598), and others.

A similar swarming of translations, adaptations, and imitations followed the appearance of Valvasone's poem on Mary Magdalen. And yet the favor it met with on every hand gives rise to some wonder. Though the purpose of the writer is undoubtedly a devout one, he sacrifices so much to the decadent tastes of the period that he turns to little advantage the possibilities here open for pious lyricism.

His poem is not nearly as long as Tansillo's, including only seventy-six stanzas in *ottava rima*, or six hundred and eight lines. Yet its author finds ample room in it for hollow amplification. He first of all represents Mary Magdalen in the cold and dreary solitude to which she is pictured as having retired after the Ascension; and then takes up the story of her life from the beginning, taking the opportunity offered here to describe, with true Italian sensuousness and relish, the beauty which was the occasion of her fall. Then follow the various incidents borrowed from the Gospel narrative: Mary Magdalen hears of the coming of a "great hero" (Christ); she dons her finest garments and jewels (another opening is found here for gaudy description) and sallies forth to meet him. At his sight a sudden change takes place in her; the horrid monster that caused her to sin comes out of her mouth in the shape of a seven-tongued flame surrounded with smoke. She feels "her lover's" glance pierce through her like lightning; throws her chains and bracelets at his feet; and then behaves toward the "divine hero, who enamors her," like a little dog who caresses his master, because he wants to be fed by him. With her golden hair she wipes away the tears with which she has watered "the holy feet." For, from now on, she begins weeping and will continue in tears until the end of the poem. Hearing that "her lover" is in prison and ill-treated, she rushes toward him like a Maenad, with torn clothes and dishevelled locks, and finds him on the cross, near which she wakens the echoes with her wailings. Then Valvasone recounts the famous scene at the tomb. After the Resurrection Mary Magdalen, like a dove seeking her spouse whom thunder has driven away, follows the footsteps of her "beloved chief," still weeping; and when he has returned to the right hand of his Father, she wanders away to mountains, crags, and caverns, where she can more easily think of heaven. There, clothed only with her flowing hair, she makes the rocks and oaks fall in love with her! Hereupon follows an apostrophe to the "sweet pains" and "fortunate horrors" that surround her, until at last her soul is carried up to the holy place where she is again to meet with "her lover."

Valvasone's work is an extreme example of the peculiar and not altogether pleasant coloring that the Italian temperament gave to the poetry of the Catholic Reformation. There is little in it that tells of the inward life of the soul; the expression of feeling is outward, not intimate. One is forcibly reminded of one of those pictures of the same period, in which there are vehement gestures, distorted features, and eyes dramatically upturned to heaven; also of Tasso's piece, included in a typical *Collection of tears* (*Raccolta di Lagrime*) of 1593, in which, according to its preface, he describes a painting of our Lady "in the act of devout contemplation; and shows in such a lively way her holy eyes full of tears, and her holy cheeks watered with drops so true and plentiful, that they deceive the sight of the onlookers and invite every pious hand to dry them."

We have here the trick of deception, so much in favor with Italian painters. More generally, in the *Lagrime*, only the external aspect of things is insisted on. Hence the really successful descriptions of nature or of plastic beauty, the glittering passages on dress and jewelry. There is about the poetry of Valvasone a remnant of Renaissance paganism; and he is strangely shy of the names of Christ or Jesus, which he does not once utter. Add to this the easy, good-humored, irreverent familiarity with which he handles the theme of Mary Magdalen's conversion at Jesus' feet; and the equally untimely display of punning wit. All this shows how much slack had to be taken up by the Catholic Reformation, before bringing Christian poetry to the chastened simplicity and intimacy which were to make it worthy of its object.

Valvasone's sensuousness, however, was not a permanent feature, and it disappeared from the works of his numerous imitators in France, Spain, and England. But the mingled tearfulness and preciosity lasted on for many decades. It reappears in a sweetly pretty series of sonnets published in 1597 at Paris under the title of *La Magdeleine repentie* (*Repentant Magdalen*) in which the saint's retired life is referred to by herself in the following words:

> For there, I hear no sound but chatty chirping
> Which feathered songsters utter in the woods,
> Their warble wedding to my woeful weeping;
>
> For if in my retreat I sing the rhymes
> Of God's great harper, herald, prophet king,
> *They* sing with me, with me their chorus chimes.

Such delicate daintiness is not always present, however, in the numberless *Tears* published at the end of the sixteenth and the beginning of the seventeenth centuries. The fashion was set in England by Robert Southwell, S.J., whose *Mary Magdalen's Tears* was printed in 1594. This was a prose work — though of a highly poetical turn — and harked back, beyond Trent, to the Franciscan mysticism of the fourteenth century. But the choice of theme betrays the influence of the Roman environment in which the author had spent many years, and it cannot be doubted that the success of his composition induced many rhymers to follow in his footsteps with *Tears* of various descriptions, many of them inferior.

While not all the authors of these poems were professedly Catholics, they all came under the influence of the Trentine movement. Gervase Markham's *Tears of the Beloved* (1600) is devoted to the "moanings" of St. John the Apostle; but the same poet published in 1604 his *Mary*

Magdalen's lamentations for the loss of her master Jesus. A similar theme is reverted to in Nicholas Breton's *Blessed Weeper* (1601) and in an anonymous poem on *Mary Magdalen's Conversion* (1603). The latter gives no proof of high poetical gifts, but we still find in it the "pleasant horrors" of the saint's retreat in the woods.

The tradition is continued by two anonymous poems, *Mary Magdalen's Lamentations* (1604) and *Saint Mary Magdalen's Pilgrimage to Paradise* (1617) and by Thomas Robinson's *Life and Death of Mary Magdalen* (1636), until we come to the most famous of the compositions of this cycle, Richard Crashaw's *Weeper*. This appeared in 1646 in London, as the first item of the author's *Steps to the Temple*. The superiority of the piece over all previous ones need hardly be stressed. It is enough to quote the best-known stanza.

> Not in the evening's eyes
> When they red with weeping are,
> For the sun that dyes,
> Sits sorrow with a face so faire.
> Nowhere but heere did ever meet
> Sweetnesse so sad, sadnes so sweet.

Yet this very example confirms what we have said of the literary ideal of the Catholic Reformation. Even here, though there be emotion of a kind, the main feature is wit. Right up to the end, the Trentine movement in letters favored preciosity. Should it be taken to task on that account, as having approved of artificiality and affectation? That it did so cannot be doubted: it had its reasons for preferring a rightly poised mind to an often misguided heart, and thus for showing partiality for an intellectual form of poetry. Yet this is not the essential point about its action. It achieved one main result, that of turning the tide of literary tastes toward pious themes treated in a devout spirit. Whatever its other faults, the new literary school was not incapable of giving expression to genuine and natural feeling. In England, in the reign of Queen Elizabeth, Catholic poetry was not merely witty. The persecuted Recusants, cheered by missionaries who brought with them from the continent the influence of Trent, sang their sufferings, comforts, and hopes in verse that often reaches to the highest pitch of plucky resolution; not to speak of the pathetic melancholy, moral earnestness, or sweet tenderness of some of their compositions. What can be more touching and more devoutly true than Richard Verstegan's poem entitled *Our Lady's Lullaby*, in which the Virgin Mary thus speaks to the Infant Jesus:

> And when I kiss his loving lips
> Then his sweet smelling breath
> Doth yield a savor to my soule,
> That feedes love, hope and faith.
> Sing lullaby my little boy,
> Sing lullaby my lives joy.

It was not lyrical poetry, however, which was destined to give an adequate expression to the militant and heroic ideal of the Catholic Reformation. This task was reserved for the drama, to which we shall now turn.

*   *   *

How the drama flourished under the direct influence of the Catholic Reformation is at present rarely suspected. No wonder, since it mostly consisted in college plays in elaborate Latin, which proficient classical scholars alone could understand. It is a pity that they should now be out of reach of the general public, for the oblivion into which they have fallen is wholly undeserved, and their influence upon the development of secular drama has been an important one.

College drama, whether reminiscent of mediaeval morality plays or of a more humanistic cast, was, in the mid-sixteenth century, far more important than the ordinary public stage; but it partook more of the rowdiness and wild spirits of the students than of the seriousness and gravity of academic pursuits. In 1553, a tragedy, *Captive Cleopatra*, and a comedy, *Eugene or the Encounter*, both by Jodelle, were acted at Boncourt College in Paris. How unsuitable the latter was for the purpose of education, is shown by its subject: the chief character is an abbot who gets his mistress, a naughty hussy, to marry a bumpkin, so that he may freely enjoy his amor with her. The same may be said of other comedies. It is not surprising, in view of such excesses, that the early regulations drafted for Jesuit teachers should have evidenced distrust toward college drama. The *rules* of the Society are quite explicit as to the type of plays the Father provincial may allow, as well as the frequency and places of their performance.

At the outset, theatrical performances in the Jesuit colleges were strictly regulated. An ordinance of Fr. Oliver Manare, visitor of the Rhine province, dated 1583, forbids the use of sacred vestments or vessels as stage properties, or the reproduction on the stage of holy ceremonies, and the singing of psalms or liturgical pieces. No priests or religious persons are allowed to act a part. Public performances should be authorized by the provincial, except in the case of an urgent order from the prince. All plays are to be examined in advance by the rector or the prefect of studies, so as to avoid — let the words be carefully noted — "anything silly, or unpolished, or lacking in gravity or seemliness." Yet Jesuit enthusiasm for letters in general, and for their embodiment of classical scholarship in the drama, prevailed in the long run; and some of the more stringent prescriptions were discarded. Female characters had been wholly barred at first. In 1603, the province of Upper Germany explained to the Father general that it was impossible not to introduce them, "whether in profane or in sacred comedies." Permission was given to do so with due moderation and decency. Later on it became a rule in German colleges that solemn performances should take place yearly or at any rate every three years.

In fact college drama, though this is not now generally realized, was to flourish astoundingly in the Jesuit houses, from the late sixteenth century to the suppression of the Society in the late eighteenth, and to play a first-rate part in the public and literary life of such towns as Paris. The plays drew large audiences, extending far beyond the immediate circle of acquaintance of the pupils, and including many noblemen and burghers. Plays were performed in every Jesuit college throughout Europe, from Düsseldorf in Germany to Coimbra in Portugal, and even in far-away Asia. *The Life of St. Francis Xavier* was put upon the stage, at the beginning of 1624, on the square before the church at Goa; and one hears of a Tamil version of *The Triumph of David over Goliath*, and even of a play called *Josaphat*, written in Tamil by the native author, Aroulanda, both of these being acted in Pondicherry.

Such outstanding success is not due to any strikingly new departure in the dramatic technique of the Jesuits. Their part, in this respect, was exactly the same as in the case of other literary forms. They invented nothing, but they adapted to a religious purpose the *genres* that were already extant. They brought back to moral purity and classical good taste the stage which in the early sixteenth century had been reveling in the full exuberance of Renaissance paganism. Their purpose is clearly outlined in a document of the province of the Upper Rhine, dated 1619:

"Let all plays be suited to the end intended by the Society, to wit, to move men's souls to detest lewd manners and perverted habits, to flee from the occasion of sin, to apply themselves to virtue, to imitate the saints. If the lives of these are represented upon the stage, let not those things, which they did worthily and holily, and which can serve as a model, be treated meagrely and casually, while ridiculous fancies, which are not in point, and childish trifles, are dealt with at full length."

The whole of the moral and literary ideal of classicism is found in the above words, as it was to appear in the plays of Corneille: heroic devotion to duty as expressed in the themes of the plays, soberness and tastefulness in the handling of the subject. Subsidiary motives also induced Jesuit educators to foster the practice of college theatricals. Their pupils, they thought, would learn on the stage how to deport themselves in public and private life, at once boldly and modestly; they would be helped in their study of rhetoric, train their memory, improve their delivery, develop their intelligence and taste; not to mention that they would be prone to imitate the noble characters whom they impersonated.

Thus did the drama gradually assume a prominent part in the life of the Jesuit and also of the Oratorian colleges. It was, however, no new departure, and here again, the Jesuits merely expanded the work which had been begun by the Christian humanists who, early in the century, had begun a reaction against the licentiousness of the stage. In 1537, Nicholas Bartholeaeus, prior of Notre-Dame de Bonne Nouvelle at Orleans, had his scholars perform his devout play, *Christus Xylonicus* (*Christ on the Cross*). The Protestants also turned the drama to religious purposes; they were early in the field with Theodore de Beze's *Sacrifice of Abraham*, a tragedy with a chorus, performed by students at Lausanne and Geneva in 1552, and with the *Holy Tragedies* of Desmazures (*David*, 1556). In 1544, Montaigne, who was a pupil at the Collège de Guyenne in Bordeaux, had acted a part there, at the age of eleven, in a pious tragedy of George Buchanan, entitled *Jephthes*. It is only in 1558 that we meet with the performance of a play in a Jesuit house at Billom; in 1570, Fr. Luis da Cruz's *Sedecias* was performed in Coimbra; while in 1579, on commencement day at the Collège de Clermont in Paris, a tragedy called *Herod* was acted "to the edification of all and the admiration of most people."

Such "admiration" the Jesuits did their best to obtain, once they had become convinced of the usefulness of college plays; and they had recourse to every resource which the stage put at their disposal, to please the eye and move the heart of the spectators. This was not done, however, in a uniform way, and one meets in Jesuit drama with the most varied kinds of inspiration and technique, ranging from blood-and-thunder Elizabethanism to the soberest French classicism. The chief models were, of course, sought in antiquity, Seneca for tragedy, for comedy Terence and Plautus — preferably Plautus, who was said to be more "moral." But there was considerable freedom in the imitation of the ancients. Verse was generally used — verse of a kind at any rate, which scarcely lends itself to scansion. Yet prose also occasionally appears, and there is an *actio oratoria* by Fr. Nicholas Caussin, *Hermenegildus,* in which the author, in his dedication to Cardinal Henry de Gondi, justifies his use of the *soluta oratio* on account of its greater freedom and naturalness. Various means were used to relieve the attention of the spectators: comedy was mixed with tragedy; interludes were introduced, in which the moral sense of the play was made clear; there were sometimes pantomimes, and, in the French province especially, extensive use was made of the ballet. The chorus played an important part in most plays. On one point only was there uniformity — though even here exceptions might be found: love between man and woman was not to be represented on the stage.

The themes were no less varied than the dramatic technique. Many, especially at the outset, were borrowed from the Old Testament, such as Luis da Cruz's *Sedecias* or *Jerusalem falling to Nabuckodonosor* and others. Other subjects were taken out of Church history, from the earliest times down to the sixteenth century. To this class belong the "martyrdom" plays, which culminated in Corneille's *Polyeucte:* Caussin's *Felicitas,* the story of St. Felicity and her seven sons; the same writer's *Hermenegildus,* a tale of the Goths and Arianism, in which two martyrs, having rejected the heresy, lay down their lives; Bernardinus Stephonius' *Flavia,* which recounts the persecution under Domitian. But there was no objection to lay subjects as long as they were treated in the proper spirit, and excursions were often made into the realm of secular history, medieval or contemporary.* Others had a purely abstract and allegorical character, such as *The Angel of Peace, On the Lord's Supper, Peace and Religion the Foundation of States.*

When one attempts to sort out those numberless Jesuit plays they seem to fall into classes, according to the countries in which they were written. There is such a thing as Italian Jesuit drama, German Jesuit drama, French Jesuit drama. If we are to judge from the plays performed at the Roman College, the stress was laid there upon the external side of the show more than on its psychological or even its properly

---

* We find in Germany two plays bearing on the Anglo-Saxon period, *Edvinus, king in England,* and *Humphredus,* and one on the reign of Edward VI, *John Dudley's Baleful Ambition;* also plays on *Conrad of Bavaria and Frederick of Austria, Hunyades and Ladislaus,* and *The Abdication of the Emperor Charles V.*

devotional value. Take for instance a tragedy in five acts, there performed five times before 1629, and "always favorably received," the *Suevia* (Souabe) of Alexander Donatus. The subject is grounded on historical data, but these have been largely modified to satisfy the tastes of an Italian audience. It is a dark and sinister story, in which the villain is a famous medieval character, Manfred, natural son of Emperor Frederick II. His machinations end in the beheading of his half-brother, Jordanus, and in the poisoning of the emperor himself. The devotional element is practically absent, except in the lines sung by the chorus at the end of Act II, when it warns men not to seek perishable kingdoms, but eternal ones instead. The action is intricate and slow, and recourse is had, to awaken and keep the interest of the spectators, to all kinds of outward means. The supernatural element is introduced. At the beginning of Act I, St. Peter Morone, the hermit, is wending his way along the stage, when Celestial Justice is seen to descend from heaven with her companions; St. Peter is rapt into ecstasy, while angels sing around him. Later, he is favored with a vision of the papal tiara and of the imperial crown, still in the midst of singing. Pageantry is largely resorted to. The Emperor and his son are seen entering the city of Naples on a chariot, amidst the full pomp of triumph, surrounded by generals, soldiers, the prefect of the town, and senators. Later on, triumphal games are exhibited, including a bout of fencing with spears.

The same partiality for the externals of the drama is met with in another five-act tragedy, several times performed at the Roman College in 1621, the *Flavia* of Bernardinus Stephonius. The villain now is the philosopher and magician, Appollonius Tyaneus, who induces the Emperor Domitian to put to death his cousin, Clemens, and the latter's two sons, because they refuse to abjure the Christian faith. The action is simple, but is made to lend itself to scenic display in a succession of tableaux surrounded with elaborate scenery. In Act I, Apollonius conjures up sixteen infernal assistants; then the scene is shifted so as to represent a "horrid solitude; here takes place an earthquake, and darkness falls; the barking of dogs is heard; flames are seen to rise from slits in the floor. Then, through the mouth of a cavern, various monsters come forward: Cerberi, hydrae, centaurs, dragons, harpies, etc." After they have left the stage, "sixteen young lads come in Aethiopian dress, for a display of games." Later on, the prefect of Rome musters his troops and the Emperor reviews them. It should be said, however, that, side by side with all that pageantry there is real pathos in the scenes in which Apollonius vainly tries to persuade his victims to renounce Christ.

As for the plays performed in the German province, their authors seem to have been occasionally partial to grotesqueness, quaintness, and buffoonery. In the directions provided for them by their Jesuit superiors, there are repeated warnings against scurrility, against the introduction of "demons, beggars, drunkards, blasphemers, fools, etc." That these cautions were not always attended to is proved by the three-act comedy of *Mopsus*. The hero, who goes by that name, is a drunken peasant. While he is dozing off his liquor in the gutter, he is picked up by the courtiers of the duke of Holland. They persuade him, on the next morning, that *he* is the duke, and he spends one day amidst the splendors of the court. He again drinks himself to sleep, and is taken back to the filth of the street, where he awakes to reality. In the first act he is seen at his potations, together with other tipplers; and in the third act, he is tipsy again. The moral lesson to be derived from the play is nevertheless clear: it shows how empty are worldly honors and pleasures. Nor should we think that *Mopsus* is the type of all German plays, many of which fall into the "martyrdom" class.

As to the French Jesuit theater, it did not from the very first produce full-blown classical plays of the type which has been made familiar to us by the works of Corneille and Racine. Fr. Caussin's *Theodoricus* (published in 1620), for instance, is in many respects reminiscent of Shakespeare — though we cannot say whether this is a case of direct influence. The plot is borrowed from Procopius and St. Gregory, and bears on the history of Gothic rule in Rome: it is the story of the philosopher, Boetius, and his son, Symmachus, falsely charged with treason by two courtiers of King Theodoric, and unjustly put to death. The subject is not in itself a Christian one, yet it is made so from the fact that Theodoric, contrary to truth, is represented as a pagan; and therefore the play offers every characteristic of the "martyrdom" class, especially in the scenes which take place in Boetius' prison, in which Theodoric threatens the philosopher, and his wife, Elpidia, expostulates with him. The action is limited to the second, third, and fourth acts, and ends in a Shakespearian way, with the madness of Theodoric. The king takes a turbot's head, which is served to him on a dish, for the head of Symmachus; he is laid on his bed, where the ghosts of his two victims, accompanied by a good genius, surround him, until he dies. At the same time, more classical elements appear. The execution of Boetius and Symmachus is not performed upon the stage, but related by a messenger. Allegory occupies an important place. The first act takes place in heaven, where Nemesis beseeches divine justice to wreck vengeance on Theodoric for having brought about the death of Pope John in a dungeon; and the fifth act is laid in heaven as well, and displays the judgment of the king, in the presence of his victims.

The chief beauty of the play, however, does not reside in scenic effects, but in the real pathos of the prison scenes. In the dialogue between Theodoric, Boetius, and Symmachus, we find that brisk word-fencing, that thrust and parry of brief questions and retorts, which was later to be used so effectively in Corneille's *Cid*. Theodoric threatens the philosopher, who, it must be remembered, was a state dignitary, and his son, with imminent death:

> BOETIUS: Words! Words!
> THEODORIC: Yet they will take effect!
> BOETIUS: As fits a tyrant, methinks, thou wilt act;
>   Whatever fits a senator, I shall suffer.
> THEODORIC: A noble speech indeed!
> BOETIUS: I'll stand true to it.
> THEODORIC: Wilt thou then try?
> BOETIUS: I'm ready when thou wilt.
>   Thou canst do much, but I can suffer more.

The same kind of word-play is found in the same author's *Nabucho-donosor*, when the Babylonian king threatens the four young Hebrews with torture if they refuse to worship his statue:

> MISAEL: Reason, and our laws too, forbid such deeds.
> NABU.:   But *I* command them, who am above your laws.
> AZARIAS: It is thy part
>   To order what thou wilt, but it is ours
>   To obey God.
> ANANIAS: A thousand times rather die
>   Than stoop to foul unholy sacrifices.
> NABU.:   Generous words indeed; but racks and fires
>   Will damp your contumacious spirits soon.
> MISAEL: Wilt thou then try what heart lies here concealed?
>   Tear up my body!

In Corneille's *Cid*, Rodrigue was to say:

> To high-born souls,
> Valour does not await the lapse of years.

One is struck when finding, sixteen years before, in *Nabuchodonosor*, words which are practically to the same effect, when Misael encourages his brother, Ananias, to die with him:

ANANIAS: O worthy soul, thou oughtest thus to speak.
Thy words surprise me not, but I felt pity
For thy young age.
MISAEL: Far older than my years
Is God, who breathed his strength into my breast.

The lyrical parts of the Jesuit plays are often moving, despite their preciosity. Ananias, in his prison, welcomes death in the following beautiful words:

O Death, thou sole fulfilment of my wishes . . .
O happy Death, thou sweet path towards Heaven,
Thou breakest prison doors, and royal threats,
Thou lettest not the pious feel thy dint.
'T is sweet and beautiful to die for God.
O Sion's youth, thy fathers' courage learn,
Learn how to seek thy trophy in the flames;
'T is sweet and beautiful to die for God.

The reminiscence of Horace's *Dulce et decorum* is used here to good effect as a preparative for martyrdom. There is enthusiasm also in other words of Ananias, which must have found a ready echo, at a time when so many young men were laying down their lives for their faith, in England and in the East:

They threaten me with blows and awful fires;
My enemies think they threaten, yet they please.
Shalt thou then die? But 'tis the law of God!
Shalt give thy life? Thou'lt give it back to God!
In thy first flower? The gardener plucks the buds!
Before thy time? Who dies thus is of age
Mature enough! To a burning pyre shalt rush?
'Tis hard, I know, but yet a happy evil . . .

Indeed, one cannot insist too much on the ardent spirit of self-devotion which is breathed by the drama of the Catholic Reformation. Further examples may be found in *Felicitas,* another tragedy of Fr. Caussin — though they might also be sought in the works of other French Jesuits dramatists, such as Fr. Cellot and Fr. Pétau.

*   *   *

Turning now to Corneille's masterpiece, *Polyeucte* (1643), one is immediately struck, despite some differences, by its unmistakable likeness with the Jesuit tragedies, in both form and matter. Nor is this surprising, if we consider Corneille's upbringing. Pierre Corneille, who was born at Rouen in Normandy in 1606, spent seven years (1615–1622) at the Jesuit college of that city. He was awarded two prizes for Latin verse in the third form and in the "Rhetoric." Now, the prize winners were generally selected to act parts in the performances of the Latin plays; and though we lack precise information on the point, there is every reason to believe that young Corneille was asked to do so. It is besides quite likely that his professor of rhetoric, Fr. Delidel, was the author of a play, *Arsaces,* performed at the Collège de Clermont in Paris in 1630. Corneille himself, in his commendatory lines prefixed to Fr. Delidel's *Treatise on the Theology of the Saints,* wrote as follows:

> What I write, that pleases, if it please, is wholly thine.

What is more, another Jesuit master of Rouen college, Fr. de la Rue, indited in 1669 a Latin epistle to "the most illustrious Corneille, the prince of tragic poets," in which he clearly assumes that the latter's purpose in writing his tragedies was the same as that of the Jesuit dramatists. Corneille may thus justifiably be considered as the greatest tragic poet of the Jesuit school, and his *Polyeucte* as the direct consequence of the Catholic Reformation, and the highest point reached by it in the field of literature.

The subject of the play is a well-known one. Pauline, the daughter of Félix, the Roman governor of Armenia, has been in love with a young Roman officer and courtier, Sévère; but as the latter is thought to have died in battle, she has married an Armenian nobleman of high rank, Polyeucte. The latter is won over to Christianity by his friend Néarque. Sévère has meanwhile reappeared, in the character of a general and a favorite of the emperor, hoping to marry Pauline. He is, of course, greatly disappointed to find her the wife of another man. Polyeucte, burning with his new zeal, induces the reluctant Néarque to come and join him in smashing up the heathen idols at a public sacrifice. Félix immediately orders Néarque put to death, but strives to persuade Polyeucte to recant in order to save his life. However, Polyeucte is absolutely proof against threats, flattery, and the entreaties of his wife; he desires Félix to have him executed, and invites Pauline and Sévère to join in wedlock and live happily after his own disappearance. He reaps the crown of martyrdom, but his constancy and magnanimity have not been useless: Félix and Pauline become Christians, and Sévère himself agrees to use his influence in order to obtain from the emperor a relaxing of the persecution.

Despite the introduction of the theme of human love, such a play is strikingly akin to the Jesuit tragedies. We find in it the same heroic tone. Pauline confesses to her confidante, Stratonice, at once her past love for Sévère and her determination to fight it down:

'T is but in such attacks that virtue shines,
And hearts that have not fought should not be trusted.

The outward form is also very much alike, with the same type of oratory — rhetorical tirades alternating with brisk dialogues, such as the beautiful passage in the fourth act, where Polyeucte is deaf to the entreaties of Pauline:

PAULINE: Renounce your fancy, dear, and love me.
POLYEUCTE: I love you,
Far less than God, but than myself far more.
PAULINE: For sweet love's sake, I pray, forsake me not.
POLYEUCTE: For sweet love's sake, I pray, follow my steps.
PAULINE: 'T is not enough to leave me, you'll seduce me?
POLYEUCTE: 'T is not enough to go to Heaven, if alone.
PAULINE: Mere dreams and fancies!
POLYEUCTE: No, celestial truths!
PAULINE: A blindness strange indeed!
POLYEUCTE: Eternal lights!
PAULINE: Prefer you death to Pauline's ardent love?
POLYEUCTE: Prefer you then the world to God above?
PAULINE: You cruel, go and die: you never loved me.
POLYEUCTE: Live happy in the world, and leave me peace.

The same dramatic motives appear in *Polyeucte* as in the Jesuit plays. Félix's menancing and cajoling, Pauline's beseeching, reminds us of the prison scenes in *Hermenegildus* or *Flavia*. Polyeucte's famous lyrical stanzas are not unlike Boetius' song in his dungeon. The theme of love itself is handled in a way which suggests St. Ignatius' "voluntarist" conception of man's moral life. Pauline refuses to give way to her natural instinct, which yearns for union with Sévère. She *will* love her husband, and she is successful in her efforts, since she cherishes him enough to wish to die with him, and flatly rejects the temptation to accept his proposal and take advantage of his death to marry Sévère. In Polyeucte's reply to her entreaties, one senses the influence of St. Ignatius' *Exercises*. The following lines are almost a verse paraphrase of the passages referring to "election."

Ambition's mine, but nobler, higher far.
Earth's greatness dies, I want eternal greatness,
Assured happiness, unmeasured, endless,
Secure above begrudging, above Fate.
Is, then, a sorry life too much to pay,
Which of a sudden, soon, may slip from me,
Which but one fleeting moment I enjoy,
Ne'er sure that other moments are to follow.

More might be said on the same subject. Corneille's idea on the co-operation between God and man in the work of grace, his insistence on divine love, his practical-mindedness in the face of temptation, all betray the influence of the Ignatian school. One might go further, and see in the utter chivalrousness of the great poet's characters a reflection of the knightly spirit of St. Ignatius himself. In any case, the heroic mood of Corneille in his tragedies suited the public of his own time; it testifies to the general temper of the period, which, as will be seen in other ways, manifests the conquering ardor of the Catholic Reformation. Thus did the latter, though hampered by the artificial side of neo-classicism, introduce an original element into literature, and produce some of the greatest works of all time.

CHAPTER IX

The Catholic Reformation and Art

IS ONE at all justified in speaking of the art of the Catholic Reformation? Doubts have been expressed on that score, and to some extent rightly so: for in technique, no original development appears as a consequence of the Trentine movement. The latter has often, it is true, been identified with neoclassicalism; but the "Jesuit" style of architecture, for instance, was no more a creation of the Society of Jesus than the Ciceronian style in letters. In either case current modes of artistic expression were adopted and adapted to serve an essentially religious purpose. But this very purpose is the reason why, in another respect, Trentine art may be said to be truly original; for while its outward aspect really belongs to the period, its inward and spiritual substance, its inspiration and subject-matter are wholly new. Nor could this be otherwise, since the work done at Trent consisted in breaking with the traditions of the Renaissance.

Indeed the reaction of the Council against the prevalent paganism was so strong that one may well wonder that art should have found any favor in its eyes. The Fathers looked askance even at the most spiritual of all forms of expression, Church music. The spirit of Paul IV, the spirit of the Theatines, was really rigid. As it was, the Council was wise enough to refrain from any sweeping condemnation. But the art which followed in its wake bore the mark of its temper. One of its most characteristic features in painting, sculpture, architecture, as well as music, is its austereness, its severity, its simplicity and concentration, its truly classical restraint. Another feature is the extraordinary intensity of its religious feeling, its spiritual depth and power, which really hark back to the Middle Ages. It is true that the Trentine movement, however fervent its inspiration, never attained to the sublime elevation of medieval art; that it developed in a period of conventions and theatricality which were averse to spontaneity and sincerity. Nevertheless, it produced works of great beauty, the value of which is due, less to the style of the moment than to the devotional feelings which they express.

Trentine art coincides in its duration with the Catholic Reformation properly so called, that is to say the period of remorsefulness for Renaissance paganism, of sadness over the woes of the Church. This period ended in Italy when peace and prosperity were restored in the early seventeenth century, and austerity and simplicity made way for the lusciousness and overdecoration of Bernini's art. In this respect as in others, the fashion spread with some delay, and in France it is only about 1650 that the soberness of the Louis XIII style was superseded by the sumptuous luxuriousness of Louis XIV's reign. A clear distinction should be made between Trentine art, which is sober and controlled, and the later exuberance of the "baroque." The former was the outcome of the work of moral reformation and theological consolidation performed by the popes; its fountainhead was in Rome, and it is from Rome that its study must start. First of all, however, it will be necessary to examine the general principles which served as guides. Though the underlying base be the same, those principles vary according as they are applied to the various forms of art, and we shall have to consider in succession painting and sculpture, architecture, and music.

*   *   *

The Council of Trent was not concerned with painting and sculpture as such, yet it had to establish dogma in regard to the worship and the images of saints, and consequently to decide whether and how the latter should be made the object of artistic representation. The question of images had been the subject of a standing debate between Catholics and Protestants. The more extreme among the latter requested their total suppression, thus aiming a death-blow at religious art. The first point, therefore, was for the Council to assert that images might legitimately be used. Its decree runs as follows:

"Let the bishops diligently teach that the story of the mysteries of our Redemption, expressed by paintings or other representations, instructs and confirms the people in remembering and assiduously rehearsing the articles of the faith; that sacred images are the source of great spiritual profit, not only because the people are thus reminded of the blessings and help which Christ has granted them, but also because the marvels and wholesome examples of God are through his saints placed before the eyes of the faithful, so that they may thank God for them, and rule their life and manners after those of the saints, and may be incited to worship and love God, and cultivate piety."

The passage is important. It assigns a religious purpose to the arts of painting and sculpture, and settles the direction they were to take after the Council of Trent. The latter did not go into particulars as to the means of reaching its aim. It was content to issue a general warning against the superstitions and abuses to which the worship of images might give rise. But its thought was interpreted by a number of theologians; and a developed theory of the art of religious painting and sculpture was expounded by Possevinus, in his *De Poesi et Pictura*.

The object of painting, Possevinus says, is like that of poetry, twofold, namely, utility and pleasure. Now, in order to be useful, painting must be true. "If it is," as St. George says, " 'the book of the unlearned,' what light can it provide if it be false?" The Protestants had frequently derided the legends mixed up with the Catholic worship of the saints. Such criticism would fall to the ground if historical truth was strictly adhered to. Possevinus complains of the painters who represent holy personages in a fanciful way and not according to sound tradition and reason. He provides several instances of what he qualifies as errors: the thieves crucified with Jesus are shown as tied with ropes, instead of being nailed to their crosses; St. Joseph standing near the crib and St. Peter standing near the cross appear as old men, whereas they ought to be young; the three Marys are painted as young girls; Mary Magdalen, at the Crucifixion, is bedecked with gems and precious clothes; St. Francis is well-combed, neat, elegant; St. Jerome wears a cardinal's red hat, a palpable anachronism; Christ on the cross seems neither sad nor afflicted.

Indeed, the painters reply, but when we show a serene, handsome, and elegant Christ, we attend to art primarily. And yet, Possevinus rejoins, the ancient Laocoon expresses pain. "I assert," he adds, "that the highest pitch of art consists in imitating reality, the martyrdoms of martyrs, the tears of those who weep, the pain of those who suffer, the glory and joy of those who come to life again."

Apocryphal Scriptures are not to be followed. In selecting themes, painters should consult first with theologians and historians. Nor should they be heedful of truth merely; they ought to respect the necessary rules of propriety in handling sacred subjects. In the Annunciation, the angel should not appear "head downwards like a dove flying and rushing down to earth, as if he were shaken out of a bag." In the Passion of Christ, one wishes "that the Angels were exerting themselves less, were not laboring with such efforts and gestures, to support the Cross, the pillar and other mystical objects so painfully. . . . More should be granted to the reverence which is due to an angel, than to art. . . ."

The third principle laid down by Possevinus is of no slight importance, and makes one understand why "expression" could be genuine in the plastic arts of the Catholic Reformation. It is necessary for the painter, he says, to feel the religious emotions which he represents. "In order that the most fatal death of Christ our Redeemer . . . should breed admiration and a sharp grief in others, it is needful that something in the soul of the painter should rouse the greatness of admiration and draw forth the rushing of grief." The artist should therefore meditate on the pains and constancy of Christ, and, "purify his soul by means of the Sacraments."

Last of all, Possevinus forbids the painting or carving of lascivious and pagan images, the two being for him one and the same thing. The first petition of the Lord's prayer, he says, is not satisfied when "shameful images" are represented. The saints are displeased to see "Jupiters, Venuses, and other unclean beings recalled from the infernal regions," when they have shed their blood to destroy them.

And here follows an illuminating description of the state of things prevalent in sixteenth-century Italy, which the Trentine movement had set out to amend. The demons, we are told, furious at being ousted from the Indies where pagodas and idols are being abolished, have tried two engines in Europe: unchaste books and lewd philosophy on the one hand, and on the other "outrageous images of nude women, of Fauns and Satyrs, infamous statues, and even fragments of idols dug out of the bowels of the earth; the which being placed on the front of houses, on towers, in the mansions of noblemen, in the innermost part of their dwellings, renew the memory of those who are confined to the eternal fires, restoring whatever was most pagan. Meanwhile the images of saints and holy mysteries of our Lord were being painted either without dignity, or for the sake of fancy rather than piety, or were placed among the images of false gods, so that religion itself was gradually removed from the souls of many."

Possevinus obviously considers the pagan sensuousness of the Renaissance as a very real danger. The setting up of heathen images, he says, is contrary to the will of the early Christians and of the holy popes. Pius V had such images removed from the Vatican; Sixtus V ordered them to be flung down from the tower of the Capitol. Besides, nudes are unchaste. No man, if he be at all virtuous, will dare to look at them. They breed sensuousness in the heart of the painter himself. They ought to be done away with at all costs. There is little to be added to Possevinus' disquisition in regard to the principles underlying the art of the Catholic Reformation. Painting and sculpture should first of all be inspired, be the outcome of the artist's own devotional upbringing and preparation; they should be moral, decent, and restrained, free from any pagan lasciviousness; they should be scrupulously true, to the extent of falling into realism; last of all, they should be Christian in regard to their themes and spirit. How these principles were applied, is now to be seen.

There is no doubt as to the fact that the artists of the Catholic Reformation, unlike those of the Renaissance, were deeply imbued with Christian devoutness. Indeed, several among them shared in the common remorsefulness of Catholic Christendom. The Italian painter, Agostino Carracci (1557–1602), whose past life had not been blameless, spent his last days with the Capuchins of Bologna, meditating, praying, and painting a picture of St. Peter lamenting his sins. Others spent their whole lifetime in piety. Il Domenechino (1581–1641) never began the picture of a saint without first praying to him. The French painter, Callot (1592–1635), would preface his working day with attendance at Mass.

But it was in Spain, in the country and at the time of the great mystics, that the artists most definitely drank in their inspiration at religious springs. Murillo (1617–1682) knew scarcely anything of the world but convents and churches. He belonged to that austere brotherhood of charity at Seville, the members of which bound themselves to gather in the bodies of drowned men, to bury those who had been murdered, and assist those who were sentenced to death at their last moments. In his will he requested four hundred Masses for the rest of his soul, and his tombstone bore the inscription: "Live in the thought of death." In the same country, many among the artists were monks who undertook the decoration of their own convents. There were painters among the religious in Italy and France also, though fewer of them.

The devotional mood of the artists accounts for the reappearance of certain elements of inspiration which dated back to the Middle Ages and had wholly disappeared from Italy during the Renaissance. The fifteenth century had been deeply absorbed in the thought of death; many of its *danses macabres* are still extant at the present time. Now the thoughts of the Catholic reformers had been turned by the evils of the times into grave and severe channels; and one need not wonder at their partiality for the meditation of the "four last things," which as a matter of fact had been recommended by St. Ignatius in his *Exercises,* and which they handled with an exalted and stormy sensibility strongly reminiscent of the late medieval period. This appears especially in the decoration of tombstones. The Renaissance had not expressed man's anguish in the presence of death, but a restfulness and serenity suggestive of ancient philosophy. In the former cloister of the Augustinian monks in Rome is the tomb of Cardinal Sclafenati, who died in 1451. It bears the following Greek inscription: "Why fear death, which brings us rest?" while another tomb in the same place, that of bishop Ottaviano Fornari, is inscribed with these words: "For thee the strife is now overpast, and the plentiful sweating of the fight." Christian prelates of the Renaissance viewed death like the wise men of ancient Greece, as a sweet repose after life's struggle.

A change took place as early as the time of the Lateran Council, and death's heads began to appear on the graves. After the Council of Trent, such representations no longer are exceptions, but the rule. They tally with the spirit of the devotional works of the period. The epitaphs on gravestones now express serious thoughts, such as "Here lies dust, and nothing more" (tomb of Cardinal Barberini in the church of the Capuchins at Rome), or "My turn yesterday, thine today." Many saints are now represented as holding a death's head in their hands and meditating over it. In the paintings of El Greco, of Zurbaran, of Caravaggio, St. Francis of Assisi no longer appears as the cheerful saint, the enraptured worshipper of God in his natural creatures, but as a lean, swarthy ascete, deeply absorbed in the contemplation of man's last end. Kindred transformations take place for St. Catherine of Siena and St. Mary Magdalen.

In the seventeenth century, whole skeletons appear in the stead of mere skulls on gravestones. Death is also represented in engravings and pictures, which become a major help to pious reflection. Thus did the spirit of the Catholic Reformation link up with that of the late Middle Ages, which as a matter of fact, in Northern Europe had never wholly died out.

In regard, not to death, but to the images of living saints, the same contrast appears between the Renaissance and the Catholic Reformation. The artists of the former painted Holy Families, for instance, as very near to common mankind, in an atmosphere of peaceful, serene, harmonious love, in the clear, sunny light of southern skies. The painting and sculpture of the Catholic Reformation no longer express contentedness and repose, but the upward, unsatisfied cravings of the soul, its dolorous striving to lose itself in God; the skies are now stormy and overcast, with dramatic effects of light and shadow. Art, in this respect, is but the reflection of the religious spirit of the period.

Never had there been such a profusion of mystics favored with visions and ecstasies. "The saints of the Middle Ages," Mr. Mâle says, "used to work miracles; those of the Catholic Reformation were themselves miracles." St. Ignatius Loyola, St. Philip Neri, St. Teresa, St. John of the Cross had mystical experiences of the highest order. Their lives and spiritual yearnings were represented by painters in a dramatic and concentrated fashion. In the fourteenth century, saintly women had been charmingly shown as engaged in homely occupations, drawing water at the well, bringing a cake to a sick woman, greeting a traveller at the monastery gates. Now they appear as wholly detached from this world, and as ecstatically beholding Christ, the Virgin, or the saints. Giotto had shown St. Francis of Assisi in the main scenes of his history, giving back his clothes to his father in the square of his town, announcing the Gospel before the Sultan of Egypt, preaching to the birds. Now, on the contrary, his life is limited to two or three scenes of ecstasy, as when he is represented as receiving into his arms the infant Christ from the Virgin Mary, in the picture by Orazio Borgiani (municipal palace at Sezze). The intentness of his gaze, the upward straining of his whole body, the supernatural light and the deep shadows, make this picture a typical work of the Catholic Reformation.

*   *   *

The second principle laid down by Possevinus is that Christian art should be, not merely chaste, but decent and dignified. We have already referred to the steps taken by the popes to counteract the moral vagaries of the Renaissance. As early as 1559, within the lifetime of Michaelangelo, Paul IV had some of the figures of the *Last Judgment* clothed in the Sistine Chapel. This work was continued by Pius V in 1566, and Clement VIII was only prevented from covering up the whole fresco by a supplication of the Academy of St. Luke. In Flanders the bishop of Ghent, James Boonen, had all indecent pictures burned and all indecent statues destroyed. The remorsefulness of the Church at large was shared by individual artists. The sculptor, Bartolomeo Ammanati, who died in 1589, toward the end of his life, wrote a letter expressive of this feeling to the Academy of Florence. He renounced the errors of his youth, and invited his fellow-artists to give up the carving of nudes. However, one should be thankful that the action of the popes was not unreasonably drastic.

But it was not enough to decide that religious subjects should be handled in a chaste mood. Needless fancifulness, the free roaming of the imagination, homeliness and vulgarity interfered with the singleness of purpose which is requisite in devotional paintings. They were to be dispensed with. In 1573, Paolo Veronese, the Venetian painter, had to answer before the Holy Office for having introduced into one of his *Lord's Supper's* figures unworthy of the dignity of his subject. "What is the point," he was asked, "of that servant whose nose is bleeding; of those armed men, dressed in the German fashion, and holding halberts in their hands?" Veronese, unable to justify himself, was sentenced to amend his picture within the space of three months. St. Ignatius had advised his disciples to concentrate their minds on the object of their meditation. Similarly, in a religious picture, nothing is now to distract attention from its main theme. This aversion from what might be called garrulousness in painting is quite in keeping with the austere moral ideal of the period and with the classical ideal in letters, that of noble, composed dignity. Carvaggio's pictures were repeatedly rejected by the Church, as being vulgar and "low." His St. Matthew (Church of St. Louis des Français, Rome) was found fault with for "coarsely showing his feet." It must be confessed, however, that on this point the art critics of the Catholic Reformation lacked breadth of outlook, and the stress they laid on "decency" eventually meant impoverishment of the art of painting.

In their eyes, a picture, like a poem, was meant primarily not to please or amuse but to serve an edifying purpose. Therefore it ought to be scrupulously true. There were reasons why exact truth should be adhered to in the painting of martyrdoms. In Rome, in the late sixteenth century, many among the clergy were daily called upon to endanger their own lives. Missionaries were being sent to England, where the persecution was raging, or to the East and West Indies, where dangers also threatened. It was necessary that they be forewarned of the fate which awaited them, and trained to long for it with their inmost souls. No wonder, therefore, that artists should have taken Possevinus' advice, and exactly represented the sufferings of early or contemporary martyrs, however horrible or frightful they might be. In 1585, Il Pomarancio painted, at the German college in Rome, some thirty frescoes representing the history of the persecutions. The most hideous torments are offered to the spectator's view. Christians, wrapped up in beasts' skins, are torn apart by dogs; others are cast alive into a furnace or into molten lead or cut into pieces or crushed with huge stones; women have their breasts cut away. The same graphic realism appears in a famous book of engravings, published in 1587 through the agency of the Jesuits, the *Theatrum crudelitatum haereticorum* (*Theatre of the Cruelties of the Heretics*) which represents contemporary martyrdoms in various countries of

Europe. It was meant to be broadcast and did in fact attain wide popularity. It represents torments which had been unknown to antiquity: a priest crucified by the Huguenots on the altar cross; religious buried up to their necks, their heads being used as targets in a game of bowls.

Painters and sculptors were guided in their presentation of martyrdoms by the discovery of the catacombs in Rome in 1578, which provided them with accurate notions on the primitive Church; also by printed works on the subject, the chief among these being Baronius' *Annales ecclesiastici,* which were published from 1588 onwards. They sought advice from competent historians. Baronius, in his *Martyrologium Romanum,* explains how St. Sebastian was tied to a post underneath an inscription which described him as a Christian. Now, Il Domenechino painted the martyr in that very position, with a board above his head on which are written the words *"Sebastianus Christianus."* The same painter, in his *Flagellation of St. Andrew,* depicted his soldiers and lictors as they are on the column of Trajan. A sober knowledge of antiquity now replaces the fancifulness of the early sixteenth century in which martyr virgins and torturing praetors wore the court dress of the period.

It should not be thought, however, that this new historical sense among the artists did away with all the legendary traditions which had lent naïve charm to religious painting and sculpture. Here again, the Catholic Reformation joined up, beyond the Renaissance, with the Middle Ages. Baronius himself refrained from extreme criticism of the fifteenth-century *Sanctuarium* of Mombritius, containing the *Acts* of the Roman martyrs. He expressed his belief in the legend of SS. Nereus and Achilleus by having it painted in a series of frescoes in the church which bears their name in Rome, which he himself had restored. Other cardinals showed the same respect for the *Acts.* In 1624 Cardinal Mellini gave orders for the decoration of the church of the Four Crowned Saints, which stands on the Monte Celio in Rome. The frescoes, painted by Giovanni da San Giovanni, tell the fanciful story of four Roman soldiers who had refused, in the Thermae of Trajan, to burn incense before the statue of Aesculapius, and of five Pannonian sculptors who had refused to work on the statue of the same god. In their church of the Gesù, in Rome, the Jesuits had the martyrdom of St. Catherine represented according to the *Golden Legend:* the wheel on which the saint has been racked bursts out and kills her tormentors. Thus were medieval traditions continued by the Catholic Reformation.

There is, however, a striking difference in the representation of martyrdoms between the Middle Ages and the late sixteenth century.

The former had shown the martyrs as triumphant, in the majestic calm of victory. The latter shows them in their struggles, their agonies, their torments, as in a series of engravings by Callot, in which St. Agatha has her breasts torn away, St. Edward has his throat cut, St. Fidelis is scourged, St. Dula stabbed, St. Dorothy branded. The Catholic reformers believed in the value of suffering. The *Sacrum sanctuarium crucis et patientiae* of Fr. Biverus, S.J. (1634) carries a set of engravings of all saints who have been crucified, as a means of exhortation to the sick. The very violence of the pictures of martyrdom was thus made to become a solace for the Christians of the times.

However, for the Catholic reformers, the purpose of the images of saints was not merely to edify but also to instruct. They were to provide teaching for the faithful on points of dogma and religious practice. The age was a controversial one, in which Catholic belief had to be asserted against Protestant tenets; and there is a striking correspondence between the themes assigned to Catholic artists — which are uniform throughout Europe — and the decrees of the Council. Not only were the artists imbued with the spirit of the times, but precise directions were issued for them. In Austria, for instance, the Jesuits prepared a detailed program for the painters who were decorating their church at Brünn: a chapel was devoted to the Cross, and to the symbols which announced it in the Old Testament: Moses' rod, the staff with the cluster of grapes, the pole and brass serpent.

The Council had defended devotion to the Virgin Mary against Protestant attacks. As a consequence of its action, there was a flowering forth of Marian literature and Marian art. The Virgin is no longer represented with her medieval serenity, but as taking part in the victorious struggle against heresy. In a fresco of Il Cavaliere d'Arpino, in the Pauline chapel of Santa Maria Maggiore, St. Gregory Thaumaturgus, the former disciple of Origen, is shown to hesitate on the doctrine he is teaching when the Virgin appears to him, to reveal to him the true symbol of the Catholic faith. The Jesuits and other religious orders promoted the belief in Mary's immaculate conception. This belief was similarly asserted by the artists who worked for them. In St. Peter's, in Rome, in one of the cupolas of the left-hand aisle, the Virgin is shown as conceived by the divine mind before the beginning of time; on the vault of San Carlo a Corso, a fresco of Giacinto Brandi shows her praying to God during the strife between St. Michael and Lucifer.

Protestant attacks had not been directed merely against veneration of the Holy Virgin and the saints. They were aimed at the authority of

the papacy as well. Catholic controversialists, such as Bellarmine, defended it, and Catholic artists followed suit, with pictures and statues
which glorified the prince of the Apostles. In the church which bears
his name in Rome, the saint was shown as walking on the waters in response to the call of Christ (Lanfranc's mosaic) or, according to various
legendary traditions, as vanquishing Simon Magus (Vanni's mosaic), or
healing the sick with his shadow (Romanelli's picture), or meeting Christ
at the gates of Rome, in the famous *Quo vadis* story (Annibale Caracci's
painting in the National Gallery, London); all these episodes being
meant to illustrate his primacy. The history of the popes, which had been
told by Ciaconius in his *Vitae pontificum romanorum,* was illustrated on
the tombs of St. Peter's by many statues or bas-reliefs; in one of the
latter, the German Emperor is shown kneeling before Gregory VII at
Canossa.

As a consequence of their attack upon indulgences, the Protestants
had denied the dogma of purgatory. The artists of the Catholic Reformation defended it in their works. The bishop of Tournai ordered from
Rubens a picture for his cathedral, representing Judas Maccabeus praying for the dead. At the Gesù, in a fresco of Federico Zuccaro, angels
are seen lifting from a furnace little figures which represent souls, which
they offer to Christ and the Virgin. Such paintings were multiplied by the
confraternities which prayed for the dead, such as that of the church
of Santa Maria del Suffragio in Rome, which was founded in 1592. The
Catholic artists also vindicated the practice of confession in pictures and
statues which represented illustrious penitents. Just as David, St. Peter,
St. Mary Magdalen had been made the subjects of literary works expressive of the remorsefulness of the period, they appeared, on the sug-
gestion of the clergy in numberless works of art. St. Peter's remorse lent
itself to the somewhat theatrical treatment which tallied with contemporary tastes: the saint was shown, as in the painting by Guido
Reni, with clasped hands, a dolorous face, and eyes upturned to heaven.
In Paris, at the Carmelite church, twin statues represent St. Peter and
St. Mary Magdalen on either side of the transept altar.

The same apologetic part was played by the art of the Catholic Reformation in regard to the Real Presence and Communion. During the
Middle Ages, the *Lord's Supper* had been shown at the moment when
Christ utters the words: "One of you shall betray me!" From the sixteenth century onward, the moment selected for representation is that
of the institution of the Eucharist, when Christ says: "This is my body,"
as in Barocio's *Lord's Supper* at Santa Maria della Minerva in Rome.

Good works are no less frequently insisted on, as against the Protestant belief in justification by faith alone. One of the heroes of Christian charity in the Trentine period, St. Charles Borromeo, was made the subject of numerous pictures. Nor were traditional points of doctrine the only ones insisted on in the works of the artists of the Catholic Reformation. Further themes were provided by the devotions introduced or revived after Trent: that of the angels, and especially that of the Guardian Angel (which had appeared in 1526), of the Holy Family, of St. Joseph, of the Child Jesus.

Lastly, one should not forget the influence which the monastic renascence had upon art, each order decorating its churches with pictures referring to the history of its patron saints, or to the devotions which it particularly favored, such as that of the scapular in the case of the Carmelites.

*   *   *

Thus was art made to contribute to the success of the Trentine revival. The older schools, however, would have been unable to achieve such a result. In Florence, the art of Giotto and Fra. Angelico had been deeply modified in the fifteenth century, owing to the prosperity and worldliness of the city: in its quest for beauty alone, it had forgotten austerity and suffering, had become uniformly sweet and smiling. Religious pictures were made to represent modern life; much attention was paid to those accessories which the Catholic Reformation was to reject, and sacred figures were turned into portraits, as in the fresco of Benozzo Gozzoli (in the chapel of the Ricardi Palace) where the Medici appear as the Wise Men. The Venetian artists, proud of the glory of their city, followed in the footsteps of the Florentine school. At Rome, on the other hand, the atmosphere of the early sixteenth century had been one of battles and political struggles, and the arts of painting and sculpture had been led to glorify force, as in Michaelangelo's *Moses*. This tendency had gradually degenerated into mere worship of physical strength, and such a work as Vasari's *Last Judgment* is chiefly noteworthy for its muscularity. Anatomical science and academic frigidity had superseded the necessary spirituality of religious painting.

No one of the extant movements was therefore qualified to express the intensely devout feelings of the Catholic Reformation. This task was taken up by a new school of painting, which had its origin in Bologna, a city especially fitted for the part which it was to play as the artistic center of the Trentine revival. It was within the States of the Church, and thus within the area of papal influence; but it was far removed from the artistic atmosphere of Florence and Rome, while, through its nearness to Parma and Milan, it regained touch with the early Florentine tradition of Giotto, which had been continued in northern Italy by Leonardo da Vinci and Correggio. Besides, it was an intellectual center of the first magnitude. Its university vied in renown with that of Padua. As the saying went, *Bologna docet* (Bologna teaches). Therefore Bologna was a suitable center for a school of painting in which the mind was to prevail over the flesh, in which all forms were to concur in the expression of thought.

In fact, Bolognese painting was a typical instance of the adaptation of extant artistic forms to a religious purpose. Therefore it was distinguished by no outstanding technical originality. Its representatives were termed the "eclectics," and were said to have borrowed the drawing of the Florentines, the coloring of the Venetians, the modelling of Correggio. Their merit lay in choosing those themes which we have described above — clear, striking scenes of the Old and New Testaments, preferably selected among the more tragic ones, and those of martyrdoms. On the other hand, their main fault lay in the very fact that their works were more intellectual than plastic, and that they painted with their heads more than with their hearts. However, they found great favor with the Church, for they were less archaic than Giotto or Fra. Angelico, and more Christian than the painters of the Renaissance.

The Bolognese school was founded and made famous by the three Carracci brothers. Agostino Carracci illustrates the intellectual character of the movement. He was a learned man, and had studied in the University of Bologna. He established an academy for painters, that of the Desiderati, in which lectures were given on the most varied subjects, so as to provide a complete culture for its disciples. He himself was not primarily a painter, though a picture of his, the *Communion of St. Jerome,* became famous, and was imitated by Il Domenechino; but he was a distinguished engraver, who believed in the value of his art as a means of dissemination of religious knowledge. A second brother, Ludovico Carracci, was both a thinker and a realist. The third brother, Annibale Carracci, was the genius of the school. Their pupils, Guercino, Guido Reni, Lanfranc, L'Albano, Il Domenechino, came to the papal court, and were entrusted with the decoration of new churches. Their influence spread throughout Europe; they numbered among their disciples Poussin and Claude Lorrain in France; Ribera, Velasquez, and Murillo in Spain; and, in Flanders, Rubens and Van Dyck; while there **Rembrandt, though freer from Italian influences, gave the most exalted** expression to the spiritual ideal of the Catholic Reformation in such a picture as his *Pilgrims of Emmaus.*

In regard to sculpture, the Catholic reformers were, to begin with, hostile to an art which had chiefly flourished in the representation of nudes. This accounts for the disappearance of native sculptors from Rome, while foreigners, who were less attached to academic traditions, were called in. At the end of the sixteenth century, there resided in the Eternal city a good many sculptors who came from other Italian towns, or even from other countries, like the Frenchman, Guillaume Bertelot, or the Fleming, Nicholas of Arras. The same reversion to the Middle Ages occurred here as in painting; and a few clothed statues were carved, some of them beautiful, such as Stefano Maderno's *Saint Cecilia.* At the same time, the influence of the Bolognese school of painters was manifested in the reappearance of the bas-relief, to adorn the tombs of the popes. There had been two figures of women, but no bas-reliefs, on the tomb of Paul III; while they plentifully decorated those of Pius V, Sixtus V, Clement VIII, and Paul V, on which they displayed the acts and triumphs of the papacy. Thus did an age of intense religious fervor, controlled by the strict use of reason, evolve, in painting and sculpture, a form of art which was far removed from the servile imitation of antiquity, but which was truly classical in the sense that the seventeenth century gave to the word.

*   *   *

In the field of architecture, the same general features appear. Monuments built during the period of the Catholic Reformation proper bear a definite character of austerity and severity, of sadness and power — truly, the monuments of an age of remorse and painful striving. They embody the artistic forms of antiquity, but while during the Renaissance these had been but a veneer laid upon surfaces for a decorative purpose, they were now incorporated into an organic whole. This whole was true to the intellectual needs of an age of clear reason, of beauty intellectually conceived, with its straight lines, it symmetry, its lack of mysteriousness: but it was also to a large extent, especially in France and Flanders, true to the traditions of the Middle Ages, the yearning of which for spiritual heights was still expressed by the upward trend of nave and steeple. Again, though there were local differences, the common source of all the architecture of the Catholic Reformation was in Rome. The religious needs of the Trentine revival turned the popes of the late sixteenth century into great builders, whose example was followed everywhere.

Indeed, here as in letters or painting, it was the practical requirements of the period which dictated the lines along which current modes of artistic expression should be adapted. Numerous churches were needed, churches which should comply with the decrees of Trent on dogma and worship, which should lend themselves easily to the task of gathering and catechizing the greatest possible number of people. Those churches had to be built in a short time, with limited financial resources. Hence their plan had to be simple and practical. The Gothic style, especially in the flamboyant stage it had reached by the fifteenth century, with its window tracery and lace-like vault-groining, was both too elaborate and too expensive, and too fanciful, while Gothic churches, with their groves of pillars, their rood-screens, and their naves darkened by stained glass, neither allowed the congregation to take part in liturgical worship nor to hear the preachers from every part of the building.

Here, again, the lead was taken by the Jesuits, who provided models which were universally followed. The common source for all later building throughout Europe was their church of the Gesù, built by Vignole at Rome in 1568, while in France the chapel at the college at Le-Puy-en-Velay, begun in 1605, was imitated in many towns. The Jesuit fathers knew that the people of the sixteenth century cared little for medieval symbolism. Therefore, they dropped the custom of orienting their churches. They aimed at the most economical and practical use of the surface at their disposal. Hence they dropped the protruding transept of the Middle Ages, and practically enclosed the building (with the exception of the apse in some cases), within an oblong, which might be conveniently placed at the angle of two streets, the front receding from the general line of one of these, so as to leave an open space for coaches to come up to the portal stairs and wheel round. The internal arrangement of the building answered three several purposes: the church being attached both to a Jesuit house and a college, and being open to the public as well. According to the *Constitutions* of the Society, the Fathers were exempt from choir duty; therefore the church had no choir properly so-called, but only a shallow apse, and oratories placed on either side of it, and screened from view, for private prayer and meditation.

The Council of Trent had defended the Mass against the Protestants, and stressed its importance in public worship. It insisted that the faithful should understand and follow it. Therefore the Jesuits built their churches so that the whole congregation should be able to see every gesture of the officiant. The rood-screen was replaced by simple altar rails; and the inside of the building was planned in such a way that the sanctuary should be visible from every part of it. In the Middle Ages, the faithful, for lack of printed books, had been unable to join in liturgical worship, and religious instruction was provided for them mostly by means of stained glass. It had now become important that they should be able to read in church. Painted windows were therefore replaced by clear glass. However, teaching by means of pictures was not given up, and a considerable space was reserved for wall-paintings. The now windowless chancel was decorated with the most important motives, that is, the life of the patron saint of the church; the cupola, the un-groined vaults of the nave and transept, the side chapels above the altars, were also covered with frescoes, as at S. Andrea della Valle in Rome.

The Council had enforced the duty of preaching upon the bishops and the whole clergy: the pulpit was now made to occupy a central position in the nave, while attention was also paid to acoustics. The building became a real lecture-hall, without those pillars and aisles in which the voice of the preacher reverberated and lost itself. The council had insisted on the practice of confession. The Jesuit architects had to provide room for numerous confessionals: hence the appearance, in place of the aisles, of side chapels, with an open passage between them in many cases, and surmounted with tribunes which provided additional accommodation for the faithful. Last of all, in agreement with the characteristic austerity of the Catholic Reformation, the altar was low and plain. In such a building as the Gesù in Rome, the main altar, which dates back to an early period, is simple, whereas the transept altars. erected in the later period of the baroque, are prodigiously rich.

How closely the building of Jesuit churches followed the directions issued at Trent and re-enforced by the Society, is shown by a couple of significant facts. First of all, the plans had to be sent up to Rome and accepted by the Father general. Secondly, the actual supervision of the building work was but seldom entrusted to lay architects, but to Fathers of the Society, with the technical help of temporal coadjutors, who had specialized in architecture. The most celebrated among the latter was Brother Martellange, a Frenchman. It is worthy of note that he had his professional training in southern France and Italy, and probably went to Rome. It is a fact that, when building the Jesuit novitiate in Paris, he imitated the church of Santa Maria dé Monti, begun in 1579 under Gregory XIII by Giacomo della Porta. He was received into the Society in 1590 and was made a temporal coadjutor in 1603. He became the regular architect for the provinces of Lyons, Toulouse, and even Paris, and designed the plans of numerous colleges together with their chapels, the first one in date being that of LePuy-en-Velay, followed notably by those of Vienne, Moulins, La Flèche, and the College of the Trinity in Lyons. He was still at work in 1625 and died in 1641 in Paris. His main quality was an austere simplicity; he avoided decorative exaggeration and mannered forms.

His Chapels were built on the lines described above. His plans for the colleges themselves were no less imbued with the severe practicality of the Society. They were meant for convenience, and were therefore simple. Besides, the city corporations which called in the Jesuits and made agreements with them for the education of youth were generally poor. The standard ground plan of a Jesuit college included two adjoining square yards, wholly surrounded with buildings. The classrooms opened out directly on one of these, one side of which was occupied by the chapel, along which ran an open gallery terminating in the main entrance. The buildings around the second yard were taken up by the lodgings of the Fathers, and later, when the colleges took in boarders, provided accommodation for them. Especial attention was paid to hygiene. This appears in the plan of Charity Hospital, at Lyons, which was drafted by Martellange. It consisted of a central yard, the buildings surrounding this being prolonged so as to create eight wings, partly enclosing eight other yards, which gave free access to the open air on their other sides. On the whole, Martellange's architectural conceptions were much in advance of his own time, and were not improved upon by the profuse decoration of a later period.

Thus did the practical requirements of the Trentine revival determine its style of building. It should not be thought, however, that beauty as such was of no interest to the Catholic reformers, or that while adapting the classical style of the Renaissance to their purpose they did not print their own stamp upon it. The Renaissance had attempted to revive the ideal of the ancients, which was one of composed harmony, measured stability, of satisfaction with the world as it was, in which there was no yearning for heaven, in which horizontal lines predominated. As soon as the new fervor of the Catholic Reformation began to manifest itself, the mystical longings of the Middle Ages reappeared along with it, as revealed by the upward trend of vertical lines or the upward soaring of towers and cupolas. The alterations made in the plan of St. Peter's in Rome are significant in this respect. As drafted by Bramante, it was hardly Christian. It consisted of a comparatively low cupola with four equal arms branching from it. A long nave, suitable for Catholic worship, was now added, while the cupola was raised by Michaelangelo, in the spirit of Gothic art. However, the drum alone had been completed at the time of his death. The work was continued by Giacomo della Porta, who made the cupola even higher and more pointed, and the lantern slenderer, so as to give the whole building the general proportions of a cathedral.

The Christian revival which followed Trent was manifested by the erection of numerous churches in the Eternal City. Though St. Peter's had been begun, no other religious edifice had been built under Julius II, Leo X, and Clement VII; whereas extensive building started under Paul IV and was continued as late as Urban VIII. It went hand-in-hand with the creation or rejuvenation of religious orders (churches of the Jesuits, Dominicans, Oratorians, Carmelites, Trinitarians, and many others), but was also due to the piety of trade guilds and of the various nations represented in Rome. Here again the spirit of the Middle Ages reappeared, and efforts were made to embody it in the new architecture. In regard to church fronts, this could not be achieved by lengthening out the pillars indefinitely, but only by the superposition of orders, which had not been used by the Greeks, but which had been tried by the Romans in their amphitheaters. Vignole's original plan for the Gesù insisted on horizontal lines; the lower story was broad, and divided up by portals, niches, and columns. Giacomo della Porta, who continued the work, tried to give the impression of height; he simplified the lower story, retrenched the lateral parts, concentrated his attention upon the center, which was prolonged in the upper story.

In France, the reversion to mediaevalism was even more striking. In the French churches of the Catholic Reformation, the front consisted of as many as three or four orders above one another, as in Saint-Gervais or Saint-Paul-Saint-Louis in Paris. However, to avoid monotony the orders were varied, the intervals between the columns were made unequal, the cornices were diversified by projections or broken pediments. On the other hand, the decoration proper was spare: the fluting of the pillars was given up, and the general impression was one of sadness, true to the spirit of the period.

But opposition to purely classical forms was even greater in the countries of the North, in Flanders and Germany. In the former country the Jesuits showed reluctance toward adopting the architecture of the Renaissance. They went on building churches in the Gothic style, long after it had disappeared from Southern Europe. This is still manifest in the Jesuit church at Luxembourg, built by Brother Jean de Blocq, from 1613 to 1621; in that of St. Omers (1615–1636) where the sanctuary has pointed windows; and elsewhere. The Gothic tradition was also long preserved in the Rhineland, where the same features are found; whereas southern influences were predominant in Bavaria. In Germany generally, music was used by the Jesuits in their struggle against Lutheranism, which had laid such stress on the chorale, and it was made an essential element of divine worship. The churches were built on a theater-like plan, with a stage-like sanctuary, side oratories akin to boxes, and, facing the altar, a double tier of galleries for the singers and the orchestra. The decoration was generally richer and appealed to the senses even more than in Flanders, both countries harking back to the profuse flowing tracery of the fifteenth century.

This, however, was a local development, and the dominant note throughout the period of the Catholic Reformation proper remains one of restraint and severity. In time, the same change of mood took place in architecture as in literature. College drama had, to begin with, been austerely and heroically devotional. In the course of the seventeenth century, it assumed a worldlier character. The Jesuits enlivened it in many ways, especially through use of the ballet. They deemed that man should be drawn to God through admiration, that nothing could be too elaborately beautiful to celebrate the glory of the Lord. Hence, in the field of architecture, the partiality they were to show for the baroque style. The overornamentation of the latter came to clothe the churches of the Catholic Reformation, so that the true spirit of these is now veiled and apt to be overlooked. No monument is more typical of the change which overlaid the early simplicity of Trentine art than the college chapel at Le-Puy-en-Velay in its present condition. The front had first of all been severely plain, with six Tuscan pilasters framing in the gate and two niches in the lower story, and four pilasters supporting a pediment in the upper story. It was remodeled in 1683, when a protruding porch was added, with six Doric columns, so as to create variety and relief. A similar change is noticed in the altar, the present highly decorated gilt wood reredos dating only to 1688.

On the whole, however, the true character of the Trentine style cannot be ignored: it was primarily Christian, as against the pagan tendencies of the Renaissance. It rejected that Greek conception of architecture, carried through by Palladio, to which the rationalizing eighteenth century was to revert. It took into account contemporary tastes by adopting classical forms, but merely made them into an outer garb for edifices which remained medieval in structure and spirit, while being adapted to the practical needs of the religious revival. It evolved no new style which might compare with the Gothic, but it did create a type of art which may rightly claim originality.

*   *   *

In music, the principles and spirit of the Catholic Reformation were the same as in literature and painting. First of all, art for art's sake was proscribed, and music was made to play its part in the work of evangelization. Again, severity and austerity were substituted for the florid exuberance of the Renaissance; this in its turn being concomitant with a reversion to the traditional simplicity of the Gregorian chant. A reaction was in fact necessary against the abuses which had gradually crept in and corrupted Church music, both morally and artistically.

Unlike literature and painting, there was, for music, no standard of good taste provided by ancient models. Add to this that the composers residing in Rome in the early sixteenth century were mostly foreigners, Flemings or Frenchmen — Josquin des Prés, Andrew Willaert, Eleazar Genet, James Arkadelt, Claude Goudimel — who, more than Italians, retained something of medieval fancifulness and grotesqueness. They went beyond the already extant tendency to substitute for the naked monody of the Gregorian chant various systems of polyphony. The contrapuntal style, which had been at first productive of great beauty, was pushed to extremes which disfigured it. While as many as eight parts were sung together, no account was taken of the liturgical words, which were now drawn into length, now hastily slurred over, now drowned under a profusion of flourishes. Worse still, the accompaniment to the liturgical themes was often derived from popular tunes. Masses, therefore, bore such names as "Farewell, My Love," "In the Shadow of the Bush," "Kiss Me," or "The Naughty Jealous One"; and while the bass sung the words of the liturgy, the tenor would troll out the very words of folk-songs, those at least which could bear a religious construction. In a *Kyrie* the tenor sang "I never saw the like of her"; in a *Benedictus,* "Madam, let me know." The accompanying instruments themselves vied with the singers in capriciousness and virtuosity, and shared in the prevailing disorder.

A reaction had already set in before the Council of Trent. Giberti, bishop of Verona, had forbidden the singing of popular or lascivious songs in church, and the seeking after theatrical effects. Morone, the bishop of Modena, prohibited, in 1537 all "figured" music in his diocese. The Fathers of Trent very nearly did the same, but thought better of it, and later reverted to the regulations issued in 1324 by the Avignon pope, John XXII. The final canon, published on September 17, 1562, dealt with the matter briefly in the following words: "Let all music, in which either through the organ or through singing is mingled anything lascivious or impure, be proscribed from churches . . . so that the House of God may truly seem and be called a house of prayer." On July 6, 1563, the council made the study of Church music compulsory for all clerics. In regard to nuns, "figured" singing, which had been at first rejected, was later permitted. The Council left it to the pope, to the bishops and provincial synods, to enforce more detailed prescriptions. On the whole, the Fathers had wisely refrained from undue puritanism, and tolerated the use of prick-song.

Pope Pius V was not long in following their lead, and on August 2, 1563, appointed a committee of cardinals, two of whom, Vitelli and Borromeo, were especially entrusted with musical and liturgical reform. They immediately recommended a style of Church music in which the words might be heard. This had been the wish expressed seven years before by Pope Marcellus II, in the course of the Holy Week offices. In the Sistine Chapel the liturgical texts had not been sung with due feeling, and the cheerfulness of the tunes had been incompatible with the sense of the words. The pope had called the singers before him, including Palestrina, and had ordered them to sing gravely and decently, and in such a way "that the words might be both heard and understood." Following his lead, the committee of cardinals decided to do away with all Masses in which additions were made to the strictly liturgical text; with Masses and other compositions on profane themes; with motets composed on words not extracted from the Mass or Divine Office. Lastly, they ordered that what was sung should in every case be clearly understood. They made the daily teaching of Gregorian chant and polyphonic music compulsory in the Roman and German colleges, to which in fact such masters as Palestrina and Vittoria were respectively appointed as *kapellmeisters*. Composers hastened to conform to the advice of the cardinals. Animuccia, in 1567; Palestrina in the same year; Ruffo, in 1574, declared that they had endeavored "to follow the reform of the Council of Trent."

The part played by Palestrina in the rejuvenation of Church music was a prominent one. Giovanni Pier Luigi, who owed the name Palestrina to his birthplace, was born in 1525. He came to Rome about 1540, and was the pupil of the Flemish composer, Firmin le Bel. His earlier works show that he studied the Flemish masters closely. His life was one of labor and poverty. The volume of his compositions is amazing — no fewer than 93 Masses, 486 antiphons, motets, offertories, and psalms, besides numerous other pieces. In 1551, while he was occupying an unimportant position in the cathedral of his native place, he was called to Rome by Pope Julius III to be choirmaster at St. Peter's. On January 13, 1555, he became one of the singers of the papal choir, but he had to relinquish that office in the following July since he was not a cleric, but a layman and married. He was later appointed choirmaster at the Lateran, and then at St. Mary Major. In 1571, he was again entrusted with the direction of the music at St. Peter's, and retained this position until his death in 1594.

Like Tansillo, he experienced a veritable conversion. He had first of all complied with the frivolous tendencies of his Italian environment and published two volumes of madrigals of an amorous character. He later repented these vagaries, and became a deeply religious man. He himself expressed his devotional purpose as a composer in the following words: "I deemed that, following the advice of the gravest and most devout men, I ought to apply all my zeal, all my pain and industry to the adorning, with a new kind of music, the greatest and most divine thing of all in the Christian religion, that is the holy sacrifice of the Mass." The "new kind of music" was not, indeed, a novelty in the technical sense of the word; it was still polyphonic and contrapuntal; but it was new in so far as it followed the directions laid down by the Council of Trent and its continuators; it borrowed its motives not from profane songs but from the Gregorian chant and its words were perfectly audible. The artistic performance of Palestrina was not inferior to the fervor of his devotional purpose; and Richard Wagner himself said that the composer's works "struck him with an indescribable emotion."

Palestrina's success as a composer had a moderating influence on those Catholic Puritans who were wholly opposed to "figured" music; and he succeeded in rescuing the latter from utter suppression. Pope Pius IV himself was not unwilling to abolish prick-song, and was on the point of proposing a decree to that effect to the Council of Trent. However, he heard Palestrina's Masses, notably the *Mass of Pope Marcellus,* and changed his mind. Later Cardinals Vitelli and Borromeo examined Church music to see whether it was in accordance with the Trentine prescriptions. They had several Masses, including, no doubt, those of Palestrina, and also those of the more fanciful Roland de Lassus, performed in their house by the choir of papal singers; and they passed judgment on them as satisfactory. In the years that followed, other composers, such as Giovanni Animuccia or Vincenzo Ruffo, were commissioned by the cardinals to write hymns, motets, psalms, and Masses. A new development in Church music took place toward the end of the sixteenth century, in connection with the meetings at St. Philip Neri's Oratory. These had been followed by singing from the first. Animuccia was one of the earliest members of the company, to which he brought some of his colleagues, who performed polyphonic motets, which he often composed himself. He published in 1563, 1565, and 1570 three collections for the use of the Oratory, in which he deliberately aimed at religious simplicity. He was later joined by Palestrina, who, toward the end of the century, came from time to time to direct the choir. However, the character of the meetings gradually altered; for the prayers, litanies, and short stories were substituted long biblical narratives, while on the musical side the polyphonic anthems, motets, and *laudi* were replaced by a monodic *recitativo*. An epic and dramatic element took the place of lyrical prayer, and was further reinforced by the tradition of the *sacre rappresentazioni,* performed on the steps of Roman churches in the month of May. Such was the origin of the Oratorio, which, however, only appeared in full-blown form in the *Teatro armonico spirituale* of G. F. Anerio, published in 1619, and which was to develop into the later Opera.

While religious prick-song thus prepared the way for the development of modern music, a rejuvenation of plainchant was attempted in connection with the liturgical revival brought about by the Council of Trent. It was necessary indeed to defend Church singing against some Protestant controversialists, who considered it a form of idolatry, and insisted that mental prayer was the only form of prayer permissible. The arguments produced against them by Cardinal Bellarmine in his *Controversies* (composed from 1576 to 1587) are of great interest. Canticles, he says, inflame the souls of the hearers; their charm makes the praise of God easier and more pleasant; they make man's heart and body to unite in it; they dispel impure thoughts, breed generosity and fortitude; they are a salve for life's sorrows and a dew which makes grace fruitful. Bellarmine's deep sense of the artistic and psychological value of music is here apparent. He also recommends the use of the organ in church, so long as it remains sober and grave. He himself, as archbishop of Capua, insisted on the performance of choir duty by the cathedral chapter, and performed his own part in it scrupulously.

While owing to the impulse of the Council of Trent revised editions of the Breviary, the Missal, and other liturgical books were published under Pius V, Gregory XIII, Sixtus V, and Clement VIII, a parallel effort was made to restore the plainchant, which had fallen into decay in the fourteenth, fifteenth, and sixteenth centuries. Gregory XIII commissioned Palestrina and his colleague, Annibal Zoilo, a singer and composer of the papal chapel, to prepare a new edition of the antiphonaries, graduales, and psalters, in order to clear them of the "numerous barbarisms, obscurities, contradictions and superfluities" with which they were filled, so that "the name of God might be praised in them reverently, distinctly and devoutly." Unfortunately the two musicians went about their work too thoroughly, and while altering the phrases of the Gregorian chant so as to transform them into suitable themes for the composition of polyphonic motets, they altered its true character and beauty beyond recognition. On the request of a Spanish musician, Don Fernando de las Infantas, and of King Philip II of Spain himself, Pope Gregory XIII interrupted the publication. However, the error of Palestrina and Zoilo was repeated in 1595, when a revised *Pontificale* was officially published by the order of Clement VIII. In 1608 the pope appointed a committee of cardinals — to which Bellarmine belonged for some time — to reform Church singing. They chose in their turn a number of well-known musicians to perform the task. These were only to "correct the mistakes which might in course of time have disfigured the melodies," but they repeated the errors of their forerunners, and the *Medicean Graduale* which they produced, though published in 1614, never received official approval, either in Rome or in the States of the Church.

Thus did the Church, at the time of the Catholic Reformation, wisely refrain, in music as well as in painting, sculpture, and architecture, from sacrificing the heritage of the early and late Middle Ages. In the artistic field, it conserved more than it created. And yet, it did exert an influence of its own, which was both narrowing and strengthening. Through compelling art to serve a definite religious purpose, through subjecting it to the laws of decency, restraint, moderation, reason, it forced it into straiter channels. The stream which had till then meandered at will through the plains, was now caught in a defile and made to flow with greater force. Nor was this force due merely to the limitations it had to accept; it was also due to what was, after all, the mainspring of the Catholic Reformation, that spiritual impulse which brought about the conversion of so many men of letters, artists, and musicians, and which was so clearly manifested in the field of mysticism.

CHAPTER X

Piety and Mysticism

THOUGH anarchy was the chief evil which afflicted the Church in the early sixteenth century, the Catholic Reformation should not be viewed as consisting essentially, or even mostly in administrative reorganization. The spiritual forces behind the movement ought not to be overlooked. They found expression in the realm of piety and mysticism. We have already had occasion to refer to them, when mentioning the development of the school of devotion founded upon St. Ignatius' *Exercises,* and its influence in education. Now, this school was not alone of its kind; there were others in various European countries, in the sixteenth and early seventeenth centuries. Their appearance was not the outcome of mere coincidence; nor did they merely follow in the wake of the great mystics of the late Middle Ages. They had an original stamp of their own, and were closely connected with the Catholic Reformation. For one thing, they derived inspiration from the spirit of Christian humanism and the principles laid down by the Council of Trent. Again, they took an important part in the actual amendment of abuses; and lastly, they provided new formulas for the practice of devotional life, which tallied with the intellectual and spiritual tendencies of the age.

Catholic Reformation piety was first and foremost optimistic, and derived much of its coloring from the Christian humanists of the Pre-Lutheran age, who proclaimed their trust in human nature and the beauty of the human soul. What is more, this optimism was confirmed and, so to say, made official by the decrees of the Council of Trent. The latter took its stand against the Protestant doctrines which stressed the unworthiness of man, and the impossibility of his doing any real good; which denied his free will, his cooperation with God, and his actual merit. In the fifth session of the Council, the fifth canon on original sin, promulgated in June, 1546, contains the following typical words:

"For God hates nothing in those who are born again. There is no condemnation for those who are buried with Christ by baptism into death (Rom. 6:4), who walk not after the flesh (Rom. 8:1) but putting off the old man, and putting on the new man, who is created after God (Eph. 4:22; Col. 3:9) have become innocent, immaculate, pure, sinless, and beloved of God, heirs of God, indeed, but joint-heirs with Christ (Rom. 8:17)."

The stress is laid here, not on the decayed nature of man, but on his bright prospects. Who could miss the eager hopefulness of those few lines? And again, in the eleventh chapter of the decree on justification:

"God, does not command impossible things, but while commanding He warns thee to do what thou canst, and to ask for what thou canst not do thyself, and helps thee to do it; whose commandments are not grievous (1 John 5:3), whose yoke is sweet and whose burden is light (Matth. 11:30). For those who are the children of God, love Christ; now those who love Him, as He Himself testifies, are true to His teachings, which they can perform always with the help of God." The same optimism pervades the whole of the decree on justification:

"God," it says, "does not desert those whom He has justified through His grace. . . . And to those who work good things unto the end and hope from God, eternal life is to be proposed, both as a grace mercifully promised to the sons of God through Jesus-Christ, and as a reward faithfully granted according to God's promise to their good works and merits."

Not only did the spiritual leaders of the Catholic Reformation believe in the fruitfulness of man's action; but they also engaged in action themselves toward the improvement of Church conditions. This need hardly be stressed in the case of St. Ignatius Loyola and St. Philip Neri, whose reforming work has been surveyed above; but everywhere in Europe the renewal of mysticism was coupled with a rejuvenation of Church discipline. The best-known work of the Italian mystical school, the *Spiritual Fight,* was produced in Theatine circles, probably by the Theatine, Lorenzo Scupoli. Another mystic, St. Magdalen de' Pazzi, a reformer of the Italian Carmelites, devoted her most fervent outpourings to prayer for the amendment of the clergy. In Spain, the Benedictine, Garcia Ximenes de Cisneros, drawing his inspiration from St. Bona-venture and Gerson, reformed the Abbey of Montserrat, from 1492 onward, by compelling the monks to perform the spiritual exercises of meditation and methodical prayer included in his *Ejercitatorio.* Later, St. Teresa's predecessor, St. Peter of Alcantara, the Franciscan mystic (1499–1562), the author of a *Treatise on Prayer and Meditation,* was also a provincial of the Discalced Minorities, and the promoter of a reform of his order. In France, the mystical revival was similarly paired with action. A Benedictine, Louis de Blois (d. 1566), improved conditions at Liessies Abbey by enforcing the practice of meditation and of exercises for the development of the inward life. The later French mystics insisted on the sanctification of the clergy; they stressed the excellence of the sacerdotal dignity, and the corresponding duties. St. Vincent de Paul exhorted his brethren of the Mission in the following words, on the eve of a retreat they were giving to future priests: "How beautiful your task, to make the clergy better! Who will understand the height of such an employment? it is the loftiest one on earth."

Lastly, as we have said, the Catholic Reformation mystics gave expression to the intellectual and spiritual needs of the period in which they were living. They did not, however, do so in a uniform way. In each of the chief European countries, the devotional movement borrowed a definite coloring from the national temperament. There was no disagreement as to essentials, but various points were stressed in various places. Hence the necessity of dividing the spiritual leaders of the age into several national groups, and to consider in succession the mystics of Spain, Italy, and France.

*   *   *

The common background for the three schools is to be found in the methodical discipline to which the later Middle Ages gradually subjected the whole of spiritual life. This was the outcome of reaction against the anarchy which then prevailed in the Church, and against the moral laxity of the early Renaissance. Where the old religious standards were disregarded, the sole remedy was personal sanctity. And, to attain this sanctity, methods were devised in spiritual treatises, leading up no less to St. Ignatius' *Exercises* than to the *Way to Perfection* of St. Teresa of Jesus.

The essential element in all these is the theory of the three ways of spiritual life. It-had first appeared in the early ages of the Church in the works of Dionysius, the Pseudo-Areopagite, where, however, the gradual ascent of the soul, through purification, illumination, and consummation, was purely intellectual. It was left for St. Bonaventure, the great thirteenth century Italian mystic, to interpret the Dionysian scheme as showing the gradual progress of the soul toward union with God through charity. Thus, in the purgative way man is converted and cleanses himself of his sins; in the illuminative way he obtains enlightenment in regard to God, Christ, and himself and tries to imitate the Savior; in the unitive way he binds himself to God and gives himself up to divine love. In each of the three ways he is guided by a graduated course of special spiritual exercises. This method was expounded by numerous mystical writers in the fourteenth and fifteenth centuries. In England, especially, there was a real flowering of devotional treatises, which described the patient ascent of the soul toward its spiritual goal, such as Alcock's *Hill of Perfection* (printed in 1497, 1499, 1501), the anonymous *Pylgrimage of Perfection* (printed in 1526, 1531), and, above all, Walter Hylton's *Ladder of Perfection* (printed in 1494, 1507, 1525, 1533). The last endeavored to sum up the whole process of sanctification by explaining "how in reason and wyll vertue begynneth, and how in loue and lykings it is made perfyte."

In all these works, the stress was laid upon interior religion, as opposed to purely outward practice; and this tendency was further strengthened by Christian humanism. The latter's attitude was a reaction against the cult of pure reason as embodied in Aristotle's philosophy, and a reversion to Platonic idealism, especially in the mystical form given to it by Plotinus. This is why the Christian humanists looked askance at the mere formalities of worship, insisted upon the ethical and inward elements of religion and recommended personal sanctification and flight from the corruption of the world; that is why they viewed Scripture, not as a storehouse of debatable "questions," but as a source of moral and spiritual inspiration; why, lastly, they adopted Plato's notion of the beauty of man's soul, and refused to consider human nature as hopelessly decayed.

Whatever may be said about the disruptive effect of Erasmus' criticism, his positive influence upon the piety of the Catholic Reformation seems beyond doubt. Like St. Ignatius' *Exercises,* his *Enchiridion militis christiani* (Manual of the Christian Soldier) is a war-like book, providing advice for man's struggle on earth. The author proposes a set of rules, first of all to help man to acquire a thorough knowledge of himself, then to strive against temptations. The "Christian soldier" will be prepared to lose everything for Christ, even his life. He will choose the narrow way. He will turn from visible to invisible things. He will gain strength in his combat from meditation on the sufferings of our Lord and the ugliness of sin, on heaven and hell, on the necessity of a holy death. He must show himself a true Christian, not by indulging in pharisaical observances, but by leading a pure life, and through a lively and intimate union of his soul with the Redeemer.

Thus did both the later medieval mystics and the Christian humanists seek union with God through personal sanctification, and pave the way for the spiritual leaders of the Catholic Reformation. Besides, their methods for the gradual ascent of the soul were averse to the spirit of Protestantism, against which, it should not be forgotten, the Catholic Reformation was also directed. Man, Luther declared, is incapable of any good; his virtuous deeds themselves are sins; he is justified by the merely external action of God; and his justification is manifested by a sudden and purely gratuitous illumination of the soul. There is no reason, therefore, why he should rise patiently, step by step, on the ladder of the spiritual life; no reason why he should find any good in himself, and seek in the depths of his own soul a refuge against the storm of worldly temptations. Indeed, there have been Protestant mystics, but there is no real similarity between the alternate certainty of salvation and terror of damnation of John Bunyan for instance, and the vicissitudes of spiritual consolation and desolation which are one main feature of the piety of the Catholic Reformation. The latter was assisted in the use of ascetical methods by directors of conscience, whereas the Protestants originally wished to do away with all intermediaries between God and the soul — however much practical necessities may have later compelled them, as in the case of Baxter, to revert to Catholic practice.

*   *   *

There had been a flourishing mystical school in Northern Europe in the fourteenth and fifteenth centuries, with masters such as Tauler and Eckhardt in Germany, Gerard Groot and the Brothers of the Common Life in the Low Countries, Hylton in England. With the Catholic Reformation the scene shifts to the South, and primarily to Spain. The latter country provided an especially favorable ground for the blossoming of mysticism, and notably for the appearance of the greatest of mystics, St. Teresa of Jesus. Many of its inhabitants were of Arabian descent. The direct influence of Mohammedanism upon the Christian devotion of the Spaniards cannot indeed be proved. But many of the newly converted Moriscos, including monks and nuns, were acquainted with the traditions of Moslem meditation, and cannot but have had a natural bent for the spiritual life.

In the national temper of Spain were blended the two contrasting features which Cervantes was soon after to characterize in the two figures of Sancho Panza and Don Quixote. On the one hand, the Spaniards were gifted with the most realistic common sense, a quality of which St. Teresa herself gave ample proof as a religious leader and a reformer. On the other hand, they were chivalrous, adventurous, even foolhardy; they loved a fight, whether in the American colonies, or in the war with France, or even, in the controversial field, against Luther and his adherents. The general atmosphere was one of feverish determination, of aspiration to high deeds, and accounts for St. Teresa's words, "One may die indeed, but be vanquished never." To this national ardor other elements were added, which fanned the flame of the saint's devotion. There were frequent performances of mystery plays, known as *autos sacramentales,* which were familiar to every class of the population, and fed the mystical imagination. Spanish society of the time was humanistic enough to be praised on that account by Erasmus himself; it was therefore open to the doctrines of Plato as thought anew by Plotinus and by Dionysius, the Pseudo-Areopagite. Luis de Granada himself expressed his admiring surprise that Plato, the pagan, should have been able to describe the greatness of God by means of his natural lights only. "The great philosopher showed how the contemplation of the Eternal Beauty necessarily bred virtue, and how on the other hand he who practiced virtue was bound to become 'the friend of the gods'; that love losing itself in 'divine madness' led to 'the contemplation of Beauty's self.' " Here we come very near indeed to Teresian mysticism.

There were, however, more direct sources. Before St. Teresa, several Spanish devotional writers had sketched out methods of gradual spiritual progress. In 1527, Francisco de Ossuna published his *Tercio abecedario espiritual* (*Third Spiritual A.B.C.*) in which the soul is subjected to a strict spiritual discipline in order to attain the prayer of recollection. The latter is reached by successive degrees; in the first, the powers of the soul are merely quieted; in the second, the understanding is still at work; in the third, the soul encloses itself as into a prison to enjoy God; in the fourth, it is rapt up into ecstasy. The whole is clothed in the garb of beautiful imagery, which St. Teresa was to borrow, as well as the general features of Ossuna's psychology and methods. After Assuna, two other Franciscans, Bernardino de Laredo, in his *Subida del Monte Sion* (Ascent of Mount Zion, 1535), and St. Peter of Alcantara, in his *Treatise on Prayer and Meditation,* showed how, when the soul is mystically united to Christ, meditation and intellectual reflection must cease in the "sleep of the powers" of the mind. A more elaborate spiritual method was supplied some time later by Luis de Granada, a Dominican, whose main purpose was to show how the spiritual life leads to the practice of Christian virtues. In his *Book on Prayer and Meditation* (1554) his main point, which was later to be taken up again by St. Francis de Sales, is that true devotion is not "a tenderness of the heart that is manifested through prayer," but "a readiness and promptitude to do good, to perform God's commandments and attend to His service." How this should be done is explained by Luis de Granada in a further work of his, the *Guia de Peccadores* (*The Guide of Sinners*, 1556), which attained to great fame, was recommended by St. Francis de Sales, and became universally popular in seventeenth-century France. The Dominican Order did not merely provide St. Teresa with models; it also supplied her with three confessors and directors, Pedro Ibañez, Domenico Bañez, and Garcia de Toledo. Ibañez induced her to write the history of her life; Bañez rescued the convent of Carmelites at Ávila, reformed by the saint, when it was about to disappear: both he and Garcia de Toledo warned her against the possible excesses of false mysticism.

St. Teresa of Jesus was born, on March 28, 1515, at Ávila, in Old Castile, an ancient fortified town of which the battlemented walls later suggested the imagery of her *Interior Castle*. She was brought up amidst the traditions of Christian knighthood, among her eleven brothers and sisters. While still a child, she thought of seeking martyrdom among the Moors, then later of becoming a hermit together with one of her brothers. But soon after she took to reading romances of chivalry, which turned her mind from her early aspirations, and led her to indulge in what she considered as sinful frivolousness, though her trespasses do not seem to have reached beyond some harmless coquetry. Her lapse into worldliness, however, was enough in her own eyes to justify the real conversion which soon followed.

In 1531, while Teresa was a boarder at the Augustinian monastery at Ávila, she felt attracted again toward the spiritual life. After struggling with her vocation for three years, she left her father's home on November 2, 1535, for the Carmelite convent of the Incarnation at Ávila, where she was to take her vows. Then followed a period of seventeen years during which she engaged in no external action, but gradually came nearer to God through the practice of prayer fostered by such readings as that of Ossuna's *Tercio abecedario espiritual*. About 1543, she became acquainted with the *Confessions* of St. Augustine, which had a lasting influence upon her. Henceforth she moved forward speedily in the progress of her soul; she felt a lively impression of the presence and love of God, and wholly gave herself up into His hands. She was favored with ecstasies and visions, such as that of the Transverberation, in 1560, in which an angel pierced her heart with a fiery spear, leaving her in the tender rapture of intimate union with God.

The very excess of such simultaneous pain and pleasure roused her scruples. Fortunately she met at that time with wise confessors, several Jesuits first, then the Franciscan Peter of Alcantara, who, in 1540, had erected the first reformed monastery of the Discalced Minors at Pedroso, in the Estremadura. They taught her to use mortification as a background for her devotions, and turned her thoughts toward practical activities. Then she had a vision, in which Christ ordered her to found a monastery dedicated to St. Joseph. Accordingly, in 1562, she created the monastery of St. Joseph at Ávila, and drafted for it her *Constitutions*, which the Father general of the Carmelites was to extend in 1607 to all the other foundations of the Order. The rule prescribed by the saint was a strict one indeed, but gave ample room for meditation, prayer, and examination of conscience, the life of the religious being one of solitude, poverty, and penitence, but steeped in a "holy and peaceful joy." No sooner was this first monastery established than St. Teresa was urged to create other houses of the same type; and thenceforth her life was a perpetual pilgrimage along the highways of Spain, despite stress of weather and the malice of men.

Her next foundation was Medina del Campo. Then she thought of establishing a monastery of men, and, while she was considering this scheme, she met a young Carmelite Father, Juan de Santo Matià, who was to become St. John of the Cross. She enlisted his help toward the foundation of a house of discalced Carmelites, where Mass was said for the first time on the first or second Sunday in Advent in 1568. Then followed other foundations, both of men and women, in rapid succession, at Toledo, at Pastrana (1569), at Salamanca (1570), at Alba de Tormes (1571), at Segovia, at Veas, at Seville. The progress was interrupted by the action of a papal nuncio, Felippo Sega, who arrived from Italy in 1577, and sided with the unreformed Carmelites. He subjected St. Teresa to a persecution of four years' duration, which very nearly ruined her work. However, the situation was restored through the intervention of King Philip II, and further monasteries were established at Villanueva de la Jara, at Palencia, at Soria (1581). On January 2, 1582, she left St. Joseph of Ávila for the last time, in the heart of winter, to found a house at Burgos, despite the grievous illness from which she had so long been suffering. After six months of labor and anguish she retired to the monastery of Alba, where in the midst of a prolonged ecstasy she departed from this world on October 15, 1582.

The outward facts of the saint's life are not the most important part of her biography. She herself has described, in the story of her *Life*, the vicissitudes of her spiritual progress, which were of far greater moment to her. It took her twenty years to reach inward stability and serenity. She was tormented by ill-health, and suffered great bodily pain, especially in the early years. She was often the butt of hostile criticism on the part of the people of her native town. She did not always meet with understanding from her confessors, several of whom ascribed her ecstasies and visions to the action of the evil one.

But these outward hardships were small compared to the struggle within her own mind and soul. Her practice of mental prayer was neither perfect from the first nor continuous. She interrupted it for as long as a year at a time, and, even when she persevered in it, was troubled by periods of religious drought and barrenness. Her very raptures were mixed with cruel pain, caused by the intensity of her longing for God. At last she was fixed on a high spiritual level. Her account of her soul's journey, her minute psychological analysis of the successive phases of prayer, her practical advice to those who wished to follow in the same tracks, are the main points of interest in her written works, the story of her *Life*, the *Foundations*, the *Way to Perfection*, the *Interior Castle*. These books make no claim to literary excellence, but they derive great beauty from the genuineness of her emotions, and the freshness of her poetical imagery.

Indeed, it was difficult for St. Teresa to convey to her readers a concrete notion of spiritual states, which were before all a matter of personal experience. Hence her use of beautiful similes to describe the soul's ascent on the mystical ladder.

While St. Teresa's spiritual raptures seem to ravish the soul from earth, it is striking that her advice to others should be severely practical and inspired by the most levelheaded common sense. No wonder, since she had had many Jesuit directors, that it should remind us of that adaptation of means to end so characteristic of the Society. One should carefully note what is most profitable in one's devotion. "Variety should be used, lest the soul tire itself by feeding on one only kind of nourishment." A soul that has reached a great intimacy with God should guard against overweening self-confidence, which might cause its ruin. Again, when in a state of "impetuous rapture," one should not give way to what might be after all but the gushing forth of an almost physical emotion, and "let the kettle boil over." On the contrary, reason should quench the fire of the soul, and bring it back to sweet serenity. When the soul falls into a state of spiritual drought, one should not tire oneself in trying to fan a fire that will not burn, but devote oneself to good works. Lastly — Jesuit influence being again visible here — however great one's longing may be for God and the eternal life, one's body should not be neglected, since it is of use for the task assigned it by God.

On no point, as a matter of fact, does the saint lay greater stress than on the fact that true devotion lies, not in "shedding tears, in feeling those spiritual pleasures and that sweetness, which are so much desired as a rule . . . but in serving God in righteousness, strength of soul and humbleness." Ecstasy itself is consequent upon good works. And the latter are not merely the necessary preparation for, and the very substance of mental prayer, they are also its fruit and its benefit. The favors granted by God "compel us to make further efforts to serve Him, and not to be ungrateful toward Him." The bliss imparted to the soul "gives it an inkling of the joys of heaven," and brings it to realize that "its happiness is not here below." Consequently "it grows in virtue and is brought nearer to true Virtue, the source of all virtues, that is God Himself." In the fourth degree of prayer, God works so swiftly upon the soul, that the same result might hardly be reached by "years of sustained efforts." The mystic who is favored with a vision is "entirely transformed" and "powerless to love aught beside God." The soul is then "seized with a huge fright, at the thought that it has been bold enough to offend such a high Majesty" and sinks deep into humility.

What is most characteristic in St. Teresa's mysticism, and we might say most Spanish mysticism, is the combination of practical efficiency with the most exalted devotional ideal. However matter-of-fact her common sense may be, there is nothing humdrum or commonplace about it. Her attitude regarding the problem of life and conduct is one of bold daring and of brave optimism. "Never let us straiten our wishes," she writes; "let us firmly believe that with the help of God and through our own efforts (one almost seems to hear in these words the ring of the previously quoted Trentine canon) we also shall be able, in time, to acquire what so many saints, helped by God, have succeeded in obtaining. . . . Our Lord requires and loves courageous souls, as long as they are humble and distrust themselves. I have not seen one single such soul dwell in the lower regions of spiritual life."

The bearing of St. Teresa is especially brave in her periods of spiritual desolation. Then she faces all the powers of hell boldly and defies them to do her harm. "I said to them," she writes: " 'Now, come on, all of you! I am the servant of the Lord, and I want to see what you can do to me.' . . . I dominate over them from aloft, and take as little account of them as if they were flies." Nobly, proudly, she rejoices in suffering. Praise and regard, she says, are irksome to her; "but if I am subjected to persecutions . . . my soul reigns like a sovereign. . . . It is quite certain that my soul then seems to be at the head of a kingdom and sees everything beneath its feet." Indeed, she does not merely triumph in bodily or mental pain; she invites it in the fulness of her love of God.

While the more chivalrous, and at the same time the more seraphic, aspect of the Spanish character is exemplified by St. Teresa, we meet with its darker, more tragic side, and its craving for the absolute, in the person of her friend and fellow-mystic, St. John of the Cross. His real name was Juan de Yepes. He was born in 1542 at Hontiveras. When twelve or thirteen he lost his father, and had to serve as an attendant at the hospital of Medina del Campo, at the same time studying at the local Jesuit college. At twenty-one he was admitted to the convent of the Carmelites in the same town, where he made his profession, in 1564, under the name of Juan de Santo Matià; next he was sent to Salamanca to study theology. He became familiar with the writings of Dionysius, the Pseudo-Areopagite, and also with those of the Flemish and German mystics.

Following his meeting with St. Teresa, in August, 1567, he decided to undertake the reform of the Carmelites, and founded at Duruelo the first discalced house of the Order. He himself took the name of John of the Cross, thus to stress his eager love of suffering. The success of his reforming efforts brought persecution upon him. He was imprisoned by the "mitigated" Carmelites, at Toledo, in a narrow dungeon, from December 4, 1577, to August 15, 1578. In his prison he began his literary career by writing the *Spiritual Canticle,* in which he described the state of the soul purified by suffering and inebriated with love. After escaping from his prison, he was made prior of the convent of the Calvary in Andalusia. Here he set out to write the *Ascent of Mount Carmel* and the *Dark Night.* These works he completed in 1583, and next wrote the *Lively Flame of Love,* in 1584, at Granada, where he was also prior. After holding the office of rector at Baeza, he founded several houses in Andalusia. His death ensued at Ubeda on December 14, 1591.

Like St. Teresa, he made mental prayer the basis of the devotional life of his reformed religious: like her, he methodically described its various stages, and the gradual ascent of the soul on its way to the contemplation of God. But his method is more austere. He divides the progress of the soul into two parts: active and passive purification. The former is the work of man himself; the latter is that of God alone.

Active purification, as described in the *Ascent of Mount Carmel*, first cleanses the senses of man, then — according to the medieval psychology adopted by St. Teresa — his understanding, his memory, and his will. The "night of the senses" does not merely consist in refraining from sin, but in utter self-renunciation. The soul should despise itself and wish for humiliation from others. Then follows the "night of the understanding," in which it not only divests itself of all knowledge, but also repudiates all mental representation, and of course all those visions, revelations, inward voices, which were the essential element of the mysticism of the illuminated sect of the "Alumbrados." Memory similarly empties itself of all recollections, through the help of hope; while the will is purified through the action of charity. The soul being thus cleared of all obstacles rises to "active" contemplation, in which "it fixes its glance affectionately upon God," and which all men can reach if they take the necessary means.

But to attain mystical union with God passive purification is necessary. Not only must the trunk of sin be cut off, but its very roots must be extirpated. How this is to be effected by God himself in those whom He chooses, is the subject of the *Dark Night*. The soul now renounces its partiality for "sensible consolations"; for virtue is not to be reached through sweetness and comfort, but through an "arduous struggle." St. Teresa had taken no such exception to the spiritual joys which cheer man on his way to perfection. After an interval which may last for years, there follows the "night of the spirit," in which "the understanding is in darkness, the will barren, memory without remembrance, and the affections of the soul are lost in grief and anguish." This is a period of cruel mental torment, in which man "is starved of all those goods that can solace him, temporal, natural, and spiritual." He thinks that God has forsaken him, and praying has become difficult for him. But his sufferings will now be rewarded.

The mystical union itself — described in the *Lively Flame of Love* and in the *Spiritual Canticle* — takes place in the "center of the soul." The latter is like a crystal that is struck by a beam of sunlight, and becomes absorbed in it. It burns with the fire of divine love; it is tenderly, delightfully wounded. Thus is supreme joy reached through heroic self-denial. Once again, as with St. Ignatius and St. Teresa, we here meet the militant spirit of old Spain.

*   *   *

We have already seen the characteristics of the Italian school when dealing with the Oratory of Divine Love, the Theatines, and St. Philip

Neri. It was less speculative than the Spanish school, and more inclined to action. It had to react against the pagan sensuousness and moral decay of the Renaissance, and therefore provided means for each man to struggle against his own depraved tendencies, and to remain unsullied in the midst of the surrounding corruption — and of the surrounding heresy as well.

However, Italian spirituality was not merely concerned with fortifying the individual against a dangerous environment; it was active in bringing about the reform of the Church. The Italian devotional writers aimed first and foremost at an improvement of the clergy. The excellence of the sacerdotal dignity had been proclaimed by the Franciscans since the time of their great founder. St. Gaetano da Thiene marveled at the "miracle of God's goodness" which had "separated him from the rest of the faithful, to raise him to the rank of God's minister"; and he ardently wished to resemble Christ the sovereign Priest. Both St. Gaetano and the other founders of the Clerks Regular insisted that the greatness of the priesthood implied a rule of conduct leading to virtue; not unduly strict or monastic indeed — for they realized that human nature should not be overtaxed — but yet austere enough. For lack of actual poverty, they prescribed poverty of the mind and heart.

The most typical work of the Italian school is the *Combattimento spirituale* (*The Spiritual Combat*) ascribed to the Theatine, Lorenzo Scupoli. Unlike the treatises of the Spanish mystics, it is not a guide through the difficult regions of prayer and ecstasy. It touches upon the devotional life indeed, but it is mainly a directory for personal sanctification. Spiritual life, Scupoli says, "does not consist in outward practices but in the knowledge of the greatness of God and of our own nothingness, in the love of the Lord and the hatred of our own selves, in our submission to the spirit of God, and to creatures for the love of God, in the complete renunciation of our will to His, and our full resignation to His sovereign decrees. Again, these virtues should be practiced solely for the glory of God, and to please Him, for the reason only that he demands and deserves to be loved and served thus." The *Spiritual Combat* purposes to enable man to reach "the summit of perfection," and outlines the necessary tactics, four weapons being recommended: distrust of self, trust in God, a good use of the faculties of the soul and body, and, lastly, the exercise of prayer. Practical advice is provided for the struggle against temptations. An "order of the day" is issued in the morning, before the beginning of the daily battle; man is to consider himself as in the lists, with Christ, the Virgin Mary, and St. Joseph on his right — the devil and his retinue on his left. The influence of St. Ignatius' meditation of the *Two Standards* is here obvious, and appears again in the stubborn optimism recommended to the soul. Even when nearly vanquished, it should never give way to despondency, but remain "of good cheer," and retain its quietness and peace. The fourth weapon, prayer, is the most important of all. Three exercises are particularly recommended, prayer or meditation, Communion, and the examination of conscience. Meditation should bear especially on the "mental" sufferings of Christ: these had already been, as early as 1490, the subject of a work of the blessed Battista Varani, a Franciscan nun, *Dolori mentali di Cristo,* which was known to Scupoli. Devotion to the Virgin Mary and to the holy angels is also advised. Direction of conscience is suggested rather than expressly mentioned: it does not yet, in the *Spiritual Combat,* assume the prominent place which it was to take in the works of St. Francis de Sales.

As for Communion, Scupoli considers it the most effective means of combatting the enemies of man who, thanks to it, gives battle "in the company of Jesus Christ." He wishes the faithful to receive the body of our Lord as often as they can get permission to do so. If permission be refused — it was not granted so easily then as it is nowadays — recourse should be had to spiritual communion, which can be repeated at every hour of the day. Indeed, at a time when the Eucharist had been largely forsaken throughout Europe, the Italian mystics were the first to revive the habit of frequent Communion, while St. Gaetano da Thiene urged his disciples to make it daily.

Undoubtedly, the devotional ideal of the Italian school was one of great moral austerity; but this austerity is less apparent than in Spain; it is, most of the time, delicately veiled. The stress is now laid on what, in Christian teaching, is beautiful and comforting, on what cheers the heart and attracts the soul. "Be cheerful, my children," St. Philip Neri used to say, ". . . the cheerful spirit acquires Christian perfection sooner than the melancholy one." And he used music as an allurement to virtue for his followers. The blending of reverence for beauty with the notion of divine love bespeaks the influence of Plato, who had been in great favor among the Italian humanists of the fifteenth century. The very name of the Oratory of Divine Love is significant in this respect. The notion of "pure love," which was later to breed such embittered controversy at the time of Fénelon and Madame Guyon, is prominent in the writings of the Italian school: "Thou must serve God," the blessed Battista Varani said, "not like a slave, for fear of bodily punishment or eternal pains, not like a sinner, in view of some reward, but like a daughter who renders to God love for love, blood for blood, death for death." The soul should not merely divest itself of all interested motives, of passion and of sin, but of all its faculties, and then it attains that "nakedness of the spirit" which is the product of pure love, and is united with God in a way which no words can express. It should be noted that in sixteenth-century Italy the love of God inspired many works of charity, and filled the hospitals with voluntary attendants.

Such optimism, cheerfulness, and lovingness played an important part in the religious upbringing of St. Francis de Sales, in whom, however, they were mingled with other elements. Both in point of date, in his origins, and also in his devotional practice, St. Francis stands midway between the Italian and the French schools. He was born at Thorens, in Savoy, in 1567. His parents belonged to the local Catholic gentry, but were on good terms with the Protestants of Geneva. He spent his childhood amidst graceful landscapes, which were later to color his poetical imagery. After five years spent at the college at Annecy, he was sent to Paris in 1581, where he remained, until 1588, as a pupil at the Jesuit Collège de Clermont. There he imbibed his literary tastes, and his sense of stylistic beauty. From Paris he went on to Padua, where he studied law for two and a half years, and met Fr. Possevin (or Possevinus).

After traveling to Rome and rambling through Italy, he came back home in 1592, and was made provost of the chapter of Geneva. Since this town was Protestant he resided at Annecy, and, in September, 1594, undertook the conversion of some districts of Savoy, especially the Chablais, which hitherto had remained obstinately Protestant. Owing to his moderation, his gentleness, his sound judgment, and his patience, he succeeded in bringing over to Catholicism the majority of the population. In 1602, he was sent to Paris by the bishop of Geneva on a diplomatic mission. There he came in touch with the saintly Madame Acarie, who was to bring the Carmel into France, and who made him her confessor. He was guided in Parisian circles by M. de Bérulle, and became a preacher of great originality and fame. Being consecrated bishop of Geneva, he resided at Annecy, and gave up much of his time to the direction of souls. His chief penitent was Madame — later St. Jeanne — de Chantal. For the rest of their lives both were united in a deep friendship and were to found together the Order of the Visitation. St. Francis' advice to the persons he directed was embodied in 1608 in the *Introduction to the Devout Life*, which has become as famous as the *Imitation;* and, in 1616, his spiritual philosophy found expression in his *Treatise on the Love of God.* His last years were troubled by a quarrel between Savoy and France and by other worries. He died in 1622. Nine days before his death he wrote: "The more I proceed in this life of mortality, the more contemptible I find it."

St. Francis de Sales provides a unique combination of sweetness and strength. The former aspect ought not to be emphasized at the expense of the latter. It is true that he has a peculiar personal charm which gives great attractiveness to his preaching of virtue. He clothes it in imagery, generally borrowed from nature, which is both pretty and touching: "A true widow," he says in the *Introduction,* "is in the Church like a small March violet, and emits a matchless sweetness, through the perfume of her devotion; she keeps hidden most of the time under the broad leaves of her abjection; and through her faint color, gives proof of mortification. She grows in cool untilled spots, being unwilling to be overborne by the conversation of the worldly, that so she may the better preserve the freshness of her heart against all the heat that might be brought by the desire of wealth, honor or even love." St. Francis advises his imaginary penitent, Philothée, to go to communion often. "Hares," he says, "become white in our mountains in the winter, because they see and eat nothing but snow; and thus, through worshipping and eating the beauty, the goodness and the purity of that divine sacrament, you will become wholly beautiful, wholly good, and wholly pure."

There is, indeed, about the piety of St. Francis a constant quality of suavity, cheerfulness, and optimism. He compares devotion to "spiritual sugar," which "makes mortification less bitter, and consolations less harmful." Despondency, according to him, ought to be shunned. "The Evil one," he writes, "delights in sadness and melancholy . . . and will be thus eternally. He would have all men like him. Now evil sadness disturbs the soul." Righteousness, on the other hand, brings joy: "Consider that virtue and devotion alone can make your soul glad in this world. See how beautiful they are. . . . Virtues . . . delight the soul with a matchless sweetness and suavity."

Like the Italian Platonists, St. Francis asserts the beauty of the soul. It is, indeed, but the reflection of the divine soul, with which it has "a secret agreement," and which is, of course, infinitely more beautiful still, especially experienced to be so when it works upon us. "What a delightful pleasure to see celestial love, which is the sun of all virtues, when, little by little . . . it sheds its light on a soul, and . . . illumines it with the perfect beauty of its own day! O how cheerful, beautiful, lovable and pleasant that dawn is."

Yet, though St. Francis insists on the pleasantness of sanctification, one ought not to consider his devotion easy-going or facile. It is the very reverse of this. He himself was of a tender and loving nature. In the preface to the *Introduction* he speaks of the "suavity" of his labors as a director. Yet he knows how to wean himself from the too human pleasures of friendship: "Cut off friendships," he wrote, "and do not waste time in untying the knots. You must take to them scissors and a knife. . . . They can be cut off but with a sharp knife. Indeed the strings are no good. Let them not be spared."

With all its sweetness, the *Introduction* is a severe book. It proposes a very high ideal of perfection, not to religious secluded from human society, but to men and especially to women living in the world; this being its most original point. True devotion consists in "working carefully, frequently and promptly" to fulfill God's will. It is, however, almost impossible for man to attain virtue by his own unaided means. It is necessary for him to submit to spiritual direction. St. Ignatius had already insisted on the importance of a director in doing the *Exercises*. St. Francis — perhaps as a reaction against the Protestant doctrine of direct inspiration by the Spirit — insists from the very first on "man's need of a conductor." The director must be a "faithful friend," and between his penitents and him there must arise "a strong and sweet friendship . . . quite holy, quite sacred, quite divine and spiritual," in which "reverence should not diminish trustfulness, nor trustfulness prevent reverence."

In order to reach perfection, one should begin with "purgation of the soul"; purgation from mortal sin first, and then from the "affections toward sin." The former should be achieved through exercises which strongly recall those of St. Ignatius. The latter extends to all "affections"; to deliberate venial sin, and even to all dangerous things which, though not evil in themselves, may be the occasion of offending God, such as "dances, banquets, pomps, comedies"; lastly, to all those "faults and failings" in our temper which are not voluntary, and therefore not sinful, but which should nonetheless be amended. In order to achieve purgation, pious exercises are necessary: daily mental prayer of one hour's duration, prayer when getting up or going to bed, examination of conscience, inward recollection or "spiritual retreat," weekly confession and frequent Communion. These were the exercises practiced by the

Clerks Regular, and recommended in the *Spiritual Combat*. St. Francis was the first to deem it possible to extend them to the laity. However there is nothing rigid about his devotional scheme. "Devotion should be differently exercised by a gentleman, by a craftsman, by a valet, by a prince, by a widow, by a maiden, by a married woman; moreover, its practice should be accommodated to the strength, business and duties of each particular person." Such "adaptation" is true to the Ignatian spirit. It plays no less a part in prayer, where no unvarying method is prescribed. If, while engaged in vocal prayer, you should feel attracted to mental prayer, "let your mind glide gently" toward the latter; if business or some other cause has prevented one from mental prayer in the morning, "try to amend that fault in the afternoon."

The same practical-mindedness appears in the scheme adopted by St. Francis for mental prayer, which is simpler than that of St. Ignatius or Luis de Granada, and more precise than that of the *Spiritual Combat*. It includes four points: preparation, considerations, affections and resolutions, and the conclusion or "spiritual bouquet." "Adaptation" to a life in the world again appears in that part of the *Introduction* which is devoted to the practice of virtue. To the monastic trinity of obedience, chastity, and poverty are now added such virtues as can develop from social relations, patience with others, humbleness, mildness toward others and toward oneself, calm in the midst of a busy life. Then, again, there are the natural qualities which should appear in friendships, in conversations, in the sober style of one's dress, in games and pastimes. The devout person, according to St. Francis, ought to be a perfect gentleman. Thus will his devotion attract love. Everyday life, as a matter of fact, provides many occasions for the exercise of the "small" virtues, which are the necessary preparation for the great ones. It is not always possible to meet with great sufferings; let us, at any rate, "patiently bear petty insults, small inconveniences, tiny losses, which occur daily . . . a headache, a toothache . . . the breaking of a glass . . . the loss of one's gloves, ring or handkerchief, the trouble of going to bed betimes or getting up early in order to pray or to go to communion. . . . All these petty sufferings, when embraced with lovingness, are extremely pleasant to the divine kindness."

The "small" virtues, "patience, meekness, mortification of the heart, humbleness . . . tenderness toward one's neighbor, forbearance toward his faults, diligence and holy favor," play an important part in St. Francis' plan for the devotional life. He insists on lowliness most. He illustrates the Ignatian *aliis deferre* in the following words: "Readily condescend to the will of your fellow-men, giving way to their opinions in what is not evil, without being quarrelsome or peevish." The stress is here laid on the passive rather than on the active virtues; and here the temper of the saint differs from that of the Jesuit, who insisted more on the exercise of the will. "It seems to me," he writes to a Parisian nun, "that I see you assiduously and restlessly seeking after perfection. . . . Let yourself be governed by God, do not think so much of yourself. . . ." One should neither overstrain oneself, nor be led by remorse to aimless self-searchings: "One must not be too finicky in the exercise of virtue, but go about it roundly, frankly, naïvely, in the old French fashion, with freedom, with good faith, . . . For I fear the spirit of constraint and melancholy."

When all is said, the dominant feature about St. Francis de Sales is the quality of ease, of simplicity, of naturalness — in one word, of liberty. "We ought to do everything," he wrote, "through love and not through force; we should love obedience rather than fear disobedience. I leave you the spirit of liberty. . . ." Add to this another humanistic trait, his partiality for balance, for the golden mean, for equability; the moderation and yet the stoic fortitude of his moral and devotional ideal. "We ought to resist evil, he says, and repress the vices of those in our charge, constantly and valiantly, yet sweetly and peacefully"; and again: "We should feel dissatisfaction for our sins, but it should be peaceful, sedate and firm; for as a judge punishes the wicked much better if he issues his sentences through reason, in a spirit of tranquillity, than if he acts rashly and passionately . . . even thus, we chastise ourselves much better through quiet and constant repentance, than if it is bitter, solicitous and angry." One of the chapters of the *Introduction* is entitled: "That one should have a just and reasonable mind." Liberty, moderation, reason: here is the true temper of the Christianized Renaissance, of that "devout humanism" which was both the cause and the consequence of the Catholic Reformation.

* * *

The same spirit is found among the French successors and imitators of St. Francis, such as Etienne Binet, Jean-Pierre Camus, Father Yves de Paris. In various ways they still represent the florid imagination and easy optimism of the Renaissance. However, such southern freedom and exuberance were really foreign to the true spirit of France. The properly so-called French school of devotion is graver and sparer in expression and temperament; it takes a gloomier view of man's nature, expects less from it and more from God's grace, and insists on human nothingness. It is

Pauline or Augustinian rather than Salesian. It is not indeed Jansenistic; but its seriousness and austerity make it possible to understand the later rise of Jansenism.

The head of the French school was Pierre de Bérulle, the founder of the French Oratory. He was born at Sérilly in the Champagne on February 4, 1575. Through both his parents he belonged to that class of lawyers, attached to the Paris "Parlement," or high court of justice, which was famous for the strictness of its moral life and for its Gallican tendencies. He imbibed from his mother a distaste for worldly pleasures and an inclination for piety. He went through his course of studies in various Parisian colleges, notably at the Collège de Clermont, then later at the Sorbonne.

While he was reading philosophy, toward 1593, he was impressed by the sovereignty of God and the dependency of all creatures upon Him. He gave expression to his ideas in a *Brief Discourse of Christian Abnegation,* published in 1597, in which the doctrine of "abnegation" appears in the following words: "There are two foundation-stones to this abnegation. The former is a very mean esteem of all created things, and of oneself more than of all others, acquired by frequent reflection on their cheapness, and by a daily experience of one's infirmity and nothingness. . . . The latter is a very high esteem of God, manifested through . . . total submission of ourselves to Him, through worshipping Him and granting Him full powers over us and what is ours." Bérulle takes pleasure in humiliating decayed human nature. This is obviously contrary to the spirit of humanism, against which he is initiating a reaction, while reverting to the pessimism of St. Augustine, whom he calls "the eagle among doctors."

Ordained a priest on June 5, 1599, he became honorary almoner to King Henry IV. He was then mostly engaged in the direction of souls, and in controversy with the Protestants, while cooperating with Madame Acarie in introducing the Reformed Carmelites into France. In 1611, he created the French Oratory, wholly consecrated to Jesus Christ, the sovereign Priest. To this foundation, and to the later career of Bérulle, who died in 1629, we shall later revert. The important fact is that he had already been struck for some years by the humiliation undergone by Christ in assuming His human nature, and the consequent necessity for us of thoroughly humbling our own selves. He composed a formula of elevation to Jesus and Mary, which was censured by the universities of Louvain and Douai. In reply to this disapproval, he wrote his master work, the *Greatness of Jesus*, divided into twelve discourses. The human nature of Christ, he says, is "essentially in a state of servitude" which is both the cause of its greatness and the condition of our salvation. We too should be in a state of servitude toward the son of God and His Mother. Bérulle reverted to that devotion to the person of Christ which had been forgotten amid the metaphysical speculations of the fifteenth century.

The essential virtue for him is the virtue of religion. Adoration of God is the chief duty of a Christian. As his disciple, Bourgoing, was to say, it was worse "to bring up souls in a certain liberty and familiarity with God, than in abasement and holy terror before Him." God ought to be worshipped, not so much on account of His kindness toward us, as on account of His sovereign majesty. The reaction against the Salesian school is here obvious. Again, following St. Augustine, Bérulle insists on the action of divine grace in our sanctification, as against that of our own will.

The essence of the doctrine of Bérulle and of his disciples, Condren and Olier, is abnegation. This is grounded on the "three nothingnesses" of man, the nothingness out of which God drew us through creation, the nothingness into which Adam cast us through sin, and the nothingness into which we must enter to adhere to Christ. Condren, the second superior of the French Oratory (1588–1641), insisted on the virtue of sacrifice. Jesus, according to him, is perpetually in the "state of a host"; we should not merely worship Him as such, but become hosts too, through the annihilation of our own selves.

The disciple of Condren, Jean-Jacques Olier, the founder of the seminary of Saint Sulpice (1608–1657), stressed the necessity of mortification. Man should utterly renounce himself, and "all desires of honor, pleasure and riches"; what is more — note the opposition with St. Francis and Richeome — he should "avoid the occasions . . . in which his heart can become filled with love and complacency for some creature." The Christian should make himself another Christ, and appropriate to himself His mysteries, chiefly His incarnation, His infancy, His crucifixion, His death, His burial, His resurrection, and His ascension. He accomplishes in himself a "small incarnation" by casting off his own self and putting on Jesus Christ. He comes into the state of infancy through the virtues of a child: utter abandonment to the guidance of Jesus, indifference to everything, simplicity, purity, sweetness, and meekness. He participates in the state of crucifixion through mortification, in the state of death through inward renunciation and peace, in the burial of Christ through the total destruction of self, in the ascension through perfect union with Jesus.

This identification with the person of Christ is even more absolute in the case of the priest, since, in the words of Bourgoing, "of all the qualities and greatnesses which the son of God has acquired in our nature, the highest and most exalted one is the dignity of a sovereign priest." Jesus preaches through the mouth of his priests, consecrates the host through them, forgives sins through them. The powers of the priest are stupendous. When he produces Christ in the Eucharist he may be compared to the Virgin Mary.

The excellence of the priesthood was asserted by another representative of the French school, St. Vincent de Paul (1581–1660). His character is an attractive blending of Berullian austerity, French common sense, and Salesian cheerfulness. Like St. Teresa and St. Francis he asserts that true love is necessarily manifested in action: "Let us love God, my brethren," he writes, "let us love God, but let this be in the labor of our arms, let it be in the sweat of our faces." He warns the alumni at the seminary of St. Sulpice against "excess to be avoided in the love of God." "His kindness," he says, "does not want us to . . . ruin our health by dint of acts of love; no, no, he does not ask us to kill ourselves."

The spiritual doctrine of St. Vincent de Paul, like that of the French school in general, is ascetical rather than mystical. Though he had experienced ecstasies and visions himself, he did not consider himself a mystic. His devotional ideal was primarily one of charitable action. "Are we ready," he asked his brother-priests, "to bear the pains that God will send us, and to stifle the motions of nature, in order to live solely the life of Jesus-Christ? Are we ready to go to Poland, to Barbary, to the Indies, in order to sacrifice to him our pleasures and our lives? If so, let us bless God. But if, on the contrary, there are some among us . . . who are still the slaves of nature, and who are given to the pleasures of the flesh . . . let them consider themselves as unworthy of the apostolic vocation to which God has called them, and enter into confusion on seeing their brethren who practice it so worthily, and on finding that they themselves are so far from the minds and hearts of these."

The attachment of the French school to the person of Jesus was manifested by the flowering forth of several new devotions. The Holy Sacrament was, of course, an object of especial worship at the seminary of St. Sulpice, since the most eminent dignity of the priest consisted, according to Olier, in consecrating the Eucharist. Bérulle, when a cardinal, instituted for the French Oratory the "Feast of Jesus" in order to honor, "not some particular mystery" of the life of Christ, but "His divine person and the whole of the adorable compound of man and God." He himself wrote the office of the feast, which was approved by Rome on February 1, 1625. This was later to develop, under the influence of St. Francis de Sales, into the feast of the Sacred Heart of Jesus, which however was not celebrated until 1672, in the congregation of religious founded by St. John Eudes.

Of all the schools of devotion, the French undoubtedly bears the strongest national stamp. National individuality is however clearly marked in all the various schools — including the English school, ranging from Thomas More to Persons, Southwell, and Crashaw, which will be dealt with later. But the differences — even the French anti-humanistic reaction — are insignificant when compared to the essential likeness. All the schools were agreed in stressing the fact that the mystical life and moral life are intimately related, that there are no raptures independent from right conduct, and that mere emotion and feeling are to be distrusted and avoided; that acts of virtue are the due preparation for mystical experiences, no less than their immediate consequence; that ecstasies are a gratuitous gift from God, not to be strained after, but only accepted when they come, and that in their absence, and in states of spiritual drouth, the only thing to do is to persevere in utter compliance with God's behests; that though love of God be at the root of all spiritual life, such love is not so much manifested by motions of the heart, as by the exercise of the obedient will. Add to this that, in every case, the ascetical and mystical writers of the various schools utilized their experiences and directed their teachings so as to lead toward the betterment of the religious orders, or the laity, or the secular clergy. From all this there emerges a body of spiritual doctrine which may truly be said to have been one of the foundations of the Catholic Reformation.

CHAPTER XI

The Catholic Reformation After Trent

THE Council of Trent was indeed a turning-point in the history of the Church, and the scandalous conditions which had prevailed in it then were never to be repeated to the same extent. The history of the papacy in the century which followed Trent discloses a succession of grave, virtuous, well-meaning popes. True, intriguing had not entirely disappeared from the conclaves; yet the cardinals sincerely tried to elect the best one among them. The work of Reformation — essentially that of applying, interpreting, and developing the Trentine code — was now proceeding apace. The very setting in which this religious action was taking place was now more favorable. Many international problems arose, it is true, in connection with the spread of Protestantism and the self-centered policy of the various European sovereigns; yet Italy was no longer torn by internal wars, and the period was for her one of peace and plenty. The moral prestige of the papacy had been restored; the Church was no longer pressed on every hand and in danger of its very life; its position was now stabilized, and it was able to take the offensive in its turn. Space forbids detailed examination of the difficulties with which the successive popes had to grapple in their struggles with the Emperor and with the kings of France, England, and Spain. We must confine ourselves to a brief rehearsal of the steps taken by each of them for the reinforcement of Church discipline and the strengthening of Christian faith and devotion.

On the death of Pius IV, the bull he had issued to provide rules for the conclave was complied with. Absolute secrecy was enforced, and all relations between the cardinals and the outer world were interrupted. The saintly Cardinal Charles Borromeo exerted a great influence on the deliberations which lasted three weeks, and ended, on January 7, 1566, in the election of Antonio Ghislieri, who was to be known later as St. Pius V.

The new pope was a pattern of monastic virtue and austerity. He was born on January 17, 1504, near Alexandria, and had, from his earliest youth, consecrated himself to the service of God. At the age of fourteen, he entered a Dominican convent. He made his profession in 1521 and was ordained a priest in 1528. For many years he was a lecturer in philosophy and theology in the house of his Order at Pavia. A strict observer of the vow of poverty, blameless in his life and utterly humble, he refused to wear a mantle, and he cherished personal cleanliness: "I have constantly loved poverty," he used to say, "but dirt never." Despite his humbleness, he rose to be prior of his convent, then definitor of the Order; and next he was appointed inquisitor of the diocese of Como, at the time threatened with the invasion of Protestantism. The discharge of his duties brought him into touch with Cardinal Caraffa, the rigid Theatine, who made him commissary general of the Inquisition. When Caraffa became Pope Paul IV, he appointed Ghislieri bishop of Sutri and Nepi and prefect of the palace of the Inquisition, then cardinal in 1577, and grand inquisitor in 1558. His insistence on regular Church discipline kept him out of favor under Pius IV; and his election to the pontificate was for him quite unexpected.

His election was due solely to his virtues, The new dignity he regarded as a heavy cross, under which he might be crushed, and he remained as pope the austere monk he had been before. He was indefatigable in his work, even at the time of the *sirocco*. He ate and drank little, and seldom allowed himself any entertainment. Much given to walking, he was likely to tire out those who followed him. He prayed much and fervently, to the point of tears, spent the whole of Holy Week in meditation, and had a special veneration for the crucifix. He took part in all religious ceremonies, and himself performed the painful pilgrimage of the seven churches, which no pope of the Renaissance had ever been seen to undertake. The feast of Corpus Christi, too, he observed with great devotion. He cherished the truth in all things, and hated dissemblers.

Not gifted with ability, either for diplomacy or politics, he was concerned first and foremost with the salvation of souls. In an address to the cardinals, five days after his election, he observed that the misbehavior of the clergy had contributed not a little to the spread of heresy. Let the cardinals reform themselves and their households. If they did so, they would enjoy his favor and trust. The prescriptions of the council should, the pope said, be complied with exactly, especially as regarded the duty of residence. He wished to establish peace between the Christian princes, to destroy heresy, and to help in repulsing the Turks.

From the beginning of his pontificate, Pius V asserted his independence and disinterestedness. He sent Dominican visitors to the Vatican back to their convents. He kept free from the influence of the Theatines and Jesuits. He held the cardinals at arm's length, especially his nephew, Bonelli, whom he compelled to monastic austerity. He banished another nephew, Paolo Ghislieri, and deprived him of all his goods, on account of his dissolute behavior. He enforced the most stringent legislation in Rome against immorality in every form. On April 1, 1566, he proclaimed severe penalties against those who disturbed divine service or broke the Sabbath; against simony, blasphemy, sodomy, and concubinage. Steps were taken to prevent excessive luxury, ruinous dowries, games on feast days, and scandalous disguises at carnival time. Physicians were made to exhort their patients to receive the sacrament of penance, and suspend their visits if they demurred. Despite the outcry of those whose financial interests were threatened, all female panders and notable courtesans were either expelled from Rome or compelled to amend their lives. Adulterers of both sexes were punished with public whipping, imprisonment, or exile. The Swiss guards were obliged to marry or forsake their concubines. In accordance with the Trentine decree, the children of Rome had to be sent to church on Sunday afternoons, and to be taught Christian doctrine, lay helpers being provided to assist in their catechizing. The charitable activity of Pius V was intense. In regard to art he was no barbarian, though he insisted on the decency of the papal palaces.

Pius V's reforming spirit was manifested in the choice of his helpers, in the remodeling of the Curia, in the administration of the diocese of Rome and the other Italian dioceses, in the steps taken toward the education of the clergy and laity, in the enforcement of monastic discipline. The pope made Borromeo his principal adviser. When the latter had returned to his archdiocese of Milan, his place was taken by his chief assistant, Niccolo Ormanetto, a Veronese priest of the school of Giberti, who severely cut down the papal establishment. The cardinals were reminded that their style of life ought to be simple, and that they ought not to eat out of silver plate. Those who were created by Pius V — four in 1568, and the unusual number of sixteen in 1570 — were men of learning and virtue, such as Jérôme Souchier, the abbot general of the Cistercians, or the Greek scholar, Antonio Carafa. Among them was the Theatine, Paolo Burali, a man of exceptional saintliness, who, as bishop of Parma, had created free schools, a seminary, an orphanage, an asylum for virgins and widows, a refuge for converted prostitutes, a convent of Capuchins and one of Theatines.

Pius V did his best to put an end to the abuses still persisting in the

Curia. Financial needs had led the popes to sell many positions, and those who had bought them at a high cost tried to squeeze out of them as much money as possible. The pope tried to put a stop to this scandal. "Better starve than lose your souls," he said to some officials of the Penitentiary, as he dismissed them. The Penitentiary was wholly remodelled in 1569; its offices were no longer for sale, and were filled with Dominicans, Observants, or Jesuits. Pius V took to heart his duties as bishop of the diocese of Rome. He undertook the visitation of the Roman churches, beginning with St. Peter's; of the hospitals, women's convents, and prisons. He subjected all secular and regular priests to an examination in order to ascertain their fitness as confessors; and candidates for the priesthood had to satisfy the pope's vicars of their qualifications, while future bishops had to appear before a papal commission. The use of the ecclesiastical dress was enforced. Churchmen who resided in Rome without valid reasons were sent back either to their dioceses, to their parishes, or to their benefices. The same measures were applied to the States of the Church and extended to the Italian dioceses.

The Trentine catechism was at last printed by the publisher, Paolo Manucci, and translated into Italian, German, and French. In 1568, the improved Breviary was issued; it answered to the new spirit of historical criticism, and many fables or dubious feasts had been replaced. The revised Missal was also sanctioned by a bull of July 14, 1570, and enforced upon all churches that had not had a proper liturgy for at least two hundred years. Four of the Greek Fathers were proclaimed doctors of the Church, together with St. Thomas Aquinas, whose theology had been victorious at Trent. A special Congregation of the Index was created on November 9, 1570. The Congregation entrusted with the interpretation of the council continued its heavy work. It declared in favor of the validity of Calvinist baptism. Pius V insisted on the universal enforcement of the decrees of Trent. Decency and reverence were now restored in the churches. Pious confraternities were encouraged, such as that of the Name of God, which purposed to heal private feuds; that of the Beheading of St. John the Baptist, which looked after persons under sentence of death; and that of the Annunciation of the Virgin, which provided dowries for poor maidens.

Pius V loathed covetousness and rejected all proposals to obtain funds for the Church by dubious means. He forbade the preaching of indulgences for the benefit of churches and hospitals. He did away with so-called confidential simony, through which a benefice was taken in charge by a bishop or cardinal in the name of a person under canonical age, sometimes a mere baby, until he should be able to occupy it; which was tantamount to hereditary succession.

Lastly, the pope made strenuous efforts toward the moral improvement of the secular and regular clergy. He supported the work of such popular missionaries as John of Ávila in Spain, and Alessandro Sauli in Corsica. The Cistercian Order had fallen into great decay; its Italian monasteries were deserted or occupied by other orders, its churches were falling to ruin. A bull of March 8, 1570, compelled the commendatory abbots to leave in their convents a sufficient number of religious, to provide for their needs, and to repair ruinous buildings. The pope dared not abolish the tenure of abbeys *in commendam*, which was widely spread, especially in France. But he suppressed the Order of the Umiliati, who, forgetful of their origins, offered a luxurious abode and life to the nobility of Lombardy. Pius V was eager to correct abuses among the Spanish Franciscans, and enrolled all the unreformed Conventuals among the Observants. The same process was applied to the other Spanish, Portuguese, and Netherlandish orders in which there were Conventuals and Observants, such as the Benedictines, Cistercians, Dominicans, Augustinian hermits, and Carmelites. The Franciscans as a whole soon followed suit, and drafted new constitutions at their general chapter of 1568.

About that time the pope launched a general reform of all religious orders, which he wanted to recall to their pristine purity, and especially to the observance of poverty. "All religious life," he said, "is ruined by private property." He limited to a short term the office of the superiors, and compelled them to give up their lordly style of life and share in the privations of the religious, which made their charges less desirable for the ambitious. A minimum age of nineteen was prescribed for the taking of vows in several orders, while monks were forbidden to wander about in search of monasteries suited to their taste. The *clausura* was enforced in women's convents, even where it had never existed or had fallen into disuse. Lastly several new or reformed orders were created under Pius V. St. Peter of Alcantara (1499–1562) founded in Spain a severer branch of the Observants, which later spread to the other Franciscan provinces. We have already mentioned the Carmelite reform effected by St. Teresa of Jesus. St. John of God founded the Brothers of Mercy for the service of the sick in hospitals. On the whole, though Pius V met with great difficulties in Spain and in the Empire, and though he did not succeed in bringing England and Scotland back to the Fold, his pontificate, which culminated in the victory of Lepanto over the Turks (October 7,

1571), was a fruitful one, in which the principles laid down at Trent began to pass into fact.

*   *   *

The work of enforcing the Trentine legislation was taken up anew when Cardinal Ugo Boncompagni was elected to succeed Pius V as Pope Gregory XIII, after a conclave of one day's duration, on May 12, 1572. Born at Bologna, on January 1, 1502, he had studied and then taught law with great success at the university of his native town. He came to Rome in 1539, and began his career as an official in the Curia, in which he occupied several legal, administrative, and diplomatic posts under Paul III and Paul IV. He was also in favor with Pius IV and had the closest personal relations with Borromeo, who brought about in him an actual conversion to the reforming spirit. He was active at Trent and enjoyed the trust of Pius V. It had been thought that he would relax the severity of the latter, but any such hopes were disappointed as soon as he began to create new dignitaries. Under the influence of Borromeo he made one of the latter's helpers, Cardinal Tolomeo Galli, Secretary of State. He showed no favor to his nephews or to the sons he had had before his priesthood. He was an indefatigable worker, a frugal eater, an austere and devout worshipper, a man of unbounded generosity. He helped, with his gifts, widows and orphans, marriageable maidens, regular and secular clerics, scholars, and converted Jews.

He was gifted with great practical sense and was a born organizer. He improved the system of government of the Church by creating new congregations of cardinals, notably for reform in general, for the reform of canon law, for the reform of the ceremonial, and for the new edition of Holy Scripture. He considered Pius V's orders enforcing compliance with the decrees of Trent to be irrevocable. That they might be applied, a committee of cardinals was created, which included the most rigid reformers: Borromeo, Paleotto, Aldobrandini, Burali. Abuses, however, die hard; and the ever-recurring work of correction falls under the same heads as in the previous pontificate. Residence was again made compulsory; non-resident cardinals were deprived of their bishoprics. The pope refused to sanction the appointment of bishops by temporal sovereigns, unless the candidates were fully qualified. The foundation of diocesan seminaries was prescribed everywhere. The virtues recommended to the bishops were prudence, charity and patience. They were urged to hold visitations, but also to proceed considerately, and mildly.

The pope's reforming activity was supported by that of Cardinal Borromeo in his archdiocese of Milan. He held numerous provincial and diocesan councils, in which the Trentine legislation was completed and made more precise. Their decrees were embodied in a book known as the *Acts of the Church of Milan,* which was published in 1582 and broadcast throughout Europe, where it served as a prototype for the decisions of other ecclesiastical assemblies. The archdiocese of Milan was a very large one, with a population of nearly 900,000 inhabitants. Ignorance and immorality flourished freely there. A number of priests did not know the words of absolution; many laymen were ignorant of the *Pater noster.* There were dances in the churches and women's convents. In order to amend this state of things, Borromeo divided his archdiocese into six districts, over which he placed capable priests, who met frequently to adjust their views and make proposals to their chief. A number of seminaries, schools, and colleges were created. The results obtained were astonishing. Borromeo congratulated himself, in 1566, on the fact that his flock "were persuaded . . . that all must henceforth embrace a new life."

A similar state of things obtained in Rome. In 1576, the great Spanish canonist, Martin Azpilcueta, deemed that of all the European cities, Rome itself gave the strongest impression of moral renovation: "For centuries past," he said, "there has not been a college of cardinals so blameless, pious, prudent, righteous, chaste and learned." There was much progress also among the religious orders, though we cannot dwell at length on the steps taken by Gregory XIII to restore discipline among them, or to support such reformers as St. Teresa of Jesus and St. Philip Neri.

The moral improvement of the clergy of all nations was largely due to the foundation of residential colleges in Rome, which were entrusted to the Society of Jesus. The German college was endowed and created in 1573. A Hungarian college followed in 1578. Gregory had subsidized the college founded at Douai in Flanders by exiles from England. In 1579, he founded at Rome the English college. A Greek college had come into existence two years before, for Catholics of the Eastern rite. Add to this again a Maronite and an Armenian college, and one for converts from Islam or Judaism. The central teaching institution for all these was the Roman college properly so-called, which was accommodated in new buildings in 1565, and became the Gregorian University, where Suarez, Bellarmine, and many other illustrious scholars lectured.

Gregory XIII, himself a learned man, did his best to help in the advancement of science. He established a printing press for Eastern languages, and augmented the Vatican library. It is hardly necessary to recall his reform of the calendar. On the whole, this generous and cultured pope, by providing extensive means of education for the clergy and laity, and by helping in the development of learning, completed the work of his predecessor, the rigid disciplinarian, Pius V.

The next pope, Sixtus V, was a commanding personality, and one who has given rise to much debate and contention both during his lifetime and afterwards. He was born on December 13, 1521, of a family of poor peasants. In his childhood he was occupied in humble farm-work: hence the legend that he was a swineherd by trade. His maternal uncle, Fra. Salvatore, a Franciscan Conventual, took the boy under his protection, brought him to his convent to live with him, and educated him very strictly. Young Felice — he had been so called from a dream of his parents, in which he was seen to wear the tiara — was eager to become a Franciscan himself, and joined the Order at the age of twelve. He threw himself into his duties as a religious with characteristic ardor, became a learned theologian and a fiery preacher, in which capacity he met with great success in Rome from 1552 onwards. He came into touch with reforming circles, and made the acquaintance of Ignatius Loyola, Philip Neri, the Capuchin Felice da Cantalice, and Cardinal Caraffa. After a difficult period during which he met with opposition as an inquisitor in Venice, he was made procurator-general of his Order in Rome. Then his patron, Cardinal Ghislieri, who had meanwhile become Pope Pius V, made him vicar-general of the Conventual Franciscans, and next bishop of St. Agatha of the Goths in southern Italy. On May 17, 1570, he became Cardinal Montalto. He was in disfavor under Gregory XIII, whose scholarly temperament could hardly agree with his vehement character. His elevation to the papacy at last opened a wide field for his impetuous activities.

Sixtus V was animated with the most ardent personal piety. His notebook, which has been preserved, began with the following beautiful words: "Prevent, we beseech thee, O Lord, our actions by Thy inspiration and further them with Thy continual help; that every prayer and work of ours may always begin from Thee, and through Thee be likewise ended." He was sincerely and ardently desirous to correct the abuses, which had never yet been wholly uprooted, and were cropping up again. It would be tedious to rehearse all the steps which, following in the wake of Pius V, he took to that end: the energetic visitation of all the churches, colleges, and religious houses in Rome; the enforcement of the *clausura* in women's convents, or residence for the bishops and even cardinals. Offences were dealt with firmly: a monk and a nun who had had guilty relations were both put to death. On one point, the reforming work of

Sixtus V was original and remarkably effective: he gave new force to the order which made it compulsory for bishops to pay regular visits to Rome, at intervals varying from three to ten years according to the distance of their sees from the Eternal City. These visits *ad limina* awakened the bishops to a keener sense of their duty and had immediate effects, especially in Germany.

Sixtus V took other steps in regard to the administration of the Church. The college of cardinals was remodeled so as to become a real deliberative assembly, the number of its members being fixed at seventy, namely six bishops, fifty priests, and fourteen deacons. The pope also realized that the Church could best be governed by committees, and therefore established, by a bull of January 22, 1588, fifteen permanent congregations, four of which were wholly new: the consistorial congregation, entrusted with the formation of new dioceses; that of the Segnatura di Grazia, which was to examine petitions and graces; that of rites and ceremonies; and lastly that of the Vatican press. The congregations took over most of the work up till then transacted in Consistory. In his creation of thirty-three new cardinals, Sixtus V was actuated by no motives of selfishness or interest; he appointed only men of virtue and integrity.

He showed favor to Camillus de Lellis (1550–1614), the founder of the "Fathers of a Good Death," an association of infirmarians, who bound themselves to give corporal and spiritual assistance to sick people in the hour of death; and likewise to the Capuchins, Felice da Cantalice (1515–1587) and Giuseppe da Leonessa (1556–1612), whose apostolic labors and saintly lives had gained popular veneration. Though he erected new tribunals of the Inquisition, he was less severe in his dealings with accused persons than might have been expected. He prepared a new Index which was not completed. He was even less fortunate in his publication of a new edition of the Vulgate, corrected by himself in an unscholarly fashion, which he dared not make the official version. Other incidents occurred under his pontificate, which made the course of the Catholic Reformation less easy. Difficulties arose in connection with the Jesuit Order, owing both to attacks from outside, and to dissensions inside the Society, which however in the long run continued true to the tradition established by its founder.

The financial policy of Sixtus V was even more deplorable. He wished to make the papacy powerful and independent, and therefore wealthy; and he went about this task with characteristic thoroughness. He subjected the population of his States to heavy taxation, and when this was not sufficient, he used more questionable means. He generalized the sale of papal offices. An auditor of the Camera had to pay 54,000 gold *scudi*, a cleric of the Camera 36,000. Knighthoods were sold profusely, too. In this respect the correction of abuses suffered a definite setback. On the whole, though Sixtus V continued the work of his predecessors to some extent, he has been aptly compared to Julius II, for his action in favor of the Church was political rather than properly religious. Nor was the Catholic Reformation much advanced under the brief pontificates of his three successors, Urban VII (September 14–24, 1590), Gregory XIV (December 5, 1590–October 15, 1591), and Innocent IX (October 29–December 30, 1591). It was only to be resumed with Clement VIII.

With the seventeenth century, we come upon a period of comparative stability and security in the history of the Church. The reforming tradition is now established. Abuses, indeed, have not been finally suppressed — how could they be as long as men are men? — but they are periodically corrected as they reappear. The administrative machinery of the papacy is now concentrated, simplified, and efficient. The general atmosphere of Rome is one of piety. The Church has not succeeded in establishing the theocratical sovereignty over the temporal rulers of Europe which even such popes as Clement VIII or Urban VIII aimed at; but its moral situation has nevertheless been consolidated, and though it cannot command obedience, it is surrounded with devotion and respect. The jubilee of the year 1600 was typical in this connection. Three million pilgrims flocked to Rome to take part in it. Under the successive pontificates of Clement VIII (1592–1605), Paul V (1605–1621), Gregory XV (1621–1623), Urban VIII (1623–1644), and Innocent X (1644–1655), papal policy developed on the lines which have been described above. The popes, indeed, had much to do with temporal affairs, in the period of the Gunpowder Plot, of the Oath of Allegiance, and of the Thirty Years' War; but they gave due attention to the religious needs of the Christian people. The duty of residence was severely enforced by the energetic Paul V. Even cardinals had to leave Rome or to resign their benefices. The latter were chosen among men of virtue and learning. Among those who were created by Clement VIII were the illustrious convert, du Perron; the learned Tolet; Bellarmine, the master of controversy; and Baronius, the master of ecclesiastical history.

The revision and publishing of liturgical books was steadily proceeding. The Breviary, amended by Clement VIII, was finally put into its present shape by Urban VIII; the former pope also issued editions of the *Index*, the *Pontificale*, the *Ceremonial of bishops*, and the *Missal*. The government of the Church was made firmer and safer by the new legislation on papal elections introduced by Gregory XV, which bound the members of the conclave to swear that their vote went to the best one among the candidates. The older religious orders were compelled to observe their rule and discipline, the wandering about of monks being again proscribed by Urban VIII. The same pope and Innocent X approved new religious societies inspired by an ardent devotional ideal: the Order of the Visitation; the Noble Widows of Dôle, founded to propagate the worship of the Immaculate Conception; and the Brothers of Christian Doctrine, established by César de Bus in 1592. That the work already accomplished by the Catholic reformers might be officially taken stock of and sanctioned, and popular devotion toward them fostered, the most illustrious among them were canonized: St. Charles Borromeo by Paul V; St. Ignatius, St. Francis Xavier, St. Philip Neri, and St. Teresa by Gregory XV; while Gaetano da Thiene and Felice da Cantalice were beatified by Urban VIII. Gregory XV did much to promote grave and serious devotions that would work as a healing balm after the Church had been so grievously wounded; he prescribed the universal veneration of St. Anne, fixed the feast of St. Joseph on the 19th of March, and forbade unedifying denials of the Immaculate Conception of the Virgin Mary. The period of the Catholic Reformation properly so-called worthily closes with the Jubilee of 1650, in which Pope Innocent X prayed with the crowd in every ceremony, and induced the Roman noblemen to lend their houses to strangers, so that Christendom, "as in the times of the primitive Church," seemed really to be but "one body and one soul."

*   *   *

It was a comparatively easy task to amend Church conditions in Rome, in the papal States, in Italy, and even in Spain, where Protestantism had gained little or no footing. Even temporal rulers there were convinced of the necessity of Catholic reform, and no resistance was to be expected save from those who profited by the ever-renascent abuses. But in Germany, in Central and Northern Europe, it was a different affair altogether. These countries were divided between Protestant and Catholic rulers; the prevailing religious confusion and social chaos made it difficult to obtain the unanimous support of civil authorities, while those who stood to suffer from the disciplinary action of the Holy See immediately threatened secession to Protestantism. In the circumstances, the first thing to do was to appeal to the authority of the Emperor — who was theoretically supreme over most of Central Europe, and always protested fidelity to the Catholic faith — and to those among the feudal princes who had remained true to the old religion, and persuade them to prevail upon their subjects to follow their lead. The principle *cujus regio, ejus religio* still obtained in the Empire; it allowed of sweeping changes; and thus the history of the partial reconquest of Germany by Catholicism is largely of a diplomatic nature. We shall not dwell at length upon the missions of the nuncios. As a matter of fact, however important their action might be, the main problem was that of education; for the Catholic Reformation could not be continued except by princes and prelates who had had a Catholic upbringing. Its foundation in the Empire and neighboring countries is therefore to be found in the erection of colleges, and is essentially the work of the Society of Jesus.

The abuses which the Jesuits had set out to correct provided ample support for the Protestant revolt. This revolt, however, was made a pretext for their continuation. To many, evangelical liberty became a synonym for moral laxity. "The scandalous conduct of the clergy," a contemporary says, "was the chief cause of sectarianism," and, according to a writing of 1561, many prelates and ecclesiastical superiors took advantage of the new doctrines "to annex the wealth of the abbeys, to marry, play the temporal lords and lead a joyous life with the money of the Churches and of the poor." But it was not merely among the favorers of Lutheranism that moral disorders prevailed. Even where outward fidelity to the old faith was still professed, the evils were quite as great. From Vienna the Jesuit, Peter Canisius, wrote in 1564: "Young men no longer care for the priesthood. From what I hear on every hand, in the space of twenty years, scarcely have two students of the university been ordained. . . . Unless God send workmen to his vineyard, the people will become, I do not say merely heretical, but like to brute beasts." "Prelates," the Jesuit Scherer said in a sermon, "do little to provide with good priests the pulpits and altars of the churches entrusted to them. They appoint the most incapable pastors, . . . that neither preach nor celebrate, that are unable to administer any sacrament, and lead such unpriestly lives that they scandalize people to the loss of their souls. . . . The few books owned by religious are gnawed away by rats, worms and dust. . . . Superiors . . . allow licence to settle down in their houses . . .; they run into debt, they spend their income in feasts and revels; they consider as their property what has only been lent to them."

These abuses were largely due to the fact that bishoprics and abbacies were invariably in the hands of noblemen, whom it was almost impossible to call to account for their misdeeds. The same cause made it especially difficult to reform cathedral chapters, which were in sore need of amendment. "Out of twenty-four, thirty, or even forty canons," the Catholic controversialist, John Eck, wrote in 1540, "scarcely are there five or six who are priests. I have lately seen a chapter where neither the bishop nor the provost, nor the dean were in holy orders." The Catholic flock as a whole had fallen into a state of listless apathy. "It seems indeed," the nuncio, Commendone, wrote in 1561, "as if it were our people themselves who teach that faith is enough without works, so little desirous do they seem to remedy present evils."

When these lines were written, however, the reaction against the state of things which they depict had already set in for twenty years. It was, at the outset, the work of three Jesuits, Peter Faber, Nicholas Bobadilla, and Claude le Jay, the first two of whom had taken a solemn vow with St. Ignatius in the chapel at Montmartre.

Peter Faber, born in Savoy in 1506, was already a priest in Worms in 1540, at the time of the Colloquy. He was convinced that the prime cause of secession from the Catholic Church was the corruption of the clergy. "One must wonder," he wrote to St. Ignatius, "that the number of apostates be not even greater than it is, for people have but too many motives to desert the old religion . . .; the true cause of the defection of so many towns and countries . . . is the scandalous life of our priests. I do not know whether, at Worms, two or three might be found who are not engaged in illegitimate bonds or given to other vices, and all this openly." In his method of apostolate, Faber thought that one ought to begin with the amendment of morals, which would automatically be followed by the correction of unorthodox doctrine. His Jesuit belief in action appears here, as well as his optimism, for he wishes to persuade the Protestants, who believe in the utter weakness of man, that with the help of God, they will be able to perform the most difficult acts of virtue.

The same ideas were shared by Claude le Jay, who came from the diocese of Geneva, and whose center of action was Ratisbon, while that of Nicholas Bobadilla, a Spaniard from the diocese of Valencia, was Vienna. Though their labors were fruitful, they were only a beginning; and the Catholic Reformation in Germany is really the work of another Jesuit, St. Peter Canisius.

Canisius was a Dutchman, descended from a respected and wealthy family of Nymegen in Guelders, within the frontiers of the Holy Roman Empire. Born on May 8, 1521, he was carefully brought up at Nymegen first, then at the gymnasium at Cologne. In the latter place he came under the influence of a priest from Brabant, Nicholas van Esche, a virtuous man and a gifted educator, who was wont to say: "One only thing matters: the service of God; all the rest is mere illusion." After taking his university degrees, he heard of Peter Faber, who was then reading theology at Mayence. He came to stay with him and in 1543 performed the *Spiritual Exercises* under his direction. From that time onward, as he himself wrote in his spiritual testament one year before his death, "my only and most important business was to imitate Jesus Christ our Lord, and to follow Him in the condition in which He had preceded me, through being poor, chaste, obedient, and painfully climbing up the way to Calvary."

His diary expresses a twofold ideal, both religious and patriotic. "When I pronounced my vows," he wrote, "I thought I heard a voice which said to me: 'Go and teach the Gospel to all creatures.' " But on the same day, he felt that God had repeatedly recommended Germany to him, and promised to work for her salvation. Moreover he viewed his adopted country as the chosen field of battle for the Society. He deemed, too, that many of his new compatriots had erred in good faith, and even conformably with their proper virtues. Hence they should be brought back to the Fold, not through controversial debates, but through sweetness and edification. In 1558, while preaching a Lenten mission at Staubing, he never once uttered the names of Luther or of his disciples; and through his moderation reaped good fruit. "Truth," he said, "must be defended, charitably, gravely, soberly, sedately."

The aptest way to defend truth, indeed, was not the writing of polemical pamphlets, but the foundation of colleges, to be used both for the upbringing of Jesuit novices, and for the education of youth in general. Canisius, who had meanwhile joined the Society of Jesus, and had become the provincial of his Order for Germany, Austria, and Bohemia on June 7, 1556, was enabled to devote his activities to this purpose, even before the Council of Trent had begun to legislate on the matter. Thanks to his influence, Jesuit houses of education were established in rapid succession. The first Jesuit college had been founded in 1555 at Cologne, where studies had fallen into a sad decay, and placed under the headship of John von Reidt, assisted by twenty members of his order. As early as 1558 the number of pupils had risen to five hundred. In 1560, the Jesuits were called to Treves, and in 1561 to Mayence and Würzburg. In Bavaria, Duke Albert V was brought over to the Catholic side by the persuasions of Canisius, and henceforth a favorable field of action opened out for the latter. In 1551, he had been made vice-chancellor of Ingolstadt University. Here he endeavored to bring back the students to the frequent reception of the sacraments, and every Sunday delivered a Latin homily to them. In 1556, Duke Albert had a large college built at Ingolstadt for the Fathers of the Society. Three years later, he founded another one at Munich. In Austria also the foundation movement had begun. A college had been created at Vienna in 1552; the number of students rose from one hundred and twenty in 1554 to five hundred in 1558.

Nor was Canisius content with the properly educational side of his untiring labors: he continued to preach with great success in Vienna, Prague, Ratisbon, Worms, Cologne, Strasbourg, Osnabrück, Würzburg. A humorous compliment was paid to his powers of persuasion when it was observed that his hearers sat out his sermons, and even stayed on till the end of the Mass, instead of leaving in the middle as they had been wont to do. The Jesuits, indeed, did not allow the remaining German Catholics to indulge their slackness and drowsiness, but made them fully alive to the moral implications of religion. "Even those among the Catholics," Canisius wrote to St. Ignatius, "who think that the Fathers are overdoing it, own that the poor and the sick heap blessings upon them; that harlots become converted, that stolen goods are restored, that many married couples once at variance, now live on good terms, all this thanks to them," so that "many Christians who had long kept aloof from the Church return to fervent practice, and many who were hostile have become friendly."

*   *   *

Canisius had anticipated the educational legislation of the Council of Trent by founding colleges; he was no less a forerunner in regard to the means of teaching the Catholic faith. The Roman catechism, the work of Dominicans mostly, was only to appear in 1566; but as early as 1556, Canisius published his first pedagogic treatise, the *Catechismus major*, also called the *Summa doctrinae Christianae*, which was in the same year translated into German. This work was meant as a counterblast to Luther's *Greater Catechism*. In the same year again Canisius printed his *Catechismus minimus*, intended for the very young, and directed against Luther's *Smaller Catechism*. Lastly, a work of the same class for the use of all the faithful was issued in 1558, the *Parvus catechismus Catholicorum*, so that altogether a graduated course of teaching was provided for all ages and all degrees of religious knowledge.

The general plan of the *Summa*, which is the prototype of all the rest, was as follows: the author first explained the Apostles' Creed; then passed on to hope and trust in God, to the Lord's prayer and the Hail

Mary; and next to the commandments of God and the Church, and to the sacraments. In the second part he discoursed on sin, its nature and forms, the means to be used to uproot it; and then came to the works of mercy, to the cardinal virtues, the gifts and fruits of the Holy Ghost, the eight beatitudes and evangelical precepts, ending with the four last things.

Owing to superstitious practices in the Church, the Protestants had a mistaken notion that Catholic doctrine made justification the work of man alone. Canisius insisted, throughout his whole work, that Christ alone was the beginning of our justice, of our strength, knowledge, and piety. Though Canisius' *Catechisms* were an exposition of Catholic principles, they were strictly non-controversial, and contained no word of abuse for his adversaries. The effect they produced is clearly demonstrated by the vehement denunciations they drew from the Protestants. These did not prevent their success, and no fewer than four hundred editions of the *Catechisms,* some of them polyglot, were published in every country in Europe, and even in Asia and Africa. It is largely thanks to their clear and coherent statement of Catholic doctrine that the old faith was maintained or restored in Bavaria, Austria, Bohemia, Swabia, Tyrol, and Switzerland.

However, the work of evangelization would have been far more difficult without the support of temporal princes, and in fact it is in those regions where the civil power buttressed the Catholic Church that progress was most decisive. We have already shown how, even before Gregory XIII launched his diplomatic campaign, Duke Albert of Bavaria had assisted the efforts of Canisius and other Jesuits. "Our duty," Canisius wrote, is to sustain the courage of Duke Albert, so that he may, with a burning zeal, take up the defence of religion on every occasion, . . . and not suffer the commandments of the Church to be despised. . . . When good examples are set from above, when religion and virtuous manners are honored at the Court, the whole of Society feels the effect: such examples are never barren, and persons of all conditions are drawn toward good." These words clearly show why the Jesuits were so anxious to provide a Catholic education for the great. However, they refrained from appearing on the political stage, and Canisius considered it a danger for their spiritual life that they should mingle with court circles, and besought the Father general of the Society, Everard Mercurian, to resist the solicitations of noblemen who wanted Jesuits as resident chaplains. He was at one on this point with Mercurian's successor, Claude Aquaviva, who in 1600, in an instruction on spiritual diseases sent to all the houses of the Society, denounced the "courtier spirit," which should be rooted out at all costs.

The turning-point for Bavaria occurred on September 5, 1564, when Duke Albert, together with the archbishop of Salzburg and other prelates, decided to observe all the decrees issued by the Council of Trent and sanctioned by the Pope. Two kinds of measures were then taken, the former of which are hardly consonant with modern liberalism, but which, it must be remembered, tallied with the current practice of the times, no matter what the religion of the nation might be. On the one hand, drastic action was begun against the "sectarian" press and "sectarian" education, young men being forbidden to attend Protestant universities even abroad. On the other hand, an earnest effort was made to Christianize such schools as were allowed, apart from any needless controversial debates. The school regulations of 1569 invite children to seek the salvation of their souls "rather in Christian deeds, and in a sincerely pious behavior, than in vain chatterings and endless disputes." The duke founded a seminary in Munich for poor children, who were educated free of charge, and two seminaries for noble children at Munich and Ingolstadt, and entrusted them all to the Jesuits.

The difficulties of the Catholic Reformation in Germany are clearly illustrated by the events which took place in the neighboring territory of Fulda. This territory was under the authority of the abbot of the Benedictine monastery of St. Boniface. The population, especially the nobility, had been largely gained over to Lutheranism. The chapter, the members of which had to be of noble blood, was composed mostly of laymen; the four remaining ecclesiastical canons dressed like secular priests, dwelt in private houses and were unable to understand Latin. The situation was almost desperate when a young man of twenty, Balthazar von Dernbach, was elected abbot in 1570. He was descended from a wholly Protestant family of Hesse. Where and how he had imbibed Catholic principles is unknown, but as soon as he had become the sovereign prince of Fulda he set about the work of reform with a firm hand. He surrounded himself with new councilors, two of whom had been educated in the Jesuit college at Treves; these in their turn directed him to the Fathers of the Society, when he undertook to found a college, in response to a request of his noble subjects. Now the present is a typical instance of the effects of Jesuit education in Germany. For this college, which opened on October 20, 1572, managed to survive all the vicissitudes with which Protestant opposition beset the path of the prince-abbot; and eventually, when after many long years he had suc-

ceeded in consolidating his position, it was found that a Catholic generation had been brought up, which quietly took possession of Fulda and
restored it to the Church.

The problem was to sway the huge mass of indifferent or lukewarm
people, who might be gained over by either side. It was really one of
superior influence. Now, Balthazar von Dernbach had to cope with a
very restive nobility and with the intervention of neighboring princes
who had embraced Lutheranism. His own chapter was by no means
willing to let him proceed with his reforming schemes. He had demanded
the immediate dismissal of concubines by the priests who kept them,
and had even had the "paramour" of the dean arrested in the public
street. Heedless of opposition, he enforced the *clausura* in the monasteries, visited a large number of convents himself, restored pilgrimages
and processions, forbade the sale of Lutheran literature, and dismissed
his Protestant servants. The canons could not bear such a "hypocritical
Jesuit" as a master. They considered it a violation of "old custom" that
they should be compelled to sing the Divine Office, assist at ceremonies,
and attend sermons. Then began a strife which lasted for thirty years,
in the course of which Balthazar was assailed with petitions by the
local nobility and guilds, threatened and even bullied by neighboring
princes, who eventually constrained him to resign his abbacy. However,
he was supported by Pope Gregory XIII, who induced the Emperor to
side with him against his adversaries. Meanwhile the college was making
headway; a papal seminary was added to it in 1584; it was meant for
forty young noblemen, for the Jesuit, Lopperz, had convinced Gregory
XIII that the future of the Church in Germany depended upon the
nobility. When at length Balthazar was restored to his power and
dignities in 1602, Jesuit education had completely renewed and transformed the chapter, and henceforth no further obstacles stood in the way
of Catholic reform.

*   *   *

The same process was exemplified in many places in Germany. From
1570 to the death of Canisius in 1596 and from that date to the outbreak
of the Thirty Years' War, new colleges, residences, and mission houses of
the Society were founded, at Aix-la-Chapelle, Coblenz, Molsheim, Erfurt,
Paderborn, and many other places. The number of pupils was everywhere high and increased rapidly. At Würzburg, for instance, it rose from
700 in 1590, to 1070 in 1604. Special provision was made for poor
scholars. Canisius had made himself responsible for two hundred of
these at Augsburg, as early as 1559. The practice of keeping poor stu-

dents free of charge gradually became general. Congregations and academies were established and soon flourished. The center for all the Jesuit schools and seminaries in the Empire was the German college at Rome. Its extraordinary influence is testified to by the bitter invectives of Protestant controversialists. Many of its pupils were young noblemen who, instead of entering cathedral chapters as laymen and leading worldly lives, now took holy orders and became learned, devout, duty-loving canons. The *Germanici* were soon disseminated throughout the Empire. Some of them were made the councillors of bishops, or preached in the courts of princes. Many others, "on Sundays and feast days, whatever the weather might be, in the heat or in the cold, in wind, rain or snow, had to rush about to three or four different parishes and to preach themselves hoarse, never getting any reward but abuse." Several died the death of martyrs.

Even the Thirty Years' War did not interrupt the steady progress of the Catholic Revival in the Empire. It was manifested in the attempts made to restore discipline in the monasteries that still remained independent, and had thus escaped supervision, by uniting them in groups or "congregations," where they stood a better chance of being reformed. The Council of Trent had attempted to correct abuses in "autocephalous" religious houses by bringing them under episcopal jurisdiction. The same purpose was kept in view when endeavors were made in the early seventeenth century to unite all the monasteries of Germany under the headship of the Benedictine Abbey of Melk or Melek, situated in the diocese of Passau on the Danube. The scheme dated back to 1460, but had succeded only in part, and had been halted by the appearance of Lutheranism, which gained a footing inside the monastery. In 1587, a new abbot, Gaspar Hoffmann, was elected. Imbued with the spirit of the Catholic Reformation, he set about restoring discipline and studies among his religious, and attempted the reassembling of the German monasteries. In 1618, six Austrian abbots gathered at Melk, and drafted constitutions for the new union. These were accepted after Hoffmann's death, in 1625, by eleven German abbots. A project of general reunion was set afoot in 1630 by the abbot of Fulda, but was interrupted by the Swedish invasion. The influence of Melk lasted on late into the following centuries, and was destroyed only by the despotism of Joseph II.

In Poland and Switzerland the Catholic Revival proceeded much on the same lines. Nuncios were sent and prevailed with the civil power — the king in the former case, the Catholic cantons in the latter — to safeguard the interests of Catholicism. In Poland, as in Germany, the higher clergy had set an evil example, monastic discipline was relaxed, and the sovereign had to contend with an unruly nobility, which was attracted by religious novelties. However, from the first he enforced the Trentine decrees, which were confirmed by the Synod of Piotrkov in 1574. Here again, the Jesuits were in the forefront of reform. Their first college was opened at Braunsberg in 1565, and was followed by those of Pultusk (1566), Jaroslav (1568), and Wilna (1570), later of Lublin and Kalisch. To even a greater extent than in Germany, the pupils belonged to the higher classes of society. Eventually the whole country was regained for Catholicism.

Switzerland largely fell to the care of St. Charles Borromeo, whose archbishopric of Milan included the three valleys of Ticino, while his protectorate extended to the whole of the country. Borromeo was fond of the Swiss; he trusted to their sterling moral qualities. He devoted much attention to them, made a visitation of Ticino twice, in 1567 and 1570, and on the latter occasion took in the whole of German-speaking Switzerland as well. In the following years the Capuchins were particularly active, and the reform of the Catholic cantons was largely their work. They settled down at Altorf in 1581, at Stans in 1582, at Lucerne in 1583, at Schwytz in 1585, at Appenzell and Solothurn in 1588. One of them, Father Philip, preached more than seven thousand times.

The Jesuits established themselves at Lucerne and in the surrounding cantons. Their sermons drew huge crowds, and Jesuit priests were not numerous enough for the administration of sacraments. In 1575, the number of communicants in the parish churches of Lucerne was 300 only; in 1588 it had risen to 10,000, and in 1589 to more than 12,000. A contemporary report of the communal secretary shows that a great change in public morals had taken place, thanks to the influence of the Society. "Men," he said, "have begun to give up drinking, dancing and gambling. . . . At night masquerades and fancy dress parades are done away with. . . . Public women are banished and many have taken a vow of chastity. . . . There has been a marvelous change in the public life of all classes." Thus was the Catholic Reformation, here as well as on the shores of the Mediterranean, a movement toward the moral regeneration, not of the clergy alone, but of the whole of the Christian people as well; and its efforts, not unparalleled by those of Calvinistic puritanism, tended to chasten the barbaric brutality of the North, no less than the pagan lasciviousness of the South.

CHAPTER XII

The Catholic Reformation in France

FROM the time of the Council of Trent, and up to the last decade of the sixteenth century, France was a prey to religious wars. The strength of the two contending parties was quite evenly matched, and thus the task of the Catholic reformers involved a bitter struggle against Protestantism, as well as the rejuvenation of the old religion. Their position was akin to what it was in Germany, and their means of action were largely the same: the popes tried, more or less successfully, to enlist the help of the civil power — i.e., of the French monarchy — against the Huguenots, while various religious orders, particularly the Jesuits, endeavored to carry on apostolic work throughout the population at large, and to bring up new generations of Catholics in their colleges. Their efforts were remarkably successful, and when Henry IV became a convert to the Roman faith, the Calvinists had been reduced to a small minority. With the beginning of the seventeenth century there opened for Catholicism in France a period of peace and prosperity, in which the seed sown in a previous age bore plentiful fruit. It was now possible to address oneself full-heartedly to such reforming tasks as the breathing of a new spirit into the secular clergy, and the performance of the works of charity demanded by the social distress of the times.

However, though the Catholic Reformation in France was of an unequalled spiritual quality, though it flourished more than in any other country, it bears a peculiar stamp, owing to the fact that it was not officially supported by the State. The Trentine decrees were never sanctioned by the French kings, as they had been by the duke of Bavaria and the German ecclesiastical princes; and thus whatever reform was effected was due to the efforts of the French Church alone, and, even more so, to those of outstanding individuals acting on their own initiative, a situation that will surprise no one at all acquainted with French history, in which it has been frequently reproduced.

The policy of popes Pius V, Gregory XIII, and Sixtus V, though fluctuating, was governed by the same motive: they wished Catholic princes to suppress Protestantism throughout their dominions, so as to restore Catholic unity in the face of the Turkish peril. In the case of France this policy suffered serious difficulties. The French kings, Charles IX and Henry III, were Catholic at heart, but they had no wish to allow Spanish supremacy in Europe, and therefore refused to molest their Protestant subjects, or to break with Queen Elizabeth of England, who were their best auxiliaries against Spain. Philip II of Spain, on the other hand, distrusted the French monarchy, especially when the Huguenot Henrí of Navarre became heir to the French throne; and he supported the rebellious and disloyal party of the French Catholic League. The popes hesitated as to whether they ought to side with the well-meaning, though wavering, French kings, or with their more determinedly Catholic subjects of the League. Hence an inextricable political and diplomatic confusion arose. Under the surface of this the Catholic reformers slowly, patiently proceeded with their apostolic labors, and eventually, where others had failed to vanquish through force, succeeded in carrying the day through persuasion.

Here as well as in the rest of Europe, the initiative came from Rome. The action of the latter was made easier from the fact that — as we learn from the Venetian ambassador, Giovanni Correro — the effect of the Huguenot uprising had been to tighten the bonds between the French Catholics and the Holy See. Direct intervention in French affairs, however, was difficult. When in 1566 Pope Pius V urgently recommended to King Charles IX the publication and enforcement of the decrees of Trent, notably on the duty of residence, on the erection of seminaries and the correction of abuses in the collation of benefices, he met with a refusal; though the French government favored the diffusion of the Roman *Catechism*. The Trentine legislation, however, was applied in the French papal dominions, at Avignon and in the surrounding province of Comtat-Venaissin. Provincial synods were held at Avignon in 1567 and 1569, while the archbishop, Felician Capitone, ordered a visitation of the whole of the territory under his authority. Meanwhile further efforts were made to obtain the ratification of the Trentine decrees. But when the assembly of the French clergy at Melun, in 1579, had failed to persuade the king to grant this, there was no hope of reformation left save by means of provincial councils. Such gatherings were held in various towns from 1581 to 1585, and through them the rules issued at Trent were to some extent enforced.

The severe trials undergone by the French Catholics at the hands of the Huguenots had had a bracing effect. It was a sign of the times that the poet, Pierre de Ronsard, should have cast upon their side the considerable weight of his influence. The dawn of the Catholic Revival could already be seen, not in the secular clergy, indeed, but among the regulars. The new orders began to appear in France. The apostolate of the Capuchins, which started in 1568, met with marked success. The general chapter of the Order sent a few of its members into France in 1573. They were Italians, and, at the outset, mingled chiefly in Italian circles. They settled down at Meudon in 1573, at Lyons and Marseilles in 1574, at Toulouse in 1581, at Rouen in 1582, at Verdun in 1585. Through their devotion in tending victims of the plague in 1576 and 1580 they gained the love of the people, and also through their strict poverty, their solemn singing of the Divine Office, and their novel practice of decorating their neatly kept churches with fresh flowers. The French king was dumbfounded when one of the most influential men in the kingdom, the brother of Cardinal de Joyeuse, joined their ranks a few days after the death of his wife, and appeared at court as Father Angel de Joyeuse, in coarse brown cloth and with bare feet.

The older orders, too, largely owing to Jesuit influence, had their share in the rejuvenation of Catholicism. Pope Gregory XIII had initiated a reform of the Cistercians in 1574, which was completed in 1580 by the abbot, John de la Barrière, according to the primitive rule of the Order. In 1580, the exempt Benedictines of France decided, in compliance with the directions of the Council of Trent, to hold general assemblies every three years.

But the reform of the older orders, and even the missionary labors of the Capuchins, pale into insignificance when compared with the apostolate of the Jesuits. The part they played in preparing the Catholic Revival in France can hardly be exaggerated. They sowed the seeds which produced the magnificent harvest of the age of Louis XIII. They understood, in France as well as in Germany, that the essential point was to get hold of the young, and they brought up a generation of great men who were to achieve distinction as reformers among the secular clergy as well as in the religious orders. Their educational campaign was conducted through their colleges. These were in fact far more than schools in the limited sense of the word. They were centers of propaganda for all ages and all classes of society. They provided the greatest scholars, preachers, and theologians of the time with a shelter in which to proceed with their literary labors and from which to issue forth upon their missions.

As early as 1540, a small colony of future Jesuits had settled down in one of the colleges of the University of Paris. But the foundation of a special college of the Society in the French capital was due to the efforts of a generous and worthy man, Guillaume du Prat, who had been elected bishop of Clermont in Auvergne in 1529, at the age of twenty-three. He had had to struggle against Protestantism in his own diocese, and coming to the conclusion that his best weapon was the education of youth, attempted to restore the decayed universities of Billom and Issoire. His counsellor, a Minim, Father Simon Guichard, had known Ignatius Loyola and his companions at Rome, and had been deeply impressed by them. At Trent, Guillaume du Prat obtained information on the Society, and found it so agreeable to his wishes, that he decided to create a seminary for it in Paris, from which he might afterwards draw helpers for his own work in Auvergne. He visited the Jesuit college in Padua, where he found, in the words of Father Ribadeneira, union, peace, and happiness. On returning to France in 1547 he went to Paris and called upon the Jesuit students at the Collège des Lombards, and soon after housed them in the residence of the bishops of Clermont, where they settled down at Easter, 1550. Everything here was according to the practice of the Roman college: the students' rooms were very simple, a small hall served as an oratory, a space had been reserved for a garden and for recreation, and at the entrance there was a porter with a bell.

The college continued for a few years as a purely Jesuit community, with a few members only. However, it was soon to be transformed into an institution for the education of the young. New premises were bought for it, though it retained the name of Collège de Clermont, and classes began on February 22, 1564. Soon the college developed and met with the most striking success. In 1571 the number of pupils had reached three thousand, and it was necessary to erect new buildings. Such prosperity was due to the presence, among the teachers, of eminent men, such as Father Venegas, the professor of humanities, and Father Maldonatus, who held the chair of philosophy. The latter, in fact, was to reach considerable fame, both as a theologian and as a preacher. He was a Spaniard, born in 1533 in the Estremadura, and was, for ten years, a student of arts and philosophy in the University of Salamanca, which had recently been remodeled on a classical basis by Anthony de Lebrixa. Next he devoted four years to the study of theology in the same university, under Dominic Soto, until finally he felt a vocation to the Society of Jesus, and fled to Rome to join it. A few years afterward, he was sent by Father Lainez, the general of the Society, to Paris, in order to establish the reputation of the Collège de Clermont.

Father Maldonatus may be said to have directed theological studies

into new channels. He was indeed the true heir of the Christian humanists, condemning the abuses of decayed scholasticism, less bitingly
indeed, but no less firmly than Erasmus. Insisting on the necessity of
keeping close to the Scriptures, Maldonatus nevertheless adhered with
characteristic moderation to the classical adage *Ne quid nimis,* refrained
from the excesses of pure scripturalism, and maintained the usefulness
of traditional theology and of true scholasticism as against false scholasticism. He recommended to future theologians to read every morning,
after prayers, a passage of the Greek scriptures, and every night, a
passage of the Hebrew Old Testament. He himself spent his whole life
in studying ancient languages: Greek, Hebrew, Syriac, Chaldean, and
Arabic, as well as all the accessory sciences which help in the interpretation of history. Unfortunately he did not live long enough to express
his views on the whole of Scripture; and before he died in 1583 he had
time to write no more than his *Commentaries on the Four Gospels,* which
enjoyed at least twenty printings in the seventeenth century.

Maldonatus lectured for many years at the Collège de Clermont,
amidst the greatest difficulties, meeting with the most stubborn opposition on the part of the adversaries of the Jesuits: the University of Paris
and especially the faculty of theology or Sorbonne. The latter was
imbued with a strongly Gallican spirit, remained true to the conciliarist
tradition, and looked askance at papal authority and its supporters. They
sought every possible means of tripping up Maldonatus and putting an
end to his lectures and preaching, finding fault with his theological
teaching. Whereas they considered the Immaculate Conception of the
Virgin Mary as an article of faith, the Jesuit professor had taken
exception to such an absolute attitude. He had also declared that he
would readily embrace the opinion of those who thought that the pains
of purgatory might possibly endure no longer than ten years' duration.
For this he was denounced by the four faculties for heretical teaching,
with which the Sorbonne charged him in a letter to Pope Gregory XIII,
dated August, 1575. Their real grievances appear from the reply that
was made to them by the Jesuit provincial, Father Mathieu, on August
19. They took exception, he wrote, to the "particular vow" through
which those of the Society bound themselves "to uphold the power of
the Sovereign Pontiff above that of the council," and sought "to
establish the authority of the pope on the ruins of the liberties of the
Gallican Church." Father Mathieu agreed to the charge, and showed
that while maintaining the supreme power of the Holy See, the Society
purposed the reformation of the clergy. "We compel," he said, "to the

recitation of the divine office all those who have received sacred orders, and those who are provided with some benefice; whereas those of the Sorbonne enforce the fulfillment of that duty upon priests only; we disapprove of pensions imposed upon benefices without the permission of the supreme Pontiff; *they* approve and allow of them. . . ." Such bickerings lasted for thirty years, until the Society, as we shall see, was driven out of France.

Meanwhile new colleges had been springing up in many places. In 1553, the plague having appeared in Paris, Msgr. de Prat invited the members of the community of the Hôtel de Clermont to Auvergne to proceed with their apostolic work there. Two Fathers, Jérome Le Bas and Jacques Morel, came accordingly, and evangelized the summer residence of the bishop at Beauregard l'Evêque and the surrounding country, then the hospital at Clermont. Their popularity increased the wish of the Auvergnat people for a college of the Society. The bishop of Clermont appealed to Ignatius Loyola for a foundation, for which he thought no place would be better suited than the ancient university town of Billom. The college was inaugurated on July 26, 1556, eight years before that of Paris, and was thus the first educational establishment of the Jesuits in France.

Other foundations followed in rapid succession: at Tournon (1560–1562), at Rodez (1561–1562), at Mauriac in Auvergne and Toulouse (1563–1564) at Avignon (1565–1570), at Chambéry and Lyons (1575–1576), at Verdun (1572), at Nevers and Bordeaux (1572), at Bourges (1575), at Dijon (1581), at Eu (1582), at Dôle (1583), at Le-Puy-en-Velay (1588), at Auch (1589), at Périgueux (1592), while a Jesuit university was created at Pont-à-Mousson (1575). Soon after an untoward event provided the adversaries of the Society with the long-awaited opportunity of getting rid of it. An attempt to assassinate King Henry IV was made, on December 27, 1594, by one Jean Chastel, who happened to have been a pupil in philosophy for two years at the Collège de Clermont. This was deemed a sufficient reason by the Parliament of Paris to turn the Jesuits out of the capital and the other towns where they had colleges. The eviction was conducted in a brutal manner, and the Society was only to be brought back by the edict of Rouen, issued by King Henry IV on September 1, 1603.

Meanwhile the missionary work of the Jesuits throughout the provinces had met with the most extraordinary success, not merely on account of its theological quality, but also because it was accompanied by works of charity in favor of the destitute, the sick, and prisoners. Father Edmund

Auger preached to packed congregations at Toulouse in 1566, 1567, and 1570; in Paris and at Lyons in 1567; in Lyons he established a society of pious ladies, to visit the hospitals twice a week; at Toulouse he founded the Confraternity of Mercy, for the relief of prisoners. At Dieppe the vicinity of England had greatly favored the spread of Protestantism; all the churches had been destroyed save one, which had been defaced. At the end of a five days' course of sermons by Father Anthony Possevin (or Possevinus), out of the six thousand Huguenots in the town, two thousand five hundred returned to the Catholic Fold; and thousands more were converted by his successor, Father Oliver Manare. At Marseilles Father Possevin obtained striking results in 1568, through getting all the confessors to deal uniformly with their penitents: the profits of usury were refunded, Sundays began to be kept, and pious processions took the place of scandalous dances and feasts. The Jesuit devoted much of his activity to the spiritual care of the three thousand galley slaves in the port, who were until then wholly forsaken, and obtained the liberation of one hundred and sixty of them. Some years later, two Jesuits sealed their apostolate with their blood.

Father James Salès, one of these victims, had been born in 1556. He was brought up at Beauregard l'Evêque, in a school founded by Msgr. du Prat, at the college of Billom, and at the university of Pont-à-Mousson, where he became a professor of theology. Being sent on to the university of Tournon, he was dispatched for a mission to the Protestant center of Aubenas, together with Brother William Saultemouche. Salès' preaching there was successful, but both Jesuits were captured in the course of a Huguenot raid upon the town, and, having refused to abjure the Eucharist, were put to death on February 7, 1593. Their case is a typical instance of life in and around the Jesuit colleges — a mingling of scholarly work and brave missionary labors. The latter were greatly assisted by the appearance of the two *Catechisms* of Father Auger, which were parallel to those of Canisius, and had a similar effect. As early as 1570, the nuncio, Frangipani, was able to announce to the pope that a veritable Catholic revival was taking place in France, and that the churches were crowded as they had not been for years.

*   *   *

The seventeenth century in France has been rightly termed *le grand siècle*. Yet if one refers, not to the worldly splendor of the French monarchy but to the spiritual life of the Church, it is the earlier half of the century which deserves the name, not the age of Louis XIV, but that of Louis XIII, of Richelieu, Pierre de Bérulle, Olier, St. Vincent de

Paul, and Pierre Corneille. Now, it is no exaggeration to say that the ground was mostly prepared for this revival between 1550 and 1600 by the Society of Jesus. One cannot help being struck by the fact that such leading figures as St. Francis de Sales, Pierre de Bérulle, Olier, and Pierre Corneille had all been pupils of Jesuit colleges. At the same time, though the work of the Society was far from finished by 1600, the task of reforming the Church was not so exclusively in its hands after that date as it had been before. Other activities developed, independent of it — activities fed at the springs of Italian and Spanish devotion, yet in which the original temper of the French nation was nevertheless reflected.

However, the part played by the Society remained a very important one. A Jesuit, Father Coton, became the confessor of King Henry IV, and the preceptor of his son, the future Louis XIII, doing much to Christianize the interior politics of France. As a consequence of the Edict of Rouen the Jesuits again occupied the colleges from which they had been expelled: at Dijon, Lyon, Bourges, Billom, Mauriac. At the same time the foundation movement continued apace right through the first half of the seventeenth century. Between 1606 and 1640, no fewer than forty-seven new colleges were opened in France, while a boarding-school was added to the Collège de Clermont in Paris (1608). The larger cities and even many smaller towns vied with each other in trying to induce the Fathers to settle down within their walls; and often they were unable to comply with the wishes of municipal bodies which had applied for houses of education. Meanwhile the Jesuit apostolate continued much on the same lines, though the controversial war with the Huguenots grew less-absorbing.

Lastly the Society, and especially Father Coton, whose influence upon the king was considerable, greatly helped in the reforming of the older orders and favored the enthusiastic movements for the creation of new orders, which was then sweeping over France. There was, toward the close of the sixteenth century, a devotional school in Provence, of which the chief representatives were César de Bus and John Baptist Romillon. De Bus, born at Cavaillon in 1544, had been brought up piously, but having spent some time as a courtier in Paris, returned to his native city as a fashionable and dissipated youth, much given to elegant verse-writing. Thanks to the efforts of a kindly peasant-woman, Antoinette, and of a simple and virtuous hatter, Louis Guyot, who struggled to bring about his conversion, he gave way to grace, changed his life, and chose Father Péquet, S.J., the rector of the college of Avignon, as his director. Romillon had been brought over from Calvinism by a relative, who had given him Luis de Granada's *Treatise on Prayer* to read, and, on the advice of the same director, studied, as a grown-up man, with the children of the Jesuit college at Tournon. Both became cathedral canons, and began to expound Christian doctrine to their flocks according to the catechetical method of Canisius. Wishing to extend their influence still further, they founded, about 1593, the Congregation of Christian Doctrine at Avignon. This "congregation" was a society of secular priests, who were to devote themselves to missionary catechizing. It was later cut up into two groups, one under César de Bus which assumed the character of a regular order and the other under Romillon, which remained true to the original foundation. Cardinal Tarugi, having sent to Romillon a description of the Roman Oratory, the latter turned his fraternity into a new congregation, modeled on the Italian society, which was approved by Pope Paul V in 1615. It already numbered eleven houses when it was absorbed into the French Oratory of Pierre de Bérulle in 1619. Father Romillon also presided at the beginnings of the Ursuline Order in France, which was introduced into Provence by Francoise de Bermont, and was to number three hundred houses by 1699.

The Jesuits again played an active part in the foundation of the order of the "Daughters of Our Lady" by the Blessed Joan de Lestonnac. The latter was born at Bordeaux in 1566. She was the niece of Michel de Montaigne, the author of the *Essays,* whose intervention defeated the plans of her Calvinist mother and aunt, who wished to win the girl to their religious views. Her brothers were among the first pupils of the college of the Society at Bordeaux, whose influence she thus indirectly felt. Having married Gaston de Montferrant in 1583, she bore several children, and lost her husband in 1597. Through the influence of the Jesuits, by whom her two sons had been brought up, she applied for admission into the Toulouse monastery of the "Feuillantines," the female branch of the Cistercians who had been reformed between 1573 to 1586 by Abbot John de la Barrière. Released, however, from her vows, owing to ill-health, she soon felt herself moved to found a new religious order, at the very same moment that two Jesuits of the Bordeaux college, Father Bordes and Father Raymond, were seeking the means of establishing a community for the education of girls. The "Institute of the Daughters of Our Lady" was accordingly created and approved by Pope Paul V on April 7, 1607. It followed the rule of St. Benedict, but in regard to education, was constructed on Ignatian principles. The classes, which were free, opened in 1609 at Bordeaux and were soon crowded; while branches were rapidly established in eight towns of southern France.

More important still was the creation of the Order of the Visitation by St. Jane Frances de Chantal. She was born at Dijon in Bourgogne on January 23, 1572, of a deeply religious and virtuous family. In 1592, she married Christopher, Baron de Chantal, and bore him six children. He was killed in a hunting accident in 1601 and thereupon she took a vow of chastity and consecrated herself wholly to God. She was greatly perturbed in her mind, however, until she came under the direction of St. Francis de Sales who wrote out a set of rules for her, thanks to which she made rapid spiritual progress. She refused a desirable marriage, and, feeling herself carried away by the Catholic Revival around her, thought of embracing the life of a religious. St. Francis, however, dissuaded her from joining the Carmelites and enlightened her as to her true vocation: to found an institute of her own. So on June 6, 1610, Jane Frances, together with two companions, Mary-Jacqueline Favre and Charlotte de Bréchard, took possession of her first convent at Annecy. The constitutions, which were drafted for her by St. Francis, differed from those of the older orders, resembling those of the Clerks Regular, and especially those of the Society of Jesus in two important points: they did away with excessive bodily mortification, which as a matter of fact might not be borne by women of delicate health, and replaced them by prayer and inward sacrifice. They required from the Sisters that they should exercise an apostolate outside their convents, through works of charity, such as visiting the poor, tending the sick, assisting the dying, and teaching the ignorant.

The original plans of St. Francis and St. Jane Frances de Chantal were, however, altered. St. Jane Frances, who had come to Lyons to found a new house of the Visitation, met with the opposition of the archbishop, Cardinal de Marquemont. He refused to allow the Sisters to leave the cloister for work outside. He wanted the Visitation to be a regular order in the traditional sense of the word. The founders had to comply with his wishes. For works of charity in the outer world, they substituted a life of prayer and perpetual adoration within strictly isolated monasteries.

The final rules of the Visitation were penned by St. Francis in 1616. The Order was placed under the rule of St. Augustine, which was supplemented by special provisions. It was to admit not merely maidens, but also widows, and sick or crippled women. Bodily asceticism was therefore reduced to a minimum. Fasting and night choir duty were done away with, whereas mortification was practiced by other means: the religious were to be utterly poor, to live in common, cheerfully to bear one another's imperfections, and to be constantly engaged in prayer. Utter obedience was due to the superior, while one of the Sisters was entrusted with the task of admonishing her of her faults. Each house was independent and placed under the direct supervision of the bishop of the diocese. The dominant features of the rules were sweetness, moderation, and common sense. The Sisters were greeted in France with uncommon enthusiasm, and soon new houses sprang up everywhere. Mother Charlotte de Bréchard founded the convent at Moulins in 1617, while others followed at Grenoble, Bourges, Paris, Montferrand, Nevers, Orléans, Valence, and many other places. They were soon to assume a different character. From the outset little girls had been admitted into the convents, and allowed to share their life. This practice was later to develop into the establishment of boarding schools. This, however, was not to take place within the lifetime of St. Jane Frances de Chantal, who died on December 13, 1641, at Moulins. Ten years after her death the number of the houses of the Visitation in France had risen to one hundred and fifteen.

*   *   *

The Visitation, it may be said, had developed under indirect Jesuit influence. There were, however, in France, other sources of spiritual life, which had existed before the Society of Jesus and had continued to exist apart from it. Thus the Capuchins — among them such prominent men as Father Archangel of Pembroke and Father Benedict of Canfeld, both Englishmen — played an important part in guiding a numerous group of devout people, formed toward the end of the sixteenth century, which had its center in the Paris house of Pierre de Bérulles' mother. Madame de Bérulle, in fact, sheltered in her home the future founder of the French Carmel, Madame Acarie, whose husband, a notorious "leaguer" and opponent of King Henry IV, had been exiled. Among the visitors to her home were many persons illustrious by their rank and piety, among them Michel de Marillac, the uncle of Louise de Marillac, who with St. Vincent de Paul was to establish the Maidens of Charity; distinguished ecclesiastics, too, came to her home, men such as M. Asseline and M. de Gamache, both professors at the Sorbonne, and M. du Val, who was to be the confessor of St. Vincent de Paul and was to suggest to him the idea of creating the Congregation of the Mission.

There was, of course, also Pierre de Bérulle himself, then a young man, but already engaged in the task of bringing over Protestants to the Fold. His confessor was a Carthusian, Dom Beaucousin, one of the most successful directors among the French aristocracy from 1593 to

1602. From 1594 onward, Madame Acarie remained under his direction, and he assisted her in the establishing of the Carmelites in France. From this center there radiated, in later years, the various movements of the French Catholic Reformation, beginning with the French Oratory, and ending with St. Vincent de Paul's Mission and M. Olier's seminaries. Just as Father Coton, S.J., had played an important part, behind the scenes, in the political life of the reign of Henry IV and during the minority of Louis XIII, so Father Joseph, the Capuchin, was to become the adviser and friend of Cardinal Richelieu, the minister of Louis XIII and the maker of modern France. His real name was Francis le Clerc du Tremblay. He was born at Paris on November 4, 1577, of an ancient and illustrious family. At the age of five, at a banquet in the house of his father, he offered to relate to the guests "how our Lord had been crucified," and did so in such a way as to move all those present. In 1585, he was admitted as a student at Boncourt College, one of the colleges of Paris University, where he became a brilliant Latin and Greek scholar. After completing his studies he lived for three years (1595–1598) under the name of Baron de Maffliers, as a young gentleman of leisure; yet religious aspirations were already uppermost in his mind. He visited Italy, where he came into touch with the Theatines and Capuchins, and then England. On coming home to France, he joined the pious circle which met at Madame de Bérulle's house and fell under the influence of the Capuchins. Then, after a period of hesitation and a struggle with his worldly minded mother, he became one of them, at Orléans, on February 2, 1599. Meeting with success as a preacher and director, he later became provincial of Touraine, and finally began to mingle in public affairs. His intervention put an end to civil war in France in 1616, when the peace of Loudun was concluded between the king and the rebellious noblemen; and he further prevented an assertion of the royal position as against the Holy See which might have developed into a French schism. He then undertook to unite the Christian princes in a Crusade against the Turks, but was unable to effect his purpose despite six years of persevering efforts.

He represented a thoroughgoing Catholic policy, which purposed both to deprive the Huguenots of all political power, and to bring about their conversion through persuasion. Therefore he was, from 1622 onwards, even more than Pierre de Bérulle, consulted on all affairs of State. His influence was such that he was able to regain the favor of the king for Cardinal Richelieu in 1619. He afterwards prevailed upon him to undertake the Béarn expedition in 1620, and upon Louis XIII to lay siege to La Rochelle. He even advised the building of the dam which eventually sealed the fate of the town.

But he never lost sight of his Catholic apostolate. He established numerous Capuchin convents in Poitou from 1610 to 1616, mostly in the "towns of safety" left by King Henry IV to the Protestants, thus laying the foundation for a mission in which he obtained wonderful success. At Christmas, 1617, more than fifty thousand people flocked to Lusignan to hear him preach; and many Huguenots embraced the Catholic faith. In the case of Béarn, military action was immediately followed by a Capuchin mission, and a monastery of the same Order was created at Pau. The same process took place after the capture of St. Jean d'Angély by the royal troops. Father Joseph also took much trouble to evangelize the besieging army there and at La Rochelle. Nor was his manifold activity limited to these tasks. From 1606 onward he assisted in the reformation of the older regular orders, the Benedictines especially. He united his efforts with those of Cardinal de la Rochefoucauld, who had been, on April 6, 1622, entrusted with the same task by Pope Gregory XV. A reformed Benedictine Order, the Congregation of Saint Maur, had been approved by the Holy See on May 27, 1621. It was joined, thanks to the efforts of Father Joseph, by all the abbeys dependent on Cluny and Chezal Benoît, the agreement gradually spreading to one hundred and fifty houses. He also helped the Bernardines, a reformed branch of the Cistercians. He had been appointed by Urban VIII prefect of the foreign missions on January 13, 1625, and was active in that field until his death, which took place on December 18, 1638. Few men have had such a varied and fruitful range of occupations.

Pierre de Bérulle also played a part on the political stage, and had a hand in the negotiations leading to the marriage of Charles I of England with Henrietta of France. But his sphere of action was more properly religious, consisting chiefly in the creation of the French Oratory, which was to be the mainspring of Catholic Reformation in France. The new foundation was suggested to Bérulle by that of St. Philip Neri; yet he did not strictly copy it, but altered it so as to make it fit the French temperament, an alteration which was indeed necessary, since the Philippine Oratory had never succeeded in taking firm root in France. The name of the new congregation indicates prayer; and indeed, according to its founder, the priest of the Oratory must be engaged in perpetual prayer. Bérulle's main idea was to restore the dignity of the priesthood, which was despised by the great, who often considered the clergy as mere servants. Therefore the priests of the Oratory were proud to wear their cassock. The actual foundation took place on November 11, 1611, when Bérulle gathered with five other priests in a house of the Rue Saint Jacques in Paris, to live there in common.

The Oratory was approved by Pope Paul V on May 10, 1613. It was to embrace all functions and all forms of employment which pertained to the sacerdotal condition: preaching, the upbringing of clerics and future priests, and even the education of youth, which was to be its main task in later years, despite Bérulle's early misgivings. The houses of the French Oratory were to be wholly dependent upon the bishops of their dioceses. Its constitutions provided that no vows should be taken beyond those of the priesthood. Whereas the houses founded by St. Philip Neri, and those of the Visitation, had each been independent, Bérulle, true to the centralizing spirit which was then prevailing in France, provided that his Order should be governed by a superior-general, subject, however, to the confirmation of a general assembly to be held every three years. The congregation soon directed its activity to the foundation of colleges, which were to emulate those of the Jesuits, and to scholarship, philosophy, and theology, in which it was to attain great fame.

Even before the Oratorians came upon the stage, several attempts had been made to provide suitable training for the clergy. Seminaries had been set up, according to the prescriptions of Trent, in some twenty towns, from 1567 onwards. Most of them, however, did not reach their twentieth year, for they lacked spiritual inspiration. The assembly of the French clergy again stressed the necessity for seminaries in 1614, and was echoed by the provincial council of Bordeaux in 1624. However, it was not the French Church as a whole, but private initiative, that was at last to provide the means of religious education so urgently required.

Indeed, the condition of the clergy at the beginning of the seventeenth century was such as to justify serious concern. Numerous writers bear witness to its debased moral and ecclesiastical condition. "They were so ignorant of our mysteries," Courtin, the biographer of Bourdoise, writes, "that some were met with who did not even know Jesus Christ and could not say how many natures there were in Him. . . . Many administered the sacraments in Church clad in a doublet. . . ." Madame de Gondi, when she went to confession, used to bring with her the written formula of absolution for the priest to read, for fear he should be ignorant of it. "The very name of priest," Father Amelote writes, "had become a by-word. . . . The priests were seen but in the market or in some low artisan's shop; their tonsure was overgrown and they feared to wear their clerical dress, as providing matter for public railing."

This was the state of things against which the Oratorians, first of all, began to strive. In 1612 they took over the seminary that had been established in Paris by the archbishop of Rouen; in 1616, that of Langres; in 1617, those of Mâcon and Luçon. But they founded only one of their own, in Paris, in the Abbey of St. Magloire. However, Bérulle's worthy successor as superior of the Oratory, Charles de Condren, and four of his disciples, Adrien Bourdoise, John Eudes, Vincent de Paul, and John James Olier, were to continue his work and execute his purpose.

Charles de Condren, born in 1588, had been, like Father Joseph, a brilliant pupil of the Sorbonne. He joined the Oratory in 1617, and founded the houses of Nevers, Langres, and Poitiers. Recalled to Paris, he became the head of the seminary of St. Magloire; then when Bérulle died in 1629, he was made superior-general of the congregation. He died in 1641. De Condren was one of the leading directors of conscience of his own time, and among those whom he guided was Olier.

The latter's predecessor, Adrian Bourdoise, however, had earlier come under the influence of the Oratory. His vocation was decided in the course of a retreat which took place there in 1611 under the direction of Father de Bérulle. He was born of a humble family in 1584 at Brou, in the diocese of Chartres. As a child he had to work as a cowherd, until a charitable parish priest, a friend of his family, took him in hand and taught him enough to enable him to attain holy orders. From the age of four he had been "thinking of the means to bring into the Church priests that should take the way to Heaven, while leading the peoples thither." He was tough and bold in his manners, and has been called a new Elias, a second John the Baptist. His ideal was to restore the parish and the parochial spirit. He objected to private chapels, and could not accept that a Christian should not be present at high Mass. He deemed that a parish should be served by priests living in common, like monks, in perfect poverty and humbleness. He considered the secular clergy as holier than the regulars: "Monks," he used to remark, "save themselves through flight, and priests through fighting." Now, "since good Capuchins or good Jesuits are the product of a good novitiate," a similar period of training should be provided for secular priests. Hence the necessity of seminaries, which ought to be diocesan, founded and directed by each bishop.

Bourdoise was unwilling to trespass on the province of the hierarchy, and was content to establish communities of priests in various parishes at Orléans, Chartres, Boinvilliers, Arles, Lyons, and many other places, especially in the dioceses of Meaux, Senlis, and Beauvais. Those communities purposed to provide future priests with an initiation into their ministry. In 1618, his own community of St. Nicholas du Chardonnet in Paris admitted young clerics to train them; and, in 1619, it became a real seminary, which was approved by the archbishop of Paris in 1631. "What we see in the Church," Bourdoise wrote, "is now silver, whereas the past was lead. But, O my God, in comparison to the gold to be wished for, this silver is but lead."

*   *   *

The first foundation of seminaries on a large scale was due to St. John Eudes. He bore the stamp of the Oratory in an even more marked fashion than Bourdoise. He was born in 1601, at Ri, a small village of Normandy, the province to which he devoted most of his labors. From his early years he had been struck by the indifference of the clergy and of the faithful toward sacred things. "Go to the houses of the great," he said, "and you will see nothing there which is not clean and orderly. Go to the churches: you will find sundry of them surrounded with rubbish, tapestried with spiders' webs, paved with mud. O God, O great God, where is the faith of Christians?" He joined the Oratory in 1623, hoping that he might remedy such evils through the foundation of seminaries. The necessity of these appeared to him even greater as a consequence of the missions which he preached, especially in Normandy, from 1632 onwards. He used to strike the minds of the people through the pomp and majesty of religious ceremonies. There were also open-air meetings, at which immoral books and drawings were publicly burned. Leagues were organized against swearing, blasphemy, and dueling. The preacher's eloquence was forceful, and equally removed from coarseness and preciosity. He founded the Congregation of the Good Shepherd, for the uplifting of fallen girls. But M. Bourgoing, then the superior general of his order, refused to allow him to create, together with a few other clerics, new seminaries. He then left the Oratory and established, on March 25, 1643, a new society, the Congregation of Jesus and Mary. No vows were required "beyond those of baptism and of the priesthood," but the activities of the *Eudistes* were confined to the training of the clergy and the preaching of missions, the former purpose generally holding the principal place. A general organization of seminaries in France, suggested by St. John Eudes to the assembly of the clergy, in 1645, miscarried. But new foundations were to appear after 1650.

A further step in the same direction was taken by St. Vincent de Paul, whose social and charitable work, however, also deserves attention. His life was an exceedingly eventful one. He was born on April 24, 1581, in Pouy, a small village in Gascony, the son of a devout family. His childhood was spent in a rural setting. He afterwards studied in the college kept by the "Cordeliers," or Franciscans, at Dax, where he made rapid progress (1595–1597). Attracted to the priesthood, he took minor orders on December 20, 1596; then, he went to study theology at Toulouse. He was ordained priest on September 23, 1600. A journey to Rome in 1605 filled him with emotion and enthusiasm. Being called to Marseilles on business, he was captured at sea on the return trip, by Barbary pirates, and sold as a slave at Tunis. He escaped in 1607 and stayed for another year in Rome. He then came to Paris and chose Pierre de Bérulle as his director. He became one of the chaplains of Queen Margaret de Valois, the divorced wife of Henry IV.

It so happened that on the foundation of the Oratory, one of the first disciples and companions of Bérulle, Francis Bourgoing, resigned his parish at Clichy, a village near Paris, to St. Vincent. Although now a successful and happy parish priest, he yet accepted the charge of tutor to Peter de Gondi, the son of Philip de Gondi, general of the royal galleys. In 1617, Madame de Gondi asked him to join two Jesuit Fathers from Amiens in preaching a mission at Folleville in Picardy, in which he taught the country people to make a general confession. That mission determined his future career. He understood that tutoring was not the proper field of activity for one who ardently desired the salvation of souls. Hence he accepted from Pierre de Bérulle the offer of a small parish, Châtillon-les-Dombes, in the Bresse, where he established his first charitable institution, the "Association of Charity of the Servants of the Poor."

Meanwhile Madame de Gondi had made plans to place a fund of sixteen thousands livres at the disposal of a community that would preach missions on her estates every five years. Vainly had St. Vincent sought to interest the Jesuits, Pierre de Bérulle, and Mons. Bourdoise in the scheme. Failing in this he returned to Paris, prepared a plan for the evangelization of the towns and villages depending on the Gondi family, and immediately began to execute it, establishing the "Charity" in every village through which he passed. This confraternity had its rules, its hierarchy, its proper functions. The sisters were to bring food to the sick, to watch the bed of the dying, and to "love one another as being persons whom Jesus-Christ has united and bound through His love."

Meanwhile St. Vincent had done much for convicts and galley slaves, and was made on February 8, 1619, royal chaplain of the galleys. In the same year, he became the superior of the first house of the Visitation in Paris. But his main creation was yet to come.

In 1624, he established the "Congregation of the Mission," intended to preach first of all on the Gondi estates, then later in the diocese of Paris. The members of the congregation were to evangelize the country-side, to be wholly dependent on the bishop of the diocese and the priest of the parish in which they were active, to preach their missions gratui-tously, and to be entirely obedient to their superior. The congregation settled down in 1632 in the priory of St. Lazare in Paris.

Meanwhile Mademoiselle Le Gras — Louise de Marillac — had chosen Vincent as a director. On the death of her husband in 1625, she became one of his auxiliaries in the organization of new "charities," and eventually helped him to fulfill St. Francis de Sales' original purpose when he had created the Visitation: to do charitable work among the poor. Together, they founded the "Company of the Maidens of Charity," on November 29, 1633. The new Order was soon to take a striking development, more than forty houses being established by 1656.

Vincent de Paul had long been impressed, in the course of his missions, by the necessity of a reformation of the clergy. He thought it impossible to correct habitually vicious priests; but conceived the notion of re-treats for ordinandi, to be conducted by himself. He began at Beauvais in September, 1628. In 1632, the archbishop of Paris, John-Francis de Gondi, struck by the idea, made it compulsory for all clerics who wished to take priests' orders to receive instruction for a fortnight on their duties and functions. Vincent de Paul was asked to take charge of them at the Mission, and this was afterwards made into a regular institution, a retreat of two weeks being given at St. Lazare every year. Neighboring dioceses then took to sending their ordinandi there. St. Vincent's re-treats attracted the most distinguished men: John James Olier; the abbot de Rancé, the future reformer of La Trappe; Bossuet; the Abbé Fleury, the famous Church historian; and many others. These retreats spread to several French dioceses, where they were entrusted to priests of the Mission, of the Oratory, of St. Nicholas, etc., penetrating next into Savoy and into Italy, beginning at Rome in 1642.

St. Vincent, however, did not think them sufficient and attempted to provide for secular priests an equivalent of a novitiate, in the shape of a minor seminary at the Collège des Bons Enfants of Paris University, of which he was the principal. It was found, however, that most of the alumni left the college without taking orders. St. Vincent, therefore, conceived the novel idea that better results would be obtained by trying to exert an influence on adult men, from twenty to thirty years of age, who would come as subdeacons, deacons, or priests. These then could be trained for the space of one or two years in the practice of virtue and prayer, the use of the liturgy and ceremonies, singing, catechizing, preaching, etc. Therefore, with the help of Cardinal Richelieu, he created, in 1642, at the Collège des Bons Enfants, a "major seminary," side by side with the already extant "minor seminary." In the following years several diocesan seminaries were entrusted to the priests of the Mission: at Annecy, Alet, Cahors, Saintes, Le Mans, St. Méen, Marseille, Tréguier, Agen, Périgueux, and in still other towns after 1650. In order to keep alive the flame of sacerdotal devotion, St. Vincent organized regular meetings of priests at St. Lazare from 1633 onwards. The Tuesday conferences soon spread to the whole of France, and sent out swarms of priests to preach missions in various provinces. They were to last on to the French Revolution.

It is not possible to follow the development of all the organizations created by St. Vincent; his reform of preaching; his attitude toward the reform of the older orders; his charitable work on behalf of foundlings, beggars, prisoners, galley slaves, war victims. When he died on September 27, 1660, he left behind him, in that age of exceptional spiritual richness, the memory of one of the most fruitful lives that have ever been recorded.

His work for the training of the clergy was paralleled by that of John James Olier, the founder of St. Sulpice. He was twenty-seven years younger than St. Vincent, having been born in 1608, in Paris, and was the son of a councillor in the Parliament of that city. In 1617, his father became the royal intendant at Lyons where he now attended the classes of the Jesuit college of the Trinity. At the age of eleven he obtained a benefice through his parents, but his fiery temperament seemed to make him unfit for the ecclesiastical state. His mother's misgivings were, however, allayed by St. Francis de Sales, who saw him in December, 1622. "Be comforted," he said to her, "God has chosen him for His glory and for the good of His Church."

After returning to Paris with his father in 1626, he received new benefices, including the Abbey of Pébrac in Auvergne. He now studied philosophy for two years at Harcourt College, and then theology in the Sorbonne. But, though a cleric, he led the dissipated life of the Latin quarter, and his actual conversion did not take place until he went to Rome to make himself proficient in the Hebrew language. There, his eyes became diseased and he made a pilgrimage to Loretto to seek recovery. No sooner had he crossed the threshold of the basilica than he was cured physically, and more than this, was seized by divine grace. He returned to Paris a different man, took to preaching to the poor in the streets of the city, and thought of becoming a Carthusian, but a dream made him conclude that the state of a *curé* was superior. He began, therefore, to prepare for the taking of holy orders, attended several of the retreats organized by St. Vincent de Paul at St. Lazare, in 1632 and 1633, and was ordained priest May 21 in the latter year. True to the spirit and directions of St. Vincent, he forthwith undertook to preach a mission in Auvergne, together with several "Lazarists."

On his arrival at Pébrac, where he attempted the reform of his abbey, the mission met with marked success, and he enthusiastically enlisted the help of several priests of the country. Returning now to Paris he became acquainted with Father Charles de Condren, who prevailed upon him to join the Oratory. He had preached several missions in France, organized one to Canada, and undergone severe spiritual trials for the space of two years, when Father de Condren gathered to him in 1640 the missionaries of the Oratory, and with them Adrian Bourdoise, in order to suggest to them the creation of a seminary. After Condren's death, the missionaries settled down at Chartres in January, 1641. They hoped now that young clerics would come to them for training. The attempt failed, but the small company soon found another abode at Vaugirard, a village close to Paris, where their community began its life on December 29, 1641.

They now established a "major seminary" for clerics only, with a permanent staff, where both masters and pupils led the same life, while serving the needs of the adjacent parish. Olier next agreed to become the curé of the parish of St. Sulpice in Paris, so that he might transfer his seminary to the interior of the city, accommodating it in two houses near his presbytery. From now on, he was the superior of two communities: the college of priests serving the parish and the seminary itself. He labored for the conversion of the Faubourg St. Germain, which was "the refuge of libertines and atheists." Meanwhile he guided the spiritual life of his disciples, and founded new seminaries in the provinces, at Nantes, Viviers, Le Puy, and Clermont. To serve them, he created the "Company of Saint Sulpice," housing his Paris seminary in new buildings before he died on April 2, 1657.

*   *   *

St. Vincent de Paul was not the only one in seventeenth-century France to try to remedy social as well as spiritual evils. As a matter of fact, most of the missions preached in the provinces at the time had a twofold character, and made for the welfare of the people as well as for moral progress. We need but instance those of John Eudes in Normandy; of Michael le Nobletz in Brittany; of St. Peter Fourier in Lorraine; of Anthony Yvan in Provence; of John Le Jeune, the blind Oratorian, throughout the whole of France. We shall here refer, however, in some detail to the missions of St. Francis Régis, S.J., the apostle of the Velay.

He was born on January 31, 1597, at Fontcouverte, a village of Languedoc. In 1612, he entered the Jesuit college at Béziers and on December 8, 1616, at Toulouse was admitted to the Society of Jesus. He was of a keen and loving temperament, and later as a teacher had a lasting influence upon his pupils. After completing his course in theology at Toulouse, he said his first Mass at Whitsuntide, in 1630. His exceptional gifts attracted the attention of his superiors, who sent him in 1632 to the city of Montpellier, one of the main citadels of Protestantism. Thereafter his life was wholly devoted to missionary labors. He organized charities, founded an association for the relief of prisoners, pleaded with the Huguenots to return to the Catholic fold and did his best to root out prostitution while finding decent employment for fallen girls.

We cannot follow the course of all his missions, but he was active from 1633 to 1636 in the Vivarais, a Huguenot stronghold. Penetrating into the deep, craggy, impenetrable valleys of the Cévennes, where the wild mountaineers had neither priests nor churches, St. Francis would go into public houses to shame the drunkards, and occasionally suffered for it. In 1636, he was called to Le-Puy-en-Velay by bishop Just de Serres, to help mend the morals of the town, which had fallen very low. Crimes were frequent, and the very judges were corrupt. In the space of fifteen years forty murders had been left unpunished. St. Francis began to preach in the Benedictine church, where the power of his speech attracted audiences of as many as five thousand people, and where all social classes met to listen to him. He established the society of the "Ladies of Mercy" to feed the poor, to clothe them and furnish their houses. Despite opposition from the debauched youth of the town, he founded a refuge for repentant prostitutes, known as the "Good Shepherd." He next penetrated the surrounding mountains, where, in the words of a parish priest of the country, "everyone was so taken with his holiness, that all ran after him. They came from very far to hear him. . . . I have seen him preach, standing on a mound of trampled snow, while neither he nor his hearers seemed to mind the cold."

In 1640, a royal edict forbade the making of lace, which was then the chief economic resource of the region. Forty thousand girls were thrown out of work, but St. Francis foretold the repeal of the edict, and was personally instrumental in bringing it about. In consequence he has remained, up to this day, the patron saint of lace-makers. Shortly afterwards, exhausted by his strenuous life, he died on December 31, 1640, in the small village of Lalouvesc. The veneration of the people for him was such that many towns claimed his mortal remains, and even wrangled for their possession.

It should not be thought, however, that Christian social work in France, in the early seventeenth century, was exclusively the work of individuals. It appeared, as well, in an organized form, as embodied in a secret society which has given rise to much historical discussion and has been judged in widely different ways — the Company of the Holy Sacrament of the Altar. Its founder was the duke of Ventadour, one of the leading noblemen of the kingdom, a valiant soldier with the soul of a Crusader. He and his wife had decided to consecrate themselves wholly to God, and therefore while she became a Carmelite, he sought means to procure the salvation of souls. The idea of the company came to him in 1627, and he confided it, first to a Capuchin, Father Philip d'Angoumois, and then to a Jesuit, Father Suffren, the confessor of Louis XIII, both of whom approved of it.

The purpose of the company was to promote all the good which might be obtained, and to prevent all the evil which might be prevented. Its spirit was universal, but no regulars were to be admitted. Its action was to remain secret. Nor was it to appear as a corporate body, but its members were to act individually, while deriving power from the union of their efforts, and spiritual strength and comfort from their common devotional exercises. Its membership included men of all social classes, both clerics and laymen united in a spirit of Christian equality. Among the clerics were most of the illustrious missioners whom we have named above — De Condren, St. Vincent de Paul, Olier, and John Eudes. It further embraced numerous archbishops and bishops, parish priests, and doctors of the Sorbonne; among the latter, the most brilliant names in the kingdom, both of noblemen and lawyers.

The Company spread rapidly to the whole of France. Fifty-three of its local branches are known today, but there were undoubtedly many more. All of them did their best to remedy the moral evils of the times which we have already referred to: destitution, prostitution, drunkenness, and profanity. The Company took over St. Vincent's work for the galley slaves; prepared the establishment of the "general hospital" intended to house paupers and beggars; created a society for the liberation of insolvent debtors; founded a refuge for repentant prostitutes; undertook the relief of the "shamefaced poor"; attempted to enforce the keeping of Sundays and feast days and to prevent the breaking of Lent; to stop the sale of lewd books, the production of immoral spectacles, and the practice of gambling. It restored the decency of public worship, took part in the reform of religious orders, and established a league against duelling.

One of its prominent members, a nobleman, M. de Renty, formed a close friendship with a pious cobbler from Luxemburg, Henri Buche, who had dedicated himself to an apostolate among the working classes. "Like two brothers," they struggled in an admirable and touching fashion against all sorts of social evils. In order to counteract the secret workingmen's union known as *compagnonnage*, which was wrongly supposed to indulge in blasphemous practices, they founded communities of artisans. The "brethren," cobblers or tailors, took no vows but lived together, wore the same dress, and worked at stated hours to the accompaniment of pious reading or singing. Henri Buche himself, though he had been appointed superior of the cobblers, did the meanest household work, and tenderly nursed the sick.

Unfortunately the activities of the Company were not confined to providing for the welfare of the lower classes. A body which not merely undertakes to further good, but also to prevent evil, tends to become a kind of pious police. In order to put a stop to blaspheming, either among the "companions" or elsewhere, a certain amount of spying and informing was necessary. It may indeed be said that greater importance was then attached to offences against God than is the case nowadays, and that the intentions of the Company were praiseworthy; nor does it always appear that it was fully responsible for the tortuous behavior of its servants. Nevertheless there is something definitely unpleasant about the mere fact that it was engaged in nosing out blasphemy and heresy. Its case is one of Catholic Puritanism, largely parallel to that of Protestant Puritanism, odium being aroused against both for kindred motives, and especially because they tried to enforce an austere moral and religious code, and interfered with what they regarded as the questionable pastimes, intellectual and otherwise, of their contemporaries. No wonder, therefore, that the Company was held up to public execration in Molière's *Tartufe,* and eventually suppressed by King Louis XIV in 1663.

Reviewing the early seventeenth century in France, we are struck by the extraordinary spiritual enthusiasm of the clergy and laity, and also by the moral unity among the various religious bodies as well as among the various classes of the population. The controversy between Gallicans and Jesuits was as yet without the bitterness it was to assume after the appearance of Jansenism. The influence of the Jesuits and that of the Sorbonne were happily blended in the Bérulle circle and among its continuators. There was emulation rather than rivalry between the various spiritual schools. The Church raised the humble and lowered the mighty, to take part in the same apostolic and charitable labors. St. Vincent, who had begun as a swineherd, associated with the noble Madame de Gondi to evangelize Picardy. On the whole, the fiery ardor of Spanish devotion, the sweetness of Italian piety, and the natural restraint and moderation of the French temper, combined in the age of Louis XIII to produce a most attractive type of Christianity, heroic and sedate, austere and tender, in which the Catholic Reformation may be said to have reached its climax.

CHAPTER XIII

The Catholic Reformation in Great Britain and Ireland

JUSTICE has never been done to the importance of the Catholic Reformation for the British Isles, and especially for England. The establishment of Protestantism in the latter country tended to isolate it from most of the continent of Europe. Church historians as a whole have failed to notice that this isolation, though officially enforced, was far less effective than it was supposed to be. The Trentine movement did not merely permeate what was left of English Catholicism after the Elizabethan settlement (and that was a very large section of the population), but also penetrated into the Anglican Church, and exerted a decisive influence upon the Laudian revival.

The attention of Catholic writers has been absorbed by the heroic side of the campaign of the Catholic missionaries in England, and by the political problem which arose on account of their twofold loyalty to the Holy See and to the sovereign. They have dwelt at length upon their trials, tortures, and executions. But they have scarcely touched upon the far more important fact that they represented a new intellectual, educational, literary, and devotional trend, which was to mold the English character quite as much as Protestantism itself and the effect of which is felt even at the present day.

In the British Isles, the Catholic Reformation took three successive forms. First of all, before the advent of Protestantism, efforts were made to amend the state of the Church according to the spirit of the Council of Trent, and various ecclesiastical assemblies were engaged in preparing a considerable body of legislation, which, however, was never allowed to take effect. Then, when Protestantism had been officially established, the Trentine revival was continued in the English, Scottish, and Irish Catholic centers abroad, through the foundation of colleges or seminaries. Meanwhile the missionaries trained there brought it along with them to their co-religionists in the home-countries. Lastly, the Episcopalian establishment itself was invaded by continental thought and devotion, and subjected especially to the influence of France in the reign of

Louis XIII. Thence followed that High-Church renascence, which only ceased temporarily upon the death of Charles I.

In the first of three phases mentioned, Scotland took the lead. Though greatly hampered by the social and political disorder prevalent in the country, the Church was free to legislate until 1560, and made a serious effort at self reform. Religious conditions in Scotland in the fifteenth and early sixteenth centuries had been much what they were in Italy and France. They offered the same curiously mixed picture: rich devotional life on the one hand, and on the other all the evils produced by the administrative mismanagement of the Church. The number of foundations during the period is significant: no fewer than forty-six collegiate churches, hospitals, and colleges — educational establishments gradually gaining the upper hand from 1500 onward. At the same time, the abuse of lay patronage had brought about an appalling state of moral laxity among the clergy. A writing of the year 1540, addressed to Cardinal Beaton, describes the Scottish Church in the following words: "How many do we see, who after spending their years in idle pastimes, after consuming the flower of their age in the most shameful things, fly to the heads of the Church, in order to obtain from them some fat benefice, where they may shield their slothfulness, and finish their old age in luxury. . . . The cure of souls is granted not merely to ignorant people, but also to children still incapable of reasoning, so that they seem to be born only to inherit. . . . Many will be loaded with a multitude of benefices, whose conversation, whose life are such, that it may be doubted, whether they be Christians, or pagans."

While the clergy as a whole provided a spectacle of moral corruption, their ranks also included men of a different cast, Christian humanists who, in the fifteenth century, prepared the reformation of the Church. Foremost among them stands William Elphinstone (1431–1514), who received part of his education in the universities of Paris and Orleans, became rector of the University of Glasgow in 1474 and bishop of Aberdeen in 1482. In 1494, he founded King's College, Aberdeen. One of the professors was Hector Boethius, the historian of Scotland, who had taught at Montaigu College in Paris, and had been in touch with Erasmus there; another one was John Adamson, the provincial and reformer of the Scottish Dominicans. Elphinstone issued new statutes for his cathedral chapter, requiring the canons to be at least licentiates in theology, "so as to announce and preach the word of God to the Christian people," and to reside in person. He was one of the first to make use of the printing-press, newly introduced into Scotland, to publish the

Aberdeen Breviary. Only in the early sixteenth century, however, was the reformation of the Scottish Church as a whole attempted by Andrew Forman, who was made, in 1514, archbishop of Saint Andrews by Pope Leo X, and held his primatial see until his death in 1521. He issued diocesan statutes, which cast a lurid light upon the state of the Church in his time. Non-resident clerics, or those who did not keep church buildings in good repair or did not provide them with the necessary utensils, were to lose one fourth the fruits of their benefices. Those who, after a third warning, still retained their concubines, were to lose their charge. Clerics who, being indicted for a crime before the ordinary, turned to the civil power for protection, were to be suspended and fined. Laymen who fought or shed blood in church were to be excommunicated. All rectors, vicars, chantry priests were to appear at high Mass and vespers on feast days and Sundays, at vespers on Saturdays, and join in singing Mass, vespers, and matins. From each one of a number of monasteries, which were named, one or two religious were to be sent to the university of Saint Andrews to complete their training.

The statutes of Archbishop Forman provide the pattern according to which all the Scottish Church legislation was drafted until 1560. Again and again we find the same prescriptions against non-residence and the keeping of concubines, the same reassertion of the jurisdiction of the Church as against the civil power, the same denunciation of lay violence and immorality, the same provisions for the education of the clergy. There were Scottish provincial councils at Edinburgh in 1536, at Linlithgow and Edinburgh in 1549, at Edinburgh in 1552 and 1559. It is not our purpose to recount how the progress of Presbyterianism in Scotland made itself felt in the decisions of the councils. It is enough to say that, as the Protestant invasion became more and more threatening, the canons of the synods increased in stringency, and struck almost a desperate note; for those very laymen whose invasion of Church rights had brought about the relaxation of ecclesiastical discipline, were the first to support the Protestant claims.

The testimony of the Catholic apologist, Quintin Kennedy, the Benedictine abbot of Crossraguel, is significant in this respect. He holds up the abuses to execration, but lays responsibility for them upon lay covetousness. Children, he says, who can scarce hold an apple in their hands, are granted parishes of five thousand souls. This is due to the avarice of their parents, who wish to draw the revenues. Monasteries are going to ruin; and yet those very men who hold them *in commendam* are the same who stand forth as the revilers of the clerical vices. If the

Church were to recover her former liberty, to elect her own abbots and bishops freely, both abuses and errors in belief would vanish.

One wonders, as a matter of fact, what would have happened had Protestant interference — which in the main was the interference of part of the nobility, egged on by England — not prevented the enforcement of the canons of these Church synods. The good-will of the assembled Fathers appears indisputable, and the principles which inspired them were those of the Council of Trent, which they repeatedly quoted. "There is a twofold cause for and root of the evils" — the Prologue to the canons of 1549 runs — "which have brought about such an outbreak of heresy; one is the corruption of manners and impurity of life among churchmen of almost every rank; the other is their gross ignorance of 'good letters and arts.' "

It is not possible to rehearse even briefly the prescriptions of the synod, but it may be pointed out that several among them are new. It lays down a method for preaching sermons: the former part of these must be devoted to the Epistle or Gospel of the day, the latter to "catechism," a novel word then, since its meaning is explained. Parish priests, "most of whom in the whole kingdom of Scotland are deficient in learning, manners and wisdom," are to be examined by the ordinaries or their deputies within the space of a few weeks, under pain of deprivation.

The following councils, and especially that of 1559, again declare heavy penalties against clerics who infringe the old canons on Church discipline. They forbid prelates and priests to bring up the children of their concubines in their own household; archbishops and prelates to provide their sons with benefices in their own churches; prelates and clerics at large to give their daughters in marriage to noblemen, and grant them dowries out of church property; prelates and other churchmen to engage in trade. They again make the wearing of clerical dress and the tonsure compulsory for all ecclesiastics, beseech priests to celebrate Mass "more frequently than they are wont to," priests and beneficiaries to say their hours daily and be present at Mass at least on Sundays and feast days. They prescribe, according to the Council of Trent, the visitation of monasteries, even if exempt. They settle the stipends of curates, and put a stop to abuses in the collection of mortuaries and tithes. Their provisions for the preaching of Christian doctrine to the people are, however, the most important and original.

Obviously the humanistic dignitaries who drafted the canons of 1552 had only a limited trust in the learning, oratorical ability, or orthodoxy of their parish priests, as appears from the rules which they laid down for their preaching or rather reciting of the catechism. "Neither the inferior orders of the clergy, nor the prelates of this kingdom," they said, "are for the most part thus advanced in the knowledge of sacred letters, that they should be able by their own efforts to instruct the people in the Catholic faith and other things necessary for salvation, or to convert those in error." The council therefore decrees that a Scottish Catechism will be published, of which a copy will be handed to every rector, vicar, or curate. Due precautions will be taken before laymen be allowed to peruse it. All priests will read it through in parts, on Sundays and feast days to the people assembled for divine service, "in a high and audible voice, distinctly, clearly and articulately, with the greatest possible gravity, from the pulpit, wearing their surplice and stole, before high Mass for the space of half an hour. They will," the council insists, read it "wholly, without any hesitancy, not adding, changing, suppressing or omitting anything." They will be careful to prepare this reading in advance "by a frequent and lengthy rehearsal." They will not allow anyone in the audience to begin a discussion, and carefully refrain from entering into controversy themselves. Should they neglect the above orders, they will be fined twenty shillings for a first offence; fifty shillings for a second offence; for a third offence, they will pay twice the amount and be imprisoned on bread and water for at least one month. The weight of those penalties, the severity of the canons, and the hugeness of the offences to be punished, show what a pitiable condition the Church of Scotland had fallen into. Unfortunately the correction of abuses came too late.

The direct appeal of Protestantism to popular rectitude and rough common sense, especially when in league with the noblemen who had despoiled the Church, had an explosive force which could not be resisted. However, the scholarly leaders of the Scottish clergy had made a brave attempt to carry it along with them on the path to Catholic reformation, and deserved a better fate.

*　　*　　*

In Ireland there prevailed, in the fifteenth century, a social and political confusion even greater than in Scotland. There was internal strife everywhere: the Church was at war with the nobility, the seculars were quarrelling with the regulars. It is hardly surprising, in the circumstances, that no comprehensive attempt at reformation should have been made before the Henrician schism, and that until then provincial and diocesan councils should have been mostly anxious to defend the privileges and jurisdiction of the Church against the encroachments of lay persons and religious orders.

Some traces of the reforming spirit, however, appeared as early as 1453, when the synod of Limerick issued canons, a few of which had to do with clerical discipline, those for instance which prescribed the singing of hours by clerics on Sundays and feast days, the wearing of clerical dress, or the payment of parish revenues to the vicar when the parson did not reside. Prescriptions of the same nature appear here and there before Henry VIII's secession from Rome. The provincial synods of Cashel (1514) and Dublin (1518) forbade priests to wear their hair over their ears, and to play football. The Council of Dublin in 1529 corrected abuses among the regulars, and established a stricter rule in Franciscan convents. But Henry VIII's efforts to separate the Irish Church from Rome put an end to all such activities, although Robert Wauchop, created archbishop of Armagh by Paul III in 1539, took a prominent part in the opening sessions of the Council of Trent.

It was only under Mary Tudor that the Catholic Reformation really made its appearance in Ireland, and, strange to say, through the instrumentality of a man who had submitted to the will of Henry VIII. In Ireland as well as in England, Henrician prelates, who had accepted the royal supremacy without realizing all its implications, stalwartly resisted the government of Edward VI when it tried to enforce the use of the Anglican liturgy and the acceptance of Protestant dogma; an attitude which qualified them, when Catholicism was restored by Mary Tudor, to become reconciled with Rome, and to resume possession of their sees. Such was the case of George Dowdall, who had been made archbishop of Armagh and primate of Ireland in 1543 by Henry VIII, despite the fact that the Holy See had already invested Robert Wauchop with the same dignities. Dowdall devoted himself to the preaching and teaching of Catholic doctrine and, under Edward VI, in 1550, put himself at the head of Irish opposition to the Book of Common Prayer, and boldly threatened the Lord Deputy St. Leger with excommunication. When Wauchop died the Irish Catholics besought the pope to choose Dowdall as his successor. The request was granted on March 1, 1553. As soon as he was reinstated in his see, the archbishop sought to heal the wounds of the Irish Church, and therefore convened, at Dublin, in 1556, a provincial council, which undertook reformation on Trentine lines. Its canons have been preserved and bear, among others, on the following points:

Bishops and other collators, who appointed priests to benefices under condition that they should pay the revenues to laymen or children, were deprived of their powers of patronage. Simoniacal bishops, who sold benefices, were to be suspended. Churchmen of all degrees were forbidden under pain of suspension to charge for the administration of sacraments. The wearing of clerical dress and tonsure were again made compulsory for priests. Severity in the collection of mortuaries was to be mitigated, especially in regard to widows and orphans. Rectors and vicars who were unable to preach in person were to pay for a substitute, who was to deliver sermons four times a year. The other canons bore upon the prosecution of heretics or the restoration of Catholic rites. There is, however, nothing in the decisions of this council which goes beyond the reinforcement of medieval Church discipline. There is no trace of anything constructive, especially in regard to the education of the clergy. Originality was scarcely to be sought for in the attempts at reformation in Scotland or Ireland. It appears in England only, where it was due to the outstanding ability and enthusiasm of one of the leaders of the Catholic revival, Cardinal Reginald Pole.

The ground had indeed long been prepared for Catholic Reformation in England. The country had been *par excellence* that of Christian humanism. One need only recall the names of Grocyn, Linacre, Colet, Erasmus, Thomas More. These men have been mistakenly described as the precursors of Protestantism. There can be no doubt, indeed, that Colet's vehement denunciations, and Erasmus' biting satire of the vices and ignorance of churchmen, helped to strengthen the current of anti-clerical opinion, which eventually merged with Protestantism. But the Christian humanists themselves felt no partiality for the methods or spirit of the religious revolution. They were aristocrats in more senses than one. They stressed the importance of Scripture, but as interpreted by means of the most searching scholarship, and not by unenlightened personal inspiration. They were lovers of peace, and disapproved of popular tumults. However much they might criticize or even ridicule clerical abuses, they had no wish to subvert the Church, and hoped for reformation from within. They were deeply attached to traditional beliefs and disinclined to embrace the new dogmatic tenets of Lutheranism. Yet they were so averse to open strife that they did not raise the standard of revolt against Henry VIII, when, to exert pressure upon the pope, he began to favor religious innovations, or, later, broke with Rome altogether. The most heroic among them, such as John Fisher and Thomas More, suffered patiently for their faith. Others, such as Stephen Gardiner, Cuthbert Tunstall, Edmund Bonner, John Stokesley, supported the king's supremacy, possibly with the idea that reformation might be achieved by Christian princes, in default of a weakened and decrepit papacy.

The years which followed the sack of Rome in 1527 were indeed a period of eclipse for the Holy See, and one need not be surprised that earnest Catholics should have turned elsewhere for the protection of their ancient faith. But as the Trentine movement gathered momentum, its influence began to be felt in England as well, and resistance to the Protestant inroads began to stiffen. Henrician oppression was so severe that it was impossible for the English prelates of the time to admit in the home-country to relations with the rising group of Catholic reformers on the Continent; and therefore direct traces of such relations are not available in the State Papers. But we know that Gardiner was at Ratisbon in 1541; and there is every reason to believe that he came into touch with German Catholics such as Latomus, Gropper, and Eck, if not with Wauchop and Peter Faber. It is not a little suggestive in any case that just as the Council of Trent was about to begin, he should have engaged in controversy with Martin Bucer, making use of the same Catholic printing-presses at Louvain, Cologne, and Ingolstadt as the continental adversaries of the Strasbourg reformer.

What is more, in the years which followed the opening sessions of the Council of Trent, there was a revival of Catholic resistance inside the Henrician, and then the Edwardine, church. Numerous treatises by English divines appeared in England or abroad, in defence of the Eucharist, the sacrifice of the Mass, and the celibacy of priests. Between 1546 and 1552, no fewer than seven of these were composed by Stephen Gardiner against English or continental Protestants, such as Hooper, Peter Martyr, or Oecolampadius; four were written by Richard Smith, D.D., and one by Cuthbert Tunstall. Meanwhile, Reginald Pole was preparing, in France and Italy, for his task as a Catholic reformer of the English church, and taking part, as a legate, in the debates of the Council of Trent.

* * *

Indeed, on the part of Catholics the *Reformatio Angliae,* like the reform of the Church at large, was a perennial undertaking; it had lasted throughout the Middle Ages, in its negative aspect at least, that is to say, the mere forbidding of malpractices. It was already in full swing at the time of Constitutions of John Peckham, archbishop of Canterbury, which date back to 1281, and later served as a basis for all disciplinary canons, including those of the sixteenth century. When Thomas

Wolsey, archbishop of York, gathered the Northern convocation in that town in 1518 to legislate on Church matters, he had but to publish a tabulated edition of the canons issued by his predecessors to cover practically the whole ground of ecclesiastical abuses. These canons refer in succession to the duties of a good archdeacon, a good archpriest, a good priest, who should not "show himself unwilling to visit the sick at any hour, and send them deacons with the Eucharist, while he himself is engaged in drinking or other pleasures"; to the residence of clerics; to the decency of worship and the expulsion of traders from the churches; to the abuses due to the hearing of confessions by others than the parish priests; to the payment of stipends to priests and especially poor vicars; to the building and repairing of churches. On no point are the canons more vigorous than against the *quaestores* or sellers of indulgences, whom Chaucer had not branded more scathingly in the prologue to his *Pardoner's Tale*. The text, formerly published by Archbishop George Neville, runs as follows: "Not without temerarious audacity, and for the deception of many souls, they have granted indulgences to the people on their own responsibility, dispensed them from fulfilling their vows, and absolved from perjury, murder, and other sins. . . . They have, as they falsely asserted, extracted from Purgatory, and led to the joys of Paradise, three or more souls of the parents or friends of those, who have brought them alms."

The negative prescriptions of the Middle Ages were again the basis of the canons issued, on the eve of the schism, by the convocation of the province of Canterbury, held at St. Paul's in London, from November 5, 1529, to April 29, 1530; which canons in their turn served as a starting-point for the debates of the same convocation, sitting at Westminster, from November 4, 1555, to February 25, 1556, in the reign of Mary Tudor. One feels, however, when reading the regulations of 1529, that there is a new spirit abroad. Beside the actual forbidding of faults, we find a beautiful portrait of the ideal priest, who should also be an ideal teacher: "Idleness being the mother of all vices, this sacred council commands and prescribes to all rectors, curates and vicars, that once they have performed their divine office, they be occupied in study, prayer, reading, or other honest business which befits their profession, namely in teaching children the alphabet, reading, singing or grammar. And let them exercise themselves on three days a week, for three or at least two hours, in the reading of Holy Scripture, or of some approved doctor. . . ."

The necessity of learning as the foundation of piety is again asserted in the passage which rehearses the duties of an ideal bishop, who should "see to it more diligently [than of yore] that the beginnings of pure faith and pure letters be proposed to pure listeners, no less in the universities, than in other schools, and increase more purely and more sincerely." Indeed, a whole section is devoted to school-teachers. The rules laid down for their choice — the fact, for instance, that they must take an oath before their appointment — obviously betray the fear of heresy; but they are also inspired by a wish to benefit the morals and intellect of the pupils. Convocation has noticed that a change of methods, consequent upon a change of masters, is detrimental to the young; consequently it decides that "one uniform mode of teaching [classical] grammar will be used throughout the province of Canterbury," after being determined by a committee of bishops, abbots, and archdeacons.

The Christian humanists had been the leading element in the convocations of York in 1518 and of Canterbury in 1529. Like Thomas More, they combined a belief in the sufficiency of learning to improve Church conditions, with a conservative position in regard to Church organization and policy; and one must wait until the Canterbury convocation of 1555–1556 to find a really new departure on Trentine lines. The settling of dogma in coherent and fixed ways, which it undertook, was however not exclusively a Catholic novelty. The Protestants also, under Edward VI, had had homilies written to be read in church, and apparently distrusted their own preachers quite as much as the representatives of the "old religion." It is nevertheless striking that the convocation of 1555–1556 should have felt it necessary to hearten and strengthen their flocks by providing them with a clear body of doctrine. Proposals were made to the effect that "for lack of preachers, four types of short sermons in English be composed, and read to the people on Sundays and feast days by vicars, rectors and parsons"; the first bearing on the Eucharist, penance, auricular confession, and other controverted subjects, such as free will and justification, good works, the authority of the Church; the second on the articles of faith, the Lord's Prayer, the Hail Mary, the commandments, and sacraments; the third on the proper feasts and saints; the fourth on ceremonies, the cardinal virtues, the capital sins. It was also proposed that a brief catechism for the young should be published in Latin and English; also guides for confession and the visitation of the sick. The Breviary and Missal were to be simplified and unified, and the same ceremonies were to be used in all dioceses.

The attempt to train a new and reformed clergy by means of seminaries is altogether more original. The assembly groped its way in that direction, before Pole, in his decrees, published a fuller scheme of clerical education. The rules proposed for cathedral churches provide for the teaching of "sacred letters." In each of these, it was suggested, a learned man should be granted a prebend, in order to expound Scripture to the clergy and people; while sixty or more boys, supported through the appropriation of benefices, should be taught grammar, in view of a future clerical career. A syllabus of courses was contemplated for the universities, where a sufficient number of scholars was to be maintained, toward the recruiting of the clergy. The teaching of theology was to include lectures on the Bible, on Peter Lombard, or some author who had "renewed" scholastic theology; that of philosophy was to rest on Aristotle alone, but the humanistic thinker, Rudolph Agricola, might also be introduced into the course. The hearing of lectures in colleges was to be made compulsory; scholarships were to be reserved for poor students, whose parents bound themselves to urge them, in due time, to join the ranks of the clergy. On the other hand, no one was to be admitted to priesthood, or to a benefice of twenty pounds sterling or above, unless he had spent three years in an "academy," and obtained at least the degree of bachelor. Card-playing and dicing were prohibited; and the endless quibblings of medieval disputations were to be done away with. Lastly such beneficiaries as were staying in the universities would be compelled to reside in colleges, to take part in disputations and attend public lectures.

When one compares the proposals made by Convocation with the decrees published by Pole on February 10, 1556, one is struck by the fact that the latter, couched in perfect Latin, are far superior to the former; this being due no less to Pole's personal ability than to the experience he had gathered on the Continent. The cardinal begins with the re-enforcement of former legislation; all clerics are bound to have a copy of the old constitutions of the English Church. Steps are then taken to prevent the spreading of false beliefs, and Catholic doctrine is rehearsed at large, on the model of the Trentine decrees. The serious strictness of Trent appears in the passage devoted to the dedication feast of churches: it condemns "the profane and irreligious habit of showing vain spectacles, of engaging in orgies, dances and other things of the same kind." On that day and other feast days, the people should "fervently apply themselves to the hearing of divine offices." The opening lines of the third decree are a beautiful warning to clerics against non-residence, to which the decay of ecclesiastical morals is almost wholly ascribed:

"Whereas the reformation of the Church," it runs, "must begin with those who have the care of others; and whereas this abuse is flourishing among them, namely that not residing in the churches committed to them, they leave them to mercenaries; which thing is the cause of almost every evil in the Church; first of all, we urgently exhort in the Lord all those who govern cathedral churches, even metropolitan, and other inferior churches, implying the cure of souls, . . . that attending to themselves, and to their whole flock . . . they exhibit to it their due presence, and, void of all cares of secular business, watch over its safety, and labor in everything according to the precept of the apostle, and fulfill their ministry."

Canons are to be granted leave of absence subject only to the approval of the majority of their chapter. Pluralities are forbidden under heavy penalties.

The fourth decree, on preaching, requests archbishops and bishops to address their flocks in person, and renews former canons for other clerics; but it strikes a new line when recommending direction of conscience: "This duty of preaching will be wholly fulfilled if, apart from public sermons, the pastor, after calling up those of the flock committed to him whom he knows to have strayed from right faith, or from good manners, warn and exhort them paternally and with all tenderness of charity, and if need be dissuade them, endeavoring to bring them back to the Catholic faith, and to a right rule of life." The fifth decree, on the life and virtues of clerics, begins with the following beautiful words: "Since the example of one's conduct adds most authority to the word, and seems to be a kind of preaching, those who are placed above others must be careful to surpass them, as well by the righteousness of their manners and the holiness of their life, as by that excellence in governing one's own house, which the apostle requires from bishops." Hereupon follows a veritable rule of life for prelates, a rule of wise moderation and simplicity, inspired by Christian humanism. They should "indulge in no pomp or luxury, wear no silken cloth, use no precious furniture; their board should be frugal and spare," with only three or at most four dishes, besides dessert; they should have few domestics and horses, and only those needful; their lay servants should wear "a modest and decent dress." The surplus of their income should be used to feed the needy and to educate children in schools. "Let them be the fathers of the poor, the refuge and protection of orphans, widows, and those oppressed." Let them apply themselves to the reading of Scripture, and abstain from profane business.

The decrees referring to the marriage of priests (which had taken root in England under Edward VI) and on clerical dress need not be dwelt on, but the prescriptions on the examination of future priests are worthy of especial attention. The bishops should not trust to others as to the qualifications of ordinandi. They should examine them in person. All who seek orders should confess their sins to an able priest, and receive Communion on the day of their ordination. Beneficiaries should be similarly examined, and promise on oath to reside. The heads of universities and colleges should be requested to supply lists of candidates "suited by their life and learning" for promotion to a living; and no benefice should be left vacant. But by far the most important decree is that which provides for the creation of diocesan seminaries and which anticipated the similar decree of Trent by several years. "Since there is in these times," it begins, "a great penury of churchmen, especially of worthy ones . . . and since the best means to remedy such an evil is to create and conserve in cathedral churches a kind of progeny and so to say a nursery [*seminarium*] of ministers . . . we decree that each metropolitan and cathedral church of this kingdom be bound to maintain a certain number of boys, according to its revenues and means." Detailed prescriptions follow: the minimum age of the alumni should be eleven or twelve; they should be able to read and write, and give fair promise of becoming priests. Poor scholars should be preferred (as in the Trentine decisions) though rich ones be not excluded, if they really wish to serve God. Their studies should begin with grammar, then proceed with religious doctrine. Those who study the latter should be divided into two classes, juniors and advanced pupils, the latter being acolytes. Both will wear clerical dress and submit to the tonsure. The acolytes will be promoted to holy orders according to age and merit, and be appointed to some ecclesiastical charge; while the gaps left in their ranks will be filled in by the most deserving of the lower class.

The grammar school will admit all sorts of suitable pupils; the ablest ones, and those most desirous of serving God, will replace the seniors who take orders. One fortieth of the diocesan revenues will serve to finance the seminary; one fortieth of the income of each benefice will be turned to the same purpose. All masters at present teaching in schools, or candidates for such posts, should be "diligently examined" by the ordinary. Pole's decrees close with a lengthy chapter on episcopal visitations, which should take place every three years, and include all priests, whether in charge of parishes or not. The visitations should bear on the condition of the churches, on the conduct of priests, and also on the morals, beliefs, and piety of the people, inquiring in regard to the latter "whether they be usurers or concubinaries, whether they live and sully themselves in sin, whether there arise among them hatred or enmity . . .; whether they spend their time devoutly in church, and hear the whole mass with attention and reverence; whether they walk about during divine offices; whether the fathers of families bring up their children, and govern their houses, piously and virtuously."

The ideal of life contemplated by the synod, for clerics as well as laymen, was both austere and harmonious. It was full of fair promise for the future. Unfortunately it was never allowed to fructify. Pope Paul IV was so ill-advised as to cancel Pole's commission as legate, and thus to put a stop to his reforming activities. Convocation had been prorogued to November 11, 1557. But both Queen Mary and the cardinal died on November 17, and Protestantism was firmly settled in England by Elizabeth. Nevertheless a beginning had been made. Such men as Allen, Campion, Parsons had received their training at the time of the Catholic Restoration, had imbibed the Trentine spirit, and were to establish it firmly in later years, among their co-religionists.

*   *   *

The English seminaries, which Pole had planned, came into being on the Continent only at the time of the Elizabethan persecution. Just as the English Protestant exiles under Mary had gathered in Lutheran or Calvinistic towns abroad, so the English Catholic exiles now sought refuge in countries stanchly loyal to the Church, at Rome, in Flanders and in Spain. The existence of those centers in turn provided the justification for the foundation of colleges.

The first of these both in date and importance, was created in 1568 at Douai by William Allen. His purpose to begin with was not to provide priests for the English mission, but to establish a spiritual rallying-point for Catholics on the Continent, to replace the universities they had lost, and to supply educational facilities for their children. Gradually it assumed the character of a seminary for the English missionary clergy. Accordingly the teaching was meant to fit the alumni for the practical part they would have to play, rather than to store them with theoretical knowledge. They were trained in preaching and debating, and made familiar with Protestant tenets.

In those early years, Jesuit influence was paramount, and there was no trace as yet of the stubborn opposition to the Society which afterward bred such unedifying dissensions. The Oxford divines who, for reasons of conscience, migrated to the Continent, enthusiastic and gifted men such as Allen, Campion, Parsons, and, later, Southwell, were conquered by the ardent spiritual ideal of St. Ignatius. Devotional life at Douai was based on the saint's method. Nor were Jesuit directors far to seek. Douai had been chosen as being, not merely the seat of a university, but also that of an educational establishment of the Society, Anchin College, where lectures were attended by the students of the English seminary. The latter soon overflowed, and it was found necessary to convert the English hospital at Rome into another residential house for English students, which was put under the direction and spiritual guidance of the Jesuits, and bore the same relation to their Roman college which Douai had borne to Anchin.

We again find the Jesuits in charge of English colleges founded by Fr. Parsons, S.J., at Valladolid (1589), at Seville (1592), at Madrid, at Lisbon, and finally in Flanders at St. Omer (1593). This last was both a seminary for priests and a school for boys. In 1600, it numbered a hundred pupils. Mention should also be made of the "institute" of Mary Ward, founded in St. Omer, in 1608, under Jesuit direction for the education of girls. Whatever truth there may be in the complaints repeatedly made against the Jesuit managment of English colleges, and although it was suspended in some of them in later years, the debt of English Catholicism to the Society appears as an important one.

It played a similar part, but with far less success, in regard to Scottish Catholicism. The efforts of Fr. Creighton, S.J., did indeed bring about, in 1576, the founding of a seminary which wandered about from town to town and finally settled down at Douai. Others were started at Braunberg (1574) and Rome (1600), while the old medieval Scottish college of Paris University was remodelled on Trentine lines. But there was little enthusiasm among the Scottish youth, and the number of students never rose above a few. The Irish colleges were far more prosperous, and as a rule, save in Spain and Portugal, were not in the hands of the Jesuits. They were founded in rapid succession in Paris (1578), Salamanca (1588), Lisbon (1593), Douai (1594), Seville (1612); then at Rouen, Bordeaux, Louvain, and other places, the older orders playing a prominent part in their creation.

In the case of each of the three nations mentioned above, the colleges did more than provide tuition for scholars: they trained the poets and prose-writers who formed the English devotional school of the Catholic Reformation. The history of this literary school has not even been attempted as yet, and will not be attempted here. It will be enough in these pages to survey its most important productions.

The considerable mass of these is dominated by one major piece, which is also a masterpiece, the *Christian Directory* of the Jesuit, Robert Parsons. This is a huge expansion — eight hundred octavo pages — of the former part of St. Ignatius' *Spiritual Exercises*, that which deals with the crucial choice man has to make between sin and Christian virtue; and therefore it is also called the *Book of Resolution*. It is a close-knit, forcible, and lucid demonstration of the reasons which induce man to throw in his lot with God and to spurn the world, profusely supported by quotations from Scripture and from the Fathers, and by elaborate scholarship. It is further divided into two parts: the first is a treatise of Christian apologetics, beginning with the proofs of God's existence going on with those of Christianity, especially the fulfillment of the prophecies. It then proceeds to show how man's purpose on earth can be attained, describes the punishment of sin in hell and purgatory, and the rewards of virtue in heaven. The second part professes to deal with the impediments which stand in the way of "resolution": mistrust of God's mercy, fear of the difficulty of virtue, procrastination, slothfulness. But the chief obstacle which prevents English Catholics from declaring themselves openly is obviously the fear of retaliation on the part of the state; and therefore Parsons lengthily describes the persecutions of the first centuries of the Church, and the fortitude of the martyrs.

As in the *Exercises*, stress is laid upon the strengthening of man's will. Another Ignatian feature is the extraordinary intensity of the pages which describe the pains of hell and the joys of heaven; though the former, with their Murillo-like tints, may be more effective than the latter.

Indeed the whole coloring of the *Christian Directory* is rather gloomy, and Parsons' devotional treatise is not bathed in that atmosphere of radiant light, of optimistic Platonism, which marked Blessed Robert Southwell's poems and prose works. He does indeed refer to "the perfection of Christian vocation, if it were fulfilled"; but he insists more upon the imperfection of man, upon the horror of sin, upon the terror of God's wrath. True to the spirit of Trentine strictness, he recommends "cutting off a great many of those worldly pleasures. . . . I mean," he says, "of those good fellowships in eating, drinking, laughing, singing, disputing, and other such vanities that distract us most." Parsons does, indeed, state that virtue is "sweet and pleasant," but he does not attract us to it as St. Francis de Sales was to do; he argues more than he allures.

Parsons' work is an appeal not to feeling, but to reason. It provides reasonable proofs of Christianity; describes the reasons why God sends crosses to man, and why one should love them; and in a colder and less homely way than that of Thomas More, expounds the reasons why we should be comforted in tribulation. The arguments are methodically, scholastically divided and subdivided. Altogether, though the *Christian Directory* be lacking in warmth of emotion, it is perfect as an intellectual construction. The author displays the most robust English commonsense: "The evil," he says, "has this prerogative above the good, in our life; that one defect only overwhelmeth and drowneth a great number of pleasures together. If man had all the felicities heaped together that this world could yield, and yet had but one tooth out of tune, all the other pleasures would not make him merry." The demonstration is clear and connected.

Parsons' prose, a full century before Dryden, may be considered as a model. Francis Bacon's seems heavy and unwieldy when compared to it. It testifies to the influence of the classical training favored by the Catholic Reformation. It is not merely terse, it is eloquent as well; and though one may dislike the rhetorical quality of some passages, others are of great beauty. One might scarcely improve upon the balanced and harmonious fulness of the following piece, on the hour of death: "Imagine now, my dear Brother, and Friend, even thou (I say) which are so fresh and frolick at this instant, and [if] the ten, twenty or two years (or perhaps two months or days), which thou hast yet to live, were to come now to an end, and that thou wert even at this present stretched out upon a bed; wearied and worn out with dolour and pain; thy carnal Friends about thee weeping, and many of them desiring thy goods; the Physicians departed with their fees, as having given thee over; and thou lying there mute and dumb, in a most pitiful agony, expecting from moment to moment the last stroke of death to be given unto thee. Tell me in this instant, what will all the pleasures and commodities of the whole Earth avail thee?"

Many passages of similar perfection might be quoted, especially those in which Parsons varies his demonstration with "similitudes." The following one is an instance of the Jesuit's vivacious and graphic manner. He wishes to show how those who have been most famous during their lives are forgotten after their death, while those who have been humble and deserving are remembered: "The world," he says, "is like . . . unto a covetous and forgetful Host; who, if he see his old Guest come by his Inn in beggarly estate, all his money being spent, he maketh semblance not to know him: And if the Guest marvel thereat, and say, that he hath come often that way, and spent much money in the house; the other answereth, it may be so, my friend, for there pass this way many, and we use not to keep account of all. But what is the way (saith one) to make this Host remember you? It is to use him evil as you pass by . . . and he will remember you as long as he liveth, and many times will talk of you, when you are far off from him."

The stylistic qualities of the *Christian Directory*, though outstanding, are secondary to its devotional purpose. It is noteworthy that it should be directed mostly against that "atheism" which prevailed in court circles during Elizabeth's reign, and which was really tantamount to religious indifference. In order to vanquish it, Parsons proposes a spiritual method which, though it be scattered through the pages of his book, is nonetheless coherent. It rests mainly on "consideration," aided by the Ignatian *applicatio sensuum*. The following might have been culled out of the *Spiritual Exercises:* "Imagine then now (my loving Brother) . . . that thou seest before thy face, this great and mighty King sitting in his Chair of Majesty, with Chariots of Fire, unspeakable Light, and infinite Millions of Angels about him. Imagine further . . . that thou seest all the Creatures in the World stand in his presence, and trembling at his Majesty, and most carefully attending to do that, for which he created them, as the Heavens to move about, the Sun, Moon, and Stars, to give light and influence, the Earth to bring forth her substance; and every other Creature diligently to labor for performance of the duty assigned unto him." Consideration should be followed by meditation, "an exact examination of [one's] thoughts and deeds," and inward "mortification of our passions, evil affections, and sinister inclinations."

The word "sinister" again suggests the somber atmosphere of most of the work; a somberness which is due to the author's horror of sin, but which however disappears when he describes the rapturous and almost mystical joys consequent upon righteous behavior. Through "cogitation" and "contemplation," he says, "we are greatly stirred up to joy, alacrity, confidence and consolation." The way of virtue is made "easy and pleasant" by "a certain hidden and secret consolation which God poureth into the heart of them that truly serve him. . . . How exceeding great and inestimable the sweetness of this Heavenly Wine is to them that taste it, no tongue of Man or Angels can express." It is a "foretaste" of the joys of heaven, and God's servant enjoys "a certain heavenly peace, serenity and tranquility of mind." Death itself is to him the object of "love and desire"; the day of its coming will be a "day of joy," and the rewards granted to the virtuous souls in heaven are described by Parsons in an ecstatic manner; "Imagine . . . what a joy it shall be unto thy soul at that day, to meet with all her godly Friends in the Kingdom of Heaven; with Father, with Mother, with Brethren, with Sisters, with Wife, with Husband, with Masters, with Scholars, with Neighbors, with Familiars, with Kindred, with acquaintance, the welcomes, the mirth, the sweet embracements, that shall be there."

Parsons is indeed at times almost lyrical. The oblivion into which the greatest men sink is handled by him almost as poetically as by Villon, Dunbar, and Southwell: "Who doth remember now one of forty thousand jolly fellows in this world, that thought themselves great people while they were here: Captains, Soldiers, Counsellors, Dukes, Earls, Princes, Prelates, Emperors, Kings, Queens, Lords and Ladies? Who remembereth them now, I say? Who once thinketh or speaketh of them? Hath not their memory perished with their sound, as the Prophet foretold?" In the face of this rare combination of clear, coherent reasoning and forceful eloquence which is found in the *Christian Directory,* one overlooks the wearisome lengthiness of many passages, their abstract character, the author's lack of critical acumen in dealing with historical problems; one rather remembers the utter good will of a man who, as he himself says, will be content if he can "understand, conceive, or hope, that any one soul . . . shall be moved to Resolution, by anything that is here said, or shall be reclaimed from the bondage of sin, and restored to the service of our Maker and Redeemer."

*　　　*　　　*

We have dwelt at length upon the *Christian Directory,* because it holds first place among the English devotional literature of the Catholic Reformation. Though it has now fallen into oblivion, its popularity in the late sixteenth and seventeenth centuries was almost beyond belief. It went through a surprising number of editions, both in Britain and abroad. Almost from the very first, it appeared in two different shapes, one authentic, professedly Catholic, and bearing the imprint of English centers on the Continent; one pirated, printed in England, and adapted for the use of the Protestant public. Of the former, only seven editions followed each other between 1582 and 1633; but the latter spread like wildfire. There were seven editions of it in 1584 and 1585, and twenty-two more between 1586 and 1640, not counting the Welsh edition of 1632. It should not be forgotten, of course, that even the continental editions were smuggled into England, while the expurgated editions testify to the deep penetration into Anglican circles of the literature of the

Catholic Revival. Nor was the fortune of Parson's work an isolated instance. One knows how Southwell imbibed, in his stay at Douai College, at Clermont Collège in Paris, and at the English College, Rome, the principles of the Catholic Reformation; how he later endeavored to introduce them into English literature; how, true to Jesuit methods, he adapted current literary forms to a religious end, and even recast well-known lyrics to make them serve a devotional purpose; how, in his *Short Rule of Good Life,* he preached the Jesuit ideal of wise moderation, orderly seemliness, and cheerful fortitude. That his influence was widespread appears from the fact that his works were repeatedly published on the Continent and in England before the end of Charles I's reign. There were three editions of *Mary Magdalen's Tears* between 1594 and 1609; four of the *Short Rule of Good Life;* seven of *Saint Peter's Complaint,* and four of the *Maenioae;* besides eight editions of the collected works, most of these being printed in England.

Parsons and Southwell are but the two figureheads of a considerable devotional school, both of prose and poetry. That this school should be overlooked in current histories of English literature may give rise to some wonder, for a mere glance at any good bibliographical catalogue will reveal its existence. It began to flourish when the colleges abroad had had time to train the first batches of pupils, at the time of the appearance of Parsons' *Christian Directory,* that is, about 1582. It attained its greatest development between 1600 and 1640, and lasted on for many years after. Most of its representatives belonged to the Society of Jesus, though a number of Benedictines were also included. It was closely connected with the French devotional school of the reigns of Henry IV and Louis XIII, and many of the books it produced were printed at Rouen and Paris. We have already mentioned, as being related to the Bérulle circle, Father Benedict Canfield, the Capuchin, alias William Fitch, whose *Rule of Perfection* was published at Rouen twice in 1609, and whose *Christian Knight* appeared in England in 1619. Many other names might be mentioned, such as that of the Catholic agent at Antwerp, Richard Verstegan, who wrote pious verse of a delicate and intimate quality; David Baker, O.S.B., who penned forty spiritual treatises, excerpts from which were afterward gathered by Father Hugh Cressy, in the famous book known as *Sancta Sophia;* and some twenty other writers, most of whom were also engaged in translating from the French, Italian, or Spanish.

It is a striking fact, the meaning of which can hardly be overstressed, that practically every important work of the continental devotional schools — but primarily of Spain — should have been translated into English, and published either in England or abroad between 1580 and 1640. The issuing of a book is generally meant as a profitable commercial venture; and it is scarcely undertaken unless the existence of a prospective public make it worthwhile. Therefore it cannot be doubted that the literature of the Catholic Reformation permeated extensive classes of the English population — and of the Scottish population as well; for Southwell's *Saint Peter's Complaint* was also published at Edinburgh.

It is not possible to mention here all of the continental works of devotion turned into English, and a few instances will suffice. The Dominican, Luis de Granada, was, it seems, extremely popular; for we find no fewer than twenty-three editions of various works of his between 1582 and 1633, twelve of these being published in England and one in Edinburgh. His *Treatise on Prayer and Meditation* alone went through ten editions within the same period. St. Teresa's *Life*, written by herself, was turned into English and published in 1611 and 1623; St. Peter of Alcantara's *Golden Treatise of Mental Prayer*, in 1632. Among the writers of the others schools, there were nine editions of the works of St. Francis de Sales between 1622 and 1637, the *Introduction to a Devout Life* being printed twice in England in 1616 and 1637; and as for his expounder, John-Peter Camus, bishop of Belley, five English editions of his works appeared in England and France between 1630 and 1639. Two editions of the *Spiritual Combat* were issued about the same time, and among the continental authors whose works were rendered into English at this period may be mentioned St. Ignatius Loyola, Father Caussin, S.J., not to speak of the compilers of catechisms such as Bellarmine and Canisius.

The effect of continental mysticism upon the English school is obvious in many places. Bl. Robert Southwell translated a Spanish mystical work, Diego de Estella's *Hundred Meditations of the Love of God*. The influence of St. Teresa's poems upon him can scarcely be doubted, though it has not hitherto been pointed out. It appears in those lyrics in which he expresses his longing for death and the life beyond, and which tender-hearted Grosart mistakenly believed to have been written in the intervals of torture. Southwell's treatment of the theme is an Euphuistic elaboration of the more direct and more passionate style of St. Teresa. The likeness is however striking. The saint had written:

> Doleful is the life,
> Bitter to excess,
> Of a lonely soul,
> Far away from thee.
> O my treasure sweet,
> How unhappy I!
> Longing to behold thee,
> I wish to die. (*Poesia 1.*)

Compare those lines with Southwell's *Life Is but Loss:*

> By force I live, in will I wish to die;
> In plaint I pass the length of lingering days;
> Free would my soul from mortal body fly,
> And tread the track of Death's desired ways . . .

Again, we find in St. Teresa's *Poesia 2* the following conceit upon the same theme:

> I live a life which is no life;
> Expect another life so high
> That longing for death makes me die.

Southwell improves upon his model:

> I live but such a life as ever dies;
> I die but such a life as never ends.
> My death to end my dying life denies,
> And life my living death no whit amends.

Half a dozen similar instances might be quoted. And in a later generation, the same influence is manifested in the poems of Crashaw, who had read St. Teresa, and written a hymn in praise of her, "when he was yet among the Protestants." The above-quoted *Poesia 2* of the saint was paraphrased by him in the following words:

> Though still I die I live again;
> Still longing so to be still slain;
> So gainful is such loss of breath
> I die even in desire of death.

*   *   *

Such direct traces of the Catholic Reformation are not frequent among the Caroline poets. It must not be forgotten that "popery" was still proscribed by the penal laws; that memories of the Gunpowder Plot still lurked in men's minds; and that it was dangerous to own up to having made use of "popish" sources. Besides George Herbert and his disciples sincerely considered themselves as Protestant; they themselves were to some extent unaware of the part which the Catholic Reformation had played in their religious upbringing. Or again, they went so far as to conceal it, as when Christopher Harvey, making use of Haeften's emblems in his *Schola cordis,* was careful to remove from them whatever was too markedly Catholic. But though genuinely Anglican, the works of George Herbert, Henry Vaughan, and Richard Crashaw in his first period unmistakably bear the stamp of the Trentine movement. It would be hard to prove this in detail, since it is, more than anything else, a question of atmosphere; and besides such a demonstration would take us too far afield. There are two points, however, on which it is possible to trace the great likeness between the works of the Anglican poets of Charles I's reign, and those of their Catholic predecessor, the Jesuit Southwell.

The latter, true to the spirit of his Order, repeatedly asserted that poetry must not confine itself to *delectare* through the handling of profane subjects, but that it should *prodesse* by devoting itself to religious themes. Now, it is not a little striking that Southwell, on the one hand, in the prose and verse prefaces to *St. Peter's Complaint,* Herbert and Vaughan on the other, should have expressed themselves on the point in practically the same words. The Jesuit had written: "Poets by abusing their talent, and making the follies and feignings of Love the customary subject of their base endeavors, have so discredited this faculty, that a Poet, a Lover, and a Liar, are by many reckoned but three words of one signification." Similarly Vaughan wrote in the preface to *Silex scintillans:* "That this kingdom hath abounded with those ingenious persons, which in the late notion are termed *Wits,* is too well known. Many of them having cast away all their fair portion of time, in no better employments, than a deliberate search, or excogitation, of *idle words,* and a most vain, insatiable desire to be reputed poets . . . *minister sin and death unto their readers."* Again, Southwell had insisted upon this idea in verse:

> Still finest wits are stilling VENUS' rose,
> In Paynim toys the sweetest veins are spent:
> To Christian works few have their talents lent.

Herbert was to give expression to the same thought almost in the same words; though more lengthily:

> My God, where is that ancient heat towards thee,
> Wherewith whole shoals of Martyrs once did burn,
> Besides their other flames? Doth poetry
> Wear Venus' livery? only serve her turn?

> Why are not sonnets made of thee? and lays
> Upon thine altar burnt? Cannot thy love
> Heighten a spirit to sound out thy praise
> As well as any she? Cannot thy dove
> Outstrip their Cupid easily in flight?

More important still is the likeness between Southwell and the Caroline poets in the practical moral ideal which they preach: the ideal of wise moderation, of staid decency, of modest gravity and sobriety. Indeed that ideal was no new thing. It was essentially that of the Christian humanists, *sustine et abstine;* and it might be considered a moot point whether it came to the Caroline poets directly from the times of Surrey and Wyatt, through a purely English tradition, or from the writers of the Catholic Reformation. The latter seems, however, the more likely. The traditional element in the Church of England had suffered a Calvinistic eclipse of thirty years' duration after the accession of Queen Elizabeth; and it is striking enough that it should have reappeared only from 1590 onwards, after the Catholic mission had had time to fructify, thus coming back to England by a circuitous route. At any rate, there is a notable similarity between the practical advice in Southwell's *Short Rule of Good Life,* and that in Herbert's *Church Porch,* and, to, some extent, in Vaughan's *Rules and Lessons.* A detailed comparison would repay the trouble spent upon it, but a few quotations must suffice here. Referring to dress, the Jesuit poet had written: "Mine apparel must be free from lightness, or more gaudiness than fitteth mine age, company, or calling: it must be decent and comely, not too open, nor with any unusual or new-fashioned dresses, that other grave persons of my quality and calling . . . do not use: it must be handsome and clean, and as much as may be without singularity, that therein the staidness and seemly estate of my soule may be perceived." Herbert reproduced the same ideas in verse:

> In clothes, cheap handsomeness doth bear the bell.
> Wisdom's a trimmer thing, than shop e'er gave.
> Say not then, This with that lace will do well;
> But, This with my discretion will be brave . . .

Southwell had deprecated excess in laughter: "My voice neither ought to be very loud, nor my laughter so vehement, as to be heard afar off, both seemly and modest. . . ." And similarly, Herbert was to say:

> Laugh not too much: the witty man laughs least . . .
> A sad wise valour is the brave complexion
> That leads the van, and swallows up the cities . . .

It is to be noted that both Herbert and Vaughan recommend the Ignatian practice of examination of conscience. The humble and orderly sweetness of the Caroline poets was already extant in Southwell's *Rule,* and in so far as it tended to complete the ideal of the English gentleman, the Catholic Reformation may be said to have had its share in molding it.

The height of its influence in the Laudian revival was manifested in the Anglican communities established by Nicholas Ferrar at Little Gidding and Lady Letice Falkland at Great Tew. Both founders expressly and sincerely asserted that they were Protestant and hostile to the Church of Rome. Yet it seems no mere chance that the *Stories* with which the inmates of Little Gidding entertained their pious gatherings (those of Sapor and Usthazanes for instance) should bear a striking likeness to the themes of Jesuit tragedies. At Great Tew, the presence of St. Francis de Sales is obvious, though never mentioned by those who were following in his wake. Lady Letice Falkland, having resolved, after the death of her husband at the battle of Newbury, to amend her life, chose an Anglican clergyman, John Duncon, as her director. The latter, who was related to the Herbert circle, wrote letters of direction for his patroness, in which he advised her on her spiritual condition, and which were published in 1648 under the following title: *The returns of spiritual comfort and grief in a devout soul.* This very title is reminiscent of the *Introduction to a Devout Life,* and in fact Duncon expounds in an orthodox way the mystical theory of St. Francis on "spiritual and sensible consolations" and on periods of spiritual drought. In the very organization of her household, Lady Letice may be considered as another Philothée; and besides turning her relatives and servants into a quasi-monastic community, she contemplated the foundation of an actual religious order of women. Deeper research into this fascinating subject must be left for further studies. Enough has been said, however, to show that the Catholic Reformation in the British Isles, though prevented from running its normal course, was far from abortive, and that it was instrumental in bringing about the reawakening of the Church of England which was to mature in the Oxford Movement.

CHAPTER XIV

The Missions

THE missionary movement of the sixteenth and early seventeenth centuries was of far greater importance than any of the other activities of the Catholic reformers, and would deserve far more attention than can possibly be given to it in a brief chapter. It spread the Catholic faith, up till then practically confined to Europe, to the four corners of the world. It laid the foundation for a truly universal Church. It brought more souls to the Fold than had been lost to it through the Protestant upheaval. Nor should it be considered as important solely in the religious field. It contributed more than anything else to the progress of civilization in newly discovered countries. It took its stand no less against the barbarity of tribal customs than against the vices, excesses, and cruelty of the European colonists. It opened schools, colleges, universities; it helped in the study of native languages, of native art and culture, and opened out wide fields to historical and geographical scholarship. It evolved methods of evangelization in agreement with the intellectual needs and liturgical practice of the times. Even in the realm of art, the results it achieved were far from negligible. In a word, it followed closely in the steps of traders and explorers, and gave its full significance to the discovery of new continents.

The missionary movement was not, any more than the Catholic Reformation itself, a direct consequence of the Protestant outbreak. As a matter of fact, it had never wholly ceased in the Church, and the proselytizing zeal of the first conquistadores, however ill-advised in many of its manifestations, was in itself a proof of its continued vitality. From the very first voyages of Columbus in 1492, and Vasco da Gama in 1498, there was an eager desire on the part of the Spaniards and Portuguese to spread the Christian faith. However, it was only as the Catholic Reformation gained momentum that the great missionary expansion began. It was to a large extent spontaneous, being due to the apostolic spirit of various religious orders: the Franciscans, Dominicans, Augustinians, and above all the newly created Society of Jesus.

Trent did not legislate on the missions, but from the very outset the popes turned their attention that way and provided directions and encouragement. In 1568, perhaps on the instigation of St. Francis Borgia, general of the Jesuits and a great founder of missions, Pope Pius V appointed a committee of cardinals for the conversion of infidels. Gregory XIII, the "pope of missions," added another committee to deal with Eastern rites and the reunion of schismatic churches. It was Clement VIII (1592–1605) who created a congregation of cardinals specially devoted to missionary questions; and Gregory XV followed this move in 1622 by proclaiming, in his constitution *Inscrutabilis divinae,* the canonical institution of the Holy Congregation for the Propagation of the faith, commonly known as the Congregation of the Propaganda.

When this final development took place, however, the missionaries had been at work for a whole century, in America, in Asia, and even in Africa. Their earliest activities outside Europe took place in Mexico, at the time of its conquest by Fernando Cortes. The latter, despite his vices, was sincerely desirous of spreading Christianity, though he went about it too hurriedly. He was accompanied by some Brothers of the Order of Mercy, who set out to establish Catholic worship and to christen natives. Little was effected until the coming of three missions, one of twelve Observant Minors, a second, of twelve Dominicans, and a third, of seven Augustinians, who arrived at Mexico in 1524, 1526, and 1533, respectively. In fact, the evangelization of the country was exclusively the work of the regulars of the three above Orders, the Franciscans occupying the land first, the Dominicans settling down where it was still free, and the Augustinians filling in the gaps.

In 1559, there resided in Mexico 380 Franciscans, 210 Dominicans, and 212 Augustinians; which numbers, though they may appear considerable, were yet wholly inadequate for such a vast region. In 1570, there were no fewer than 140 monasteries or foundations: 61 Franciscan, 40 Dominican, and 39 Augustinian. The number of baptisms, in the first few years of the mission, was extremely great. It is estimated at five million for the period beginning in 1524 and ending in 1536. In a letter of 1529, Brother Peter of Ghent, the foremost apostle of Mexico, speaks of fourteen thousand baptisms daily. There is, indeed, no cause for surprise at this remarkably swift spreading of Christianity; nor should the sincerity of most of the converts be doubted. Their deities had failed to rescue them from the foreign invader, whose God was apparently all-powerful; they felt like children in the presence of a superior race, and the Spaniards had no difficulty in making religious instruction compulsory for them. Paganism persisted locally, but there is no reason to ascribe to its survival present-day Mexican superstition. The work of evangelization was performed ably and thoroughly.

It gave rise indeed to a number of problems which are worth our detailed study, since they were, on the whole, to be faced — with local variants — in every mission field. First of all, what attitude was to be observed in regard to native religious beliefs? Should they be considered as wholly false and wicked, and to be therefore ruthlessly rejected, or as containing an approach to Christian truth, which might be used as a starting-point? The question was particularly in point in Mexico, from the fact that the native religion included baptism and a kind of confession. Nevertheless, the fear of heresy, especially on the part of the Dominicans, was such that no attempt was made to utilize local beliefs as a basis for Christian apologetics. The method of catechizing used was that of the *tabula rasa*. Temples and idols were destroyed, and native religion uncompromisingly denounced. At the same time the missionaries — to their praise — did not try to Europeanize their flock, except in a very few cases. They did not, in the face of a great variety of local dialects, enforce the use of Castilian as an overriding tongue, but they chose for that purpose the most widely used of the local languages, *nahuatl*. This, of course, entailed one major difficulty, that of finding words to express Christian notions. If use was made of native words, the sense of which more or less approximated that of Spanish religious vocables, there was a danger that pagan notions might be perpetuated, as when the name of the goddess Tonantzin was applied to the Virgin Mary. On the other hand, if Castilian words were imported into the native tongue, the ideas to be imparted might very well remain foreign to the Indian mind. The latter solution was, however, generally adopted.

In any case, the missionaries did their best to provide Christian substitutes for the pagan customs which they abolished, in the spirit of adaptation which was later to be that of the Jesuits. Before the coming of the Europeans, the Indians had continual religious feasts and ceremonies. Every effort was now made to satisfy them in that respect: "Ornaments and pomp in the churches," a Franciscan writer says, "are very necessary to elevate the soul of the Indians and bring them to divine things, for their nature is lukewarm and forgetful of inward realities, and they must be helped by means of outward appearances."

The Indians' taste for music was taken into account. They were taught to sing plain chant, in which they are said to have done as well as any Spanish choir. They were also made to play instruments in church: flutes, bugles, cornets, trombones, oboes, guitars, drums. We hear of one of them composing an entire Mass. Solemn processions were organized. In addition to all this, it was necessary to afford the natives a chance of giving vent to their animal spirits through singing and dancing. Spanish songs were translated into *nahuatl*, or Christian words adapted to local tunes. Dancing sometimes took place in the very churches. However the enthusiasm of the Indians soon led to abuses, which had to be prohibited by the provincial councils of Mexico in 1555 and 1565. The native temper was also taken into account in the case of religious drama, which was used as a means of evangelization almost solely by the Franciscans. The equivalent of Spanish *autos sacramentales* was performed in Mexico, the subjects being scriptural themes such as the sacrifice of Isaac or the adoration of the Magi. All the actors, singers, dancers were Indian; and the text, spoken or sung, was in a native tongue, generally *nahuatl*.

Apart from all those auxiliary modes of teaching, the Indians were duly catechized by the missionaries. Wherever there was a convent, catechism took place on Sundays and feast days. The population of each village came in procession headed by a cross and reciting prayers. A roll call was taken of those present, and those who absented themselves unduly were subjected to penalties. Catechisms were published in the *nahuatl* tongue. The expounding of dogma in them was entirely similar to what it was in Spain; but huge pictures were used to bring home to the Indian mind the elements of religious truth, God in His glory, amidst angels and saints, some of them Indian, the pains of hell, with some Indians among the damned, and other kindred subjects. The Franciscans were too few to deal with the crowds they had to teach. They were assisted by lay helpers chosen from among the Indians themselves, the *fiscales* or *mandones,* who also acted as censors of the manners of their fellow-villagers, saw to the administration of baptism and confirmation, repressed adultery, drunkenness, and sorcery, and organized worship where there were no priests to do so.

The children of the Indian aristocracy were brought up with especial care in residential schools established within the convents themselves. They learned Latin, often gaining remarkable proficiency in that language, and later formed a most distinguished native élite. Colleges were established for them by the Augustinians in Mexico in 1537 and by the Franciscans in the suburb of Santiago in 1536. The pupils of both led an altogether monastic life, and the founders of the latter intended to prepare for the upbringing of a native clergy. Most unfortunately, in

Mexico as well as in most colonial countries, there was an anti-native party, which was bitterly opposed to the granting of the priesthood to Indians. Fear was expressed lest they should be incapable of the virtues necessary for the sacerdotal ministry; and also in strange contrast to this — lest they should, if sufficiently educated, discern and condemn the vices of the European colonists. The opposition was such that the Provincial Council of 1555 forbade the ordaining of natives and half-castes. This was the more deplorable as some Indians had been notable for their sanctity.

Indeed, the notion that the Indians were not to be fully trusted, that they were to be treated like children, was the reason why the otherwise remarkable work of the regulars in Mexico did not reach the results that might have been expected. The intentions of the missionaries were no doubt excellent: they wanted to withdraw the natives from the habits of a nomadic life, to plant them firmly in agricultural communities where they might lead a thrifty existence; also to keep them wholly apart from the Europeans, whose corrupting influence and cruelty were but too well known. From the first, therefore, they gathered the Indians in villages, all of these built on the same plan, taught them to till and irrigate the land, to ply various trades, to produce silk; they forbade Europeans to stay for more than three days in the native settlements. The advantages and the drawbacks of such a policy are clear. It undoubtedly established Christian communities and civilized the Indians; but it required the continued presence of the missionaries among them, kept them under perpetual tutelage, and did not make them morally and religiously self-dependent.

When all is said, however, the work of the Franciscans, Dominicans, and Augustinians is in many ways a model of Christian charity. They loved the natives deeply, passionately; they respected their personality, and they treated them with the utmost disinterestedness. "The Indians marveled," the Dominican Davila Padilla writes, "at seeing the perseverance of the preachers, and even more to see them so little affected by the gold and silver the Spanish laymen hold in such esteem; and so experiencing how the religious despised the riches of the world, they were fortified in their belief in the proper wealth of the soul."

The religious of the three Orders always objected to the payment of tithes by the Indians; and they led austere lives amidst the sumptuous surroundings which were provided by their beautiful churches and cloisters, which are still one of the glories of Mexico. Brother Francis of Ghent was so humble that he insisted on remaining a lay Brother and refused the priesthood, which would have ensured to him the arch-bishopric of Mexico. When he died in 1572, after having "broken several idols, brought down several temples of idolaters, built more than a hundred churches, converted several thousand infidels," many Indians went into mourning. In fact, whatever may be said of the shortcomings of Mexican evangelization, there was good reason for the enthusiasm of Brother Martin of Valencia, one of the original twelve Franciscans, who wrote on June 12, 1531, referring to the Indians: "Their women are very chaste, and embellished with that modesty which makes their sex agreeable. . . . Their confessions, especially those of the women, are full of matchless purity and candor, of unbelievable subtlety, and of the greatest sincerity. They receive the sacrament of the Altar with plentiful tears."

The conditions were largely the same in the province of Lima, which included not only modern Peru, but most of South America except Brazil. The spread of Christianity was hampered from the very first by the vices, cruelty, and covetousness of Spanish laymen and even secular priests. When Pizarro first invaded Peru, he held a conference with the ruler of the country, Atahualpa. According to the Augustinian chronicle, a Dominican who was present, Vincent de Valverde, asked him to believe in Christ and pay a tribute. On his refusal, he was presented with a breviary. The Indian turned over the leaves, and failing to understand what the print meant, threw away the book and spat upon it. "What, you Christians," Valverde cried, "is the Gospel trampled down? Justice and revenge against the idolaters!" Whereupon the Spaniards came out of their hiding-places with a great uproar, and slaughtered five thousand Indians without suffering a single wound. Atahualpa was made a prisoner, then killed despite the promises made to him. Such a beginning was obviously inauspicious.

Before the arrival of the Augustinians, the chronicle runs, "there was no talk of divine law or Christian doctrine: people were merely intent on defending themselves or attacking, in repulsing or inflicting violence, in stealing other men's goods or preserving their own. As to teaching those poor vagrants [the Indians], there was no news of that." The change was really no less due to the work of four other religious orders: the Dominicans — despite Valverde — who remained confined to Peru proper; the Franciscans, who migrated to Rio de la Plata; the Order of Mercy, which spread to the whole of South America; and the Jesuits, who arrived at Lima in 1568, but whose expansion was also very swift, since they had five colleges in Peru by 1582.

It is a fact that the low moral and intellectual level of the secular clergy seriously compromised the evangelization of Peru. The Spanish government had placed at the head of each district an *encomendero*, who was supposed to ensure to the Indians the *doctrina,* i.e., the teaching of the catechism, the exercise of divine worship, and the administration of the sacraments, and therefore to provide a priest. But the *encomenderos* were often remiss, and entrusted the ministry of the Gospel, the Augustinian chronicle runs, to certain "caymans, vagabonds, men of no standing, who hired themselves to teach doctrine to their Indian subjects, and even baptized children against the will of their fathers." The Indians called them *Bixatrayques,* that is to say, the slaves of their bellies, though they called themselves "doctrinarians." In fact, the bishops complained that Spain sent them "scandalous priests," who dressed gaudily, used weapons, traded, gambled, obtained wills in their favor by underhand means, or were even guilty of simony. Add to this that they often had charge of too many Indians over too large an extent of territory, that they were very frequently ignorant of the native language, and that they compelled the Indians by force to work for their sustenance. Even the cathedral chapters were not above reproof.

On the other hand, though it cannot be contended that the regulars were always faultless, it is in any case certain that they were inspired with the highest apostolical ideal. Read the "articles" which were prepared for the Augustinian missionaries: they were to lead a perfect life and set a good example; to suffer hunger, thirst, the weather, and the insults of men, even unto death.

In particular they were "to serve the Indians with a free and disinterested heart; to take neither gold nor silver nor rewards; to make it clearly understood that the religious did not seek riches in those lands like the other Spaniards, but . . . sought to plant faith and virtues in souls as the ministers of Jesus Christ; . . . to accommodate themselves to the capacity of each man, and suffer with forbearance and patience stupidity and ignorance; and season with loving sweetness and affability all their speeches and 'doctrine,' so as to draw the Indians by that charm, while it was forbidden to treat them harshly or to chastise them."

The missionaries were further admonished "that going out there to serve, and not to be served, they should request no service from any Indian man or woman; however, that they should induce them to build churches and found hospitals, and themselves nurse the sick; that they should morning and night teach Christian doctrine and good morals; that they should try to establish schools wherein to teach reading, writing, and reckoning, as well as the trades necessary for social life, such as those of goldsmiths, painters, carpenters and others; that they should instruct the Indians in regard to divine worship, founding chapels, where music should be sung to the accompaniment of flutes, and organs, and other instruments, so as to impress upon the heart of those pagans, through that luster, a greater respect and devotion; . . . lastly, that they should seek out those savages in the mountains, in caves and marshes, where they hid, and gather them whenever possible that they might preach Jesus to them, and put them in the way of their salvation, without ever shrinking from the fatigue implied by such a search."

The document is a capital one, because it outlines the whole of the evangelizing and civilizing policy of the regulars. They had gathered the natives of Mexico and the Antilles into *pueblos* or villages; and according to their advice and to that of St. Pius V, the Christian-minded viceroy of Peru, Francis Toledo, did the same from 1568 onwards, by establishing "reductions" for the Indians. These were to be placed in the best possible locations, and provided with public buildings. As to the beauty of divine worship, which was meant to impress the Indian mind, the Augustinians complacently insist on the splendor and wealth of their monastery and church at Lima. The reredos, they say, is finer than anything in Spain; the pews are of delicately carved cedar. The articles made for the refining of Indian manners by Father Anthony Ramirez provide that each Saturday there will be a Mass for the members of the Confraternity of Our Lady, the brethren holding lighted tapers; while on Sundays and feast days, after Catechism, "the girls will come to church in procession, crowned with wreaths of flowers. . . ." In the first Augustinian women's convent, that of the Incarnation, established at Lima in 1558, "one hears . . . the most beautiful music in the Indies, in which there are nine choirs of viols, bassoons, harps, lutes, guitars and other instruments, the which marrying their sounds and accents with the voices and trills of fifty girls . . . make a concert, the most delectable and harmonious that can be heard."

The main obstacle to the evangelization of the Indians was, however, their ignorance of the Castilian tongue. It had been the ideal of the Augustinians to bring them to "imitate the Spaniards in dress, food and conversation," but this proved impracticable. It was necessary for the clergy to study and learn the native languages, among which *quichua* held the same position as *nahuatl* in Mexico. A *quichua* grammar had been composed by a Dominican, but the Jesuits were the first to tackle the problem seriously.

Father Alonzo Barzana, S.J., traveled to the East of the Andes and made himself master of five Indian dialects. His successor was Father Diego Gonzalez Halguin, who devoted himself to the *quichua* tongue. A printing-press was established at the Jesuit college of Juli, where grammars, dictionaries, and books of devotion were published in several native languages. Nor were the Fathers content with philological studies; they investigated the history, geography, and customs of the country, and such a work as Father José de Acosta's *Natural History of the Indies* has remained invaluable down to the present day.

There was considerable fervor and enthusiasm among the Spanish regulars in the late fifteenth and early sixteenth centuries: and their contribution to the Catholic Revival was no less great in America than in the Spanish home-country. They forestalled the Trentine movement and they also joined in it later on. Most of the reforming bishops of the New World, who followed the directions of Trent, belonged to the Franciscan and Dominican Orders. The first archbishop of Lima (1540–1575), Francis Jerome de Loaysa, was a Dominican, who held two provincial councils. His successor (1579–1606), St. Toribio (or Turibius) de Mogrovejo, was a secular, but one who was deemed worthy of the title "apostle of Peru." He was born in 1538 at Mayorga, in the Spanish province of Leon. His reforming zeal was no less ardent than his devotion to the native population. He held no fewer than thirteen diocesan councils, and three provincial councils in 1583, 1591, and 1601, extending to the whole of Spanish South America. In order better to direct and supervise the evangelization of the Indians, he made three general visitations of his huge diocese, penetrating to the remotest valleys of the Andes at the peril of his life, everywhere preaching and improving religious conditions. In 1594, he wrote to the king of Spain that he had journeyed more than three thousand leagues, and confirmed five hundred thousand persons. He founded churches, convents, seminaries, almshouses. In the course of his third episcopal visitation, he was taken by death at Sana, on March 23, 1606.

The Provincial Council of 1583 — that which is meant when one refers to the Council of Lima — undertook to reform the church of Peru. It prescribed the appointment of one priest for the *doctrinas* of one thousand to two thousand souls; and of two priests for the *doctrinas* of more than two thousand souls. Villages with a population of less than one thousand souls were to be gathered together into "reductions." Each priest was to be helped by two *majordomos,* in charge of the material organization of the parish, and two overseers exactly similar to the *fiscales* of Mexico.

The Council of 1567 had organized the teaching of catechism, which was to take place twice a week, early in the morning, before work; attendance was compulsory. Variations in the teaching of the *doctrina* were a stumbling-block for the Indians, whose quibbling minds were easily perturbed. Therefore the Council of Lima ordered the drafting of three catechisms, based on that of Trent, and of graded difficulty, like those of Canisius. Stress was laid in them on the idolatrous character of pre-Columbian religions; warnings were issued against an anthropomorphic conception of the Creed and against abuses in the worship of images; and carnal vices were condemned with especial force.

The Council also insisted upon the necessity of beautifying divine worship, and on the importance of training singers and instrument players. All sacraments were to be open to the Indians, save holy orders. The "superior" catechism, however, allows of Communion only when permission is granted by a confessor. In regard to baptism, the Council of 1567 had forbidden the christening of unwilling or unprepared adults; for children, the consent of one parent at least was required. Considering the weightiness and efficiency of the work of the Council of Lima, it is surprising that its members should have, as in Mexico, overlooked the true interests of evangelization by denying to the Indians access to the priesthood and the religious life. They had a poor opinion of their minds, which, according to them, "were not guided by reason." The Church was identified with the Spaniards, and even with the Spanish crown, which enjoyed the rights of *padronado* in America; and it stood to lose much on the day on which governmental support was to be withdrawn, owing to the secession of the colonies from the home-country.

Brazil stood apart from the rest of Latin America, belonging, as it did, to the Portuguese, and also owing its evangelization mostly to the Jesuits. But the conditions of religious life were largely the same as in Peru. The country was being conquered by Europeans, who enslaved the natives and considered them as brute beasts; while the task of the missionaries, on the contrary, was to protect, educate, and civilize the Indians, whose paganism easily gave way to Christianity. It was important, therefore, to induce them to give up their nomadic life and settle down in villages or *aldeos*.

This work was performed first and foremost by the Jesuit, Father José d' Anchieta, whose fame is due no less to his Latin verse than to his apostolic labors. He was born at Teneriffe in 1533, and studied at the University of Coimbra. Joining the Society when still very young, he was sent to Brazil in 1553. In 1576, he became the rector of the college of San Vicente and, in 1578, provincial of his Order in the country. He penetrated into the most remote wildernesses and, through his gentleness, won the respect of the wildest tribes. He also composed a grammar and a dictionary of the Brazilian tongue. His death took place in retirement on June 9, 1597. A great deal has been said about his thaumaturgic powers, to which he no doubt owed much of his influence. His work was continued by another Jesuit, Anthony de Vieira (1608–1697), who ran up against the opposition of the slave-drivers; his activity, however, belongs mostly to the late seventeenth century, and therefore need not detain us here.

In Paraguay the Jesuits had a chance to experiment with their notion of a Christian community. They were here given a free hand by the Spanish government, and found the natives isolated from the Spaniards, whose vices were too often an excuse for those of the Indians who refused to accept Christian morality. The first three Jesuits were called to Paraguay by the bishop of Tucuman, Don Francis Vittoria, on account of the failure of previous attempts to convert the natives. They penetrated into pathless forests, gained a few souls through their gentle and peaceful demeanor, and then rowed down the rivers with the neophytes, singing hymns accompanied by instruments. Their work was fruitful, and in 1609 they established "reductions," to which the Spanish crown granted independence, and from which all foreigners were carefully excluded. The Indians were attracted, Muratori remarks, not merely by the moving exhortations of the Jesuits, but also by the prospect of obtaining plentiful victuals. The reductions soon gathered from four to six thousand inhabitants each, the district of Gayra alone numbering one hundred thousand souls in 1629.

Paraguay soon became a Christian republic, with the missionaries acting not merely in their spiritual capacity, but as administrators as well. The land was the property of the community as a whole, according to local custom. Work was made cheerful, as in the European colleges of the Society. Every morning, after Mass, the people went to their several tasks to the accompaniment of flutes and tabors, and solemnly carrying the image of a saint. Absolute equality prevailed; all wore the same uniform dress. The education of the young was much on the same lines as in Mexico or in Peru. The religious fervor of the people was both extraordinary and touching. "They shed floods of tears while confessing sins so slight that it is doubtful whether they provide matter for absolution. . . . They declare their sins with such pain and groaning, that the confessor is moved and cannot help joining his tears to those of the penitent." In fact, devotional practice was pushed very far, and there were "congregations" of St. Michael and the Virgin Mary, the members of which were accustomed to frequent Communion. All the wealth and splendor available were, as in Mexico and in Peru, concentrated upon public worship. On the whole the experiment was, both from the Christian and the purely human angle, an undoubted success, and has compelled the admiration even of Montesquieu and Voltaire.

*   *   *

Conditions in Latin America favored the wholesale conversion of the Indians. Huge tracts of land had been wholly conquered by the Spaniards, who could exert pressure over the natives. These were largely barbarians, and found themselves face to face with a superior civilization, which could not but impress them. Their paganism could not hold its own against Christianity. But the problems confronting the missionaries in the East Indies were of a more difficult kind. The Portuguese colonial empire in Asia and Malaya really consisted of little more than trading-posts, beyond which lay vast unconquered countries, where no support was to be expected from the civil power. The peoples of Asia had attained a high degree of civilization, and many of them professed religions — such as Mohammedanism, Buddhism, or Confucianism — which were capable of offering stubborn resistance. One point there was, however, in common between the West and East Indies: the European colonists were given to all manner of vices, and evangelization had to begin with them, if any measure of success was to be reached with the natives.

As in America, the older religious orders had followed in the footsteps of the Portuguese adventurers. In 1500, eight Franciscans of the Strict Observance had accompanied Alvarez Cabral, and three of them had suffered martyrdom at Calicut. In 1510, when Alphonse Albuquerque took Goa, he turned over to the Franciscans the use of a mosque for a convent. In 1540, Father Anthony Patroni made a small cabin for himself under the walls of the town of San Thomé, where "he stayed in prayer, meditation, fasting and abstinence," while ever and again he went into the city. Here he always gained some soul to God, so that in a little time he converted to the faith more than thirteen hundred of the infidels. He then built the monastery of St. Thomas, where he died. The Franciscans settled down at Goa in 1542. One of their number, Father Vincent, founded, "for eighty children of converted Gentiles," the college at Cranganor, which educated fourteen native priests to serve churches in their own country, and fourteen more who became canons of the cathedral church of Cochin. The same Father brought over to the Christian faith the king of Tanor, who persevered to the end. By the close of the sixteenth century, the Franciscan province of St. Thomas numbered twelve convents, six colleges, and sixteen residences. As for the Dominicans, they established a house at Goa in 1549.

The work done by the older orders was no doubt considerable. However, the history of Christian expansion in the East is wholly dominated by the figure of St. Francis Xavier, S.J., "the apostle of the Indies and of Japan." His career flashed like a shooting star across the Asiatic skies. His story is a fascinating tale of spiritual adventure. His character, to the present day, retains surpassing attractiveness. He was young — barely forty-six when he died, after a life packed with action. He was handsome, cheerful, gentle, heroic withal. He was no doubt an exceptional personality, gifted with extraordinary powers. In any case, he evidenced a startling penetration into men's motives and thoughts, and a surprising foreknowledge of future or distant events; and no doubt the remarkable influence which he exerted over those who came near him accounts for much in the success of his apostolic labors.

He was born at the foot of the Pyrenees, at the Castle of Xavier, on April 7, 1506, of a noble Spanish family. When he was eighteen years old, his father sent him to study philosophy in the Collège Sainte Barbe of the University of Paris. He took his degree of master of arts, and was judged worthy to teach philosophy at the Collège de Beauvais. Ignatius Loyola, arriving at Paris about that time, judged him to be a highly suitable person for the teaching of the Gospel, and therefore began to lay siege to him and to his companion, Peter Faber, taking lodgings with them for that purpose.

Xavier, who was of a haughty spirit, and whose head was filled with ambitious thoughts, resisted Ignatius for some time; but the latter absolutely won his trust, and afterwards "weaned him from the world." Xavier was one of the six disciples of Ignatius who, together with him, took vows in the chapel at Montmartre on Assumption day, 1534. He accompanied his leader to Venice, where he tended the sick in the hospital of the incurables, then to Rome, then back to Venice, where he took holy orders. Next he went to Bologna and again to Rome, participating everywhere in the apostolic work of the young Society.

It was now that John III of Portugal asked Pope Paul III to grant him six Jesuits to evangelize the East Indies. Ignatius appointed only two, one of these being Xavier. The latter accordingly repaired to Lisbon, where he stayed for some months, laboring so successfully for the reformation of the Church and laity, that the king wanted to keep him in Portugal. He was, however, unwilling to remain, and Ignatius insisted upon his departure. The pope issued four briefs for the benefit of St. Francis, ranging in date from July 27 to October 2, 1540, in which he constituted him apostolic nuncio, and recommended him to the sovereigns of the east coast of Africa and the south of Asia. Throughout that immense territory Xavier was entrusted, both by Paul III and by the king of Portugal with a general mission of information, inspection, and organization; which accounts for the apparently disconcerting swiftness and extent of his movements in the course of the brief ten years that were to elapse before his death. He embarked for the Indies on April 7, 1541. Wherever Xavier happened to be throughout his life, he sowed the seeds of Christianity. On board ship he made himself all things to all men, at the hospital of Mozambique, in Melinda, he vainly tried to convert Moslems, as also at Socotora which he was loath to leave. He arrived at Goa on May 6, 1542.

Henceforth the brief career of St. Francis Xavier — apart from his attempt to penetrate into China in the last phase — was divided between three main theaters of activity. First came the south of India, with the Portuguese settlements of Goa, Cochin, San Thomé, and regions such as the coast of Fishery and Travancore, where Christianity had been more or less firmly planted but where it was languishing for lack of priests. Secondly, he entered the Portuguese colonies in Malaya, Malacca, and in the Moluccas, Amboyna, and Ternate; with the background of half-heathen islands, such as the terrible island, Del Moro, where the inhabitants scarcely remembered that they had been baptized. Thirdly, he arrived in Japan, which lay altogether outside the pale of European rule, though the Portuguese traders had some influence there.

Xavier was active in South India for more than three years, from his arrival at Goa until September, 1545; in Malaya for two and a half years, since he was back at Goa on March 20, 1548, spending seventeen months there; in Japan for more than two years, from his arrival at Cangoxima (Kagoshima) on Assumption day, 1549, to his departure from Figi on November 20, 1551. The remainder of his life was spent at Goa, and on the island of Sancian (San Choan) near Canton, where he died of a fever on December 2, 1552. We shall not attempt to follow Xavier in his journeys by land or sea. It is of more interest to study his missionary methods and assess the value of the results which he obtained.

*   *   *

It should not be forgotten that St. Francis was, first and foremost, a Jesuit, one who had thoroughly imbibed the spirit of the nascent Society.

"It is impossible to relate," Father Bouhours writes, "with what tenderness he loved the Society." His devotion to St. Ignatius was unspeakable. "My only, dear Father, in the bowels of Jesus Christ," he wrote to him from Cochin, "father of my soul for whom I have a most profound respect, I write this to you upon my knees, as if you were present and I beheld you with my eyes." It is not surprising, under the circumstances, that Xavier's apostolate should have been imbued with the spirit of the Society, and in particular with its practical-mindedness. He made it a rule always to apply his effort where it was likely to be most effective. When he sent Father Barzeus to Ormuz, he issued instructions to him, in which the following words occur: "Always prefer those employments which are of a large extent, to those which are more limited. According to that rule you shall never omit a sermon in public in order to hear a private confession. You shall not set aside the catechizing that you may visit any particular person, or for any good work of the like nature."

He himself applied this principle, and determined the order of importance of his tasks according to the profit which might be expected. He began his apostolic work with the Europeans, whose Christian beliefs provided a starting-point for the reformation of their manners, and whose good example might carry much weight with the natives. He was never weary of writing to Europe, to ask for preachers for the Portuguese stations. "We must remedy our own miseries first," he wrote; "then we shall go to the rescue of the Infidels." Next in order of preference came those natives who had become Christians through baptism, but whose religion had often sadly deteriorated, as in the neighborhood of Cape Comorin. Then followed those who were still infidels, but who were asking for priests, as at Travancore. After these, Xavier attended to those whose natural moral qualities and intellectual gifts fitted them for the acceptance of the truth, like the Japanese, and their masters in regard to civilization, the Chinese.

In the Portuguese settlements, colonial vices flourished amidst a population of adventurers. At Goa, "the Portuguese themselves lived more like idolaters, than Christians. . . . Every man kept as many mistresses as he pleased, and maintained them openly in his own house. . . . They bought women, or took them away by force, either for their service, or to make money of them. . . . Justice was sold at the tribunals, and the most enormous crimes escaped punishment when the criminals had wherewithal to corrupt the judges. All methods for heaping up money were accounted lawful. . . . Murder was reckoned but a venial trespass, and was boasted of as a piece of bravery."

Religious conditions were no better: "The use of confession, and the communion, were in a manner abolished; and if anyone by chance was struck with remorse of conscience . . . he was constrained to steal to his devotions by night, to avoid being seen by his neighbor." The lack of priests contributed to this state of things, which also prevailed at Meliapore, Malacca, and Ternate. It needed some pluck on the part of Xavier to undertake the amendment of such a lawless crowd. At Malacca, "walking the streets at night, with his bell in his hand, he would cry with a loud voice, 'Pray to God for those who are in the state of mortal sin.' . . ." However, he realized how important it was to get hold of young people. He gathered them into the church at Goa for catechism, and "it was through those babes that the town began to change its face."

According to another principle, which the Society had borrowed from St. Paul, Xavier consistently made himself all things to all men, managing to gain the confidence even of hardened sinners. Once he told a gamester who used to swear, "that gaming required a composed spirit," and thus brought him "to show a kindness for a man who was so much concerned about his advantage," and who eventually converted him. He would visit concubinaries, asking to see the children and their mother, and would treat her respectfully. If she were beautiful, he would praise her, and recommend marriage. If she were a "swarthy, ugly Indian," he would advise dismissal. It was by all these means that "he left the town (of Meliapore, or San Thomé) so different from what it was at his coming, that it could hardly be known for the same place."

With the nominal Christians or infidels, Xavier was not in a position to do any elaborate work. There was, first of all, the language difficulty. Few of the natives had a smattering of Portuguese, and interpreters were necessary. There was next the question of time — with the Paravas, the saint spent one month only in each center. His methods had to be swift and simple. He generally managed, even in Japan, to compose a translation into the local tongue of a few essential religious texts — the sign of the cross, the apostles' creed, the commandments, the Lord's prayer, the Hail Mary, the confiteor, and the Salve Regina. He would then, as with the Paravas, gather the adults and children, and recite to them the various prayers in their own tongue, that they might repeat them after him. "This being done," he says, "I repeated the Creed singly, and insisting on every particular article, asked if they certainly believed it. They all protested to me with loud cries, and their hands across their breasts, that they firmly believed it." The same procedure was followed with the commandments, which were interspersed with resolutions uttered in common. It is clear that such a lesson, in which the audience were made to take part through their words and gestures, must have impressed the native mind. Nor was Xavier averse to the use of a measure of compulsion in addition to persuasion. The natives with whom he had to deal were generally half-barbarians, low caste or outcaste people, who might be treated with paternal authority. He made use of the Paravas children to "break in pieces as many idols as they could get into their power. . . . Xavier went often in their company, to make a search of . . . suspected houses; and if he discovered any idols, they were immediately destroyed."

As a matter of fact, the Portuguese were, in his eyes, to play the same part in their Asiatic dominions toward the spread of Christianity that the Spaniards had played in America. He obtained orders from the king of Portugal to the effect that "no toleration should be granted to the superstitions of the infidels in the isle of Goa." Houses should be searched for idols, and the latter broken. Those who concealed them should be punished. Brahmins should be banished if they opposed the publication of the Gospel. Xavier, in fact, went to the length of calling the Portuguese to arms against the king of Jafanapatan (Ceylon) who had slaughtered the Christian population of the island of Manar. Nor was he above using wise diplomacy, and appealing to the temporal interests of prospective Christians, as he eventually did with the king of Jafanapatan, advising him to accept, for his own good, the protectorate and the faith of the Portuguese. But of course he kept in view the ultimate spiritual welfare, no less than the temporal welfare, of his proselytes; for he also obtained from King John III "that no exaction should remain unpunished; that no slaves should henceforth be sold, either to Mahometans, or to Gentiles; that the pearl fishing should only be in the hands of Christians, and that nothing should be taken from them, without paying them the due value."

*   *   *

Firm fatherliness was suitable for a primitive population, especially where support was available from the civil power. It was altogether out of place in Japan, and Xavier modified his plans, with a true Jesuit sense of adaptation. When he and his companion, Fernandez, preached at Amanguchi (Yamagutsi), without permission from the king, "people admired their courage, according to the humor of the Japonians, whose inclinations are naturally noble, and full of esteem for actions of generosity." Their noble-mindedness, however, implied no respect for poverty, and when Xavier appeared at the court of Bungo, his miserable attire was likely to draw contempt upon him. He therefore agreed with the Portuguese merchants who had brought him, "that he should present himself with all the pomp and magnificence they could devise," even to the extent of his donning a new cassock, which was much against the grain. Besides, the Japanese were almost on a par with Europeans in regard to their intellectual faculties. On no point does the saint insist so much as upon the fact that they are "ingenious and very rational," "of docible and reasonable minds." With true scholastic and humanistic belief in the compelling power of reason, Xavier again and again reverts to the necessity of proving to the Japanese, "according to the rules of the schools," that "the Christian doctrine is most conformable to good sense." Hence his spectacular disputations at the court of Bungo, with the chief bonze of the kingdom. More than forty years later, his successor, Father Valignani, recommended the confutation by means of arguments, of erroneous beliefs: "We must," he said, "follow reason as did our leader."

His work, however, did not end with convincing the infidels. Steps had to be taken to maintain religious life in the Christian communities, after the departure of the saint. With the Paravas, Xavier "called together the most intelligent amongst them, and gave them in writing what he had taught, to the end that as masters of the rest, on Sundays and Saints' days, they might congregate the people, and have them repeat, according to his method, that which they had learned formerly. He committed to these catechists (who in their own tongue are called *canacapoles*), the care of the churches . . . and recommended to them the ornament of those sacred buildings." The same was done at Ternate and in Japan.

Meanwhile the saint was painstakingly and patiently organizing the missions of the East. He was constantly writing to Europe to obtain more priests, and allotting to each newcomer a sphere of action. Even before the Society had become fully conscious in Europe of the part it was to play in the realm of education, the saint began to create Jesuit colleges in the East. He had founded one at Malacca in 1548, and he took over from the Portuguese principal, James de Borba, on behalf of the Society, the Seminary of Holy Faith at Goa. His ambitions were huge: "Whatever he performed, he looked on it, as no more than an essay." He purposed to convert China, and then "to return to Europe by the North, that he might labor in the reduction of heretics; . . . after this, he planned to go over into Africa." The results which he actually obtained, though not proportionate to his wishes, were considerable. He is said to have brought over seven hundred thousand souls to the Christian faith. This, of course, would apply mostly to the mass conversions in southern India and Malaya. In Japan, the figures given are more modest: five hundred persons in the first two months at Amanguchi, the number soon rising to three thousand.

In fact, though the work done by Xavier was merely preparatory, it laid down a solid foundation for further conquests. Christianity was firmly planted and has remained prosperous in every one of the regions he visited, save in Japan, where it was suppressed by severe persecution. Whatever the practical results, in any case, the life of St. Francis is one of supreme spiritual beauty. He was a great mystic as well as a great preacher. His thirst for martyrdom is revealed in the admirable lines which he wrote to the Fathers at Rome: "Let our brethren then, who desire to shed their blood for Jesus Christ, be of good courage, and anticipate their future joy. For behold a seminary of martyrdom is ready for them; and they will have wherewithal to satisfy their longings."

Xavier trusted much to the effect produced upon the common people by the fearless proclamation of Christian belief. Yet, true to the invariable practice of the Jesuits, he aimed at conquering influential individuals, who might carry along with them whole sections of the population. Hence his efforts to gain over the local rulers of Japan, and his scheme of an embassy to the emperor of China. In India, however, he failed to win over the Brahmins, who despised low caste converts, and also foreigners who used cow leather and ate cow meat.

In 1608, another Jesuit, Father Robert de Nobili, devised a new method for the religious conquest of the Brahmins, and consequently of the whole of India. He adopted their dress and the mode of life, and withdrew to a hut made of turf, where he lived for one year as a hermit, feeding on vegetables and drinking only water. At the same time he studied the sacred books of the Hindoos. His renown gradually spread. He was consulted by Brahmins, and, like St. Paul preaching the "unknown God," explained to them that the Christian faith was the fourth *veda,* which had not as yet been revealed. This interpretation of the Hindoo religion met with prodigious success. It scandalized some of the inhabitants of Goa, however, who denounced it to the Holy See; but in 1623, Pope Gregory XV expressly approved of it. In 1639, De Nobili instituted two classes of missionaries: the first, called *Saniasis,* were subjected like him to the etiquette of the Brahmins; the second, called *Pandara-swamis,* were to mingle with all classes. When he died in 1656, the Madura mission numbered one hundred thousand Christians.

In Japan, Xavier's work was continued by the Jesuits, Franciscans,

Dominicans, and Augustinians. A huge movement of conversions took place, especially under a wise and ambitious ruler, Nobunaga, who reigned from 1565 to 1582, and favored Christianity. During this period, the number of Christians rose to 200,000, with 250 churches; it was to reach the figure of 600,000 in 1622; "Christians, mark," the Franciscan chronicle runs, "not like ours, who are mostly hermaphrodites in their belief; but Christians faithful unto death, yea unto death on the Cross." The truth of these words had been proved as early as 1596, when a bloody persecution began. The captain of a stranded Spanish galleon, to save his cargo, attempted to intimidate the ruler, Hydeyoski, by describing to him the dominions of the king of Spain, which, he said, had been acquired by first converting the natives. This roused the suspicions of the sovereign. All the Franciscans in Japan were arrested and sentenced to crucifixion, together with seventeen tertiaries and three Jesuits. The traditional Japanese contempt of death was now turned to a Christian purpose. "It was a fine thing to see some of the first of the town of Nagasaki running about the streets, saying in a loud voice, 'I too want to be a martyr.'" A new and terrible persecution began in 1610; it was renewed in 1624, when 30,000 Christians were put to death. The final blow was struck in 1640, when Christianity was utterly proscribed in Japan.

The situation was more favorable in China for almost a century. Until the Spanish Dominicans arrived in 1631, the Jesuits had a free hand in the Empire, and obtained the most remarkable results. In 1562, they settled down in the newly founded Portuguese colony of Macao, where a college was to be established in 1595. But the method still followed was to Europeanize the converts. It was Father Valignani who directed the Far Eastern apostolate into apter channels, by prescribing to the new missionaries the study of Chinese characters.

Xavier's principle for the conversion of China was applied by Father Matthew Ricci (1552–1610). His plan was to start from above, and to gain the people through the scholarly class of the mandarins; while these were in turn to be gained by means of European science. Ricci was qualified for the performance of such a task, for he was scientifically gifted, and had studied mathematics and astronomy in Rome. Besides, like De Nobili in India, he lived, as far as he could, the life of the people among whom he had to move; he first dressed like a bonze, then more advisedly like a mandarin. His progress through China was slow and patient. He obtained the favor of dignitaries through gifts of European instruments, especially clocks. He gradually made his way to Peking, rendered himself agreeable to the emperor, and converted a number of men and women in all classes of society. His successors continued his work on the same lines. Father John Adrian Schall, a Rhinelander, became an official character through his reform of the Chinese calendar. Father John de Rocha, in charge of the Nanking residence, brought over to Christianity an illustrious doctor, Paul Siu Koank-k'i, who traveled to Macao to make himself better acquainted with Catholic life, and there went through St. Ignatius' *Exercises*. About 1650, there were in Shanghai 30,000 baptized Christians, and the annual increase was from two to three thousand. It is even reported, though perhaps too optimistically, that there were 100,000 Christians in the province of Nanking in 1641. This remarkable development was checked, from 1630 onward, by the unfortunate quarrel which broke out between the Jesuits and Dominicans over the question of Chinese rites, such as "ancestor worship," which the Jesuits, stretching "adaptation" to its utmost possibilities, sanctioned as compatible with Christian belief, obviously excluding, of course, the intention of giving divine honors. The controversy, which was to last on until 1705, had been fatal to the Catholic apostolate in China.*

* * *

Just as the Spanish revival initiated by St. Peter of Alcantara and St. Teresa was responsible for the planting of Christianity in Central and South America; just as Jesuit enthusiasm and militancy gave it a firm footing in Asia; so also was its establishment in North America a consequence of the French Catholic renascence of the early seventeenth century. New Spain cannot be considered apart from Castile and Aragon; nor can Canada, "New France," be separated from the home-country. There are, however, essential differences between the Spanish and French apostolates. The former, in its dreams of political and religious aggrandizement, enjoyed the whole-hearted support of the State, whereas the latter received but niggardly help from the crown. The king of France had to reckon with the Calvinists, who were numerous among oversea traders, and who were opposed to Catholic expansion. Fur merchants, as a rule, regarded Canada as their private preserve, the ownership of which would be endangered if colonists became too numerous or if the natives became civilized. Besides there was in France an anti-colonial

---

* It is interesting to note in this connection the regulations issued by the S. Congregation of the Propagation of the Faith, Dec. 8, 1939. One section of this Instruction specifically deals with "Ceremonies in Honor of Confucius Permitted as Purely Civil Acts." There is question here of ceremonies in honor of a Chinese sage who died in the fifth century before Christ.

party, the party of the "stay-at-home," who thought that any expenditure of strength in far-away countries would be a needless drain upon national resources. For these reasons the French apostolate in Canada was, like the reformation of the Church in France, due chiefly to the private initiative of regular or secular priests, and very often of laymen. Again, apart from English or Dutch raids on coastal posts, the Spaniards were left in undisturbed possession of their American colonies; and their ecclesiastical policy met on the whole with little opposition. The French in Canada, on the other hand, were subject to ceaseless attacks from their Protestant adversaries of England, New England, and the Netherlands, who went so far as to arm and egg on against them the Indian tribes, such as the ferocious Iroquois. The evangelization of Canada was carried on amidst constant dangers and hardships; that it obtained such deep and lasting results proves the stintless devotion to Catholicism of the French pioneers.

It is not possible here to rehearse the religious history of Canada. The chief events are well-known: the landing of two Jesuits in Acadia in 1611; the destruction of the colony by the English in 1613; the arrival of the Franciscans at Quebec in 1615; their work among the Hurons; the appearance of the Jesuits in 1625; the departure of the Franciscans after the capture of Quebec by the Kirke brothers in 1629; the Jesuit apostolate as far as Lake Superior; the foundation of Montreal as an advanced post in 1641; and finally, the slaughter of the Christianized Hurons by the Iroquois in 1648–1649.

The essential fact, throughout that chain of events, is the close connection between the activities of the Catholic reformers in France and the Canadian apostolate. The exalted religious atmosphere of the home-country provided a fit preparation for the missionaries and for lay settlers imbued with the missionary spirit. It is a significant fact that out of 450 books on far-away countries printed in France from 1600 to 1661, one hundred and seventy-three were missionary works, published in twenty-seven different towns. The Jesuit college at La Fléche was a center of propaganda for the evangelization of Canada. Father Massé, who had preached Christianity in Acadia, was minister of the college in 1615, and imparted his enthusiasm to his pupils. In 1647, a miscellany of Latin verse by Father John Chevalier was adopted for use in the classes. It included five poems devoted to the Canadian apostolate, and was imbued with the chivalrous heroism of the period.

It is, therefore, not surprising that we should find every prominent Catholic of the reigns of Henry IV and Louis XIII associated in some degree with the mission to Canada. Father Caton, the provincial of the Society of Jesus in Paris, and the duke of Ventadour, the founder of the Company of the Holy Sacrament and viceroy of Canada from 1624 onward, were both instrumental in sending Jesuit Fathers across the Atlantic. Everywhere among the French aristocracy and bourgeoisie, in the world or in religious houses, missionary vocations occurred. The aspirations of an Ursuline nun, Mother Mary of the Incarnation, were turned toward the teaching of young native girls in Canada by the rector of the Jesuit college at Tours, Father Dinet. She was accompanied in her exile by Madame de la Peltrie, a gentlewoman of Caen, who had been encouraged in her purpose by Father de Condren the Oratorian and St. Vincent de Paul, and helped by M. de Bernières, a prominent member of the Company of the Holy Sacrament. The Duchess of Aiguillon sent Hospitaller nuns to found a hospital in Quebec. M. de la Dauversière, a former pupil of the college of La Fléche, who shared in the devotion of the Fathers toward St. Francis Xavier, founded, with the approval of M. Olier, the Society of Our Lady of Montreal, to colonize the island of the same name. A suitable governor was found by the Jesuits for the new settlement. He was a gallant Christian soldier, M. de la Maisonneuve. The Montreal Society was also mentioned by the Jesuits to a clever and virtuous woman, Mademoiselle Jeanne Mance, who joined the group of the emigrants. Division had not yet crept into French Catholicism; and all energies were united toward one purpose, which has been rightly described as a "crusade."

The settlers were prepared to live and die for the advancement of Christianity. Champlain had served in the army of the League. He was "in everything a religious and God-fearing man," who tolerated no blasphemy on board ship, who conducted prayers there, morning and night, and who desired, whenever possible, the assistance of a chaplain. "The conversion of a single infidel," he wrote in his *Travels*, "is worth more than the conquest of a kingdom." His companion, Louis Hébert, formerly an apothecary, now become a tiller of the soil, asked for a grant of land, "so as to make a beginning of a Christian people."

The communities of colonists established in Canada recalled the purity and fraternity of the early Church. In the fort of Quebec, of which Champlain was the governor, "some good book of history was read aloud during the midday meal, and the Lives of Saints in the evening. Everyone examined his conscience at night in his room, and then took part in prayers, which were said kneeling. The angelus was rung at dawn, at noon and at dusk." The "gentlemen" who founded Montreal did not consider themselves as traders, but as working for "the glory of God," and for "the salvation of the savages." When they had settled down in their colony, "they all lived in common as in a sort of inn, and all were one heart and one soul in Jesus-Christ. . . . The vice of impurity was not even heard of. . . . If by any chance they offended each other, they asked each other's forgiveness at night before going to bed." This devotional spirit culminated in the heroism shown in times of stress by the settlers themselves and by their spiritual advisers, the Jesuit Fathers, who had to put up with severe hardships, and several of whom, such as Jogues, De Brébeuf, and Lalemant, suffered martyrdom.

Even where it did not end in martyrdom, the task proposed to the efforts of religious and lay missionaries was a difficult one, the more difficult as their aim in regard to the natives was noble and exalted. Contrary to Spanish practice, they raised no barrier between the Reds and the Whites. They wanted the former, once Christianized, to become the equals of the latter. Their religious ideal was humanitarian, with its settled belief in equality of the races. Richelieu stipulated that a baptized native was to become in every respect similar to a French subject, to the extent of enjoying all his legal privileges, without having to take out letters of naturalization. At Sillery, toward 1639, the governor of Quebec and Madame de la Peltrie went to Communion side by side with the natives. No wonder, under these circumstances, if, as Fr. Lalemant wrote in 1631 after the capture of Quebec, "the savages longed after the return of the French, who treat them far otherwise than the English."

About the same time earnest efforts were made at Quebec by the Jesuits to establish a seminary for the natives, in order to turn them, when grown up, into Christian propagandists. Unfortunately, the attempt ended in failure. The Redskins were captivated by their new surroundings at the outset; but soon they began to pine after their life of freedom in the woods, and fled from the seminary. They were indeed a ticklish population to deal with. They were often friendly to the missionaries, and listened to them willingly; but afterwards proved elusive and disappointing. "Even after baptism [which some accepted as a guarantee of bodily health] there was little change in them," Father Biard wrote in 1611. Father Le Jeune did not remember "having seen them do one single act of true moral virtue; they had," he said, "but their pleasure and satisfaction in view. They were gluttonous, vindictive, pitiless with the old and sick, superstitious, morally and physically unclean." It required especial good will on the part of the missionaries to conclude that their soul, though spoiled by long neglect, "was naturally an excellent soil." Besides, the variety in their modes of life required a corresponding adaptation of missionary methods. When the Jesuits had to deal with nomads, the Algonquins for instance, they endeavored, as in Paraguay, to establish agricultural "reductions." In some cases, they met with no little success. At St. Joseph de Sillery near Quebec, they built a residence for themselves, houses for the neophytes, a fort, a hospital, and a chapel. In 1638, two large families of Algonquins agreed to settle down there; in 1645, the number of families had grown to thirty. The same happened in other cases. The problem was wholly different for sedentary tribes like that of the Hurons, who lived in villages, and who were too far from the centers of white population for the latter to exert a lasting influence. The Jesuit apostolate had to proceed among them on other lines. The Fathers, under De Brébeuf, built a hut in Ihonatiria, including a storehouse, a common room, and a chapel, and tried to attract the natives by displaying objects which to them were marvels: a prism, a magnet, a microscope, joiner's tools, a handmill for flour, a clock. They gathered the children together and taught them the elements of Christian belief; but the elders were more obdurate. It was soon found that it was impracticable to multiply such establishments, and new methods were adopted by Father Lalemant. A single central residence, named Sainte Marie, was established, not in an already extant village, but in a vacant site suitable for the purpose. Thence flying missions were to issue forth to other tribes from time to time; while their members were to come back periodically for rest and spiritual refreshment. In their apostolate the Jesuits were assisted by a new class of servants who devoted themselves freely to the service of the mission, and who, because they made a gift of themselves, were called the *donnés*. No provision had been made in the rules of the Society for such helpers, who were akin to tertiaries; they were authorized, however, by the Father general Vitelleschi, after Father Lalemant had provided that they should take no vows and wear no clerical dress.

The difficulties of the apostolate, especially among the Western tribes, were increased by the fact that the English and Dutch colonists conducted among the savages a merciless anti-Jesuit propaganda. The Dutch supplied the Iroquois with firearms, while the military support which would have kept them in check was sadly lacking. As early as 1634, Father Le Jeune bemoaned the reluctance of the French to display their strength to impress the natives, as the Portuguese had done in India. Champlain had asked Richelieu to send him one hundred and fifty well-armed soldiers, who would have sufficed to reinforce the Hurons and Algonquins. But the cardinal needed every available resource for his war against the house of Austria, and refused to grant a single man. That in such circumstances, the hard-beset mission should have gained a firm footing in Canada may give rise to some wonder.

Indeed, the results obtained are not expressed by such huge figures as those which we have quoted in the case of the West and East Indies. The country was thinly populated, and such important tribes as the Hurons and Algonquins ran only to tens of thousands. Therefore baptisms were necessarily few. The Huron mission reported 22 in 1633; 115 in 1636; more than 300 in 1637. In 1640, Father Le Jeune wrote to Richelieu that the Gospel had been preached to more than 10,000 savages, and that more than 1000 had been christened during epidemics. In the new settlement of Villemarie (Montreal), seventy to eighty natives were baptized in 1643. In the following years considerable progress was made to such an extent that in 1650 Father Lalemant could write that "on departing from the country, he scarcely left one Huron, Algonquin, or 'montagnaise' family, that was not altogether Christian." This may sound too optimistic; but the missionaries repeatedly testify to the genuine piety and devotion of the converts. Their apostolic zeal, Mother Mary of the Incarnation wrote, knew no bounds. "A Christian woman has gone on purpose to a very remote nation, to catechize those who dwelt there; in which she succeeded so well, that she brought them all to Quebec, where they were christened." And when Father de Brébeuf was tortured by the Iroquois, the Christian Hurons who were with him replied to his exhortations: "Never fear, Father, our souls will be in Heaven while our bodies suffer here below."

Indeed, the beginnings of French Canada were of great spiritual beauty, and worthily close the history of the Catholic Reformation. There were also secondary mission fields, such as Constantinople, Syria, Ethiopia, Morocco, Congo, and South Africa, which it is not possible to deal with here in detail. Both these and the larger ones in America and Asia confirm the views which have been expressed above, on the continued vitality of the Church, both before and after the Lutheran outbreak.

Conclusion

THE Catholic Reformation has been presented, in the preceding pages, in a somewhat bewildering diversity of aspects — administrative, moral, devotional, literary, artistic; while further diversity has been shown to have come from the variety of national temperaments. It is time to pause and to point out, despite such seeming confusion, the underlying unity. This unity, to begin with, was manifested in the revival of traditional piety among Western Europeans, in the late fifteenth and early sixteenth centuries. We have seen how the printing presses of the time turned out book after book of devotion and mysticism — books which were the direct predecessors of the works of St. Teresa and St. Francis de Sales. Deep religious cravings were united, in every country of the West, with humanistic learning applied to the study of Scripture and the Fathers. Both, in turn, were coupled with sporadic efforts to heal the sores of Christendom. Every element of the Catholic Reformation was already present there.

Such influences, too, were everywhere obscurely at work, at the very time which is considered the darkest one in the history of the Church, that of the scandalous pontificate of Alexander VI. It was in those years — and this should not be forgotten — that young men, engaged in study and meditation, received the religious upbringing which was to turn them into the Catholic reformers of the next phase. Such of the Fathers of Trent, at the opening of the Council, as were fifty years old, had spent their decisive years of formation between 1500 and 1510. The movement as a whole was bound to come to a head sooner or later — though of course it was lashed into prompt action by the Protestant outbreak. It would not, however, have become the Catholic Reformation had it not been unified and strengthened by the Council of Trent, the latter in its turn being made possible through the authority of a centralized hierarchy.

The Middle Ages had frittered away the organization of the Roman Empire. Sovereignty had become divided and subdivided into innumerable local powers, in the Church no less than in civil society. The Renaissance, on the other hand, with its ideal of classical orderliness, made for unification; and in fact, feudalism was coming to an end, in the sixteenth century, to some degree, in every country in Europe. For the picturesque tangle of the previous centuries in the building art was substituted the harmonious composition of ancient architecture. So too we behold to some extent the process of simplification and concentration in the Church.

"Reason" alone, however, would not have been sufficient to ensure the improvement of ecclesiastical conditions; and while the Catholic Reformation did away with the cumbrous machinery of the Middle Ages, it really harked back to them for religious inspiration. There is no definite break between the mysticism of St. Francis of Assisi or St. Bonaventure, and that of St. Teresa and St. John of the Cross. Palestrinian music had much in common with Gregorian plainchant. The spirit of the builders of the cathedrals still appears in the upward trend of the churches of the late sixteenth century, and the Jesuits once again made St. Thomas Aquinas the prince of theological studies. From the religious upheaval of the fifteenth century to that of the Catholic Reformation the distance is not so great as might at first appear.

The unity of the Trentine movement was further enhanced by the fact that it implicitly proclaimed its purely spiritual character. In the Middle Ages the dependence of the Church upon the civil power had been — as in Scotland — the source of many evil practices. Provincial councils had repeatedly bewailed this state of things, and asserted that it barred the way to thorough reformation. At Constance and Basle national rivalries had had the same effect of weakening any central authority in the Church. At Trent, the position was reversed. The ambassadors of temporal princes could no longer sway the Council at will. The independence and universality of the Church were restored; and while the agreement of sovereigns was sought to enforce the decisions of the Fathers, they were nevertheless carried out, as in France, even in the face of their opposition. On no point was the action of the Council more decisive. By proclaiming that the Church ought to be above worldly interests, it enhanced its prestige considerably. It prepared the saintly pontificates of the late sixteenth and early seventeenth centuries. Looking further ahead we can see how it enabled the papacy to gain the moral position which it enjoys today, and to play its part in the international field as an agency of reconcilement, and a help in healing the injuries of a sorely bruised world.

Nor is this the only point wherein the Catholic Reformation contributed to the creation of modern civilization. It resisted a very natural impulse wholly to destroy the work of the Renaissance. The moral evils produced by the latter were so flagrant that any reformer might well wonder whether anything of it should be allowed to stand. And in fact the Fathers of Trent stood on the brink of taking drastic measures which would have been untrue to the spirit of Christian humanism. The latter, however, prevailed; the legacy of classical antiquity, insofar as it might be reconciled with Christian belief, was saved for later generations, and was made the basis of an academic culture which has left its mark, to the present day, on the educational systems of the whole civilized world. The diffusion of this culture was mainly the work of the Society of Jesus. The fact has been mentioned repeatedly, and should be mentioned again here, because of the prominent part it played in the Catholic Reformation. If the latter was truly "modern," it was largely thanks to the Jesuits. They crystallized into a system many tendencies which were already manifest among the Christian humanists, the Brothers of the Common Life, the new Italian Orders. They broke loose from the fetters of old monasticism; they proclaimed the paramount value of action; they made use of the most up-to-date psychology in their devotional and educational schemes toward the training of the will; they understood the value of the practical adaptation of means to ends. They realized that individual efforts toward reformation would be unavailing if these were not co-ordinated and sanctioned from above; and hence, more than any others they were instrumental in establishing the authority of the papacy on a firm basis. They themselves, in their *Constitutions,* combined the absolute power of the Father general with representative government. In the mission field, no less than in literature and art they used "adaptation." They refrained from presenting Christianity to the natives as something foreign and strange; they made it, as far as might be, fit in with their customs and social environment; they favored the creation of a native clergy, thus anticipating the decisions of twentieth-century popes. Nor should it be forgotten that their first generations were afire with the most ardent enthusiasm, an enthusiasm which was contagious, and carried along with it many distinguished men. Whatever may have been urged against them in later days, their part in bringing the Church into line with the world of today can hardly be overstressed.

Taken as a whole, the results obtained by the Catholic Reformation appear monumental. We might speak of it almost as a second birth of the Church: a Church, indeed, greatly reduced, at least in Europe, and from which all abuses had not been weeded out; a Church, nevertheless, purified and strengthened, concentrated, more sinewy, more capable of endurance, of bearing persecution at home and abroad, and of expanding in the mission field; a Church with its dogma clearly defined and firmly settled, fit to serve as a rallying point; a Church spiritually independent, and suited to play its part in dealing with great moral, social, and charitable issues; last but not least, a Church which was supported in its reforming action by literature and art, and which created a cultural movement of lasting value. A sure sense indeed, of what was best in Renaissance letters and erudition was found among the Christian humanists who became the Fathers of Trent. At any rate, they undoubtedly had the leading part in preserving the heritage of ancient culture, and all that it means for man, while raising it to the level of the highest spiritual life; and in so doing they may be said to have largely contributed to the molding of the modern world.

Index

Acarie, Madame, and French Carmel, 236 f

Acts of Martyrs, in reformation art, 167

Adaptation, Jesuit teaching, 106

Adrian VI, Pope, character, 39; and Germany, 42; and reform of Curia, 83; reform efforts, 40 ff

Alexander VI, Pope, reform efforts, 23; and reform in France, 24; and religious Orders, 21; sale of ecclesiastical offices, 14; scandals of pontificate, 15; and Spain, 12

Allen, William, and seminary at Douai, 263 f

Amboise, Cardinal d', legate in France, reform efforts, 25 f

America, *see,* North America; South America; individual countries

Anarchy, in Church, 1 ff

Anchieta, Fr. José d', S.J., in Brazil, 284 f

Animuccia, Giovanni, composer, 180 f

Annales ecclesiastici, 136

Architecture, pre-reformation, 18

Architecture, reformation, 172 f; Churches in Rome, 176; influence of Middle Ages on, 175; Jesuit influence on, 173; and the Mass, 173; in Northern Europe, 176; preaching and, 174

Archithrenius, de Hantville's, 142

Art, and Catholic reformation, 159 ff; pre-reformation, 170; reformation, 170 f; reformation, attitude toward death in, 163 f; reformation, decency in, 165; reformation, realism in, 166

Asia, missions in, 286 f

Assisi, St. Francis of, in reformation art, 164, 165

Augustinians, reform, 94

Bankers, and papacy, 14

Barnabites, 95 ff, 98

Baronius, Caesar, 135 f; and *Acts* of Martyrs, 167; *Annales ecclesiastici,* 167; *Martyrologium Romanorum,* 167

Bascio, Matteo da, and Franciscan reform, 94; preaching, 95

Basle, Council of, and nationalism, 2

Bavaria, reform in, 221 f

Bellarmine, Robert Cardinal, St., 135; on music, 181

Bérulle, Madame de, 236

Bérulle, Pierre de, 236 ff; and French spirituality, 202 f; and Jesuits, 131

Bible, *see* Scripture

Biblia idiotorum, 20

Billom, Jesuit college of, 123; Jesuit school at, 119

Bishops, and Council of Trent, 65; powers of, and Council of Trent, 71, 77 ff; and reformation, 4 f; residence of, and reform, 72

Biverus, Fr., *Sacrum sanctuarium crucis et patientiae,* 168

Bobadilla, Nicholas, S.J., reform work of, 218

Bologna, school of painting, 170 f

Boncompagni, Cardinal Ugo, *see* Gregory XIII, pope

Borgia, Caesar, 15

Borgia, Lucrece, 15

Borromeo, Charles, Cardinal, St., character of, 84 f; and Council of Trent, 68; reform in Milan, 211 f; and reform in Switzerland, 225

Bourdoise, Adrien, 240 f

Brazil, missions in, 284

Brebeuf, St. Jean de, S.J., 299

Brenton, Nicholas, *Blessed Weeper,* 147

Breviary, reform of, 86 f; reform under Urban VIII, 215; revised, 209

Brothers of the Common Life, and education, 116 f

Butzbach, Johannes, on classical studies, 30

Caccia, Giovan Battista, on state of Church, 54

Cajetan, Thomas, 33; at Lateran Council, 26

Callot, painter, 163

Camaldolese, reform of, 93

Camillus de Lellis, St., 214

Campeggio, Cardinal, proposal for reform, 40 f

Canada, missions in, 295 ff

Canisius, Peter, St., catechism of, 86, 220 f; reform work of, 218 ff

Capuchins, foundation, 94; in France, 228, 236

Caraffa, Gian-Pietro, 93; called to Vatican, 42; in "pre-council," 59; and reform of Curia, 62; and Theatines, 96 f

Carracci, Agostino, and Bolognese school of art, 171; painter, 163

Carracci, Annibale, and Bolognese school of art, 171

Carracci, Ludovico, and Bolognese school of art, 171

Carthusians, 20

Carvaggio, 166

Carvajal, Cardinal, speech on reform, 40

Catechism, Roman, publication, 86

Catechisms, French, of Fr. Auger, 232; in Peru, 284; of St. Peter Canisius, 220 f

Cathedral chapters, 5; and Council of Trent, 79

Catholic reformation, and Council of Trent, 301 f

Caussin, Fr., Felicitas, 151; Hermenegildus, 151; Nabuchodonosor, 154; Theodoricus, 153

Censures, ecclesiastical, misuse of, 15

Chant, see plainchant

Chantal, St. Jane F. de, and Order of the Visitation, 235 f

Charles V, emperor, 67; and Clement VII, 44 f; and council, 49 f, 56; and Council of Trent, 70

Charles VIII, King of France reform efforts, 24 f

Chieregati, nuncio to Germany, 42

China, missions in, 294 f

Christian Directory, by Fr. Parsons, 265 ff; Protestant use of, 268

Christian Humanism, and piety, 183; and reform, 3, 28 ff; and reform in England, 259

Churches, pre-reformation, 19; in Rome, after Trent, 176

Citeaux, reform efforts, 25

Classics, attitudes toward, 129 f; use of, in study, 31

Clement VII, Pope, 43; character, 48; death, 51; and international politics, 46; reform efforts, 45, 51

Clement VIII, Pope, and Church music, 182; and missions, 276; and Vulgate, 87

Clergy, higher, state of, 9 f; lower, state of, 10; qualified, and Council of Trent, 80; reform of, aim of Italian devotional writers, 195; regular, in Peru, 281; secular, in Peru, 281; work of St. Vincent de Paul with, 243 f

Clermont, Collége de, foundation and influence, 228 ff

Clichtoue, works on eloquence, 31

Cluny, reform efforts, 25

Cölde, Dederich, catechism, 19

Colle, Bonifazio da, and Theatines, 96

Colleges, English, growth of, 123; Irish, 264; Jesuit, 223 f; Jesuit, in France, 228 ff; Jesuit, Peter Canisius and, 219 f; Scottish, 264; in Spain, 264

Colloquia, policy of, 57

Combattimento spirituale, and Italian spirituality, 195 f

Commendone, Nuncio to Poland, 90

Company of the Holy Sacrament of the Altar, 247 ff

Company of the Maidens of Charity, established, 243

Company of St. Sulpice, established, 245

Condren, Charles de, Fr., 240; on education, 131

Confession, practice of, in art, 169

Congregation of the Council, formed, 86

Congregation of the Good Shepherd, foundation, 241

Congregation of the Mission, established, 243

Congregations, formed under Sixtus V, 214

Consilium, evils denounced by, 59 ff; see also "pre-council"

Constance, Council of, and nationalism, 2

Contarini, Gaspare, made cardinal, 58 f; and reform of Curia, 62

Corneille, Pierre, Polyeucte, 151, 155 ff

Cortes, Fernando, 176

Council, general, necessity for, 47; political obstacles to, 47 f; problems of, 57 f; religious obstacles to, 49

Crashaw, Richard, Weeper, 147

Curia, powers of, and Council of Trent, 78; and reform, 3; reform of, 62 f; Roman, and reform, 36

Danses macabres, in art, 163
Da Thiéne, Gaetano, 20
Death, attitude toward, in reformation art, 163 f
Dernbach, Balthazar von, and reform at Fulda, 222 f
Diet of Augsburg, 70
Dominican Order, reform, 94
Donatus, Alexander, *Suevia*, 152
Douai, English college at, 264
Dowdall, George, 255
Drama, Catholic reformation, 148 ff; pre-reformation, 20; prose in, 151; Protestant interest in, 150; reformation, martyrdom plays, 151; reformation, verse in, 151

Eastern Churches, see Oriental churches
Eck, Johann, report to Adrian VI, 42
Education, 115 ff; Peter Canisius and, 220; prescriptions of Council of Trent, 122; Protestant, 118 ff; Protestant *vs* Catholic, 120 f
Edward IV, King of England, 25
Elphinstone, William, 251
Emulation, in Jesuit education, 127
England, Catholic reformation in, 256 ff; poetry in, 147; reform literature, 264 ff
Episcopate, powers of, and Council of Trent, 71
Erasmus, Desiderius, *Enchiridion militis christiani*, 186; on humanistic schools, 115 f; Leo X and, 35 f
Estinne, Robert, *Les larmes du Sainct Pierre*, 144
Eudes, St. John, 240, 241
Europe, northern, reform in, 216 ff
Exemption, 5; and religious Orders, 21

Faber, Peter, S.J., reform work of, 218
Farnese, Alessandro Cardinal, see Paul III, Pope
Ferreri, Zaccaria, and Breviary hymns, 35
Forman, Andrew, 252
Fossombrone, Lodovico, and Franciscan reform, 94
France, and American Missions, 295 f; concordat with (1516), 26; mysticism in, 201 ff; provincial Councils in, 227; reformation in, 226 ff; reform efforts in, 24; Trentine decrees in, 88 f

Francis of Assisi, St., in reformation art, 164, 165
Franciscan, reform, 94 f
Francisco de Ossuna, mystic, 188
Francis de Sales, St., 197; and Order of the Visitation, 235 f; spirituality of, 197 ff
Francis I, King of France, and Adrian VI, 44; and council, 49 f, 56; and Italy, 38
Francis Régis, St., work of, 246 f
Fregoso, Federigo, made cardinal, 62; in "pre-council," 59

Gaguin, *Ars versificatoria*, 31
Gazzella, Tommaso, called to Vatican, 42
Germany, Catholic princes, and emperor, 56; reform in, 216 ff; reform of, and Catholic princes, 221; Trentine decrees in, 88
Ghinucci, Cardinal, and reform of Curia, 62
Ghislieri, Antonio, see Pius V, St.
Giberti, Gian Matteo, Christian humanist, 45; in "pre-council," 59; reforms of, 52 f
Gierusalemne liberato, Tasso's, 141 f
Giles of Viterbo, 33; at Lateran Council, 26; and reform of Augustinians, 94
Good Shepherd, Congregation of, foundation, 241
Good works, in art, 170
Gothic, survival of, in north of Europe, 176
Granada, Luis de, mystic, 188, 189
Great Britain, Catholic reformation in, 250 ff; see also, England; Scotland
Gregory XIII, Pope, 211 ff; and missions, 276; and Oratory of Divine Love, 101; and plainchant, 182
Gregory XV, Pope, and missions, 276
Guilds, pre-reformation, 17

Hantville, Jean de, 142
Henry II, King of France, 67; and Council of Trent, 70
Henry VII, King of England, 25
Henry VIII, King of England, and Clement VII, 44, 48; and Council, 49 f, 55 f; and Turks, 38
Herolt, Johann, sermons, 19
Holy See, and Council of Trent, 64 f

Homes, pre-reformation, 18 f
Humanism, Christian *see* Christian humanism

Ignatius Loyola, St., *see* Loyola, St. Ignatius
Il Domenechino, painter, 163; realism of, 167
Il Pomarancio, frescoes on persecutions, 166
Il Vendemmiatore, Tansillo's, 142
Immaculate Conception of Blessed Virgin Mary, in art, 168
Index, Congregation of, created, 209; of forbidden books, revised, 86
India, missions in, 286
Indians, French and, in Canada, 298
Indulgences, for completion of St. Peter's, Cardinal Ximenes protests, 36; Venice forbids, 36
Inquisition, 67
Introduction to a Devout Life, 197, 198, 199
Ireland, attempts at reform in, 254 ff; Catholic reformation in, 250 ff
Italy, mysticism in, 194 ff; nobility of, 13; Trentine decrees in, 87

Jane Frances de Chantal, St., *see* Chantal
Japan, Francis Xavier in, 291 f; missions in, 293 f; persecution in, 294
Jay, Claude le, S.J., reform works of, 218
Jesuits, art of, 159; in Asia and India, 287; in Brazil, 284 f; in Canada, 297 ff; and college drama, 148 f; and Council of Trent, 68; and educational prescriptions of Trent, 122; and English seminaries, 263 f; features of teaching, 134 f; in France, 228 ff; in Paraguay, 285 f; qualifications of, 111 f; and reformation art, 173; *see also* Society of Jesus
Jesus and Mary, Congregation of, 241
John of the Cross, St., 190, 193 f
John Eudes, St., *see* Eudes
Joseph, Father, influence in France, 237 f
Julius II, Pope, 13; and bankers, 14; pontificate of, 15; and religious Orders, 21
Julius III, Pope, and Council of Trent, 64, 66; and reformation of religious Orders, 83

Kennedy, Quintin, on religious abuses in Scotland, 252 f

Lagrime della Maddalena, Valvasone's, 144 ff
Lagrime di San Pietro, Tansillo's, 142 ff
Laity, education of, 122 ff; St. Francis de Sales and, 200
Lalemant, Fr., S.J., in Canada, 299
La Magdeleine repentie, 146
Laredo, Bernardino de, mystic, 188
Lascaris, Jan, rector Greek college, 36
Lateran, Council of, and reform, 26 f; results, 32
Laynez (Lainez), James, Jesuit, at Trent, 68
Leo X, Pope, and bankers, 14; and concordat with France, 27 f; concordats, 27 f; pontificate of, 33 f; and Turkish invasion, 37 f
Lestonnac, Blessed Joan de, and "Daughters of Our Lady," 234
Lichetto, Francesco, and Franciscan reform, 94
Literature, and Catholic reformation, 137 ff; religious, 17
Louis XII, King of France, and Italy, 38; and nationalism, 12; reform efforts, 25
Loyola, St. Ignatius, 17, 103 ff; influence of Brothers of the Common Life on, 120
Luigi, Giovanni Pier, *see* Palestrina
Lutheran Church, founded in Germany, 43
Luther, Martin, 20, 28, 33, 44; and mysticism, 187

Machiavelli, *Prince,* 38
Maldonatus, Fr., S.J., work of, in France, 229 ff
Mantua, Council convened in, 56
Manucci, Aldo (Aldus Manutius), and Leo X, 36
Manutius, Paulus, printer, called to Rome, 87
Marcellus II, Pope, 66; and music, 179
Marillac, Louise de, and St. Vincent de Paul, 243
Markham, Gervase, *Mary Magdelen's lamentations for the loss of her*

master Jesus, 146 f; *Tears of the Beloved,* 146

Martellange, S.J., Brother, and Jesuit architecture, 174 f

"Martyrdom," plays, 151

Martyrdom, in reformation art, 166

Mary, Blessed Virgin, devotion to, 168

Mary of the Incarnation, Mother, 297

Mass, relation of, to reformation architecture, 173

Maximilian II, Emperor, and reform, 38; and Trentine decrees, 88

Melk, Abbey of, and reform, 224

Merici, St. Angela, founder of Ursulines, 131

Mexico, missions in, 276 f

Miani, Girolamo (Hieronymus Aemilianus), and Somaschi, 97 f

Milan, reform of, 85

Missal, reform of, 86 f; revised, 209

Missions, sixteenth-seventeenth century, 275 ff

Monastic influence, in 15th century, 6

Money, importance of, 7 f; in church, 2; *see also* Taxation

Montaigu, College of, 116 ff

Montalvo, Luys Galves de, *El llanto de Sant Pedro,* 144

More, St. Thomas, 4, 20

Morone, Cardinal, tried for heresy, 67

Murillo, 163

Music, church, Council of Trent on, 178 f; popular themes in, 178; pre-Trent reaction to, 178; protestant view of, 181; spirit of Catholic reformation in, 178 ff

Mysticism, English, 270; in France, 201 ff; in Italy, 194 ff; Protestantism and, 187; reformation, 183 ff; of St. Teresa, 191 ff; in Spain, 187 ff

Mystics, reformation, 164 f

Nationalism, 38; in Council of Trent, 69; effect of, on reform, 43 f; and papacy, 12; and reform, 3

Nepotism, 6

Neri, St. Philip, and Italian spirituality, 196; and Oratory of Divine Love, 99 ff; as spiritual director, 102

Nicholas de Cusa, Cardinal, reform efforts of, 21 ff

Nicholas V, Pope, reform under, 21

Nobili, Fr. Robert de, S.J., work in India, 293

North America, missions in, 295 ff

Nuremberg, Diet of, Adrian VI and, 42

Observant Franciscans, and reform, 25

Ochino, Bernardino, apostacy, 55; apostate, 95

Olier, Jean-Jacques (John James), 240; and French mysticism, 203 f; work of, 244 f

Opera, origin of, 181

Oratorio, origin, 181

Oratory, French, 238 f; and seminaries, 240

Oratory of Divine Love, 92 f; foundation and history, 99 ff; founded, 20; French, and education, 131 f

Oratory of St. Philip Neri, and music, 181

Orders, religious, and reform, 21

Oriental churches, and Council of Trent, 64

Ormaneto, Niccoló, and Charles Borromeo, 85

Our Lady's Lullaby, Verstegan's 148

Palestrina (Giovanni Pier Luigi), 179 ff; influence on music, 180; and plainchant, 182

Papacy, authority of, in art, 169

Paraguay, missions in, 285 f

Parsons, Robert, S.J., 264; *Christian Directory,* 265 ff

Paul III, Pope, character, 53 f; Council of Trent under, 66

Paul IV, Pope, and Council of Trent, 66; and reform of Curia, 83; and simony, 84

Perugia, revolt in, 55

Peru, missions in, 280 f

Peter of Alcantara, St., mystic, 188, 190

Peter Canisius, St., *see* Canisius

Philip Neri, St., *see* Neri, St. Philip

Philip II, King of Spain, and decrees of Trent, 89 f; and France, 227

Pico della Mirandula, Giovanni-Francesco, Christian Platonist, 36; at Lateran Council, 37

Piety, on "Eve of Reformation," 1; influence of Erasmus, 186; reformation, 183 ff

Pisa, Council of, 12, 26

Pius II, Pope, reform efforts of, 23

Pius III, Pope, 23

Pius IV, Pope, and Council of Trent, 64; and nepotism, 84; reconvenes Council of Trent, 67
Pius V, St., Pope, 85, 206 ff; and music, 179
Pizarro, 280
Plainchant, restoration, 182
Poetry, Catholic reformation, 140 ff; Christian, Leo X and, 36
Poland, Catholic revival in, 224 f; Trentine decrees in, 90
Pole, Reginald, Cardinal, in "pre-council," 59; and reform in England, 260 ff; tried for heresy, 67
Politics, international, and Council, 56; local, and popes, 14
Polyeucte, Corneille's, 155 ff; influence of *Spiritual Exercises* in, 157 f
Polyphony, *see* Music
Pontanus, Jacobus, 140; *Institutiones poeticae,* 138 f; on literature, 137
Pontanus, Jorianus, writings of, 137
Popes, burdens of, 32; and France, 226 f; and reform, 3
Portugal, Trentine decrees in, 89
Possevinus, *De Poesi et Pictura,* 161 f
Prat, Guillaume de, and education of laity, 122
Prato, Giovanni Andrea, on monks, 37
Preaching, pre-reformation, 19; and reformation architecture, 174
"Pre-council," Paul III forms, 59
Princes, Catholic, aid of, in reforms, 221
Protestants, and council, 49; and Council of Trent, 64; education of, 118 ff
Punishment of pupils, in Jesuit education, 127
Purgatory, dogma of, in art, 169

Quebec, religious spirit, in, 297 f

Ragazzoni, Hieronimo, oration at end of Council of Trent, 73
Raimundus, Franciscus, epigram, 140
Raphael, work of, in Sistine Chapel, 34
Ratio Studiorum, analysis of, 124 ff
Ratisbon, "colloquy" at, 70
Real presence of Christ in Eucharist, in art, 169 f
Reductions, Jesuit, in Paraguay, 285 f
Reform, Catholic, obstacles to, 49
Reformation, Catholic, and missionary movement, 275; need of, in Church, 1

Regulars, state of, 10; *see also* Religious Orders
Religion, practices of, in Jesuit education, 129
Religious Orders, Clement VII reform efforts in, 51; in France, 228; reforms in, 52; reform under Pius V, 210; revival, 92 ff
Renaissance spirit, Catholic reformers and, 139 f
Reni, Guido, 169
Retreats, St. Vincent de Paul and, 243
Ricci, Fr. Mathew, S.J., work in China, 294 f
Richelieu, Cardinal, influence of Fr. Joseph on, 257 f
Roman College, foundation, 122
Rome, reform in, 212; Sack of, 46 f
Rowland, Samuel, *Betraying of Christ,* 144
Ruff, Vincenzo, composer, 180

Sack of Rome, *see* Rome
Sadolet, Christian humanist, 34 f, 45; in "pre-council," 59; on Sack of Rome, 47
St. Peter's, alterations in, plans of, 175 f
Salmeron, Jesuit, at Trent, 68
Savonarola, Jerome, 24
Schall, Fr. John Adrian, S.J., work in China, 295
Schinner, Cardinal, proposal for reform, 40
Scholarship, 115 ff
Scotland, attempts at reform in, 251 ff
Scripture, Jesuit views on teaching, 134
Sculpture, reformation, 172
Seminaries, created by Council of Trent, 80; English, 263 f; French, 239
Sens, Provincial Council, reform canons of, 24
Seripando, Girolamo, and reform of Augustinians, 94
Sermons, *see* Preaching
Sigismund, Augustus, King of Poland, and decrees of Trent, 90
Sigismund, duke of Tyrol, 23
Simonetta, Cardinal, and reform of Curia, 62
Sixtus IV, Pope, 14; and bankers, 14; and religious Orders, 21
Sixtus V, Pope, 213 ff

Society of Jesus, 103 ff; *Constitutions,* 108 ff; foundation, 108; growth of, 114; and reformation culture, 303; *see also* Jesuits; Loyola, St. Ignatius; *Spiritual Exercises*

Somaschi, 95 ff

South America, missions in, 280 f

Southwell, Robert, 269; *Mary Magdalen's Tears,* 146; *St. Peter's Complaint,* 144

Spain, mysticism in, 187 ff; reformation art in, 163; Trentine decrees in, 89 f

Spiritual Exercises of St. Ignatius, 104 ff

Spiritual life, three ways of, in mysticism, 185

Spirituality, *see* Mysticism

Stafileo, Bishop, speech to Rota, 47

Standonck, Jean (John), 24; founder of Montaigu community, 116

Stephonius, Bernardinus, *Flavia,* 151, 152

Sturm, John, and Protestant education, 119

Sublimis Deus, bull, 59

Switzerland, Catholic revival in, 225

Tansillo, Luigi, 142 ff

Tasso, Torquato, 141 f

Taxation, Church, 13 f; *see also* Money

Teresa of Avila, St., 187, 188 ff; and English mysticism, 270 ff; spiritual teaching, 191 f; writings of, 191

Theatines, 95 ff

Theatrum Crudelitatum haereticorum, 166 f

Theology, Jesuit views on teaching, 134

Thiene, Gaetano di, 93; and Theatines, 96 f

Thomas More, St., *see* More

Tiron, reform efforts, 25

Tizio, Sigismundo, on financial practices, 37

Toribio (Turibius) de Mogrovejo, St., apostle of Peru, 283

Torsellinus, Franciscus, ode, 140

Trent, choice of, for Council, 65; council convoked at, 57

Trent, Council of, 64 ff; and art, 59 f;

cardinal-legates in, 68; and Catholic reformation, 301 f; and Church music, 178 f; classical influence in, 138; decrees of, and French kings, 226 f; evaluation of, 73 ff; makeup in third period, 67 f; nature, 92; and piety, 183 f; results, 89 ff

Trithemius, on classical studies, 30

Tudor, Mary, and Catholic Reformation in Ireland, 255

Turkey, invasion from, 32, 54; invasion threats from, 37 f

Turks, *see* Turkey

Tyndale, 4

Ursulines, schools of, 132 ff

Valvasone, Erasmo de, *Lagrime della Maddalena,* 142, 144 ff

Venice, and indulgence for St. Peter's, 36; and nationalism, 12; and Turks, 38

Vermigli, Pietro Martyr, apostasy, 55

Vernacular, and Protestant schools, 121

Veronese, Paolo, 166

Verstegan, Richard, *Our Lady's Lullaby,* 147 f

Vicenza, council shifted to, 56 f

Vincent de Paul, St., 240, 242 ff; spirituality of, 204

Vittoria, 179

Vives, Luis, 120; proposal for reform, 40

Vulgate, Vatican edition, 87

Wills, 17 f

Wolsey, Cardinal, and nationalism, 45

Xavier, St. Francis, S.J., life and work, 287 ff

Ximenes, Cardinal, protest against indulgence, 36

Zaccaria, Antonio Maria, founder of Barnabites, 98

Zano, Bernardino, at Lateran Council, 26

Zoilo, Annibal, and plainchant, 182